Exploring Ethics

An Introductory Anthology

FIFTH EDITION

Edited by

STEVEN M. CAHN
The City University of New York Graduate Center

New York   Oxford
OXFORD UNIVERSITY PRESS

Oxford University Press is a department of the University of Oxford. It furthers the University's objective of excellence in research, scholarship, and education by publishing worldwide. Oxford is a registered trade mark of Oxford University Press in the UK and certain other countries.

Published in the United States of America by Oxford University Press
198 Madison Avenue, New York, NY 10016, United States of America.

For titles covered by Section 112 of the US Higher Education Opportunity Act, please visit www.oup.com/us/he for the latest information about pricing and alternate formats.

Library of Congress Cataloging-in-Publication Data

Names: Cahn, Steven M., editor.
Title: Exploring ethics: an introductory anthology / [edited by] Steven M. Cahn.
Description: Fifth Edition. | New York: Oxford University Press, 2019. | Includes bibliographical references and index. | Description based on print version record and CIP data provided by publisher; resource not viewed.
Identifiers: LCCN 2019013957 (print) | LCCN 2019018897 (ebook) | ISBN 9780190887933 (epub) | ISBN 9780190887902 (pbk.: alk. paper)
Subjects: LCSH: Ethics.
Classification: LCC BJ1012 (ebook) | LCC BJ1012.E97 2019 (print) | DDC 170—dc23
LC record available at https://lccn.loc.gov/2019013957

Printing number: 9 8 7 6 5 4 3 2 1

Printed by LSC Communications Inc.
United States of America

To my wife,
Marilyn Ross, M.D.

Contents

Preface

Most anthologies in ethics contain far more material than can be covered in one course, and the readings are often daunting in their complexity. The few simpler and more concise collections usually stress moral problems while deemphasizing discussion of the concepts and methods of ethics.

This book can be completed in a single semester, and the readings have been edited, wherever appropriate, to enhance their accessibility. Moral theory is given its due alongside a selection of contemporary moral issues.

The first part, Challenges to Morality, considers questionable assumptions sometimes brought to the study of ethics. The second part, Moral Theories, focuses on competing explanations of why certain actions are right and others wrong. The third part, Moral Problems, features opposing readings on a variety of controversial issues, such as world hunger, immigration, and the environment.

Those who wish to learn more about any particular subject can consult the *Encyclopedia of Ethics*, second edition (Routledge, 2001), edited by Lawrence C. Becker and Charlotte B. Becker. It contains detailed entries with bibliographies on every significant topic in the field.

New to This Edition

- Sections have been added on immigration, injustice, and prostitution.
- Other articles have been added on subjectivism, the treatment of animals, and global change.
- The selections by Kant, Mill, Pojman, Longino, Feinberg, Sober, Thomson (39), Warren (40), Steinbock (44), and Vitrano have been re-edited.
- A glossary has been added.
- Nearly half of the readings are authored by women.

Some selections found in the previous edition have been omitted, including those by Walter Berns, Carl Cohen, Karen Hanson, Daniel

J. Hill, Lionel K. McPherson, Stephen Nathanson, Henry Shue, Laurence Thomas, Michael Walzer, three by Tom Regan, and one by the editor. Martin Luther King, Jr.'s "Letter from a Birmingham Jail," which appeared in every previous edition, could not be included here due to the rights holder imposing a prohibitive permissions fee.

Readings Added to This Edition

- Julia Driver, "Subjectivism"
- David Miller, "Immigration: The Case for Limits"
- Michael Huemer, "Is There a Right to Immigrate?"
- Kwame Anthony Appiah, "Racisms"
- Ann E. Cudd and Leslie E. Jones, "Sexism"
- Elizabeth Anderson, "Value and the Gift of Sexuality"
- Martha Nussbaum, "Taking Money for Bodily Services"
- Debra Satz, "Markets in Women's Sexual Labor"
- Peter Singer, "Equality for Animals"
- Bonnie Steinbock, "Speciesism and the Idea of Equality"
- Christine Korsgaard, "Getting Animals in View"
- Dale Jamieson, "Ethics and Global Change"

Instructor and Student Resources

The Oxford University Press Ancillary Resource Center (ARC) at http://www.oup.com/us/cahn houses an Instructor's Manual with Test Bank and PowerPoint Lecture Outlines for instructor use. Student Resources are available on the Companion Website at www.oup.com/us/cahn and include brief overviews, flashcards that highlight key terms, and essay questions that reaffirm the main ideas and arguments.

Acknowledgments

I am grateful to Robert Miller, executive editor at Oxford University Press, for his encouragement and guidance; to associate editor Alyssa Palazzo and assistant editor Sydney Keen, who helped in so many ways; to manuscript editor Marianne Paul for her conscientiousness; and to the staff at Oxford University Press for generous assistance throughout production.

I would also like to express my appreciation to those reviewers, chosen by the publisher, who offered valuable suggestions for the Fifth Edition:

Heath Allen, *Oklahoma State University*
Daniel Gluch, *California State University-Sacramento*
Jeremy Morris, *Ohio University*
Max Pensky, *Binghamton University*
Dr. Elizabeth Scarbrough, *Florida International University*
Susanne Sreedhar, *Boston University*
Nathan Stout, *Tulane University*
Harvey Whitney, *Miami Dade College-Wolfson*
Elaine Yoshikawa, *Arizona State University*

Note

Some of the selections were written when the custom was to use the noun "man" and the pronoun "he" to refer to all persons regardless of gender, and I have retained the authors' original wording. With this proviso, we begin our readings.

Introduction

CHAPTER 1

Morality and Moral Philosophy

William K. Frankena

The terms "ethics" and "moral philosophy" may be used interchangeably. "Ethics" is derived from the Greek word *ethos* meaning "character"; "moral" is from the Latin *moralis*, relating to "custom." But what is the nature of the subject referred to as "ethics" or "moral philosophy"? That question is addressed here by William K. Frankena (1908–1994), who was Professor of Philosophy at the University of Michigan.

Suppose that all your life you have been trying to be a good person, doing your duty as you see it and seeking to do what is for the good of your fellowmen. Suppose, also, that many of your fellowmen dislike you and what you are doing and even regard you as a danger to society, although they cannot really show this to be true. Suppose, further, that you are indicted, tried, and condemned to death by a jury of your peers, all in a manner which you correctly consider to be quite unjust. Suppose, finally, that while you are in prison awaiting execution, your friends arrange an opportunity for you to escape and go into exile with your family. They argue that they can afford the necessary bribes and will not be endangered by your escaping; that if you escape, you will enjoy a longer life; that your wife and children will be better off; that your friends will still be able to see you; and that people generally will think that you should escape. Should you take the opportunity?

This is the situation Socrates, the patron saint of moral philosophy, is in at the opening of Plato's dialogue, the *Crito*. The dialogue gives us his answer to our question and a full account of his reasoning in arriving at it. It will, therefore, make a good beginning for our

From William K. Frankena, *Ethics*, 2nd edition. Copyright © 1973. Reprinted by permission of Pearson Education, Inc., Upper Saddle River, NJ.

study. Socrates first lays down some points about the approach to be taken. To begin with, we must not let our decision be determined by our emotions, but must examine the question and follow the best reasoning. We must try to get our facts straight and to keep our minds clear. Questions like this can and should be settled by reason. Secondly, we cannot answer such questions by appealing to what people generally think. They may be wrong. We must try to find an answer we ourselves can regard as correct. We must think for ourselves. Finally, we ought never to do what is morally wrong. The only question we need to answer is whether what is proposed is right or wrong, not what will happen to us, what people will think of us, or how we feel about what has happened.

Having said this, Socrates goes on to give, in effect, a threefold argument to show that he ought not to break the laws by escaping. First: we ought never to harm anyone. Socrates' escaping would harm the state, since it would violate and show disregard for the state's laws. Second: if one remains living in a state when one could leave it, one tacitly agrees to obey its laws; hence, if Socrates were to escape he would be breaking an agreement, which is something one should not do. Third: one's society or state is virtually one's parent and teacher, and one ought to obey one's parents and teachers.

In each of these arguments Socrates appeals to a general moral rule or principle which, upon reflection, he and his friend Crito accept as valid: (1) that we ought never to harm anyone, (2) that we ought to keep our promises, and (3) that we ought to obey or respect our parents and teachers. In each case he also uses another premise which involves a statement of fact and applies the rule or principle to the case in hand: (1a) if I escape I will do harm to society, (2a) if I escape I will be breaking a promise, and (3a) if I escape I will be disobeying my parent and teacher. Then he draws a conclusion about what he should do in his particular situation. This is a typical pattern of reasoning in moral matters. . . .

At some point you . . . will almost inevitably raise the question of how ethical judgments and principles . . . are to be justified . . . ; and this is likely to lead to the further question of what is meant by saying that something is right, good, virtuous, just, and the like. . . .

When this happens the discussion has developed into a full-fledged philosophical one. Ethics is a branch of philosophy; it is *moral philosophy* or philosophical thinking about morality, moral problems, and moral judgments. What this involves is illustrated by the sort of thinking Socrates was doing in the *Crito*. . . .

Moral philosophy arises when, like Socrates, we pass beyond the stage in which we are directed by traditional rules and even beyond the stage in which these rules are so internalized that we can be said to be inner-directed, to the stage in which we think for ourselves. . . . We may . . . distinguish three kinds of thinking that relate to morality in one way or another.

1. There is descriptive empirical inquiry, historical or scientific, such as is done by anthropologists, historians, psychologists, and sociologists. Here, the goal is to describe or explain the phenomena of morality or to work out a theory of human nature which bears on ethical questions.

2. There is normative thinking of the sort that Socrates was doing in the *Crito* or that anyone does who asks what is right, good, or obligatory. This may take the form of asserting a normative judgment like
"I ought not to try to escape from prison,"
"Knowledge is good," or
"It is always wrong to harm someone,"
and giving or being ready to give reasons for this judgment. Or it may take the form of debating with oneself or with someone else about what is good or right in a particular case or as a general principle, and then forming some such normative judgment as a conclusion.

3. There is also "analytical," "critical," or "meta-ethical" thinking. This is the sort of thinking we imagined that Socrates would have come to if he had been challenged to the limit in the justification of his normative judgments. . . . It does not consist of empirical or historical inquiries and theories, nor does it involve making or defending any normative or value judgments. It does not try to answer either particular or general questions about what is good, right, or obligatory. It asks and tries to answer . . . questions like the following: What is the meaning or use of the expressions "(morally) right" or "good"? How can ethical and value judgments be established or justified? Can they be justified at all? . . .

We shall take ethics to include meta-ethics as just described, but as also including normative ethics or thinking of the second kind. . . . In fact, we shall take ethics to be primarily concerned with . . . answering problems about what is right or ought to be done, and as being interested in meta-ethical questions mainly because it seems necessary to answer such questions before one can be entirely satisfied with one's normative theory (although ethics is also interested in meta-ethical questions for their own sakes). However, since certain psychological and anthropological theories are considered to have a bearing on the answers to normative and meta-ethical questions, as we shall see in discussing egoism . . . and relativism, we shall also include some descriptive or empirical thinking of the first kind.

Study Questions

1. What is a typical pattern of reasoning in moral matters?
2. In answering moral questions, do we need factual knowledge?
3. What are the differences among descriptive morality, normative ethics, and meta-ethics?
4. How does moral reasoning differ from mathematical reasoning?

CHAPTER 2

Crito

Plato

Here is the *Crito*, discussed in the previous selection. Plato (c. 428–347 B.C.E.), the famed Athenian philosopher, authored a series of such dialogues, most of which feature his teacher Socrates (469–399 B.C.E.), who himself wrote nothing but in conversation was able to befuddle the most powerful minds of his day.

SOCRATES: Why have you come at this hour, Crito? It's still very early, isn't it?

CRITO: Yes, very.

SOCRATES: About what time?

CRITO: Just before daybreak.

SOCRATES: I'm surprised the prison-warder was willing to answer the door.

CRITO: He knows me by now, Socrates, because I come and go here so often; and besides, I've done him a small favour.

SOCRATES: Have you just arrived, or have you been here for a while?

CRITO: For quite a while.

SOCRATES: Then why didn't you wake me up right away instead of sitting by me in silence?

CRITO: Well *of course* I didn't wake you, Socrates! I only wish I weren't so sleepless and wretched myself. I've been marvelling all this time as I saw how peacefully you were sleeping, and I deliberately kept from waking you, so that you could pass the time as peacefully as possible. I've often admired your disposition in the past, in fact all your life; but more than ever in your present plight, you bear it so easily and patiently.

SOCRATES: Well, Crito, it really would be tiresome for a man of my age to get upset if the time has come when he must end his life.

CRITO: And yet others of your age, Socrates, are overtaken by similar troubles, but their age brings them no relief from being upset at the fate which faces them.

SOCRATES: That's true. But tell me, why *have* you come so early?

CRITO: I bring painful news, Socrates—not painful for you, I suppose, but painful and hard for me and all your friends—and hardest of all for me to bear, I think.

SOCRATES: What news is that? Is it that the ship has come back from Delos,[1] the one on whose return I must die?

CRITO: Well no, it hasn't arrived yet, but I think it will get here today, judging from reports of people who've come from Sunium,[2] where they disembarked. That makes it obvious that it will get here today; and so tomorrow, Socrates, you will have to end your life.

SOCRATES: Well, may that be for the best, Crito. If it so please the gods, so be it. All the same, I don't think it will get here today.

CRITO: What makes you think that?

SOCRATES: I'll tell you. You see, I am to die on the day after the ship arrives, am I not?

CRITO: At least that's what the authorities say.

SOCRATES: Then I don't think it will get here on the day that is just dawning, but on the next one. I infer that from a certain dream I had in the night—a short time ago, so it may be just as well that you didn't wake me.

CRITO: And what was your dream?

SOCRATES: I dreamt that a lovely, handsome woman approached me, robed in white. She called me and said, "Socrates, Thou shalt reach fertile Phthia upon the third day."[3]

CRITO: What a curious dream, Socrates.

SOCRATES: Yet its meaning is clear, I think, Crito.

CRITO: All too clear, it would seem. But please, Socrates, my dear friend, there is still time to take my advice, and make your escape—because if you die, I shall suffer more than one misfortune: not only shall I lose such a friend as I'll never find again, but it will look to many people, who hardly know you or me, as if I'd abandoned you—since I could have rescued you if I'd been willing to put up the money. And yet what could be more shameful than a reputation for valuing money more highly than friends? Most people won't believe that it was you who refused to leave this place yourself, despite our urging you to do so.

SOCRATES: But why should we care so much, my good Crito, about what most people believe? All the most capable people, whom we should take more seriously, will think the matter has been handled exactly as it has been.

CRITO: Yet surely, Socrates, you can see that one must heed popular opinion too. Your present plight shows by itself that the populace can inflict not the least of evils, but just about the worst, if someone has been slandered in their presence.

SOCRATES: Ah Crito, if only the populace *could* inflict the worst of evils! Then they would also be capable of providing the greatest of goods, and a fine thing that would be. But the fact is that they can do neither: they are unable to give anyone understanding or lack of it, no matter what they do.

CRITO: Well, if you say so. But tell me this, Socrates: can it be that you are worried for me and your other friends, in case the blackmailers[4] give us trouble, if you escape, for having smuggled you out of here? Are you worried that we might be forced to forfeit all our property as well, or pay heavy fines, or even incur some further penalty? If you're afraid of anything like that, put it out of your mind. In rescuing you we are surely justified in taking that risk, or even worse if need be. Come on, listen to me and do as I say.

SOCRATES: Yes, those risks do worry me, Crito—amongst many others.

CRITO: Then put those fears aside—because no great sum is needed to pay people who are willing to rescue you and get you out of here. Besides, you can surely see that those blackmailers are cheap, and it wouldn't take much to buy them off. My own means are available to you and would be ample, I'm sure. Then again, even if—out of concern on my behalf—you think you shouldn't be spending my money, there are visitors here who are ready to spend theirs. One of them, Simmias from Thebes, has actually brought enough money for this very purpose, while Cebes and quite a number of others are also prepared to contribute. So, as I say, you shouldn't hesitate to save yourself on account of those fears.

And don't let it trouble you, as you were saying in court, that you wouldn't know what to do with yourself if you went into exile. There will be people to welcome you anywhere else you may go: if you want to go to Thessaly,[5] I have friends there who will make much of you and give you safe refuge, so that no one from anywhere in Thessaly will trouble you.

Next, Socrates, I don't think that what you propose—giving yourself up, when you could be rescued—is even just. You are actually hastening to bring upon yourself just the sort of thing which your enemies would hasten to bring upon you—indeed, they have done so—in their wish to destroy you.

What's more, I think you're betraying those sons of yours. You will be deserting them, if you go off when you could be raising and educating them: as far as you're concerned, they will fare as best they may. In all likelihood, they'll meet the sort of fate which usually befalls orphans once they've lost their parents. Surely, one should either not have children at all, or else see the toil and trouble of their upbringing and education through to the end; yet you seem to me to prefer the easiest path. One should rather choose the path that a good and resolute man would choose, particularly if one professes to cultivate goodness all one's life. Frankly, I'm ashamed for you and for us, your friends: it may appear that this whole predicament of yours has been handled with a certain feebleness on our part. What with the bringing of your case to court when that could have been avoided, the actual conduct of the trial, and now, to crown it all, this absurd outcome of the business, it may seem that the problem has eluded us through some fault or feebleness on our part—in that we failed to save you, and you failed to save yourself, when that was quite possible and feasible, if we had been any use at all.

Make sure, Socrates, that all this doesn't turn out badly, and a disgrace to you as well as us. Come now, form a plan—or rather, don't even plan, because the time for that is past, and only a single plan remains. Everything needs to be carried out during the coming night; and if we go on waiting around, it won't be possible or feasible any longer. Come on, Socrates, do all you can to take my advice, and do exactly what I say.

SOCRATES: My dear Crito, your zeal will be invaluable if it should have right on its side; but otherwise, the greater it is, the harder it makes matters. We must therefore consider whether or not the course you urge should be followed—because it is in my nature, not just now for the first time but always, to follow nothing within me but the principle which appears to me, upon reflection, to be best.

I cannot now reject the very principles that I previously adopted, just because this fate has overtaken me; rather, they appear to me much the same as ever, and I respect and honour the same ones that I did before. If we cannot find better ones to maintain in the present situation, you can be sure that I won't agree with you—not even if the power of the populace threatens us, like children, with more bogeymen than it does now, by visiting us with imprisonment, execution, or confiscation of property.

What, then, is the most reasonable way to consider the matter? Suppose we first take up the point you make about what people will think. Was it always an acceptable principle that one should pay heed to some opinions but not to others, or was it not? Or was it acceptable before I had to die, while now it is exposed as an idle assertion made for the sake of talk, when it is really childish nonsense? For my part, Crito, I'm eager to look into this together with you, to see whether the principle is to be viewed any differently, or in the same way, now that I'm in this position, and whether we should disregard or follow it.

As I recall, the following principle always used to be affirmed by people who thought they were talking sense: the principle, as I was just saying, that one should have a high regard for some opinions held by human beings, but not for others. Come now, Crito: don't you think that was a good principle? I ask because you are not, in all foreseeable likelihood, going to die tomorrow, and my present trouble shouldn't impair your judgement. Consider, then: don't you think it a good principle, that one shouldn't respect all human opinions, but only some and not others; or, again, that one shouldn't respect everyone's opinions, but those of some people, and not those of others? What do you say? Isn't that a good principle?

CRITO: It is.

SOCRATES: And one should respect the good ones, but not the bad ones?

CRITO: Yes.

SOCRATES: And good ones are those of people with understanding, whereas bad ones are those of people without it?

CRITO: Of course.

SOCRATES: Now then, once again, how were such points established? When a man is in training, and concentrating upon that, does he pay heed to the praise or censure or opinion of each and every man, or only to those of the individual who happens to be his doctor or trainer?

CRITO: Only to that individual's.

SOCRATES: Then he should fear the censures, and welcome the praises of that individual, but not those of most people.

CRITO: Obviously.

SOCRATES: So he must base his actions and exercises, his eating and drinking, upon the opinion of the individual, the expert supervisor, rather than upon everyone else's.

CRITO: True.

SOCRATES: Very well. If he disobeys that individual and disregards his opinion, and his praises, but respects those of most people, who are ignorant, he'll suffer harm, won't he?

CRITO: Of course.

SOCRATES: And what is that harm? What does it affect? What element within the disobedient man?

CRITO: Obviously, it affects his body, because that's what it spoils.

SOCRATES: A good answer. And in other fields too, Crito—we needn't go through them all, but they surely include matters of just and unjust, honourable and dishonourable, good and bad, the subjects of our present deliberation—is it the opinion of most people that we should follow and fear, or is it that of the individual authority—assuming that some expert exists who should be respected and feared above all others? If we don't follow that person, won't we corrupt and impair the element which (as we agreed) is made better by what is just, but is spoilt by what is unjust? Or is there nothing in all that?

CRITO: I accept it myself, Socrates.

SOCRATES: Well now, if we spoil the part of us that is improved by what is healthy but corrupted by what is unhealthy, because it is not expert opinion that we are following, are our lives worth living once it has been corrupted? The part in question is, of course, the body, isn't it?

CRITO: Yes.

SOCRATES: And are our lives worth living with a poor or corrupted body?

CRITO: Definitely not.

SOCRATES: Well then, are they worth living if the element which is impaired by what is unjust and benefited by what is just has been corrupted? Or do we consider the element to which justice or injustice belongs, whichever part of us it is, to be of less value than the body?

CRITO: By no means.

SOCRATES: On the contrary, it is more precious?

CRITO: Far more.

SOCRATES: Then, my good friend, we shouldn't care all that much about what the populace will say of us, but about what the expert on matters of justice and injustice will say, the individual author- ity, or Truth. In the first place, then, your proposal that we should care about popular opinion regarding just, honourable, or good actions, and their opposites, is mistaken.

"Even so," someone might say, "the populace has the power to put us to death."

CRITO: *That's* certainly clear enough; one might say that, Socrates.

SOCRATES: You're right. But the principle we've rehearsed, my dear friend, still remains as true as it was before—for me at any rate. And now consider this further one, to see whether or not it still holds good for us. We should attach the highest value, shouldn't we, not to living, but to living well?

CRITO: Why yes, that still holds.

SOCRATES: And living well is the same as living honourably or justly? Does that still hold or not?

CRITO: Yes, it does.

SOCRATES: Then in the light of those admissions, we must ask the following question: is it just, or is it not, for me to try to get out of here, when Athenian authorities are unwilling to release me? Then, if it does seem just, let us attempt it; but if it doesn't, let us abandon the idea.

As for the questions you raise about expenses and reputation and bringing up children, I suspect they are the concerns of those who cheerfully put people to death, and would bring them back to life if they could, without any intelligence, namely, the populace. For us, however, because our principle so demands, there is no other question to ask except the one we just raised: shall we be acting justly—we who are rescued as well as the rescuers themselves—if we pay money and do favours to those who would get me out of here? Or shall we in truth be acting unjustly if we do all those things? And if it is clear that we shall be acting unjustly in taking that course, then the question whether we shall have to die through standing firm and holding our peace, or suffer in any other way, ought not to weigh with us in comparison with acting unjustly.

CRITO: I think that's finely *said*, Socrates; but do please consider what we should *do*.

SOCRATES: Let's examine that question together, dear friend; and if you have objections to anything I say, please raise them, and I'll listen to you—otherwise, good fellow, it's time to stop telling me, again and again, that I should leave here against the will of Athens. You see, I set great store upon persuading you as to my course of action, and not acting against your will. Come now, just consider whether you find the starting point of our inquiry acceptable, and try to answer my questions according to your real beliefs.

CRITO: All right, I'll try.

SOCRATES: Do we maintain that people should on no account whatever do injustice willingly? Or may it be done in some circumstances but not in others? Is acting unjustly in no way good or honourable, as we frequently agreed in the past? Or have all those former agreements been jettisoned during these last few days? Can it be, Crito, that men of our age have long failed to notice, as we earnestly conversed with each other, that we ourselves were no better than children? Or is what we then used to say true above all else? Whether most people say so or not, and whether we must be treated more harshly or more leniently than at present, isn't it a fact, all the same, that acting unjustly is utterly bad and shameful for the agent? Yes or no?

CRITO: Yes.

SOCRATES: So one must not act unjustly at all.

CRITO: Absolutely not.

SOCRATES: Then, even if one is unjustly treated, one should not return injustice, as most people believe—given that one should act not unjustly at all.

CRITO: Apparently not.

SOCRATES: Well now, Crito, should one ever ill-treat anybody or not?

CRITO: Surely not, Socrates.

SOCRATES: And again, when one suffers ill-treatment, is it just to return it, as most people maintain, or isn't it?

CRITO: It is not just at all.

SOCRATES: Because there's no difference, I take it, between ill-treating people and treating them unjustly.

CRITO: Correct.

SOCRATES: Then one shouldn't return injustice or ill-treatment to any human being, no matter how one may be treated by that person. And in making those admissions, Crito, watch out that you're not agreeing to anything contrary to your real beliefs. I say that because I realize that the belief is held by few people, and always will be. Those who hold it share no common counsel with those who don't; but each group is bound to regard the other with contempt when they observe one another's decisions. You too, therefore, should consider very carefully whether you share that belief with me, and whether we may begin our deliberations from the following premise: neither doing nor returning injustice is ever right, nor should one who is ill-treated defend himself by retaliation. Do you agree? Or do you dissent and not share my belief in that premise? I've long been of that opinion myself, and I still am now; but if you've formed any different view, say so, and explain it. If you stand by our former view, however, then listen to my next point.

CRITO: Well, I do stand by it and share that view, so go ahead.

SOCRATES: All right, I'll make my next point—or rather, ask a question. Should the things one agrees with someone else be done, provided they are just, or should one cheat?

CRITO: They should be done.

SOCRATES: Then consider what follows. If we leave this place without having persuaded our city, are we or are we not ill-treating certain people, indeed people whom we ought least of all to be ill-treating? And would we be abiding by the things we agreed, those things being just, or not?

CRITO: I can't answer your question, Socrates, because I don't understand it.

SOCRATES: Well, look at it this way. Suppose we were on the point of running away from here, or whatever else one should call it. Then the Laws, or the State of Athens, might come and confront us, and they might speak as follows:

"Please tell us, Socrates, what do you have in mind? With this action you are attempting, do you intend anything short of destroying us, the Laws and the city as a whole, to the best of your ability? Do you think that a city can still exist without being overturned, if the legal judgments rendered within it possess no force, but are nullified or invalidated by individuals?"

What shall we say, Crito, in answer to that and other such questions? Because somebody, particularly a legal advocate,[6] might say a great deal on behalf of the law that is being invalidated here, the one requiring that judgements, once rendered, shall have authority. Shall we tell them, "Yes, that is our intention, because the city was treating us unjustly, by not judging our case correctly"? Is that to be our answer, or what?

CRITO: Indeed it is, Socrates.

SOCRATES: And what if the Laws say, "And was that also part of the agreement between you and us, Socrates? Or did you agree to abide by whatever judgments the city rendered?"

Then, if we were surprised by their words, perhaps they might say, "Don't be surprised at what we are saying, Socrates, but answer us, seeing that you like to use question-and-answer. What complaint, pray, do you have against the city and ourselves, that you should now attempt to destroy us? In the first place, was it not we who gave you birth? Did your father not marry your mother and beget you under our auspices? So will you inform those of us here who regulate marriages whether you have any criticism of them as poorly framed?"

"No, I have none," I should say.

"Well then, what of the laws dealing with children's upbringing and education, under which you were educated yourself? Did those of us Laws who are in charge of that area not give proper direction, when they required your father to educate you in the arts and physical training?"[7]

"They did," I should say.

"Very good. In view of your birth, upbringing, and education, can you deny, first, that you belong to us as our offspring and slave, as your forebears also did? And if so, do you imagine that you are on equal terms with us in regard to what is just, and that whatever treatment we may accord to you, it is just for you to do the same thing back to us? You weren't on equal terms with your father, or your master (assuming you had one), making it just for you to return the treatment you received—answering back when you were scolded, or striking back when you were struck, or doing many other things of the same sort. Will you then have licence against your fatherland and its Laws, if we try to destroy you, in the belief that that is just? Will you try to destroy us in return, to the best of your ability? And will you claim that in doing so you are acting justly, you who are genuinely exercised about goodness? Or are you, in your wisdom, unaware that, in comparison with your mother and father and all your other forebears, your fatherland is more precious and venerable, more sacred and held in higher esteem among gods, as well as among human beings who have any sense; and that you should revere your fatherland, deferring to it and appeasing it when it is angry, more than your own father? You must either persuade it, or else do whatever it commands; and if it ordains that you must submit to certain treatment, then you must hold your peace and submit to it: whether that means being beaten or put in bonds, or whether it leads you into war to be wounded or killed, you must act accordingly, and that is what is just; you must neither give way nor retreat, nor leave your position; rather, in warfare, in court, and everywhere else, you must do whatever your city or fatherland commands, or else persuade it as to what is truly just; and if it is sinful to use violence against your mother or father, it is far more so to use it against your fatherland."

What shall we say to that, Crito? That the Laws are right or not?

CRITO: I think they are.

SOCRATES: "Consider then, Socrates," the Laws might go on, "whether the following is also true: in your present undertaking you are not proposing to treat us justly. We gave you birth, upbringing, and education, and a share in all the benefits we could provide for you along with all your fellow citizens. Nevertheless, we proclaim, by the formal granting of permission, that any Athenian who wishes, once he has been admitted to adult status,[8] and has observed the conduct of city business and ourselves, the Laws, may—if he is dissatisfied with us—go wherever he pleases and take his property. Not one of us Laws hinders or forbids that: whether any of you wishes to emigrate to a colony, or to go and live as an alien elsewhere, he may go wherever he pleases and keep his property, if we and the city fail to satisfy him.

"We do say, however, that if any of you remains here after he has observed the system by which we dispense justice and otherwise manage our city, then he has agreed with us by his conduct to obey whatever orders we give him. And thus we claim that anyone who fails to obey is guilty on three counts: he disobeys us as his parents; he disobeys those who nurtured him; and after agreeing to obey us he neither obeys nor persuades us if we are doing anything amiss, even though we offer him a choice, and do not harshly insist that he must do whatever we command. Instead, we give him two options: he must either persuade us or else do as we say; yet he does neither. Those are the charges, Socrates, to which we say you too will be liable if you carry out your intention; and among Athenians, you will be not the least liable, but one of the most."

And if I were to say, "How so?" perhaps they could fairly reproach me, observing that I am actually among those Athenians who have made that agreement with them most emphatically.

"Socrates," they would say, "we have every indication that you were content with us, as well as with our city, because you would never have stayed home here, more than is normal for all other Athenians, unless you were abnormally content. You never left our city for a festival—except once to go to the Isthmus[9]—nor did you go elsewhere for other purposes, apart from military service. You never travelled abroad, as other people do; nor were you eager for acquaintance with a different city or different laws: we and our city sufficed for you. Thus, you emphatically opted for us, and agreed to be a citizen on our terms. In particular, you fathered children in our city, which would suggest that you were content with it.

"Moreover, during your actual trial it was open to you, had you wished, to propose exile as your penalty; thus, what you are now attempting to do without the city's consent, you could have done with it. On that occasion, you kept priding your-self that it would not trouble you if you had to die: you would choose death ahead of exile, so you said. Yet now you dishon-our those words, and show no regard for us, the Laws, in your effort to destroy us. You are acting as the meanest slave would act, by trying to run away in spite of those compacts and agree-ments you made with us, whereby you agreed to be a citizen on our terms.

"First, then, answer us this question: are we right in claiming that you agreed, by your conduct if not verbally, that you would be a citizen on our terms? Or is that untrue?"

What shall we say in reply to that, Crito? Mustn't we agree?

CRITO: We must, Socrates.

SOCRATES: "Then what does your action amount to," they would say, "except breaking the compacts and agreements you made with us? By your own admission, you were not coerced or tricked into making them, or forced to reach a decision in a short time: you had seventy years in which it was open to you to leave if you were not happy with us, or if you thought those agreements unfair. Yet you preferred neither Lacedaemon nor Crete[10]—places you often say are well governed—nor any other Greek or foreign city: in fact, you went abroad less often than the lame and the blind or other cripples. Obviously, then, amongst Athenians you were exceptionally content with our city and with us, its Laws—because who would care for a city apart from its laws? Won't you, then, abide by your agreements now? Yes you will, if you listen to us, Socrates; and then at least you won't make yourself an object of derision by leaving the city.

"Just consider: if you break those agreements, and commit any of those offences, what good will you do yourself or those friends of yours? Your friends, pretty obviously, will risk being exiled themselves, as well as being disenfranchised or losing their prop-erty. As for you, first of all, if you go to one of the nearest cit-ies, Thebes or Megara[11]—they are both well governed—you will arrive as an enemy of their political systems, Socrates: all who are concerned for their own cities will look askance at you, regarding you as a subverter of laws. You will also confirm your jurors in their judgment, making them think they decided your case cor-rectly: any subverter of laws, presumably, might well be thought to be a corrupter of young, unthinking people.

"Will you, then, avoid the best-governed cities and the most respectable of men? And if so, will your life be worth living? Or will you associate with those people, and be shameless enough to converse with them? And what will you say to them, Socrates? The things you used to say here, that goodness and justice are most precious to mankind, along with institutions and laws? Don't you think that the predicament of Socrates will cut an ugly figure? Surely you must.

"Or will you take leave of those spots, and go to stay with those friends of Crito's up in Thessaly? That, of course, is a region of the utmost disorder and licence; so perhaps they would enjoy hearing from you about your comical escape from jail, when you dressed up in some outfit, wore a leather jerkin or some other runaway's garb, and altered your appearance. Will no one observe that you, an old man with probably only a short time left to live, had the nerve to cling so greedily to life by violating the most important laws? Perhaps not, so long as you don't trouble anyone. Otherwise, Socrates, you will hear a great deal to your own discredit. You will live as every person's toady and lackey; and what will you be doing—apart from living it up in Thessaly, as if you had travelled all the way to Thessaly to have dinner? As for those principles of yours about justice and goodness in general—tell us, where will they be then?

"Well then, is it for your children's sake that you wish to live, in order to bring them up and give them an education? How so? Will you bring them up and educate them by taking them off to Thessaly and making foreigners of them, so that they may gain that advantage too? Or if, instead of that, they are brought up here, will they be better brought up and educated just because you are alive, if you are not with them? Yes, you may say, because those friends of yours will take care of them. Then will they take care of them if you travel to Thessaly, but not take care of them if you travel to Hades? Surely if those professing to be your friends are of any use at all, you must believe that they will.

"No, Socrates, listen to us, your own nurturers: do not place a higher value upon children, upon life, or upon anything else, than upon what is just, so that when you leave for Hades, this may be your whole defence before the authorities there: to take that course seems neither better nor more just or holy, for you or for any of your friends here in this world. Nor will it be better for you when you reach the next. As things stand, you will leave this world (if you do) as one who has been treated unjustly not by us Laws, but by human beings; whereas if you go into exile, thereby shamefully returning injustice for injustice and ill-treatment for ill-treatment, breaking the agreements and compacts you made with us, and inflicting harm upon the people you should least harm—yourself, your friends, your fatherland, and ourselves—then we shall be angry with you in your lifetime; and our brother Laws in Hades will not receive you kindly there, knowing that you tried, to the best of your ability, to destroy us too. Come then, do not let Crito persuade you to take his advice rather than ours."

That, Crito, my dear comrade, is what I seem to hear them saying, I do assure you. I am like the Corybantic revellers[12] who think they are still hearing the music of pipes: the sound of those arguments is ringing loudly in my head, and makes me unable to hear the others. As far as these present thoughts of mine go, then, you may be sure that if you object to them, you will plead in vain. Nonetheless, if you think you will do any good, speak up.

CRITO: No, Socrates, I've nothing to say.

SOCRATES: Then let it be, Crito, and let us act accordingly, because that is the direction in which God is guiding us.

Notes

1. The small island of Delos was sacred to the god Apollo. A mission sailed there annually from Athens to commemorate her deliverance by Theseus from servitude to King Minos of Crete. No executions could be carried out in Athens until the sacred ship returned.
2. The headland at the southeastern extremity of Attica, about 50 kilometres from Athens. The winds were unfavourable at the time; so the ship may have been taking shelter at Sunium when the travellers left it there.
3. In Homer's *Iliad* (ix. 363) Achilles says, "on the third day I may return to fertile Phthia," meaning that he can get home in three days.
4. Athens had no public prosecutors. Prosecutions were undertaken by private citizens, who sometimes threatened legal action for personal, political, or financial gain.
5. The region of northern Greece, lying 200–300 kilometres northwest of Attica.
6. It was customary in Athens to appoint a public advocate to defend laws which it was proposed to abrogate.

7. The standard components of traditional Athenian education.
8. Admission to Athenian citizenship was not automatic, but required formal registration by males at the age of 17 or 18, with proof of age and parental citizenship.
9. The Isthmus was the strip of land linking the Peloponnese with the rest of Greece. Socrates may have attended the Isthmian Games, which were held every two years at Corinth.
10. Lacedaemon was the official name for the territory of Sparta. Sparta and Crete were both authoritarian and "closed" societies, which forbade their citizens to live abroad.
11. Thebes was the chief city in Boeotia, the region lying to the northwest of Attica; Megara was on the Isthmus. Both lay within easy reach of Athens.
12. The Corybantes performed orgiastic rites and dances to the sound of pipe and drum music. Their music sometimes induced a state of frenzy in emotionally disordered people, which was followed by a deep sleep from which the patients awoke cured.

Study Questions

1. According to Socrates, should one heed popular opinion about moral matters?
2. If you reside in a country, do you implicitly agree to abide by its laws?
3. Does Socrates accept the fairness of the laws under which he was tried and convicted?
4. Do you believe Socrates would have been wrong to escape?

CHAPTER 3

Phaedo

Plato

The *Phaedo*, one of Plato's greatest and most complex works, is set in the
Athenian prison on the day of Socrates's death. The discussion focuses
on Plato's attempts to prove the immortality of the soul. Near the end
of the dialogue, Socrates utters his last thoughts, drinks poison, and
dies. This scene, reprinted here, has had an enormous impact on the
conscience of countless succeeding generations.

When he'd spoken, Crito said: "Very well, Socrates: what instructions
have you for these others or for me, about your children or about
anything else? What could we do, that would be of most service
to you?"

"What I'm always telling you, Crito," said he, "and nothing very
new: if you take care for yourselves, your actions will be of service
to me and mine, and to yourselves too, whatever they may be, even
if you make no promises now; but if you take no care for yourselves,
and are unwilling to pursue your lives along the tracks, as it were,
marked by our present and earlier discussions, then even if you make
many firm promises at this time, you'll do no good at all."

"Then we'll strive to do as you say," he said; "but in what fashion
are we to bury you?"

"However you wish," said he: "provided you catch me, that is, and
I don't get away from you." And with this he laughed quietly, looked
towards us and said: "Friends, I can't persuade Crito that I am

---

From *Phaedo*, translated by David Gallop. Copyright © 1975 by Oxford University Press.
Reprinted by permission of the publisher. The notes are by Andrea Tschemplik and are
used with her permission.

Socrates here, the one who is now conversing and arranging each of the things being discussed; but he imagines I'm that dead body he'll see in a little while, so he goes and asks how he's to bury me! But as for the great case I've been arguing all this time, that when I drink the poison,[1] I shall no longer remain with you, but shall go off and depart for some happy state of the blessed, this, I think, I'm putting to him in vain, while comforting you and myself alike. So please stand surety for me with Crito, the opposite surety to that which he stood for me with the judges: his guarantee was that I *would* stay behind, whereas you must guarantee that, when I die, I shall *not* stay behind, but shall go off and depart; then Crito will bear it more easily, and when he sees the burning or interment of my body, he won't be distressed for me, as if I were suffering dreadful things, and won't say at the funeral that it is Socrates they are laying out or bearing to the grave or interring. Because you can be sure, my dear Crito, that misuse of words is not only troublesome in itself, but actually has a bad effect on the soul. Rather, you should have confidence, and say you are burying my body; and bury it however you please, and think most proper."

After saying this, he rose and went into a room to take a bath, and Crito followed him but told us to wait. So we waited, talking among ourselves about what had been said and reviewing it, and then again dwelling on how great a misfortune had befallen us, literally thinking of it as if we were deprived of a father and would lead the rest of our life as orphans. After he'd bathed and his children had been brought to him—he had two little sons and one big one—and those women of his household had come, he talked with them in Crito's presence, and gave certain directions as to his wishes; he then told the women and children to leave, and himself returned to us.

By now it was close to sunset, as he'd spent a long time inside. So he came and sat down, fresh from his bath, and there wasn't much talk after that. Then the prison official came in, stepped up to him and said: "Socrates, I shan't reproach you as I reproach others for being angry with me and cursing, whenever by order of the rulers I direct them to drink the poison. In your time here I've known you for the most generous and gentlest and best of men who have ever come to this place; and now especially, I feel sure it isn't with me that you're angry, but with others, because you know who are responsible. Well now, you know the message I've come to bring: good-bye, then, and try to bear the inevitable as easily as you can." And with this he turned away in tears, and went off.

Socrates looked up at him and said: "Goodbye to you too, and we'll do as you say." And to us he added: "What a civil man he is! Throughout my time here he's been to see me, and sometimes talked with me, and been the best of fellows; and now how generous of him to weep for me! But come on, Crito, let's obey him: let someone bring in the poison, if it has been prepared; if not, let the man prepare it."

Crito said: "But Socrates, I think the sun is still on the mountains and hasn't yet gone down. And besides, I know of others who've taken the draught long after the order had been given them, and after dining well and drinking plenty, and even in some cases enjoying themselves with those they fancied. Be in no hurry, then: there's still time left."

Socrates said: "It's reasonable for those you speak of to do those things—because they think they gain by doing them; for myself, it's reasonable not to do them; because I think I'll gain nothing by taking the draught a little later: I'll only earn my own ridicule by clinging to life, and being sparing when there's nothing more left. Go on now; do as I ask, and nothing else."

Hearing this, Crito nodded to the boy who was standing nearby. The boy went out, and after spending a long time away he returned, bringing the man who was going to administer the poison, and was carrying it ready-pounded in a cup. When he saw the man, Socrates said: "Well, my friend, you're an expert in these things: what must one do?"

"Simply drink it," he said, "and walk about till a heaviness comes over your legs; then lie down, and it will act of itself." And with this he held out the cup to Socrates.

He took it perfectly calmly, Echecrates, without a tremor, or any change of colour or countenance; but looking up at the man, and fixing him with his customary stare, he said: "What do you say to pouring someone a libation from this drink? Is it allowed or not?"

"We only prepare as much as we judge the proper dose, Socrates," he said.

"I understand," he said: "but at least one may pray to the gods, and so one should, that the removal from this world to the next will be a happy one; that is my own prayer: so may it be." With these words he pressed the cup to his lips, and drank it off with good humour and without the least distaste.

Till then most of us had been fairly well able to restrain our tears; but when we saw he was drinking, that he'd actually drunk it, we could do so no longer. In my own case, the tears came pouring out in spite of myself, so that I covered my face and wept for myself—not for him, no, but for my own misfortune in being deprived of such a man for a companion. Even before me, Crito had moved away, when he was unable to restrain his tears. And Apollodorus, who even earlier had been continuously in tears, now burst forth into such a storm of weeping and grieving, that he made everyone present break down except Socrates himself.

But Socrates said: "What a way to behave, my strange friends! Why, it was mainly for this reason that I sent the women away, so that they shouldn't make this sort of trouble; in fact, I've heard one should die in silence. Come now, calm yourselves and have strength."

When we heard this, we were ashamed and checked our tears. He walked about, and when he said that his legs felt heavy he lay down on his back—as the man told him—and then the man, this one who'd given him the poison, felt him, and after an interval examined his feet and legs; he then pinched his foot hard and asked if he could feel it, and Socrates said not.

After that he felt his shins once more; and moving upwards in this way, he showed us that he was becoming cold and numb. He went on feeling him, and said that when the coldness reached his heart, he would be gone.

By this time the coldness was somewhere in the region of his abdomen, when he uncovered his face—it had been covered over—and spoke; and this was in fact his last utterance: "Crito," he said, "we owe a cock to Asclepius: please pay the debt, and don't neglect it."[2]

"It shall be done," said Crito; "have you anything else to say?"

To this question he made no answer, but after a short interval he stirred, and when the man uncovered him his eyes were fixed; when he saw this, Crito closed his mouth and his eyes.

And that, Echecrates, was the end of our companion, a man who, among those of his time we knew, was—so we should say—the best, the wisest too, and the most just.

Notes

1. The poison was hemlock, frequently used in ancient executions.
2. Asclepius was the hero or god of healing. A provocative, but disputed, interpretation of Socrates's final instruction is that he considers death the cure for life and, therefore, wishes to make an offering in gratitude to the god of health.

Study Questions

1. According to Socrates, how could Crito be of most service?
2. Why, according to Socrates, will he have to be caught in order to be buried?
3. What lessons can be drawn from the equanimity with which Socrates faced death?
4. Is death an evil?

PART I

Challenges to Morality

CHAPTER 4

Subjectivism

Julia Driver

Faced with an ethical issue, some people challenge the supposition that the problem can be resolved through reasoned discussion. They claim that moral judgments are merely matters of individual opinion. Thus "right" and "wrong" express only personal preferences. This position, known as "subjectivism," is here examined and found unconvincing by Julia Driver, Professor of Philosophy at Washington University in St. Louis.

[T]here are some people who are very skeptical about morality—about whether there is such a thing as a truly universal moral system, and whether any moral claims are true or "just a matter of opinion." . . .

On this view of moral evaluation, normative claims will be radically different from descriptive claims. For example, if someone were to make the descriptive claim

(1) Wombats are mammals.

she would be stating something that has a truth-value that does not vary across individual beliefs, or across cultures. If (1) is true, it is true not in virtue of what someone happens to believe. The truth-value of (1) is not a relative matter. How do we find out whether or not (1) is true or false? We look at the features of wombats relevant to their classification as mammals—Are they warm-blooded and furry, and do they give birth to live young? The answers to all of these questions are affirmative, so (1) is true. In determining the truth-value of

From Julia Driver, *Ethics: The Fundamentals* (Malden, MA: Blackwell Publishing, 2007). Reprinted by permission of the publisher.

(1), we don't look at what people happen to believe about wombats. After all, people can be mistaken.

Moral relativists hold that normative claims, such as moral ones, however, are quite different from descriptive claims such as (1) and do have truth-values that can vary. . . .

One form of moral relativism . . . [holds] that the truth-value of moral claims can vary from individual to individual. This view is sometimes referred to as . . . *subjectivism*. Consider the claim

(2)   Abortion is always wrong.

There are some people who believe that (2) is true and others who believe that (2) is false. If we think that the correct way to relativize moral truth is to the beliefs or attitudes of individuals, then we need to hold that (2) is true for those who believe it, but false for those who believe it false. Then (2) is both true and false—but false for one person, and true for another.

One way to spell out this theory more plausibly is to hold that claims such as (2) are just reports of approval or disapproval, so that when Mary utters (2) sincerely, that is just the same as saying something like

(3)   I (Mary) disapprove of abortion.

If Mary is being sincere, then (3) must be true. If (3) is the same as (2), then (2) must be true as well. But note that if Ralph says

(4)   Abortion is always permissible.

which is the same (on this theory) as

(5)   I (Ralph) do not disapprove of abortion.

then if Ralph sincerely utters (4), (4) must be true as well. Thus, (2) and (4) are both true, albeit relativized to different subjects. This has the very odd result that when Ralph and Mary argue about abortion, there is really nothing that they are disagreeing about. How can Mary disagree with Ralph, really, when all he is actually saying is that he does not disapprove of abortion? But this goes against our views about what takes place in moral argumentation—we do believe that something more substantive, more objective, is at stake.

Subjectivism seems to be an attractive view to some because it seems highly tolerant. What is "right" for me may not be "right" for you, since you have different beliefs. We sometimes hear people talking as though, for example, "Abortion is right for some, but for me would be murder," but—upon reflection—most people find the view that "right" is purely a matter of opinion to lack plausibility. It seems quite counter-intuitive, since it would result in the truth—albeit subjective truth—of claims such as "For me, mass killing is perfectly permissible," as long as the person making the utterance actually believed that mass killings were permissible. But a genocidal maniac cannot be acting rightly just because he happens to believe that he is acting rightly. There are lots of cases to which we could refer to show how unappealing such a criterion of rightness would be. There have been many people who have done terrible things and yet have felt very self-righteous about their actions. The Nazi commander Heinrich Himmler, for example, believed that morality demanded that he obey his leader for the sake of German society: of course, he was horribly wrong about this, and his individual beliefs in no way provide justification for what he did, and the horrors that he inflicted on others. So mere individual belief about what is right and what is wrong cannot morally justify someone's actions. In doing anything, whether it is right or wrong, a person is not acting rightly or wrongly just because she happens to believe that what she is doing is right or wrong. There must be something else that justifies her action (or not), some moral reasons for or against the action.

Study Questions

1. According to subjectivism, what is meant by saying that "lying is wrong"?
2. Why does Driver reject subjectivism?
3. In what ways, if any, do moral judgments differ from descriptive ones?
4. Do you suppose that those who believe moral judgments are a matter of personal preference would say the same about non-moral normative claims, such as "Susan is a good swimmer"?

CHAPTER 5

God and Morality

Steven M. Cahn

A widespread belief is that morality depends on the will of God. In this selection I focus on some problems with this theological conception of right and wrong. The view I defend is that whether God exists, morality requires an independent justification.

According to many religions (although not all), the world was created by God, an all-powerful, all-knowing, all-good being. Although God's existence has been doubted, let us for the moment assume its truth. What implications of this supposition would be relevant to our lives?

Some people would feel more secure in the knowledge that the world had been planned by an all-good being. Others would feel insecure, realizing the extent to which their existence depended on a decision of this being. In any case, most people, out of either fear or respect, would wish to act in accord with God's will.

Belief in God by itself, however, provides no hint whatsoever of which actions God wishes us to perform or what we ought to do to please or obey God. We may affirm that God is all-good, yet have no way of knowing the highest moral standards. All we may presume is that, whatever these standards, God always acts in accordance with them. We might expect God to have implanted the correct moral standards in our minds, but this supposition is doubtful in view of the conflicts among people's intuitions. Furthermore, even if consensus prevailed, it might be only a means by which God tests us to see whether we have the courage to dissent from popular opinion.

Some would argue that if God exists, then murder is immoral, because it destroys what God with infinite wisdom created. This argument, however, fails on several grounds. First, God also created germs, viruses, and disease-carrying rats. Because God created these things, ought they not be eliminated? Second, if God arranged for us to live, God also arranged for us to die. By killing, are we assisting the work of God? Third, God provided us with the mental and physical potential to commit murder. Does God wish us to fulfill this potential?

Thus God's existence alone does not imply any particular moral precepts. We may hope our actions are in accord with God's standards, but no test is available to check whether what we do is best in God's eyes. Some seemingly good people suffer great ills, whereas some seemingly evil people achieve happiness. Perhaps in a future life these outcomes will be reversed, but we have no way of ascertaining who, if anyone, is ultimately punished and who ultimately rewarded.

Over the course of history, those who believed in God's existence typically were eager to learn God's will and tended to rely on those individuals who claimed to possess such insight. Diviners, seers, and priests were given positions of great influence. Competition among them was severe, however, for no one could be sure which oracle to believe.

In any case, prophets died, and their supposedly revelatory powers disappeared with them. For practical purposes what was needed was a permanent record of God's will. This requirement was met by the writing of holy books in which God's will was revealed to all.

But even though many such books were supposed to embody the will of God, they conflicted with one another. Which was to be accepted? Belief in the existence of God by itself yields no answer.

Let us suppose, however, that an individual becomes persuaded that a reliable guide to God's will is contained in the Ten Commandments. This person, therefore, believes that to murder, steal, or commit adultery, is wrong.

But why is it wrong? Is it wrong because God says so, or does God say so because it *is* wrong?

This crucial issue was raised more than two thousand years ago in Plato's remarkable dialogue, the *Euthyphro*. Plato's teacher, Socrates, who in most of Plato's works is given the leading role, asks the overconfident Euthyphro whether actions are right because God says they are right, or whether God says actions are right because they are right.

In other words, Socrates is inquiring whether actions are right because of God's fiat, or whether God is subject to moral standards. If actions are right because of God's command, then anything God commands would be right. Had God commanded adultery, stealing, and murder, then adultery, stealing, and murder would be right—surely an unsettling and to many an unacceptable conclusion.

Granted, some may be willing to adopt this discomforting view, but then they face another difficulty. If the good is whatever God commands, to say that God's commands are good amounts to saying that God's commands are God's commands, a mere tautology or repetition of words. In that case, the possibility of meaningfully praising the goodness of God would be lost.

The lesson here is that might does not make right, even if the might is the infinite might of God. To act morally is not to act out of fear of punishment, not to act as one is commanded. Rather, it is to act as one ought to act, and how one ought to act is not dependent on anyone's power, even if the power be divine.

Thus actions are not right because God commands them; on the contrary, God commands them because they are right. What is right is independent of what God commands, for to be right, what God commands must conform to an independent standard.

We could act intentionally in accord with this standard without believing in the existence of God; therefore morality does not rest on that belief. Consequently those who do not believe in God can be highly moral (as well as immoral) people, and those who do believe in the existence of God can be highly immoral (as well as moral) people. This conclusion should come as no surprise to anyone who has contrasted the benevolent life of the Buddha, the inspiring teacher and an atheist, with the malevolent life of the monk Torquemada, who devised and enforced the boundless cruelties of the Spanish Inquisition.

In short, believing in the existence of God does not by itself imply any specific moral principles, and knowing God's will does not provide any justification for morality. Thus regardless of our religious commitments, the moral dimension of our lives remains to be explored.

Study Questions

1. If God exists, is murder immoral?
2. Is murder wrong because God prohibits it, or does God prohibit murder because it is wrong?
3. Can those who do not believe in God be highly moral people?
4. Can people who practice different religions agree about how to resolve a moral disagreement?

CHAPTER 6

The Challenge of Cultural Relativism

James Rachels

The search for universal answers to moral questions is often said to be futile because morality differs from one culture to another. This view, known as cultural relativism, maintains that while we can seek understanding of a particular culture's moral system, we have no basis for judging it.

In the next section James Rachels (1941–2003), who was Professor of Philosophy at the University of Alabama at Birmingham, examines cultural relativism and finds that it has serious shortcomings.

How Different Cultures Have Different Moral Codes

Darius, a king of ancient Persia, was intrigued by the variety of cultures he encountered in his travels. He had found, for example, that the Callatians (a tribe of Indians) customarily ate the bodies of their dead fathers. The Greeks, of course, did not do that—the Greeks practiced cremation and regarded the funeral pyre as the natural and fitting way to dispose of the dead. Darius thought that a sophisticated understanding of the world must include an appreciation of such differences between cultures. One day, to teach this lesson, he summoned some Greeks who happened to be present at his court and asked them what they would take to eat the bodies of their dead fathers. They were shocked, as Darius knew they would be, and replied that no amount of money could persuade them to do such a thing. Then Darius called in some Callatians, and while the Greeks listened asked them what they would take to burn their dead fathers'

From James Rachels, *The Elements of Moral Philosophy*, 2nd edition. Copyright © 1993 by McGraw-Hill. Reprinted by permission of The McGraw-Hill Companies.

bodies. The Callatians were horrified and told Darius not even to mention such a dreadful thing.

This story, recounted by Herodotus in his *History*, illustrates a recurring theme in the literature of social science: different cultures have different moral codes. What is thought right within one group may be utterly abhorrent to the members of another group, and vice versa. Should we eat the bodies of the dead or burn them? If you were a Greek, one answer would seem obviously correct; but if you were a Callatian, the opposite would seem equally certain.

It is easy to give additional examples of the same kind. Consider the Eskimos. They are a remote and inaccessible people. Numbering only about 25,000, they live in small, isolated settlements scattered mostly along the northern fringes of North America and Greenland. Until the beginning of this century, the outside world knew little about them. Then explorers began to bring back strange tales.

Eskimo customs turned out to be very different from our own. The men often had more than one wife, and they would share their wives with guests, lending them for the night as a sign of hospitality. Moreover, within a community, a dominant male might demand—and get—regular sexual access to other men's wives. The women, however, were free to break these arrangements simply by leaving their husbands and taking up with new partners—free, that is, so long as their former husbands chose not to make trouble. All in all, the Eskimo practice was a volatile scheme that bore little resemblance to what we call marriage.

But it was not only their marriage and sexual practices that were different. The Eskimos also seemed to have less regard for human life. Infanticide, for example, was common. Knud Rasmussen, one of the most famous early explorers, reported that he met one woman who had borne twenty children but had killed ten of them at birth. Female babies, he found, were especially liable to be destroyed, and this was permitted simply at the parents' discretion, with no social stigma attached to it. Old people also, when they became too feeble to contribute to the family, were left out in the snow to die. So there seemed to be, in this society, remarkably little respect for life.

To the general public, these were disturbing revelations. Our own way of living seems so natural and right that for many of us it is hard to conceive of others living so differently. And when we do hear of such things, we tend immediately to categorize those other peoples as "backward" or "primitive." But to anthropologists and sociologists, there was nothing particularly surprising about the Eskimos. Since the time of Herodotus, enlightened observers have been accustomed to the idea that conceptions of right and wrong differ from culture to culture. If we assume that *our* ideas of right and wrong will be shared by all peoples at all times, we are merely naive.

Cultural Relativism

To many thinkers, this observation—"Different cultures have different moral codes"—has seemed to be the key to understanding morality. The idea of universal truth in ethics, they say, is a myth. The customs of different societies are all that exist. These customs cannot be said to be "correct" or "incorrect," for that implies we have an independent standard of right and wrong by which they may be judged. But there is no such independent standard; every standard is culture-bound. The great pioneering sociologist William Graham Sumner, writing in 1906, put the point like this:

> The "right" way is the way which the ancestors used and which has been handed down. The tradition is its own warrant. It is not held subject to verification by experience. The notion of right is in the folkways. It is not outside of them, of independent origin, and brought to test them. In the folkways, whatever is, is right. This is because they are traditional, and therefore contain in themselves the authority of the ancestral ghosts. When we come to the folkways we are at the end of our analysis.

This line of thought has probably persuaded more people to be skeptical about ethics than any other single thing. *Cultural Relativism*, as it has been called, challenges our ordinary belief in the objectivity and universality of moral truth. It says, in effect, that there is no such thing as universal truth in ethics; there are only the various cultural codes, and nothing more. Moreover, our own code has no special status; it is merely one among many.

As we shall see, this basic idea is really a compound of several different thoughts. It is important to separate the various elements of the theory because, on analysis, some parts of the theory turn out to be correct, whereas others seem to be mistaken. As a beginning, we may distinguish the following claims, all of which have been made by cultural relativists:

1. Different societies have different moral codes.
2. There is no objective standard that can be used to judge one societal code better than another.

3. The moral code of our own society has no special status; it is merely one among many.
4. There is no "universal truth" in ethics—that is, there are no moral truths that hold for all peoples at all times.
5. The moral code of a society determines what is right within that society; that is, if the moral code of a society says that a certain action is right, then that action *is* right, at least within that society.
6. It is mere arrogance for us to try to judge the conduct of other peoples. We should adopt an attitude of tolerance toward the practices of other cultures.

Although it may seem that these six propositions go naturally together, they are independent of one another, in the sense that some of them might be true even if others are false. In what follows, we will try to identify what is correct in Cultural Relativism, but we will also be concerned to expose what is mistaken about it.

The Cultural Differences Argument

Cultural Relativism is a theory about the nature of morality. At first blush it seems quite plausible. However, like all such theories, it may be evaluated by subjecting it to rational analysis; and when we analyze Cultural Relativism we find that it is not so plausible as it first appears to be.

The first thing we need to notice is that at the heart of Cultural Relativism there is a certain *form of argument*. The strategy used by cultural relativists is to argue from facts about the differences between cultural outlooks to a conclusion about the status of morality. Thus we are invited to accept this reasoning:

1. The Greeks believed it was wrong to eat the dead, whereas the Callatians believed it was right to eat the dead.
2. Therefore, eating the dead is neither objectively right nor objectively wrong. It is merely a matter of opinion, which varies from culture to culture.

Or, alternatively:

1. The Eskimos see nothing wrong with infanticide, whereas Americans believe infanticide is immoral.
2. Therefore, infanticide is neither objectively right nor objectively wrong. It is merely a matter of opinion, which varies from culture to culture.

Clearly, these arguments are variations of one fundamental idea. They are both special cases of a more general argument, which says,

1. Different cultures have different moral codes.
2. Therefore, there is no objective "truth" in morality. Right and wrong are only matters of opinion, and opinions vary from culture to culture.

We may call this the *Cultural Differences Argument.* To many people, it is very persuasive. But from a logical point of view, is it a *sound* argument?

It is not sound. The trouble is that the conclusion does not really follow from the premise—that is, even if the premise is true, the conclusion still might be false. The premise concerns what people *believe*: in some societies, people believe one thing; in other societies, people believe differently. The conclusion, however, concerns *what really is the case.* The trouble is that this sort of conclusion does not follow logically from this sort of premise.

Consider again the example of the Greeks and Callatians. The Greeks believed it was wrong to eat the dead; the Callatians believed it was right. Does it follow, *from the mere fact that they disagreed*, that there is no objective truth in the matter? No, it does not follow; for it *could* be that the practice was objectively right (or wrong) and that one or the other of them was simply mistaken.

To make the point clearer, consider a very different matter. In some societies, people believe the earth is flat. In other societies, such as our own, people believe the earth is (roughly) spherical. Does it follow, *from the mere fact that they disagree*, that there is no "objective truth" in geography? Of course not; we would never draw such a conclusion because we realize that, in their beliefs about the world, the members of some societies might simply be wrong. There is no reason to think that if the world is round everyone must know it. Similarly, there is no reason to think that if there is a moral truth everyone must know it. The fundamental mistake in the Cultural Differences Argument is that it attempts to derive a substantive conclusion about a subject (morality) from the mere fact that people disagree about it.

It is important to understand the nature of the point that is being made here. We are *not* saying (not yet, anyway) that the conclusion of the argument is false. Insofar as anything being said here is concerned, it is still an open question whether the conclusion is true. We *are* making a purely logical point and saying that the conclusion does not *follow from* the premise. This is important, because in order to determine whether the conclusion is true, we need arguments in its support. Cultural Relativism proposes this argument, but unfortunately the argument turns out to be fallacious. So it proves nothing.

The Consequences of Taking Cultural Relativism Seriously

Even if the Cultural Differences Argument is invalid, Cultural Relativism might still be true. What would it be like if it were true?

In the passage quoted above, William Graham Sumner summarizes the essence of Cultural Relativism. He says that there is no measure of right and wrong other than the standards of one's society: "The notion of right is in the folkways. It is not outside of them, of independent origin, and brought to test them. In the folkways, whatever is, is right."

Suppose we took this seriously. What would be some of the consequences?

1. *We could no longer say that the customs of other societies are morally inferior to our own.* This, or course, is one of the main points stressed by Cultural Relativism. We would have to stop condemning other societies merely because they are "different." So long as we concentrate on certain examples, such as the funerary practices of the Greeks and Callatians, this may seem to be a sophisticated, enlightened attitude.

However, we would also be stopped from criticizing other, less benign practices. Suppose a society waged war on its neighbors for the purpose of taking slaves. Or suppose a society was violently anti-Semitic and its leaders set out to destroy the Jews. Cultural Relativism would preclude us from saying that either of these practices was wrong. We would not even be able to say that a society tolerant of Jews is *better* than the anti-Semitic society, for that would imply some sort of transcultural standard of comparison. The failure to condemn *these* practices does not seem "enlightened": on the contrary, slavery and anti-Semitism seem wrong *wherever* they occur. Nevertheless, if we took Cultural Relativism seriously, we would have to admit that these social practices also are immune from criticism.

2. *We could decide whether actions are right or wrong just by consulting the standards of our society.* Cultural Relativism suggests a simple test for determining what is right and what is wrong: all one has to do is ask whether the action is in accordance with the code of one's

society. Suppose a resident of South Africa is wondering whether his country's policy of *apartheid*—rigid racial segregation—is morally correct. All he has to do is ask whether this policy conforms to his society's moral code. If it does, there is nothing to worry about, at least from a moral point of view.

This implication of Cultural Relativism is disturbing because few of us think that our society's code is perfect—we can think of ways it might be improved. Yet Cultural Relativism would not only forbid us from criticizing the codes of *other* societies; it would stop us from criticizing our *own*. After all, if right and wrong are relative to culture, this must be true for our own culture just as much as for others.

3. *The idea of moral progress is called into doubt.* Usually, we think that at least some changes in our society have been for the better. (Some, of course, may have been changes for the worse.) Consider this example: Throughout most of Western history the place of women in society was very narrowly circumscribed. They could not own property; they could not vote or hold political office; with a few exceptions, they were not permitted to have paying jobs; and generally they were under the almost absolute control of their husbands. Recently much of this has changed, and most people think of it as progress.

If Cultural Relativism is correct, can we legitimately think of this as progress? Progress means replacing a way of doing things with a *better* way. But by what standard do we judge the new ways as better? If the old ways were in accordance with the social standards of their time, then Cultural Relativism would say it is a mistake to judge them by the standards of a different time. Eighteenth-century society was, in effect, a different society from the one we have now. To say that we have made progress implies a judgment that present-day society is better, and that is just the sort of transcultural judgment that, according to Cultural Relativism, is impermissible.

Our idea of social *reform* will also have to be reconsidered. A reformer, such as Martin Luther King, Jr., seeks to change his society for the better. Within the constraints imposed by Cultural Relativism, there is one way this might be done. If a society is not living up to its own ideals, the reformer may be regarded as acting for the best: the ideals of the society are the standard by which we judge his or her proposals as worthwhile. But the "reformer" may not challenge the ideals themselves, for those ideals are by definition correct. According to Cultural Relativism, then, the idea of social reform makes sense only in this very limited way.

These three consequences of Cultural Relativism have led many thinkers to reject it as implausible on its face. It does make sense, they say, to condemn some practices, such as slavery and anti-Semitism, wherever they occur. It makes sense to think that our own society has made some moral progress, while admitting that it is still imperfect and in need of reform. Because Cultural Relativism says that these judgments make no sense, the argument goes, it cannot be right.

Why There Is Less Disagreement Than It Seems

The original impetus for Cultural Relativism comes from the observation that cultures differ dramatically in their views of right and wrong. But just how much do they differ? It is true that there are differences. However, it is easy to overestimate the extent of those differences. Often, when we examine what *seems* to be a dramatic difference, we find that the cultures do not differ nearly as much as it appears.

Consider a culture in which people believe it is wrong to eat cows. This may even be a poor culture, in which there is not enough food; still, the cows are not to be touched. Such a society would *appear* to have values very different from our own. But does it? We have not yet asked why these people will not eat cows. Suppose it is because they believe that after death the souls of humans inhabit the bodies of animals, especially cows, so that a cow may be someone's grandmother. Now do we want to say that their values are different from ours? No; the difference lies elsewhere. The difference is in our belief systems, not in our values. We agree that we shouldn't eat Grandma; we simply disagree about whether the cow *is* (or could be) Grandma.

The general point is this: Many factors work together to produce the customs of a society. The society's values are only one of them. Other matters, such as the religious and factual beliefs held by its members and the physical circumstances in which they must live, are also important. We cannot conclude, then, merely because customs differ, that there is a disagreement about *values*. The difference in customs may be attributable to some other aspect of social life. Thus there may be less disagreement about values than there appears to be.

Consider the Eskimos again. They often kill perfectly normal infants, especially girls. We do not approve of this at all; a parent who did this in our society would be locked up. Thus there appears to be a great difference in the values of our two cultures. But suppose we ask *why* the Eskimos do this. The explanation is not that they have less affection for their children or less respect for human life. An Eskimo family will always protect its babies if conditions permit. But they live in a harsh environment, where food is often in short supply. A fundamental postulate to Eskimo thought is, "Life is hard, and the margin of safety small." A family may want to nourish its babies but be unable to do so.

As in many "primitive" societies, Eskimo mothers will nurse their infants over a much longer period of time than mothers in our culture. The child will take nourishment from its mother's breast for four years, perhaps even longer. So even in the best of times there are limits to the number of infants that one mother can sustain. Moreover, the Eskimos are a nomadic people—unable to farm, they must move about in search of food. Infants must be carried, and a mother can carry only one baby in her parka as she travels and goes about her outdoor work. Other family members can help, but this is not always possible.

Infant girls are more readily disposed of because, first, in this society the males are the primary food providers—they are the hunters, according to the traditional division of labor—and it is obviously important to maintain a sufficient number of food gatherers. But there is an important second reason as well. Because the hunters suffer a high casualty rate, the adult men who die prematurely far outnumber the women who die early. Thus if male and female infants survived in equal numbers, the female adult population would greatly outnumber the male adult population. Examining the available statistics, one writer concluded that "were it not for female infanticide . . . there would be approximately one-and-a-half times as many females in the average Eskimo local group as there are food-producing males."

So among the Eskimos, infanticide does not signal a fundamentally different attitude toward children. Instead, it is a recognition that drastic measures are sometimes needed to ensure the family's survival. Even then, however, killing the baby is not the first option considered. Adoption is common; childless couples are especially happy to take a more fertile couple's "surplus." Killing is only the last resort. I emphasize this in order to show that the raw data of the anthropologists can be misleading; it can make the differences in values between cultures appear greater than they are. The Eskimos' values are not all that different from our values. It is only that life forces upon them choices that we do not have to make.

How All Cultures Have Some Values in Common

It should not be surprising that, despite appearance, the Eskimos are protective of their children. How could it be otherwise? How could a group survive that did *not* value its young? This suggests a certain argument, one which shows that all cultural groups must be protective of their infants:

1. Human infants are helpless and cannot survive if they are not given extensive care for a period of years.
2. Therefore, if a group did not care for its young, the young would not survive, and the older members of the group would not be replaced. After a while the group would die out.
3. Therefore, any cultural group that continues to exist must care for its young. Infants that are *not* cared for must be the exception rather than the rule.

Similar reasoning shows that other values must be more or less universal. Imagine what it would be like for a society to place no value at all on truth telling. When one person spoke to another, there would be no presumption at all that he was telling the truth—for he could just as easily be speaking falsely. Within that society, there would be no reason to pay attention to what anyone says. (I ask you what time it is, and you say, "Four o'clock." But there is no presumption that you are speaking truly; you could just as easily have said the first thing that came into your head. So I have no reason to pay attention to your answer—in fact, there was no point in my asking you in the first place!) Communication would then be extremely difficult, if not impossible. And because complex societies cannot exist without regular communication among their members, society would become impossible. It follows that in any complex society there must be presumption in favor of truthfulness. There may of course be exceptions to this rule: there may be situations in which it is thought to be permissible to lie. Nevertheless, these will be exceptions to a rule that is in force in the society.

Let me give one further example of the same type. Could a society exist in which there was no prohibition on murder? What would this be like? Suppose people were free to kill other people at will, and no one thought there was anything wrong with it. In such a "society," no one could feel secure. Everyone would have to be constantly on guard. People who wanted to survive would have to avoid other people as much as possible. This would inevitably result in individuals trying to become as self-sufficient as possible—after all, associating with others would be dangerous. Society on any large scale would collapse. Of course, people might band together in smaller groups with others that they *could* trust not to harm them. But notice what this means: they would be forming smaller societies that *did* acknowledge a rule against murder. The prohibition of murder, then, is a necessary feature of all societies.

There is a general theoretical point here, namely, that *there are some moral rules that all societies will have in common, because those rules are necessary for society to exist.* The rules against lying and murder are two examples. And in fact, we do find these rules in force in all viable cultures. Cultures may differ in what they regard as legitimate exceptions to the rules, but this disagreement exists against a background of agreement on the larger issues. Therefore, it is a mistake to overestimate the amount of difference between cultures. Not *every* moral rule can vary from society to society.

What Can Be Learned from Cultural Relativism

At the outset, I said that we were going to identify both what is right and wrong in Cultural Relativism. Thus far I have mentioned only its mistakes: I have said that it rests on an invalid argument, that it has consequences that make it implausible on its face, and that the extent of cultural disagreement is far less than it implies. This all adds up to a pretty thorough repudiation of the theory. Nevertheless, it is still a very appealing idea, and the reader may have the feeling that all this is a little unfair. The theory *must* have something going for it, or else why has it been so influential? In fact, I think there *is* something right about Cultural Relativism, and now I want to say what that is. There are two lessons we should learn from the theory, even if we ultimately reject it.

1. Cultural Relativism warns us, quite rightly, about the danger of assuming that all our preferences are based on some absolute rational standard. They are not. Many (but not all) of our practices are merely peculiar to our society, and it is easy to lose sight of that fact. In reminding us of it, the theory does a service.

Funerary practices are one example. The Callatians, according to Herodotus, were "men who eat their fathers"—a shocking idea, to us at least. But eating the flesh of the dead could be understood as a sign of respect. It could be taken as a symbolic act that says, We wish this person's spirit to dwell within us. Perhaps this was the understanding of the Callatians. On such a way of thinking, burying the dead could be seen as an act of rejection, and burning the corpse as positively scornful. If this is hard to imagine, then we may need to have our imaginations stretched. Of course we may feel a visceral repugnance at the idea of eating human flesh in any circumstances. But what of it? This repugnance may be, as the relativists say, only a matter of what is customary in our particular society.

There are many other matters that we tend to think of in terms of objective right and wrong, but that are really nothing more than social conventions. Should women cover their breasts? A publicly exposed breast is scandalous in our society, whereas in other cultures it is unremarkable. Objectively speaking, it is neither right nor wrong—there is no objective reason why either custom is better. Cultural Relativism begins with the valuable insight that many of our practices are like this—they are only cultural products. Then it goes wrong by concluding that, because *some* practices are like this, *all* must be.

2. The second lesson has to do with keeping an open mind. In the course of growing up, each of us has acquired some strong feelings: we have learned to think of some types of conduct as acceptable, and others we have learned to regard as simply unacceptable. Occasionally, we may find those feelings challenged. We may encounter someone who claims that our feelings are mistaken. For example, we may have been taught that homosexuality is immoral, and we may feel quite uncomfortable around gay people and see them as alien and "different." Now someone suggests that this may be a mere prejudice; that there is nothing evil about homosexuality; that gay people are just people, like anyone else, who happen, through no choice of their own, to be attracted to others of the same sex. But because we feel so strongly about the matter, we may find it hard to take this seriously. Even after we listen to the arguments, we may still have the unshakable feeling that homosexuals *must*, somehow, be an unsavory lot.

Cultural Relativism, by stressing that our moral views can reflect the prejudices of our society, provides an antidote for this kind of dogmatism. When he tells the story of the Greeks and Callatians, Herodotus adds,

> For if anyone, no matter who, were given the opportunity of choosing from amongst all the nations of the world the set of beliefs which he thought best, he would inevitably, after careful consideration of

their relative merits, choose that of his own country. Everyone without exception believes his own native customs, and the religion he was brought up in, to be the best.

Realizing this can result in our having more open minds. We can come to understand that our feelings are not necessarily perceptions of the truth—they may be nothing more than the result of cultural conditioning. Thus when we hear it suggested that some element of our social code is *not* really the best and we find ourselves instinctively resisting the suggestion, we might stop and remember this. Then we may be more open to discovering the truth, whatever that might be.

We can understand the appeal of Cultural Relativism, then, even though the theory has serious shortcomings. It is an attractive theory because it is based on a genuine insight—that many of the practices and attitudes we think so natural are really only cultural products. Moreover, keeping this insight firmly in view is important if we want to avoid arrogance and have open minds. These are important points, not to be taken lightly. But we can accept these points without going on to accept the whole theory.

Study Questions

1. What is the cultural differences argument?
2. According to Rachels, why is that argument unsound?
3. If the cultural differences argument is unsatisfactory, might cultural relativism still be true?
4. According to Rachels, what can be learned from cultural relativism?

CHAPTER 7

Right and Wrong

Thomas Nagel

Another challenge to morality claims that we have no good reason to care about others. In the next selection Thomas Nagel, who is University Professor of Philosophy and Law Emeritus at New York University, responds that, as a matter of consistency, if you agree that another person has a reason not to harm you, then in similar circumstances you have a reason not to harm that other person.

Suppose you work in a library, checking people's books as they leave, and a friend asks you to let him smuggle out a hard-to-find reference work that he wants to own.

You might hesitate to agree for various reasons. You might be afraid that he'll be caught, and that both you and he will then get into trouble. You might want the book to stay in the library so that you can consult it yourself.

But you may also think that what he proposes is wrong—that he shouldn't do it and you shouldn't help him. If you think that, what does it mean, and what, if anything, makes it true?

To say it's wrong is not just to say it's against the rules. There can be bad rules which prohibit what isn't wrong—like a law against criticizing the government. A rule can also be bad because it requires something that *is* wrong—like a law that requires racial segregation in hotels and restaurants. The ideas of wrong and right are different from the ideas of what is and is not against the rules. Otherwise they couldn't be used in the evaluation of rules as well as of actions.

If you think it would be wrong to help your friend steal the book, then you will feel uncomfortable about doing it: in some way you won't want to do it, even if you are also reluctant to refuse help to a friend. Where does the desire not to do it come from; what is its motive, the reason behind it?

There are various ways in which something can be wrong, but in this case, if you had to explain it, you'd probably say that it would be unfair to other users of the library who may be just as interested in the book as your friend is, but who consult it in the reference room, where anyone who needs it can find it. You may also feel that to let him take it would betray your employers, who are paying you precisely to keep this sort of thing from happening.

These thoughts have to do with effects on others—not necessarily effects on their feelings, since they may never find out about it, but some kind of damage nevertheless. In general, the thought that something is wrong depends on its impact not just on the person who does it but on other people. They wouldn't like it, and they'd object if they found out.

But suppose you try to explain all this to your friend, and he says, "I know the head librarian wouldn't like it if he found out, and probably some of the other users of the library would be unhappy to find the book gone, but who cares? I want the book; why should I care about them?"

The argument that it would be wrong is supposed to give him the reason not to do it. But if someone just doesn't care about other people, what reason does he have to refrain from doing any of the things usually thought to be wrong, if he can get away with it: what reason does he have not to kill, steal, lie, or hurt others? If he can get what he wants by doing such things, why shouldn't he? And if there's no reason why he shouldn't, in what sense is it wrong? . . .

There is no substitute for a direct concern for other people as the basis of morality. But morality is supposed to apply to everyone: and can we assume that everyone has such a concern for others? Obviously not: some people are very selfish, and even those who are not selfish may care only about the people they know, and not about everyone. So where will we find a reason that everyone has not to hurt other people, even those they don't know?

Well, there's one general argument against hurting other people which can be given to anybody who understands English (or any other language), and which seems to show that he has *some* reason to care about others, even if in the end his selfish motives are so strong that he persists in treating other people badly anyway. It's an argument that I'm sure you've heard, and it goes like this: "How would you like it if someone did that to you?"

It's not easy to explain how this argument is supposed to work. Suppose you're about to steal someone else's umbrella as you leave a restaurant in a rainstorm, and a bystander says, "How would you like it if someone did that to you?" Why is it supposed to make you hesitate, or feel guilty?

Obviously the direct answer to the question is supposed to be, "I wouldn't like it at all!" But what's the next step? Suppose you were to say, "I wouldn't like it if someone did that to me. But luckily no one *is* doing it to me. I'm doing it to someone else, and I don't mind that at all!"

This answer misses the point of the question. When you are asked how you would like it if someone did that to you, you are supposed to think about all the feelings you would have if someone stole your umbrella. And that includes more than just "not liking it"—as you wouldn't "like it" if you stubbed your toe on a rock. If someone stole your umbrella you'd *resent* it. You'd have feelings about the umbrella thief, not just about the loss of the umbrella. You'd think, "Where does he get off, taking my umbrella that I bought with my hard-earned money and that I had the foresight to bring after reading the weather report? Why didn't he bring his own umbrella?" and so forth.

When our own interests are threatened by the inconsiderate behavior of others, most of us find it easy to appreciate that those others have a reason to be more considerate. When you are hurt, you probably feel that other people should care about it: you don't think it's no concern of theirs, and that they have no reason to avoid hurting you. That is the feeling that the "How would you like it?" argument is supposed to arouse.

Because if you admit that you would *resent* it if someone else did to you what you are now doing to him, you are admitting that you think he would have a reason not to do it to you. And if you admit that, you have to consider what that reason is. It couldn't be just that it's *you* that he's hurting, of all the people in the world. There's no special reason for him not to steal *your* umbrella, as opposed to anyone else's. There's nothing so special about you. Whatever the reason is, it's a reason he would have against hurting anyone else in the same way. And it's a reason anyone else would have too, in a similar situation, against hurting you or anyone else.

But if it's a reason anyone would have not to hurt anyone else in this way, then it's a reason *you* have not to hurt someone else in this way (since *anyone* means *everyone*). Therefore it's a reason not to steal the other person's umbrella now.

This is a matter of simple consistency. Once you admit that another person would have a reason not to harm you in similar circumstances, and once you admit that the reason he would have is very general and doesn't apply only to you, or to him, then to be consistent you have to admit that the same reason applies to you now. You shouldn't steal the umbrella, and you ought to feel guilty if you do.

Someone could escape from this argument if, when he was asked, "How would you like it if someone did that to you?" he answered, "I wouldn't resent it at all. I wouldn't *like* it if someone stole my umbrella in a rainstorm, but I wouldn't think there was any reason for him to consider my feelings about it." But how many people could honestly give that answer? I think most people, unless they're crazy, would think that their own interests and harms matter, not only to themselves, but in a way that gives other people a reason to care about them too. We all think that when we suffer it is not just bad *for us* but *bad, period.*

The basis of morality is a belief that good and harm to particular people (or animals) is good or bad not just from their point of view, but from a more general point of view, which every thinking person can understand. That means that each person has a reason to consider not only his own interests but the interests of others in deciding what to do. And it isn't enough if he is considerate only of some others—his family and friends, those he specially cares about. Of course he will care more about certain people, and also about himself. But he has some reason to consider the effect of what he does on the good or harm of everyone. If he's like most of us, that is what he thinks others should do with regard to him, even if they aren't friends of his.

Study Questions

1. Can a duly enacted law be morally wrong?
2. Do you have any reason to care about others?
3. Do others have any reason to care about you?
4. Does consistency require that your answers to questions 2 and 3 be the same?

CHAPTER 8

Egoism and Moral Skepticism

James Rachels

Morality involves taking into account interests apart from our own. Do we ever do so? According to psychological egoism we don't, because all human behavior is motivated only by self-interest. According to ethical egoism, even if we could act in the interest of others, we ought not do so but should be concerned only with ourselves. In the selection that follows, James Rachels, whose work we read previously, considers both psychological and ethical egoism, concluding that neither is acceptable. He refers to the writings of Joseph Butler (1692–1752), an English philosopher and Anglican bishop.

1. Our ordinary thinking about morality is full of assumptions that we almost never question. We assume, for example, that we have an obligation to consider the welfare of other people when we decide what actions to perform or what rules to obey; we think that we must refrain from acting in ways harmful to others, and that we must respect their rights and interests as well as our own. We also assume that people are in fact capable of being motivated by such considerations, that is, that people are not wholly selfish and that they do sometimes act in the interests of others.

Both of these assumptions have come under attack by moral sceptics, as long ago as by Glaucon in Book II of Plato's *Republic*. Glaucon recalls the legend of Gyges, a shepherd who was said to have found a magic ring in a fissure opened by an earthquake. The ring would make its wearer invisible and thus would enable him to go anywhere and do anything undetected. Gyges used the power of the ring to gain

From Steven M. Cahn, ed., *A New Introduction to Philosophy.* Copyright © 1971. Reprinted by permission of Steven M. Cahn.

entry to the Royal Palace, where he seduced the Queen, murdered the King, and subsequently seized the throne. Now Glaucon asks us to imagine that there are two such rings, one given to a man of virtue and one given to a rogue. The rogue, of course, will use his ring unscrupulously and do anything necessary to increase his own wealth and power. He will recognize no moral constraints on his conduct, and, since the cloak of invisibility will protect him from discovery, he can do anything he pleases without fear of reprisal. So, there will be no end to the mischief he will do. But how will the so-called virtuous man behave? Glaucon suggests that he will behave no better than the rogue: "No one, it is commonly believed, would have such iron strength of mind as to stand fast in doing right or keep his hands off other men's goods, when he could go to the market-place and fearlessly help himself to anything he wanted, enter houses and sleep with any woman he chose, set prisoners free and kill men at his pleasure, and in a word go about among men with the powers of a god. He would behave no better than the other; both would take the same course."[1] Moreover, why shouldn't he? Once he is freed from the fear of reprisal, why shouldn't a man simply do what he pleases, or what he thinks is best for himself? What reason is there for him to continue being "moral" when it is clearly not to his own advantage to do so?

These sceptical views suggested by Glaucon have come to be known as *psychological egoism* and *ethical egoism*, respectively. Psychological egoism is the view that all men are selfish in everything that they do, that is, that the only motive from which anyone ever acts is self-interest. On this view, even when men are acting in ways apparently calculated to benefit others, they are actually motivated by the belief that acting in this way is to their own advantage, and if they did not believe this, they would not be doing that action. Ethical egoism is, by contrast, a normative view about how men *ought* to act. It is the view that, regardless of how men do in fact behave, they have no obligation to do anything except what is in their own interests. According to ethical egoists, a person is always justified in doing whatever is in his own interests, regardless of the effect on others.

Clearly, if either of these views is correct, then "the moral institution of life" (to use Butler's well-turned phrase) is very different than what we normally think. The majority of mankind is grossly deceived about what is, or ought to be, the case, where morals are concerned.

2. Psychological egoism seems to fly in the face of the facts. We are tempted to say, "Of course people act unselfishly all the time. For

example, Smith gives up a trip to the country, which he would have enjoyed very much, in order to stay behind and help a friend with his studies, which is a miserable way to pass the time. This is a perfectly clear case of unselfish behavior, and if the psychological egoist thinks that such cases do not occur, then he is just mistaken." Given such obvious instances of "unselfish behavior," what reply can the egoist make? There are two general arguments by which he might try to show that all actions, including those such as the one just outlined, are in fact motivated by self-interest. Let us examine these in turn:

a. The first argument goes as follows: If we describe one person's action as selfish, and another person's action as unselfish, we are overlooking the crucial fact that in both cases, assuming that the action is done voluntarily, *the agent is merely doing what he most wants to do.* If Smith stays behind to help his friend, that only shows that he wanted to help his friend more than he wanted to go to the country. And why should he be praised for his "unselfishness" when he is only doing what he most wants to do? So, since Smith is only doing what he wants to do, he cannot be said to be acting unselfishly.

This argument is so bad that it would not deserve to be taken seriously except for the fact that so many otherwise intelligent people have been taken in by it. First, the argument rests on the premise that people never voluntarily do anything except what they want to do. But this is patently false; there are at least two classes of actions that are exceptions to this generalization. One is the set of actions which we may not want to do, but which we do anyway as a means to an end which we want to achieve, for example, going to the dentist in order to stop a toothache, or going to work every day in order to be able to draw our pay at the end of the month. These cases may be regarded as consistent with the spirit of the egoist argument, however, since the ends mentioned are wanted by the agent. But the other set of actions are those which we do, not because we want to, nor even because there is an end which we want to achieve, but because we feel ourselves *under an obligation* to do them. For example, someone may do something because he has promised to do it, and thus feels obligated, even though he does not want to do it. It is sometimes suggested that in such cases we do the action because, after all, we want to keep our promises; so, even here, we are doing what we want. However, this dodge will not work: if I have promised to do something, and if I do not want to do it, then it is simply false to say that I want to keep my promise. In such cases we feel a conflict precisely because we do *not* want to do what we feel obligated to do. It is reasonable to think that Smith's action falls roughly into this second category: he might stay behind, not because he wants to, but because he feels that this friend needs help.

But suppose we were to concede, for the sake of the argument, that all voluntary action is motivated by the agent's wants, or at least that Smith is so motivated. Even if this were granted, it would not follow that Smith is acting selfishly or from self-interest. For if Smith wants to do something that will help his friend, even when it means forgoing his own enjoyments, that is precisely what makes him *un*selfish. What else could unselfishness be, if not wanting to help others? Another way to put the same point is to say that it is the *object* of a want that determines whether it is selfish or not. The mere fact that I am acting on *my* wants does not mean that I am acting selfishly; that depends on *what it is* that I want. If I want only my own good, and care nothing for others, then I am selfish; but if I also want other people to be well-off and happy, and if I act on *that* desire, then my action is not selfish. So much for this argument.

b. The second argument for psychological egoism is this: Since so-called unselfish actions always produce a sense of self-satisfaction in the agent,[2] and since this sense of satisfaction is a pleasant state of consciousness, it follows that the point of the action is really to achieve a pleasant state of consciousness, rather than to bring about any good for others. Therefore, the action is "unselfish" only at a superficial level of analysis. Smith will feel much better with himself for having stayed to help his friend—if he had gone to the country, he would have felt terrible about it—and that is the real point of the action. According to a well-known story, this argument was once expressed by Abraham Lincoln:

> Mr. Lincoln once remarked to a fellow-passenger on an old-time mud-coach that all men were prompted by selfishness in doing good. His fellow-passenger was antagonizing this position when they were passing over a corduroy bridge that spanned a slough. As they crossed this bridge they espied an old razor-backed sow on the bank making a terrible noise because her pigs had got into the slough and were in danger of drowning. As the old coach began to climb the hill, Mr. Lincoln called out, "Driver, can't you stop just a moment?" Then Mr. Lincoln jumped out, ran back, and lifted the little pigs out of the mud and water and placed them on the bank. When he returned, his companion remarked: "Now, Abe, where does selfishness come in on this little episode?" "Why, bless your soul, Ed, that was the very essence

of selfishness. I should have had no peace of mind all day had I gone on and left that suffering old sow worrying over those pigs. I did it to get peace of mind, don't you see?"[3]

This argument suffers from defects similar to the previous one. Why should we think that merely because someone derives satisfaction from helping others this makes him selfish? Isn't the unselfish man precisely the one who *does* derive satisfaction from helping others, while the selfish man does not? If Lincoln "got peace of mind" from rescuing the piglets, does this show him to be selfish, or, on the contrary, doesn't it show him to be compassionate and good-hearted? (If a man were truly selfish, why should it bother his conscience that *others* suffer—much less pigs?) Similarly, it is nothing more than shabby sophistry to say, because Smith takes satisfaction in helping his friend, that he is behaving selfishly. If we say this rapidly, while thinking about something else, perhaps it will sound all right; but if we speak slowly, and pay attention to what we are saying, it sounds plain silly.

Moreover, suppose we ask *why* Smith derives satisfaction from helping his friend. The answer will be, it is because Smith cares for him and wants him to succeed. If Smith did not have these concerns, then he would take no pleasure in assisting him; and these concerns, as we have already seen, are the marks of unselfishness, not selfishness. To put the point more generally: if we have a positive attitude toward the attainment of some goal, then we may derive satisfaction from attaining that goal. But the *object* of our attitude is *the attainment of that goal*; and we must want to attain the goal *before* we can find any satisfaction in it. We do not, in other words, desire some sort of "pleasurable consciousness" and then try to figure out how to achieve it; rather, we desire all sorts of different things—money, a new fishing boat, to be a better chess player, to get a promotion in our work, etc.—and because we desire these things, we derive satisfaction from attaining them. And so, if someone desires the welfare and happiness of another person, he will derive satisfaction from that; but this does not mean that this satisfaction is the object of his desire, or that he is in any way selfish on account of it.

It is a measure of the weakness of psychological egoism that these insupportable arguments are the ones most often advanced in its favor. Why, then, should anyone ever have thought it a true view? Perhaps because of a desire for theoretical simplicity: In thinking about human conduct, it would be nice if there were some simple formula that would unite the diverse phenomena of human behavior under a single explanatory principle, just as simple formulae in physics bring together a great many apparently different phenomena. And since it is obvious that self-regard is an overwhelmingly important factor in motivation, it is only natural to wonder whether all motivation might not be explained in these terms. But the answer is clearly No; while a great many human actions are motivated entirely or in part by self-interest, only by a deliberate distortion of the facts can we say that all conduct is so motivated. This will be clear, I think, if we correct three confusions which are commonplace. The exposure of these confusions will remove the last traces of plausibility from the psychological egoist thesis.

The first is the confusion of selfishness with self-interest. The two are clearly not the same. If I see a physician when I am feeling poorly, I am acting in my own interest but no one would think of calling me "selfish" on account of it. Similarly, brushing my teeth, working hard at my job, and obeying the law are all in my self-interest but none of these are examples of selfish conduct. This is because selfish behavior is behavior that ignores the interests of others, in circumstances in which their interests ought not to be ignored. This concept has a definite evaluative flavor; to call someone "selfish" is not just to describe his action but to condemn it. Thus, you would not call me selfish for eating a normal meal in normal circumstances (although it may surely be in my self-interest); but you would call me selfish for hoarding food while others about are starving.

The second confusion is the assumption that every action is done *either* from self-interest or from other-regarding motives. Thus, the egoist concludes that if there is no such thing as genuine altruism then all actions must be done from self-interest. But this is certainly a false dichotomy. The man who continues to smoke cigarettes, even after learning about the connection between smoking and cancer, is surely not acting from self-interest, not even by his own standards— self-interest would dictate that he quit smoking at once—and he is not acting altruistically either. He *is*, no doubt, smoking for the pleasure of it, but all that this shows is that undisciplined pleasure-seeking and acting from self-interest are very different. This is what led Butler to remark that "the thing to be lamented is, not that men have so great regard to their own good or interest in the present world, for they have not enough."[4]

The last two paragraphs show (*a*) that it is false that all actions are selfish, and (*b*) that it is false that all actions are done out of self-interest. And it should be noted that these two points can be made, and were, without any appeal to putative examples of altruism.

The third confusion is the common but false assumption that a concern for one's own welfare is incompatible with any genuine concern for the welfare of others. Thus, since it is obvious that everyone (or very nearly everyone) does desire his own well-being, it might be thought that no one can really be concerned with others. But again, this is false. There is no inconsistency in desiring that everyone, including oneself *and* others, be well-off and happy. To be sure, it may happen on occasion that our own interests conflict with the interests of others, and in these cases we will have to make hard choices. But even in these cases we might sometimes opt for the interests of others, especially when the others involved are our family or friends. But more importantly, not all cases are like this: sometimes we are able to promote the welfare of others when our own interests are not involved at all. In these cases not even the strongest self-regard need prevent us from acting considerately toward others.

Once these confusions are cleared away, it seems to me obvious enough that there is no reason whatever to accept psychological egoism. On the contrary, if we simply observe people's behavior with an open mind, we may find that a great deal of it is motivated by self-regard, but by no means all of it; and that there is no reason to deny that "the moral institution of life" can include a place for the virtue of beneficence.[5]

3. The ethical egoist would say at this point, "Of course it is possible for people to act altruistically, and perhaps many people do act that way—but there is no reason why they *should* do so. A person is under no obligation to do anything except what is in his own interests."[6] This is really quite a radical doctrine. Suppose I have an urge to set fire to some public building (say, a department store) just for the fascination of watching the spectacular blaze: according to this view, the fact that several people might be burned to death provides no reason whatever why I should not do it. After all, this only concerns *their* welfare, not my own, and according to the ethical egoist the only person I need think of is myself.

Some might deny that ethical egoism has any such monstrous consequences. They would point out that it is really to my own advantage not to set the fire—for, if I do that I may be caught and put into prison (unlike Gyges, I have no magic ring for protection). Moreover, even if I could avoid being caught it is still to my advantage to respect the rights and interests of others, for it is to my advantage to live in a society in which people's rights and interests are respected. Only in such a society can I live a happy and secure life; so, in acting kindly toward others, I would merely be doing my part to create and maintain the sort of society which it is to my advantage to have.[7] Therefore, it is said, the egoist would not be such a bad man; he would be as kindly and considerate as anyone else, because he would see that it is to his own advantage to be kindly and considerate.

This is a seductive line of thought, but it seems to me mistaken. Certainly it is to everyone's advantage (including the egoist's) to preserve a stable society where people's interests are generally protected. But there is no reason for the egoist to think that merely because *he* will not honor the rules of the social game, decent society will collapse. For the vast majority of people are not egoists, and there is no reason to think that they will be converted by his example— especially if he is discreet and does not unduly flaunt his style of life. What this line of reasoning shows is not that the egoist himself must act benevolently, but that he must encourage *others* to do so. He must take care to conceal from public view his own self-centered method of decision making, and urge others to act on precepts very different from those on which he is willing to act.

The rational egoist, then, cannot advocate that egoism be universally adopted by everyone. For he wants a world in which his own interests are maximized; and if other people adopted the egoistic policy of pursuing their own interests to the exclusion of his interests, as he pursues his interests to the exclusion of theirs, then such a world would be impossible. So he himself will be an egoist, but he will want others to be altruists.

This brings us to what is perhaps the most popular "refutation" of ethical egoism current among philosophical writers—the argument that ethical egoism is at bottom inconsistent because it cannot be universalized.[8] The argument goes like this:

To say that any action or policy of action is *right* (or that it *ought* to be adopted) entails that it is right for *anyone* in the same sort of circumstances. I cannot, for example, say that it is right for me to lie to you, and yet object when you lie to me (provided, of course, that the circumstances are the same). I cannot hold that it is all right for me to drink your beer and then complain when you drink mine. This is just the requirement that we be consistent in our evaluations; it is a requirement of logic. Now it is said that ethical egoism cannot meet this requirement because, as we have already seen, the egoist would not want others to act in the same way that he acts. Moreover, suppose he *did* advocate the universal adoption of egoistic policies: he would be saying to Peter, "You ought to pursue your own interests even if it means destroying Paul"; and he would be saying to Paul, "You ought to pursue your own interests even if it means destroying Peter." The attitudes expressed in these two recommendations seem clearly inconsistent—he is urging the advancement of Peter's interest at one moment, and countenancing their defeat at the next. Therefore, the argument goes, there is no way to maintain the doctrine of ethical egoism as a consistent view about how we ought to act. We will fall into inconsistency whenever we try.

What are we to make of this argument? Are we to conclude that ethical egoism has been refuted? Such a conclusion, I think, would be unwarranted; for I think that we can show, contrary to this argument, how ethical egoism can be maintained consistently. We need only to interpret the egoist's position in a sympathetic way: we should say that he has in mind a certain kind of world which he would prefer over all others; it would be a world in which his own interests were maximized, regardless of the effects on the other people. The egoist's primary policy of action, then, would be to act in such a way as to bring about, as nearly as possible, this sort of world. Regardless of however morally reprehensible we might find it, there is nothing *inconsistent* in someone's adopting this as his ideal and acting in a way calculated to bring it about. And if someone did adopt this as his ideal, then he would not advocate universal egoism; as we have already seen, he would want other people to be altruists. So, if he advocates any principles of conduct for the general public, they will be altruistic principles. This could not be inconsistent; on the contrary, it would be perfectly consistent with his goal of creating a world in which his own interests are maximized. To be sure, he would have to be deceitful; in order to secure the good will of others, and a favorable hearing for his exhortations to altruism, he would have to pretend that he was himself prepared to accept altruistic principles. But again, that would be all right; from the egoist's point of view, this would merely be a matter of adopting the necessary means to the achievement of his goal—and while we might not approve of this, there is nothing inconsistent about it. Again, it might be said, "He advocates one thing, but does another. Surely *that's* inconsistent." But it is not; for what he advocates and what he does are both calculated as means to an end (the *same* end, we might note); and as such, he is doing what is rationally required in each case. Therefore, contrary to the previous argument, there is nothing inconsistent in the ethical egoist's view. He cannot be refuted by the claim that he contradicts himself.

Is there, then, no way to refute the ethical egoist? If by "refute" we mean show that he has made some *logical* error, the answer is that there is not. However, there is something more that can be said. The egoist challenge to our ordinary moral convictions amounts to a demand for an explanation of why we should adopt certain policies of action, namely, policies in which the good of others is given importance. We can give an answer to this demand, albeit an indirect one. The reason one ought not to do actions that would hurt other people is other people would be hurt. The reason one ought to do actions that would benefit other people is other people would be benefited. This may at first seem like a piece of philosophical sleight-of-hand, but it is not. The point is that the welfare of human beings is something that most of us value *for its own sake*, and not merely for the sake of something else. Therefore, when *further* reasons are demanded for valuing the welfare of human beings, we cannot point to anything further to satisfy this demand. It is not that we have no reason for pursuing these policies, but that our reason *is* that these policies are for the good of human beings.

So if we are asked, "Why shouldn't I set fire to this department store?" one answer would be, "Because if you do, people may be burned to death." This is a complete, sufficient reason which does not require qualification or supplementation of any sort. If someone seriously wants to know why this action shouldn't be done, that's the reason. If we are pressed further and asked the sceptical question, "But why shouldn't I do actions that will harm others?" we may not know what to say—but this is because the questioner has included in his question the very answer we would like to give: "Why shouldn't you do actions that will harm others? Because, doing those actions would harm others."

The egoist, no doubt, will not be happy with this. He will protest that *we* may accept this as a reason, but *he* does not. And here the argument stops: there are limits to what can be accomplished by argument, and if the egoist really doesn't care about other people—if he honestly doesn't care whether they are helped or hurt by his actions—then we have reached those limits. If we want to persuade him to act decently toward his fellow humans, we will have to make our appeal to such other attitudes as he does possess, by threats, bribes, or other cajolery. That is all that we can do.

Though some may find this situation distressing (we would like to be able to show that the egoist is just *wrong*), it holds no embarrassment for common morality. What we have come up against is simply a fundamental requirement of rational action, namely, that the existence of reasons for action always depends on the prior existence of certain attitudes in the agent. For example, the fact that a certain course of action would make the agent a lot of money is a reason for doing it only if the agent wants to make money; the fact that practicing at chess makes one a better player is a reason for practicing only if one wants to be a better player; and so on. Similarly, the fact that a certain action would help the agent is a reason for doing the action only if the agent cares about his own welfare, and the fact that an action would help others is a reason for doing it only if the agent cares about others. In this respect ethical egoism and what we might call ethical altruism are in exactly the same fix: both require that the agent *care* about himself, or about other people, before they can get started.

So a nonegoist will accept "It would harm another person" as a reason not to do an action simply because he cares about what happens to that other person. When the egoist says that he does *not* accept that as a reason, he is saying something quite extraordinary. He is saying that he has no affection for friends or family, that he never feels pity or compassion, that he is the sort of person who can look on scenes of human misery with complete indifference, so long as he is not the one suffering. Genuine egoists, people who really don't care at all about anyone other than themselves, are rare. It is important to keep this in mind when thinking about ethical egoism; it is easy to forget just how fundamental to human psychological makeup the feeling of sympathy is. Indeed, a man without any sympathy at all would scarcely be recognizable as a man; and that is what makes ethical egoism such a disturbing doctrine in the first place.

4. There are, of course, many different ways in which the sceptic might challenge the assumptions underlying our moral practice. In this essay I have discussed only two of them, the two put forward by Glaucon in the passage that I cited from Plato's *Republic*. It is important that the assumptions underlying our moral practice should not be confused with particular judgments made within that practice. To defend one is not to defend the other. We may assume—quite properly, if my analysis has been correct—that the virtue of beneficence does, and indeed should, occupy an important place in "the moral institution of life"; and yet we may make constant and miserable errors when it comes to judging when and in what ways this virtue is to be exercised. Even worse, we may often be able to make accurate moral judgments, and know what we ought to do, but not do it. For these ills, philosophy alone is not the cure.

Notes

1. *The Republic of Plato*, translated by F. M. Cornford (Oxford, 1941), p. 45.
2. Or, as it is sometimes said, "It gives him a clear conscience," or "He couldn't sleep at night if he had done otherwise," or "He would have been ashamed of himself for not doing it," and so on.
3. Frank C. Sharp, *Ethics* (New York, 1928), pp. 74–75. Quoted from the Springfield (IL) *Monitor* in the *Outlook*, vol. 56, p. 1059.
4. *The Works of Joseph Butler*, edited by W. E. Gladstone (Oxford, 1896), vol. II, p. 26. It should be noted that most of the points I am making against psychological egoism were first made by Joseph Butler. Butler made all the important points; all that is left for us is to remember them.
5. The capacity for altruistic behavior is not unique to human beings. Some interesting experiments with rhesus monkeys have shown that these animals will refrain from operating a device for securing food if this causes other animals to suffer pain. See Jules H. Masserman, Stanley Wechkin, and William Terris, "'Altruistic' Behavior in Rhesus Monkeys," *American Journal of Psychiatry*, vol. 121 (1964), pp. 584–85.
6. I take this to be the view of Ayn Rand, insofar as I understand her confused doctrine.
7. Cf. Thomas Hobbes, *Leviathan* (London, 1651), chap. 17.
8. See, for example, Brian Medlin, "Ultimate Principles and Ethical Egoism," *Australasian Journal of Philosophy*, vol. 35 (1957), pp. 111–18; and D. H. Monro, *Empiricism and Ethics* (Cambridge, 1967), chap. 16.

Study Questions

1. Explain the distinction between psychological and ethical egoism.
2. In the story about Abraham Lincoln, was his action motivated by selfishness?
3. Is a concern for one's own welfare incompatible with a concern for the welfare of others?
4. Is it self-defeating for an ethical egoist to urge everyone to act egoistically?

CHAPTER 9

Happiness and Immorality

Steven M. Cahn and Jeffrie G. Murphy

An additional challenge to morality comes from those who believe that sometimes a person may achieve happiness by acting immorally. Is the happiness supposedly attained in this way illusory, or does it provide a reason to disregard moral considerations? I discuss the issue here with Jeffrie G. Murphy, Regents' Professor of Law and Philosophy at Arizona State University. He refers to the work of Sören Kierkegaard (1813–1855), the Danish philosopher and theologian. Regarding Philippa Foot, see chapter 11.

A. The Happy Immoralist

Steven M. Cahn

"Happiness," according to Philippa Foot, "is a most intractable concept." She commits herself, however, to the claim that "great happiness, unlike euphoria or even great pleasure, must come from something related to what is deep in human nature, and fundamental in human life, such as affection for children and friends, the desire to work, and love of freedom and truth."[1] I am not persuaded by this characterization of happiness and offer the following counterexample.

Consider Fred, a fictitious person but an amalgamation of several individuals I have known. Fred's life has been devoted to achieving three aims: fame, wealth, and a reputation for probity. He has no interest whatsoever in friends or truth. Indeed, he is treacherous and thoroughly dishonest. Nevertheless, he has attained his three goals and is, in fact, a rich celebrity renowned for his supposed integrity.

Parts A and B are from *Journal of Social Philosophy*, Vol. 35. Copyright © 2004. Reprinted by permission of Blackwell Publishing Ltd. Parts C and D are reprinted by permission of the author.

His acquiring a good name while acting unscrupulously is a tribute to his audacity, cunning, and luck. Now he rests self-satisfied: basking in renown, delighting in luxuries, and relishing praise for his reputed commitment to the highest moral standards.

That he enjoys great pleasure, even euphoria, is undeniable. But, according to Philippa Foot, he is not happy. I would say, rather, that *we* are not happy with *him*. We do not wish to see shallowness and hypocrisy rewarded. Indeed, while numerous works of literature describe good persons who are doomed to failure, few works tell of evil persons who ultimately flourish. (An exception to the rule is Natasha in Chekhov's *The Three Sisters*, a play that causes most audiences anguish.)

We can define "happiness" so as to falsify the claim that Fred is happy. This philosophical sleight-of-hand, though, accomplishes little, for Fred is wholly contented, suffering no worries or anxieties. Indeed, he is smug, as he revels in his exalted position.

Happiness may be, as Philippa Foot says, an "intractable concept." Yet surely Fred is happy. Perhaps later in life he won't be. Or perhaps he will. He may come to the end of his days as happy as he is now. I presume his case provides a reason why God is supposed to have created hell, for if Fred suffers no punishment in the next world, he may escape punishment altogether. And believing in that prospect is yet another reason he is happy.

B. The Unhappy Immoralist

Jeffrie G. Murphy

> All that you've just noted merely confirms my belief . . . that if we are to talk philosophy to any purpose, language must be re-made from the ground up.
>
> —*Doctor Glas*, Hjalmar Söderberg

When presenting his version of the ancient and well-known challenge that the Sophists long ago posed to Socrates, Professor Cahn seems to be assuming at the outset—and asking us to grant—that the man he describes *is* happy. But such an assumption begs the whole question at issue here.

In both *Republic* and *Gorgias*, Plato has Socrates argue that the immoral man—even a tyrant with great power—may of course be happy as the ignorant world understands happiness but will not be happy as this concept will be truly understood by the wise philosopher.

Professor Cahn dismisses this as verbal "sleight-of-hand," but I think that such dismissal is hasty. Plato is trying to advance our philosophical understanding by making a conceptual or linguistic claim— no doubt a revisionary one—and surely not all such claims are merely useless verbal tricks. As I read Plato, he (like Philippa Foot) is suggesting that full human happiness is to be understood as the satisfaction one takes in having a personality wherein all elements required for a fully realized human life are harmoniously integrated. The immoralist lacks some of these attributes—integrity, moral emotions, and the capacity for true friendships, for example. Given what he lacks, it can be granted that he may indeed be happy in some limited way—e.g., enjoying a great deal of pleasure—while insisting that he cannot be happy in the full sense.

As a matter of common language, of course, many people do not use the word "happiness" in this rich sense but tend to mean by it something like "has a whole lot of fun." Because of this, the Greek word *eudaimonia*, which in the past was generally translated as "happiness," is now often rendered as "flourishing" to avoid confusion. But some are not so quick to give up the older and deeper usage.

> [Realizing how little the clergyman cared about his wife's health or even his own] I began to think that Markel and his Cyrenäics are right: people care nothing for happiness, they look only for pleasure. They seek pleasure even flat in the face of their own happiness. (*Doctor Glas* again)

Some of the spirit of Plato and Socrates is to be found in Kierkegaard's *Purity of Heart Is to Will One Thing*—where he seeks to expose the conflicts and deficiencies present in the "double-minded" person who does not organize his life around the moral good, a person whom Kierkegaard regards as self-deceived if he thinks of himself as truly happy. Kierkegaard argues for this with a blending of conceptual and psychological claims—claims about the nature of those desires he calls "temporal." The person who wills only in pursuit of temporal rather than eternal (i.e., ethico-religious) desires will, he maintains, ultimately fall into boredom and despair since the objects of these desires are vulnerable to the vicissitudes of fate and fortune and carry only temporary satisfaction. The apparent happiness of the person in bondage to temporal desires will be momentary and will mask what is in fact that person's desperate attempt to generate and satisfy new desires as the old ones become boring or their objects pass away. Kierkegaard, in *Either/Or*, calls this boredom avoidance strategy "the rotation of crops." The person who lives solely for temporal values will, according to Kierkegaard, remain in his deficient state unless he experiences and listens to the moral emotions of regret and remorse—those "emissaries from eternity" that call us to our full humanity.

Is Professor Cahn's "happy immoralist" captured by Kierkegaard's diagnosis? I think that he is. He does, after all, "relish praise," "bask in renown," and smugly "revel in his exalted position." This suggests that, like the tyrant discussed by Plato, he is attached to temporal values that are *vulnerable*—e.g., dependent on the responses of others. Since these are ultimately out of his control, must he not consciously feel or repress *fear*—a fear that may not be compatible with happiness? Professor Cahn admits that there may be a future time when his immoralist becomes unhappy, and I am inclined to think that the immoralist's conscious or repressed realization of this possibility would at the very least pose a serious obstacle to his being fully happy now. And is happiness simply a matter of *now* anyway? Perhaps, as Aristotle sometimes suggests, happiness is better understood as an attribute, not of a present moment of one's life, but of a whole life—the wisdom in the ancient Greek saying that we should call no man happy until he is dead. Finally, if there is any truth in the idea that love and friendship are among the constituents of the happiest of human lives, must not the immoralist's nature—his inability to make and honor binding commitments—forever foreclose these goods to him?

There is no doubt that Plato's and Kierkegaard's understanding of happiness does not capture everyone's understanding of the concept, and thus it must be admitted that some conceptual or linguistic revision is going on here—just as Socrates was engaged in such revision when he made the revolutionary suggestion (*Apology*) that a good person cannot be harmed because harm (*kakon*), when properly understood, will be understood as loss of moral integrity and not as personal pain or disgrace. And if this was "sleight-of-hand," it strikes me that our concept of morality—indeed our civilization—was enriched by it. Professor Cahn's attempt to undermine the Platonic happiness tradition with his story of "the happy immoralist" thus strikes me as no more successful than an attempt to refute Socrates's claim about a good man's insulation from harm by finding a good man and hitting him in the head with a baseball bat. Doctor Glas's friend certainly overstated the case when he said that philosophy requires that language be remade from the ground up, but it is true,

I think, that conceptual or linguistic revision can sometimes enlarge and deepen our moral understanding—perhaps bringing to consciousness something that was latent all along.

To sum up: When I think of the man described by Professor Cahn, I find that I *pity* him—pity him because, with Plato, I think that he is punished simply by being the kind of person that he is. But why would I pity him if I thought that he was truly happy?

C. A Challenge to Morality

Steven M. Cahn

Why have so many philosophers, past and present, been loath to admit even the possibility of a happy immoralist? I believe they rightly regard the concept as a threat to morality. For the greater the divergence between morality and happiness, the greater the loss of motivation to choose the moral path.

Most of us, fortunately, have moral compunctions. But when our moral values and our happiness conflict, what are we to do? Those who doubt that such a situation can ever arise should consider the following example inspired by the plot of Woody Allen's thought-provoking movie *Crimes and Misdemeanors*.

Suppose a man who is happily married and highly respected as a physician makes the mistake of embarking on an affair with an unmarried woman whom he meets while she is working as a flight attendant. When he tries to break off this relationship, she threatens to expose his adultery and thereby wreck his marriage and career.

All he has worked for his entire life is at risk. He knows that if the affair is revealed, his wife will divorce him, his children will reject him, and the members of his community will no longer support his medical practice. Instead of being the object of people's admiration, he will be viewed with scorn. In short, his life will be shattered.

As the flight attendant is about to take the steps that will destroy him, he confides in his brother, who has connections to the criminal underworld. The brother offers to help him by arranging for the flight attendant to be murdered, with minimal danger that the crime will be traced to either the physician or his brother.

Should the physician consent to the killing? Doing so is clearly immoral, but, if all goes as planned, he will avoid calamity.

The physician agrees to the murder, and when it is carried out and the police investigate, they attribute it to a drifter who eventually dies of alcoholism, and the case is closed. The physician's life goes on without further complications from the matter, and years later he is honored at a testimonial dinner where, accompanied by his loving wife and adoring children, he accepts the effusive gratitude of the community for his lifetime of service. He is a happy man, taking pride in both the affection of his family and the admiration of his patients and friends.

Even most of those who might take issue with my claim that the physician is happy would agree that he is happier than he would have been had his life been destroyed. Hence his immorality enhanced his chances for happiness.

But then the feared question arises: What persuasive reasons, if any, can be offered to demonstrate that in securing his own happiness the physician acted unwisely? Here is a serious challenge to morality, of a sort we may face quite frequently in our lives, although usually the stakes are less momentous. How we decide tells us not only about morality and happiness but also about the sort of persons we choose to be.

D. A Further Challenge

Steven M. Cahn

For those who find farfetched the case of the adulterous physician, I offer the following fictional but realistic story from the world of academia.

* * *

TWO LIVES

Joan earned a doctoral degree from a first-rate university and sought appointment to a tenure-track position in which she could teach and pursue her research. Unfortunately, she received no offers and reluctantly was about to accept nonacademic employment when an unexpected call came inviting her for an interview at a highly attractive school. During her visit she was told by the dean that the job was hers. The dean, however, had one condition: Joan was expected to teach a particular course each year in which numerous varsity athletes would enroll, and she would be required to award them all passing grades, even if their work was in every respect unsatisfactory. Only the dean would know of this special arrangement.

Joan rejected the position on moral grounds and continued trying to obtain a suitable opportunity in academic life. Never again, however, was she offered a faculty position, and she was forced to pursue a career path that gave her little satisfaction. Her potential as a teacher went unfulfilled, and her planned research was left undone. Throughout her life she remained embittered.

Kate also earned a doctoral degree from a first-rate university and sought appointment to a tenure-track position in which she could teach and pursue her research. She, too, received no offers and reluctantly was about to accept nonacademic employment when an unexpected call came inviting her for an interview at the same school Joan had visited. The dean made Kate the identical offer that had been made to Joan. After weighing the options, Kate accepted the appointment, even though she recognized that doing so would require her to act unethically.

Kate went on to a highly successful academic career, became a popular teacher and renowned researcher, moved to one of the nation's most prestigious universities, and enjoyed all the perquisites attendant to her membership on that school's renowned faculty. Occasionally she recalled the conditions of her initial appointment but viewed the actions she had taken as an unfortunate but necessary step on her path to a wonderful life.

* * *

Joan acted morally but lived unhappily ever after, while Kate acted immorally but lived happily ever after. So I leave you with this dilemma: Which of the two was the wiser?

Note

1. Philippa Foot, "Moral Relativism," in *Moral Dilemmas and Other Topics in Moral Philosophy* (Oxford: Clarendon, 2002), p. 35.

Study Questions

1. Do you believe Fred can be happy?
2. How might Jeffrie G. Murphy try to convince Fred that he is not happy?
3. Can the adulterous physician ever be truly happy?
4. If you desired an academic position and were offered one under the conditions proposed by the dean, would you accept?

CHAPTER 10

The Nature of Ethical Disagreement

Charles L. Stevenson

A basic challenge to morality contends that, unlike scientific claims, moral claims cannot be tested, and therefore ethical disputes are pointless. An influential reply is provided in the next selection, written by Charles L. Stevenson (1908–1979), who was Professor of Philosophy at the University of Michigan. Stevenson believes that ethical disagreements often involve factual disputes, which are open to possible resolution by the methods of science. Once we agree on the relevant facts, our ethical disagreement may also be resolved. But which facts, if any, are in question? We can tell only by analyzing the reasons that support our moral judgments.

1

When people disagree about the value of something—one saying that it is good or right and another that it is bad or wrong—by what methods of argument or inquiry can their disagreement be resolved? Can it be resolved by the methods of science, or does it require methods of some other kind, or is it open to no rational solution at all?

The question must be clarified before it can be answered. And the word that is particularly in need of clarification, as we shall see, is the word "disagreement."

Let us begin by noting that "disagreement" has two broad senses: In the first sense it refers to what I shall call "disagreements in belief." This occurs when Mr. A believes *p*, when Mr. B believes *not-p*, or something incompatible with *p*, and when neither is content to let the

From Charles L. Stevenson, *Facts and Values.* Copyright © 1963. Reprinted by permission of Yale University Press.

belief of the other remain unchallenged. Thus doctors may disagree in belief about the causes of an illness; and friends may disagree in belief about the exact date on which they last met.

In the second sense the word refers to what I shall call "disagreement in attitude." This occurs when Mr. A has a favorable attitude to something, when Mr. B has an unfavorable or less favorable attitude to it, and when neither is content to let the other's attitude remain unchanged. The term "attitude" . . . designates any psychological disposition of being *for* or *against* something. Hence love and hate are relatively specific kinds of attitudes, as are approval and disapproval, and so on.

This second sense can be illustrated in this way: Two men are planning to have dinner together. One wants to eat at a restaurant that the other doesn't like. Temporarily, then, the men cannot "agree" on where to dine. Their argument may be trivial, and perhaps only half serious; but in any case it represents a disagreement *in attitude*. The men have divergent preferences and each is trying to redirect the preference of the other—though normally, of course, each is willing to revise his own preference in the light of what the other may say.

Further examples are readily found. Mrs. Smith wishes to cultivate only the four hundred; Mr. Smith is loyal to his old poker-playing friends. They accordingly disagree, in attitude, about whom to invite to their party. The progressive mayor wants modern school buildings and large parks; the older citizens are against these "newfangled" ways; so they disagree on civic policy. These cases differ from the one about the restaurant only in that the clash of attitudes is more serious and may lead to more vigorous argument.

The difference between the two senses of "disagreement" is essentially this: the first involves an opposition of beliefs, both of which cannot be true, and the second involves an opposition of attitudes, both of which cannot be satisfied.

Let us apply this distinction to a case that will sharpen it. Mr. A believes that most voters will favor a proposed tax and Mr. B disagrees with him. The disagreement concerns attitudes—those of the voters—but note that A and B are *not* disagreeing in attitude. Their disagreement is *in belief about* attitudes. It is simply a special kind of disagreement in belief, differing from disagreement in belief about head colds only with regard to subject matter. It implies not an opposition of the actual attitudes of the speakers but only of their beliefs about certain attitudes. Disagreement *in* attitude, on the other hand, implies that the very attitudes of the speakers are opposed.

A and B may have opposed beliefs about attitudes without having opposed attitudes, just as they may have opposed beliefs about head colds without having opposed head colds. Hence we must not, from the fact that an argument is concerned with attitudes, infer that it necessarily involves disagreement *in* attitude.

2

We may now turn more directly to disagreement about values, with particular reference to normative ethics. When people argue about what is good, do they disagree in belief, or do they disagree in attitude? . . . It must be readily granted that ethical arguments usually involve disagreement in belief; but they *also* involve disagreement in attitude. And the conspicuous role of disagreement in attitude is what we usually take, whether we realize it or not, as the distinguishing feature of ethical arguments. For example:

Suppose that the representative of a union urges that the wage level in a given company ought to be higher—that it is only right that the workers receive more pay. The company representative urges in reply that the workers ought to receive no more than they get. Such an argument clearly represents a disagreement in attitude. The union is *for* higher wages; the company is *against* them, and neither is content to let the other's attitude remain unchanged. *In addition* to this disagreement in attitude, of course, the argument may represent no little disagreement in belief. Perhaps the parties disagree about how much the cost of living has risen and how much the workers are suffering under the present wage scale. Or perhaps they disagree about the company's earnings and the extent to which the company could raise wages and still operate at a profit. Like any typical ethical argument, then, this argument involves both disagreement in attitude and disagreement in belief.

It is easy to see, however, that the disagreement in attitude plays a unifying and predominating role in the argument. This is so in two ways:

In the first place, disagreement in attitude determines what beliefs are *relevant* to the argument. Suppose that the company affirms that the wage scale of fifty years ago was far lower than it is now. The union will immediately urge that this contention, even though true, is irrelevant. And it is irrelevant simply because information about the wage level of fifty years ago, maintained under totally different circumstances, is not likely to affect the present attitudes of either party. To be relevant, any belief that is introduced into the argument must be one that is likely to lead one side or the other to have a different attitude, and so reconcile disagreement in attitude. Attitudes are often functions of beliefs. We often change our attitudes to something when we change our beliefs about it; just as a child ceases to *want* to touch a live coal when he comes to *believe* that it will burn him. Thus in the present argument any beliefs that are at all likely to alter attitudes, such as those about the increasing cost of living or the financial state of the company, will be considered by both sides to be relevant to the argument. Agreement in belief on these matters may lead to agreement in attitude toward the wage scale. But beliefs that are likely to alter the attitudes of neither side will be declared irrelevant. They will have no bearing on the disagreement in attitude, with which both parties are primarily concerned.

In the second place, ethical argument usually terminates when disagreement in attitude terminates, even though a certain amount of disagreement in belief remains. Suppose, for instance, that the company and the union continue to disagree in belief about the increasing cost of living, but that the company, even so, ends by favoring the higher wage scale. The union will then be content to end the argument and will cease to press its point about living costs. It may bring up that point again, in some future argument of the same sort, or in urging the righteousness of its victory to the newspaper columnists; but for the moment the fact that the company has agreed in attitude is sufficient to terminate the argument. On the other hand: suppose that both parties agreed on all beliefs that were introduced into the argument, but even so continued to disagree in attitude. In that case neither party would feel that their dispute had been successfully terminated. They might look for other beliefs that could be introduced into the argument. They might use words to play on each other's emotion. They might agree (in attitude) to submit the case to arbitration, both feeling that a decision, even if strongly adverse to one party or the other, would be preferable to a continued impasse. Or, perhaps, they might abandon hope of settling their dispute by any peaceable means.

In many other cases, of course, men discuss ethical topics without having the strong, uncompromising attitudes that the present example has illustrated. They are often as much concerned with redirecting their own attitudes, in the light of greater knowledge, as with redirecting the attitudes of others. And the attitudes involved are often altruistic rather than selfish. Yet the above example will serve, so long as that is understood, to suggest the nature of ethical disagreement. Both disagreement in attitude and disagreement in belief are involved, but the former predominates in that (1) it determines what sort of disagreement in belief is relevantly disputed in a given ethical argument, and (2) it determines by its continued presence or its resolution whether or not the argument has been settled. We may see further how intimately the two sorts of disagreement are related: since attitudes are often functions of beliefs, an agreement in belief may lead people, as a matter of psychological fact, to agree in attitude.

3

Having discussed disagreement, we may turn to the broad question that was first mentioned, namely, By what methods of argument or inquiry may disagreement about matters of value be resolved?

It will be obvious that to whatever extent an argument involves disagreement in belief, it is open to the usual methods of the sciences. If these methods are the *only* rational methods for supporting beliefs—as I believe to be so, but cannot now take time to discuss—then scientific methods are the only rational methods for resolving the disagreement in *belief* that arguments about values may include.

But if science is granted an undisputed sway in reconciling beliefs, it does not thereby acquire, without qualification, an undisputed sway in reconciling attitudes. We have seen that arguments about values include disagreement in attitude, no less than disagreement in belief, and that in certain ways the disagreement in attitude predominates. By what methods shall the latter sort of disagreement be resolved?

The methods of science are still available for that purpose, but only in an indirect way. Initially, these methods have only to do with establishing agreement in belief. If they serve further to establish agreement in attitude, that will be due simply to the psychological fact that altered beliefs may cause altered attitudes. Hence scientific methods are conclusive in ending arguments about values only to the extent that their success in obtaining agreement in belief will in turn lead to agreement in attitude.

In other words, the extent to which scientific methods can bring about agreement on values depends on the extent to which a commonly accepted body of scientific beliefs would cause us to have a commonly accepted set of attitudes.

How much is the development of science likely to achieve, then, with regard to values? To what extent *would* common beliefs lead to common attitudes? It is, perhaps, a pardonable enthusiasm to *hope* that science will do everything—to hope that in some rosy future, when all men know the consequences of their acts, they will all have common aspirations and live peaceably in complete moral accord. But if we speak not from our enthusiastic hopes but from our present knowledge, the answer must be far less exciting. We usually *do not know*, at the beginning of any argument about values, whether an agreement in belief, scientifically established, will lead to an agreement in attitude or not. It is logically possible, at least, that two men should continue to disagree in attitude even though they had all their beliefs in common, and even though neither had made any logical or inductive error, or omitted any relevant evidence. Differences in temperament, or in early training, or in social status, might make the men retain different attitudes even though both were possessed of the complete scientific truth. Whether this logical possibility is an empirical likelihood I shall not presume to say; but it is unquestionably a possibility that must not be left out of account.

To say that science can always settle arguments about value, we have seen, is to make this assumption: Agreement in attitude will always be consequent upon complete agreement in belief, and science can always bring about the latter. Taken as purely heuristic, this assumption has its usefulness. It leads people to discover the discrepancies in their beliefs and to prolong enlightening argument that *may* lead, as a matter of fact, from commonly accepted beliefs to commonly accepted attitudes. It leads people to reconcile their attitudes in a rational, permanent way, rather than by rhapsody or exhortation. But the assumption is *nothing more*, for present knowledge, than a heuristic maxim. It is wholly without any proper foundation of probability. I conclude, therefore, that scientific methods cannot be guaranteed the definite role in the so-called normative sciences that they may have in the natural sciences. Apart from a heuristic assumption to the contrary, it is possible that the growth of scientific knowledge may leave many disputes about values permanently unsolved. Should these disputes persist, there are nonrational methods for dealing with them, of course, such as impassioned, moving oratory. But the purely intellectual methods of science, and indeed, *all* methods of reasoning, may be insufficient to settle disputes about values even though they may greatly help to do so.

Study Questions

1. How do disagreements in belief differ from disagreements in attitude?
2. Can science ever help resolve a moral disagreement?
3. Are disagreements in belief about attitudes the same as disagreements in attitude?
4. Do disagreements in attitude predominate in a moral disagreement?

CHAPTER 11

The Rationality of Moral Action

Philippa Foot

Whereas Charles L. Stevenson maintains that reason alone does not yield moral judgments, a view sometimes referred to as "noncognitivism," an opposing position is defended by Philippa Foot (1920–2010), who was Professor of Philosophy at the University of California, Los Angeles, and an Honorary Fellow of Somerville College of the University of Oxford. She argues that moral beliefs are grounded in facts about human life that rational people take as reasons for action. Thus morality is not dependent on an agent's feelings, passions, or desires.

As I see it, the rationality of, say, telling the truth, keeping promises, or helping a neighbour is *on a par* with the rationality of self-preserving action, and of the careful and cognizant pursuit of other innocent ends; each being a part or aspect of practical rationality. . . .

How can I now find a way of showing that reason may demand that promises be kept, truth told, or succour given, even when that is contrary to self-interest or to heart's desire?

The demonstration should start, I believe, with some observations on the nature of a moral virtue. It is in the concept of a moral virtue that in so far as someone possesses it his actions are good; which is to say that he acts well. Moral virtues bring it about that one who has them acts well, and we must enquire as to what this does and does not mean.

What, for instance, distinguishes a just person from one who is unjust? The fact that he keeps his contracts? That cannot be right, because circumstances may make it impossible for him to do so. Nor

---

From Philippa Foot, *Moral Dilemmas*, Oxford University Press, 2002. Reprinted by permission of the publisher.

is it that he saves life rather than kills innocent people, for by blameless mishap he may kill rather than save. 'Of course,' someone will say at this point, 'it is the just person's intention not what he actually brings about that counts.' But why not say, then, that it is the distinguishing characteristic of the just that *for them certain considerations count as reasons for action?* (And as reasons of a certain weight.) And will it not be the same with other virtues, as for instance the virtues of charity, courage, and temperance? Those who possess these virtues possess them insofar as they recognize certain considerations (such as the fact of a promise, or of a neighbour's need) as powerful, and in many circumstances compelling, reasons for acting. They recognize the reasons, and act on them.

Thus the description 'just', as applied to a man or woman, speaks of how it is with them in respect of the acceptance of a certain group of considerations as reasons for action. If justice is a virtue, this is what the virtue of justice rectifies, i.e. makes good. It is no part of moral goodness—which is goodness of character—that someone should be physically strong, should move well, or talk well, or see well. But he must act well, in a sense that is given primarily at least by his recognition of the force of particular considerations as reasons for acting: that and the influence that this has on what he does. The just person aims at keeping his promises, paying what he owes, and defending those whose rights are being violated, so far as such actions are required by the virtue of justice. Likewise, he recognizes certain limitations on what he may do even for some virtue-given end; as he may not kill an innocent person even for the sake of stopping someone else from killing a greater number, though he may, as Elizabeth Anscombe has remarked, destroy someone's property to stop the spread of a fire. And again he acts accordingly. Similarly, if charity is a virtue, this is because it makes its possessor's action good in the area of aims such as the relief of poverty. Here again, recognizing particular considerations as reasons for action, he acts on these reasons as he should.

Now in describing moral virtues in terms of (*a*) the recognition of particular considerations as reasons for acting, and (*b*) the relevant action, I have only been expressing very familiar and time-honoured ideas of moral goodness. But how can it be denied that I have at the same time been talking about practical rationality? The discussion has been about human goodness in respect of reason-recognition and reason-following, and if this is not practical rationality I should like to know what is! . . .

But it is just here that some of my noncognitivist opponents will move in, scenting victory. For they will insist that the fact of an agent's having reason to do something (say to keep promises) is itself dependent on his feelings, passions, or desires. And so, they will argue, if a moral judgement about what I ought to do implies that I have reason so to act, the judgement would seem to imply not just 'cognitions' but also something 'conative': something having to do with an engagement of the will. . . .

Take as an example that of someone who throws away his supply of cigarettes. He does so because he wants to give up smoking. And he wants to give up smoking because he wants a healthy old age. The series goes on—A for the sake of B—but it can't go on forever. And must it not end with something that the agent 'just wants'; in other words with some 'conative' element in his individual psychological state?

The question is meant to be rhetorical; but the answer to it is 'No'. For what, we must ask, gives the agent this goal? Does he find himself trembling at the thought of cancer at 50? Is he in a state of anxiety at the thought of how much he smokes? Perhaps. But nothing of this kind has to be part of the story. . . . So why do we say that what gets the whole thing going must be a desire or other 'conative' element in the subject's 'psychological state'? Suppose instead that it is the recognition that there is reason for him, as for anyone else, to look after his future so far as circumstances allow? Why should not this be where the series of questions 'why?' comes to an end? . . . Recognition of a reason gives the rational person a goal; and this recognition is, according to the argument of the present paper, based on facts and concepts, not on some prior attitude, feeling, or goal. The only fact about the individual's state of mind that is required for the explanatory force of the proposition about the requirement of rationality is that he does not (for some bizarre reason) deny its truth. He only needs to know, like most adults, that it is silly to disregard one's own future without special reason to do so. No special explanation is needed of why men take reasonable care of their own future; an explanation is needed when they do not. Nor does human cooperation need a special explanation. Most people know that it is, for instance, unreasonable to take benefits and give nothing in return. . . .

What then is to be said about the relation between 'fact' and 'value'? The thesis of this paper is that the grounding of a moral argument is ultimately in facts about human life—facts of the kind . . . that I spoke of in saying why it was a part of rationality for human beings to take special care each for his or her own future. In my view, therefore, a moral evaluation does not stand over against the statement of a matter of fact, but rather has to do with facts about a particular subject matter, as do evaluations of such things as sight and hearing in animals, and other aspects of their behaviour. Nobody would, I think, take it as other than a plain matter of fact that there is something wrong with the hearing of a gull that cannot distinguish the cry of its own chick, as with the sight of an owl that cannot see in the dark. Similarly, it is obvious that there are objective, factual evaluations of such things as human sight, hearing, memory, and concentration, based on the life form of our own species. Why, then, does it seem so monstrous a suggestion that the evaluation of the human will should be determined by facts about the nature of human beings and the life of our own species? Undoubtedly the resistance has something to do with the thought that the goodness of good action has a special relation to choice. But as I have tried to show, this special relation is not what noncognitivists think it, but rather lies in the fact that moral action is rational action, and in the fact that human beings are creatures with the power to recognize reasons for action and to act on them.

Study Questions

1. What is a moral virtue?
2. What does Foot mean by "practical rationality"?
3. Do you agree with Foot that no special explanation is needed for why people take reasonable care of their own futures?
4. What does Foot believe is the relation between facts and values?

PART II

Moral Theories

CHAPTER 12

The Categorical Imperative

Immanuel Kant

Having considered various challenges to morality, we turn next to some of the most important moral theories, competing explanations of why certain actions are right and others wrong. One of the most influential of all ethical systems is that developed by the German philosopher Immanuel Kant (1724–1804), a dominant figure in the history of modern philosophy. Because his views are not easy to grasp, I shall offer a brief overview of them.

Kant argues that the moral worth of an action is to be judged not by its consequences but by the nature of the maxim or principle that motivates the action. Thus right actions are not necessarily those with favorable consequences but those performed in accordance with correct maxims. But which maxims are correct? According to Kant, the only correct ones are those that can serve as universal laws because they are applicable without exception to every person at any time. In other words, you should act only on a maxim that can be universalized without contradiction.

To see what Kant has in mind, consider a specific example he uses to illustrate his view. Suppose you need to borrow money, but it will be lent to you only if you promise to pay it back. You realize, however, that you will not be able to honor the debt. May you promise to repay the money, knowing you will not keep the promise? Kant argues that doing so is not permissible, because if it were a universal law that promises could be made with no intention of keeping them, then the practice of promising would be destroyed.

Kant refers to his supreme moral principle as the "categorical imperative"—categorical because it does not depend on anyone's particular desires, and an imperative because it is a command of reason. Kant also claims that the categorical imperative can be reformulated as

---

follows: So act that you treat humanity, whether in your own person or in any other person, always at the same time as an end, never merely as a means. Using this version, Kant argues that a deceitful promise is immoral because a person making such a promise is using another person only as a means, not treating that individual as an end, a rational being worthy of respect.

It is impossible to imagine anything at all in the world, or even beyond it, that can be called good without qualification—except a *good will.* Intelligence, wit, judgement, and the other mental talents, whatever we may call them, or courage, decisiveness, and perseverance, are, as qualities of *temperament,* certainly good and desirable in many respects; but they can also be extremely bad and harmful when the will which makes use of these *gifts of nature* and whose specific quality we refer to as *character,* is not good. It is exactly the same with *gifts of fortune.* Power, wealth, honour, even health and that total well-being and contentment with one's condition which we call "happiness," can make a person bold but consequently often reckless as well, unless a good will is present to correct their influence on the mind, thus adjusting the whole principle of one's action to render it conformable to universal ends. It goes without saying that the sight of a creature enjoying uninterrupted prosperity, but never feeling the slightest pull of a pure and good will, cannot excite approval in a rational and impartial spectator. Consequently, a good will seems to constitute the indispensable condition even of our worthiness to be happy.

Some qualities, even though they are helpful to this good will and can make its task very much easier, nevertheless have no intrinsic unconditional worth. Rather, they presuppose a good will which puts limits on the esteem in which they are rightly held and forbids us to regard them as absolutely good. Moderation in emotions and passions, self-control, and sober reflection are not only good in many respects: they may even seem to constitute part of the inner worth of a person. Yet they are far from being properly described as good without qualification (however unconditionally they were prized by the ancients). For without the principles of a good will those qualities may become exceedingly bad; the passionless composure of a villain makes him not merely more dangerous but also directly more detestable in our eyes than we would have taken him to be without it.

A good will is not good because of its effects or accomplishments, and not because of its adequacy to achieve any proposed end: it is good only by virtue of its willing—that is, it is good in itself. Considered in itself it is to be treasured as incomparably higher than anything it could ever bring about merely in order to satisfy some inclination or, if you like, the sum total of all inclinations. Even if it were to happen that, because of some particularly unfortunate face or the miserly bequest of a step-motherly nature, this will were completely powerless to carry out its aims; if with even its utmost effort it still accomplished nothing, so that only good will itself remained (not, of course, as a mere wish, but as the summoning of every means in our power), even then it would still, like a jewel, glisten in its own right, as something that has its full worth in itself. . . .

We must thus develop the concept of a will estimable in itself and good apart from any further aim. This concept is already present in the natural, healthy mind, which requires not so much instruction as merely clarification. It is this concept that always holds the highest place in estimating the total worth of our actions and it constitutes the condition of all the rest. Let us then take up the concept of *duty*, which includes that of a good will, the latter however being here under certain subjective limitations and obstacles. These, so far from hiding a good will or disguising it, rather bring it out by contrast and make it shine forth more brightly. . . .

It is a duty to help others where one can, and besides this many souls are so compassionately disposed that, without any further motive of vanity or self-interest, they find an inner pleasure in spreading joy around them, taking delight in the contentment of others, so far as they have brought it about. Yet I maintain that, however dutiful and kind an action of this sort may be, it still has no genuinely moral worth. It is on a level with other inclinations—for example, the inclination to pursue honour, which if fortunate enough to aim at something generally useful and consistent with duty, something consequently honourable, deserves praise and encouragement but not esteem. For its maxim lacks the moral merit of such actions done not out of inclination but out of *duty*. Suppose then that the mind of this humanitarian were overclouded by sorrows of his own which extinguished all compassion for the fate of others, but that he still had the power to assist others in distress; suppose though that their adversity no longer stirred him, because he is preoccupied with his own; and now imagine that, though no longer moved by any inclination, he nevertheless tears himself out of this deadly apathy and does the action without any inclination, solely out of duty. Then for the first time his action has its genuine moral worth. Furthermore, if nature had put little sympathy into this or that person's heart; if he, though an honest man, were cold in temperament and indifferent to the sufferings of others—perhaps because he has the special gifts of patience and fortitude in his own sufferings and he assumes or even demands the same of others; if such a man (who would in truth not be the worst product of nature) were not exactly fashioned by nature to be a humanitarian, would he not still find in himself a source from which he might give himself a worth far higher than that of a good-natured temperament? Assuredly he would. It is precisely in this that the worth of character begins to show—a moral worth, and incomparably the highest—namely, that he does good, not out of inclination, but out of duty. . . .

The moral worth of an action done out of duty has its moral worth, not *in the objective* to be reached by that action, but in the maxim in accordance with which the action is decided upon; it depends, therefore, not on actualizing the object of the action, but solely on the *principle of volition* in accordance with which the action was done, without any regard for objects of the faculty of desire. It is clear from our previous discussion that the objectives we may have in acting, and also our actions' effects considered as ends and as what motivates our volition, can give to actions no unconditional or moral worth. Where then can this worth be found if not in the willing of the action's hoped for effect? It can be found nowhere but *in the principle of the will,* irrespective of the ends that can be brought about by such action. . . .

Duty is the necessity of an act done out of respect for the law. While I can certainly have an *inclination* for an object that results from my proposed action, I can never *respect* it, precisely because it is nothing but an effect of a will and not its activity. Similarly I cannot respect any inclination whatsoever, whether it be my own inclination or that of another. At most I can approve of that towards which I feel an inclination, and occasionally I can like the object of somebody else's inclination myself—that is, see it as conducive to my own advantage. But the only thing that could be an object of respect (and thus a commandment) for me is something that is conjoined with my will purely as a ground and never as a consequence, something that does not serve my inclination but overpowers it or at least excludes it entirely from my decision-making—consequently, nothing but the law itself. Now if an action done out of duty is supposed to exclude totally the influence of inclination, and, along with inclination, every object of volition, then nothing remains that could determine the will except objectively *the law* and subjectively *pure respect* for this practical law. What is left therefore is the maxim, to obey this sort of law even when doing so is prejudicial to all my inclinations.

Thus the moral worth of an action depends neither on the result expected from that action nor on any principle of action that has to borrow its motive from this expected result. For all these results (such as one's own pleasurable condition or even the promotion of the happiness of others) could have been brought about by other causes as well. It would not require the will of a rational being to produce them, but it is only in such a will that the highest and unconditional good can be found. That pre-eminent good which we call "moral" consists therefore in nothing but *the idea of the law* in itself, which certainly *is present only in a rational being*—so far as that idea, and not an expected result, is the determining ground of the will. And this pre-eminent good is already present in the person who acts in accordance with this idea; we need not await the result of the action in order to find it. . . .

Everything in nature works in accordance with laws. Only a rational being has the power to act in accordance with the idea of laws—that is, in accordance with principles—and thus has a will. . . .

The idea of an objective principle, in so far as it constrains a will, is called a commandment (of reason), and the formulation of this commandment is called an Imperative. . . .

All imperatives command either hypothetically or categorically. Hypothetical imperatives declare a possible action to be practically necessary as a means to the attainment of something else that one wants (or that one may want). A categorical imperative would be one that represented an action as itself objectively necessary, without regard to any further end.

Since every practical law presents a possible action as good and therefore as necessary for a subject whose actions are determined by reason, all imperatives are therefore formulae for determining an action which is necessary according to the principle of a will in some way good. If the action would be good only as a means to something else, the imperative is hypothetical; if the action is thought of as good in itself and therefore as necessary for a will which of itself conforms to reason as its principle, then the imperative is categorical. . . .

There is, however, *one* end that we may presuppose as actual in all rational beings (so far as they are dependent beings to whom imperatives apply); and thus there is one aim which they not only *might* have, but which we can assume with certainty that they all *do* have by a necessity of nature and that aim is *perfect happiness*. The hypothetical imperative which affirms the practical necessity of an action as a means to the promotion of perfect happiness is an assertoric imperative. We must not characterize it as necessary merely for some uncertain, merely possible purpose, but as necessary for a purpose that we can presuppose a priori and with certainty to be present in everyone because it belongs to the essence of human beings. Now we can call skill in the choice of the means to one's own greatest well-being "prudence" in the narrowest sense of the word. So the imperative concerning the choice of means to one's own happiness—that is, the precept of prudence—still remains hypothetical; the action is commanded not absolutely but only as a means to a further end.

Finally, there is one imperative which commands a certain line of conduct directly, without assuming or being conditional on any further goal to be reached by that conduct. This imperative is categorical. It is concerned not with the material of the action and its anticipated result, but with its form and with the principle from which the action itself results. And what is essentially good in the action consists in the [agent's] disposition, whatever the result may be. This imperative may be called the imperative of morality. . . .

The question now arises "How are all these imperatives possible?" This question does not ask how an action commanded by the imperative can be performed, but merely how we can understand the constraining of the will, which imperatives express in setting us a task. How an imperative of skill is possible requires no special discussion. Whoever wills the end also wills (so far as reason has decisive influence on his actions) the means which are indispensably necessary and in his power. . . .

By contrast, "How is the imperative of morality possible?" is beyond all doubt the one question in need of solution. For the moral imperative is in no way hypothetical, and consequently the objective necessity, which it affirms, cannot be supported by any presupposition, as was the case with hypothetical imperatives. . . .

If I think of a *hypothetical* imperative as such, I do not know beforehand what it will contain—not until I am given its condition. But if I think of a *categorical imperative*, I know right away what it contains. For since this imperative contains, besides the law, only the necessity that the maxim conform to this law, while the law, as we have seen, contains no condition limiting it, there is nothing left over to which the maxim of action should conform except the universality of a law as such; and it is only this conformity that the imperative asserts to be necessary.

There is therefore only one categorical imperative and it is this: "Act only on that maxim by which you can at the same time will that it should become a universal law." . . .

We shall now enumerate some duties. . . .

1. A man feels sick of life as the result of a mounting series of misfortunes that has reduced him to hopelessness, but he still possesses enough of his reason to ask himself whether it would not be contrary to his duty to himself to take his own life. Now he tests whether the maxim of his action could really become a universal law of nature. His maxim, however, is: "I make it my principle out of self-love to shorten my life if its continuance threatens more evil than it promises advantage." The only further question is whether this principle of self-love can become a universal law of nature. But one sees at once that a nature whose law was that the very same feeling meant to promote life should actually destroy life would contradict itself, and hence would not endure as nature. The maxim therefore could not possibly be a general law of nature and thus it wholly contradicts the supreme principle of all duty.

2. Another finds himself driven by need to borrow money. He knows very well that he will not be able to pay it back, but he sees too that nobody will lend him anything unless he firmly promises to pay it back within a fixed time. He wants to make such a promise, but he still has enough conscience to ask himself, "Isn't it impermissible and contrary to duty to get out of one's difficulties this way?" Suppose, however, that he did decide to do it. The maxim of his action would run thus: "When I believe myself short of money, I will borrow money and promise to pay it back, even though I know that this will never be done." Now this principle of self-love or personal advantage is perhaps quite compatible with my own entire future welfare; only there remains the question "Is it right?" I therefore transform the unfair demand of self-love into a universal law and frame my question thus: "How would things stand if my maxim became a universal law?" I then see immediately that this maxim can never qualify as a self-consistent universal law of nature, but must necessarily contradict itself. For the universality of a law that permits anyone who believes himself to be in need to make any promise he pleases with the intention of not keeping it would make promising, and the very purpose one has in promising, itself impossible. For no one would believe he was being promised anything, but would laugh at any such utterance as hollow pretense.

3. A third finds in himself a talent that, with a certain amount of cultivation, could make him a useful man for all sorts of purposes.

But he sees himself in comfortable circumstances, and he prefers to give himself up to pleasure rather than to bother about increasing and improving his fortunate natural aptitudes. Yet he asks himself further "Does my maxim of neglecting my natural gifts, besides agreeing with my taste for amusement, agree also with what is called duty?" He then sees that a nature could indeed endure under such a universal law, even if (like the South Sea Islanders) every man should let his talents rust and should be bent on devoting his life solely to idleness, amusement, procreation—in a word, to enjoyment. Only he cannot possibly *will* that this should become a universal law of nature or should be implanted in us as such a law by a natural instinct. For as a rational being he necessarily wills that all his powers should be developed, since they are after all useful to him and given to him for all sorts of possible purposes.

4. A fourth man, who is himself flourishing but sees others who have to struggle with great hardships (and whom he could easily help) thinks to himself: "What do I care? Let every one be as happy as Heaven intends or as he can make himself; I won't deprive him of anything; I won't even envy him; but I don't feel like contributing anything to his well-being or to helping him in his distress!" Now admittedly if such an attitude were a universal law of nature, the human race could survive perfectly well and doubtless even better than when everybody chatters about sympathy and good will, and even makes an effort, now and then, to practise them, but, when one can get away with it, swindles, traffics in human rights, or violates them in other ways. But although it is possible that a universal law of nature in accord with this maxim could exist, it is impossible to *will* that such a principle should hold everywhere as a law of nature. For a will that intended this would be in conflict with itself, since many situations might arise in which the man needs love and sympathy from others, and in which, by such a law of nature generated by his own will, he would rob himself of all hope of the help he wants. . . .

If we now look at ourselves whenever we transgress a duty, we find that we in fact do not intend that our maxim should become a universal law. For this is impossible for us. What we really intend is rather that its opposite should remain a law generally; we only take the liberty of making an *exception* to it, for ourselves or (of course just this once) to satisfy our inclination. Consequently if we weighed it all up from one and the same perspective—that of reason—we should find a contradiction in our own will, the contradiction that a certain principle should be objectively necessary as a universal law and yet subjectively should not hold universally but should admit of exceptions. . . .

Suppose, however, there were something *whose existence in itself* had an absolute worth, something that, as an end *in itself,* could be a ground of definite laws. Then in it and in it alone, would the ground of a possible categorical imperative, that is, of a practical law, reside.

Now, I say, a human being, and in general every rational being, *does exist* as an end in himself, *not merely as a means* to be used by this or that will as it pleases. In all his actions, whether they are directed to himself or to other rational beings, a human being must always be viewed *at the same time as an end.* . . . Beings whose existence depends not on our will but on nature still have only a relative value as means and are therefore called *things,* if they lack reason. Rational beings, on the other hand, are called *persons* because, their nature already marks them out as ends in themselves—that is, as something which ought not to be used *merely* as a means—and consequently imposes restrictions on all choice making (and is an object of respect). Persons, therefore, are not merely subjective ends whose existence as an effect of our actions has a value *for us.* They are *objective ends*—that is, things whose existence is in itself an end, and indeed an end such that no other end can be substituted for it, no end to which they should serve *merely* as a means. For if this were not so, there would be nothing at all having *absolute value* anywhere. But if all value were conditional, and thus contingent, then no supreme principle could be found for reason at all.

If then there is to be a supreme practical principle and a categorical imperative for the human will, it must be such that it forms an objective principle of the will from the idea of something which is necessarily an end for everyone because *it is an end in itself,* a principle that can therefore serve as a universal practical law. The ground of this principle is: *Rational nature exists as an end in itself.* This is the way in which a human being necessarily conceives his own existence, and it is therefore a *subjective* principle of human actions. But it is also the way in which every other rational being conceives his existence, on the same rational ground which holds also for me; hence it is at the same time an *objective* principle from which, since it is a supreme practical ground, it must be possible to derive all laws of the will. The practical imperative will therefore be the following: *Act in such a way that you treat humanity, whether in your own person or in any other person, always at the same time as an end, never merely as a means.* We will now see whether this can be carried out in practice.

Let us keep to our previous examples.

First, . . . the man who contemplates suicide will ask himself whether his action could be compatible with the Idea of humanity as *an end in itself.* If he damages himself in order to escape from a painful situation, he is making use of a person *merely as a means* to maintain a tolerable state of affairs till the end of his life. But a human being is not a thing—not something to be used *merely* as a means: he must always in all his actions be regarded as an end in himself. Hence I cannot dispose of a human being in my own person, by maiming, corrupting, or killing him. (I must here forego a more precise definition of this principle that would forestall any misunderstanding—for example, as to having limbs amputated to save myself or exposing my life to danger in order to preserve it, and so on—this discussion belongs to ethics proper.)

Secondly, . . . the man who has in mind making a false promise to others will see at once that he is intending to make use of another person *merely as a means* to an end which that person does not share. For the person whom I seek to use for my own purposes by such a promise cannot possibly agree with my way of treating him, and so cannot himself share the end of the action. This incompatibility with the principle of duty to others can be seen more distinctly when we bring in examples of attacks on the freedom and property of others. For then it is manifest that a violator of the rights of human beings intends to use the person of others merely as a means without taking into consideration that, as rational beings, they must always at the same time be valued as ends—that is, treated only as beings who must themselves be able to share in the end of the very same action.

Thirdly, . . . it is not enough that an action not conflict with humanity in our own person as an end in itself: it must also *harmonize with this end.* Now there are in humanity capacities for greater perfection that form part of nature's purpose for humanity in our own person. To neglect these can perhaps be compatible with the *survival* of humanity as an end in itself, but not with the *promotion* of that end.

Fourthly, . . . the natural end that all human beings seek is their own perfect happiness. Now the human race might indeed exist if everybody contributed nothing to the happiness of others but at the same time refrained from deliberately impairing it. This harmonizing with humanity *as an end in itself* would, however, be merely negative and not positive, unless everyone also endeavours, as far as he can, to further the ends of others. For the ends of any person who is an end in himself must, if this idea is to have its full effect in me, be also, as far as possible, *my* ends.

Study Questions

1. According to Kant, what is the only thing in the world that is good without limitation?
2. What does Kant mean by acting from duty?
3. How does Kant differentiate between a hypothetical and a categorical imperative?
4. By what argument does Kant seek to prove that the first formulation of the categorical imperative demonstrates the immorality of your making a promise you don't intend to keep?

CHAPTER 13

A Simplified Account of Kant's Ethics

Onora O'Neill

Onora O'Neill is an Emeritus Professor of Philosophy at the University of Cambridge and a member of the House of Lords. In the next selection she explains Kant's second formulation of his categorical imperative, the requirement that each person be treated as an end and never merely as a means.

Kant's moral theory has acquired the reputation of being forbiddingly difficult to understand and, once understood, excessively demanding in its requirements. I don't believe that this reputation has been wholly earned, and I am going to try to undermine it. . . .

The main method by which I propose to avoid some of the difficulties of Kant's moral theory is by explaining only one part of the theory. This does not seem to me to be an irresponsible approach in this case. One of the things that makes Kant's moral theory hard to understand is that he gives a number of different versions of the principle that he calls the Supreme Principle of Morality, and these different versions don't look at all like one another. . . .

Kant calls his Supreme Principle the *Categorical Imperative*; its various versions also have sonorous names. . . . The one on which I shall concentrate is known as the *Formula of the End in Itself.* . . .

The Formula of the End in Itself

Kant states the Formula of the End in Itself as follows:

> Act in such a way that you always treat humanity, whether in your own person or in the person of any other, never simply as a means but always at the same time as an end.

To understand this we need to know what it is to treat a person as a means or as an end. According to Kant, each of our acts reflects one or more *maxims*. The maxim of the act is the principle on which one sees oneself as acting. A maxim expresses a person's policy, or if he or she has no settled policy, the principle underlying the particular intention or decision on which he or she acts. Thus, a person who decides, "This year I'll give 10 percent of my income to famine relief," has as a maxim the principle of tithing his or her income for famine relief. In practice, the difference between intentions and maxims is of little importance, for given any intention, we can formulate the corresponding maxim by deleting references to particular times, places, and persons. In what follows I shall take the terms "maxim" and "intention" as equivalent.

Whenever we act intentionally, we have at least one maxim and can, if we reflect, state what it is. (There is of course room for self-deception here—"I'm only keeping the wolf from the door," we may claim as we wolf down enough to keep ourselves overweight, or, more to the point, enough to feed someone else who hasn't enough food.)

When we want to work out whether an act we propose to do is right or wrong, according to Kant, we should look at our maxims and not at how much misery or happiness the act is likely to produce, and whether it does better at increasing happiness than other available acts. We just have to check that the act we have in mind will not use anyone as a mere means, and, if possible, that it will treat other persons as ends in themselves.

Using Persons as Mere Means

To use someone as a *mere means* is to involve them in a scheme of action *to which they could not in principle consent*. Kant does not say that there is anything wrong about using someone as a means. Evidently we have to do so in any cooperative scheme of action. If I cash a check I use the teller as a means, without whom I could not lay my hands on the cash; the teller in turn uses me as a means to earn his or her living. But in this case, each party consents to her or his part in the transaction. Kant would say that though they use one another as means, they do not use one another as *mere* means. Each person assumes that the other has maxims of his or her own and is not just a thing or a prop to be manipulated.

But there are other situations where one person uses another in a way to which the other could not in principle consent. For example, one person may make a promise to another with every intention of breaking it. If the promise is accepted, then the person to whom it was given must be ignorant of what the promisor's intention (maxim) really is. If one knew that the promisor did not intend to do what he or she was promising, one would, after all, not accept or rely on the promise. It would be as though there had been no promise made. Successful false promising depends on deceiving the person to whom the promise is made about what one's real maxim is. And since the person who is deceived doesn't know that real maxim, he or she can't in principle consent to his or her part in the proposed scheme of action. The person who is deceived is, as it were, a prop or a tool—a mere means—in the false promisor's scheme. A person who promises falsely treats the acceptor of the promise as a prop or a thing and not as a person. In Kant's view, it is this that makes false promising wrong.

One standard way of using others as mere means is by deceiving them. By getting someone involved in a business scheme or a criminal activity on false pretenses, or by giving a misleading account of what one is about, or by making a false promise or a fraudulent contract, one involves another in something to which he or she in principle cannot consent, since the scheme requires that he or she doesn't know what is going on. Another standard way of using others as mere means is by coercing them. If a rich or powerful person threatens a debtor with bankruptcy unless he or she joins in some scheme, then the creditor's intention is to coerce; and the debtor, if coerced, cannot consent to his or her part in the creditor's scheme. To make the example more specific: If a moneylender in an Indian village threatens not to renew a vital loan unless he is given the debtor's land, then he uses the debtor as a mere means. He coerces the debtor, who cannot truly consent to this "offer he can't refuse." (Of course the outward form of such transactions may look like ordinary commercial dealings, but we know very well that some offers and demands couched in that form are coercive.)

In Kant's view, acts that are done on maxims that require deception or coercion of others, and so cannot have the consent of those others (for consent precludes both deception and coercion), are wrong. When we act on such maxims, we treat others as mere means, as things rather than as ends in themselves. If we act on such maxims, our acts are not only wrong but unjust: such acts wrong the particular others who are deceived or coerced.

Study Questions

1. According to Kant, is using someone as a means always wrong?
2. What does Kant mean by the maxim of an action?
3. Why is it wrong to deceive others?
4. Can you imagine circumstances in which breaking a promise would not be wrong?

CHAPTER 14

Utilitarianism

John Stuart Mill

John Stuart Mill (1806–1873) was the leading English philosopher of the nineteenth century. Whereas Kant's ethical system concentrates exclusively on the reason for an action and does not take account of its results, Mill's system focuses only on consequences. Mill defends utilitarianism, the view that the supreme principle of morality is to act so as to produce as much happiness as possible, each person counting equally. By "happiness" Mill means pleasure and the absence of pain. He grants, however, that some pleasures are more worthwhile than others. "It is . . . better to be Socrates dissatisfied than a fool satisfied." His evidence for this claim is that anyone who knew the lives of both would choose the former rather than the latter.

Utilitarianism provides a means of dealing with the quandary of conflicting obligations. For instance, suppose you promised to meet someone for lunch but on the way encounter a child in need of immediate aid. What should you do? Utilitarianism solves the problem by telling you to give priority to helping the child because that course of action will produce more happiness. Shouldn't we keep our promises? Mill says that usually we should because the practice of keeping one's promises produces important social benefits. An exception should be made, however, on those occasions when more happiness will be produced by not keeping a promise.

What Utilitarianism Is

. . . The creed which accepts as the foundation of morals "utility" or the "greatest happiness principle" holds that actions are right in proportion as they tend to promote happiness; wrong as they tend to produce the reverse of happiness. By happiness is intended pleasure

---

From John Stuart Mill, *Utilitarianism* (1863).

and the absence of pain; by unhappiness, pain and the privation of pleasure. To give a clear view of the moral standard set up by the theory, much more requires to be said; in particular, what things it includes in the ideas of pain and pleasure, and to what extent this is left an open question. But these supplementary explanations do not affect the theory of life on which this theory of morality is grounded— namely, that pleasure and freedom from pain are the only things desirable as ends; and that all desirable things (which are as numerous in the utilitarian as in any other scheme) are desirable either for pleasure inherent in themselves or as means to the promotion of pleasure and the prevention of pain.

Now such a theory of life excites in many minds, and among them in some of the most estimable in feeling and purpose, inveterate dislike. To suppose that life has (as they express it) no higher end than pleasure—no better and nobler object of desire and pursuit—they designate as utterly mean and groveling, as a doctrine worthy only of swine. . . .

But there is no known . . . theory of life which does not assign to the pleasures of the intellect, of the feelings and imagination, and of the moral sentiments a much higher value as pleasures than to those of mere sensation. It must be admitted, however, that utilitarian writers in general have placed the superiority of mental over bodily pleasures chiefly in the greater permanency, safety, uncostliness, etc., of the former—that is, in their circumstantial advantages rather than in their intrinsic nature. And on all these points utilitarians have fully proved their case; but they might have taken the other and, as it may be called, higher ground with entire consistency. It is quite compatible with the principle of utility to recognize the fact that some kinds of pleasure are more desirable and more valuable than others. It would be absurd that, while in estimating all other things quality is considered as well as quantity, the estimation of pleasure should be supposed to depend on quantity alone.

If I am asked what I mean by difference in quality in pleasures, or what makes one pleasure more valuable than another, merely as a pleasure, except its being greater in amount, there is but one possible answer. Of two pleasures, if there be one to which all or almost all who have experience of both give a decided preference, irrespective of any feeling of moral obligation to prefer it, that is the more desirable pleasure. If one of the two is, by those who are competently acquainted with both, placed so far above the other that they prefer it, even though knowing it to be attended with a greater amount of

discontent, and would not resign it for any quantity of the other pleasure which their nature is capable of, we are justified in ascribing to
the preferred enjoyment a superiority in quality so far outweighing
quantity as to render it, in comparison, of small account.

Now it is an unquestionable fact that those who are equally
acquainted with and equally capable of appreciating and enjoying
both do give a most marked preference to the manner of existence
which employs their higher faculties. Few human creatures would
consent to be changed into any of the lower animals for a promise of
the fullest allowance of a beast's pleasures; no intelligent human
being would consent to be a fool, no instructed person would be an
ignoramus, no person of feeling and conscience would be selfish and
base, even though they should be persuaded that the fool, the dunce,
or the rascal is better satisfied with his lot than they are with theirs.
They would not resign what they possess more than he for the most
complete satisfaction of all the desires which they have in common
with him. If they ever fancy they would, it is only in cases of unhappiness so extreme that to escape from it they would exchange their
lot for almost any other, however undesirable in their own eyes. A
being of higher faculties requires more to make him happy, is capable probably of more acute suffering, and certainly accessible to it at
more points, than one of an inferior type; but in spite of these liabil-
ities, he can never really wish to sink into what he feels to be a lower
grade of existence. . . . It is better to be a human being dissatisfied
than a pig satisfied; better to be Socrates dissatisfied than a fool satisfied. And if the fool, or the pig, are of a different opinion, it is because they only know their own side of the question. The other party
to the comparison knows both sides.

It may be objected that many who are capable of the higher pleasures occasionally, under the influence of temptation, postpone them
to the lower. But this is quite compatible with a full appreciation of
the intrinsic superiority of the higher. Men often, from infirmity of
character, make their election for the nearer good, though they know
it to be the less valuable; and this no less when the choice is between
two bodily pleasures than when it is between bodily and mental. They
pursue sensual indulgences to the injury of health, though perfectly
aware that health is the greater good. It may be further objected that
many who begin with youthful enthusiasm for everything noble, as
they advance in years, sink into indolence and selfishness. But I do not
believe that those who undergo this very common change voluntarily
choose the lower description of pleasures in preference to the higher.

I believe that, before they devote themselves exclusively to the one, they have already become incapable of the other. Capacity for the nobler feelings is in most natures a very tender plant, easily killed, not only by hostile influences, but by mere want of sustenance; and in the majority of young persons it speedily dies away if the occupations to which their position in life has devoted them, and the society into which it has thrown them, are not favorable to keeping that higher capacity in exercise. Men lose their high aspirations as they lose their intellectual tastes, because they have not time or opportunity for indulging them; and they addict themselves to inferior pleasures, not because they deliberately prefer them, but because they are either the only ones to which they have access or the only ones which they are any longer capable of enjoying. It may be questioned whether anyone who has remained equally susceptible to both classes of pleasures ever knowingly and calmly preferred the lower, though many, in all ages, have broken down in an ineffectual attempt to combine both.

From this verdict of the only competent judges, I apprehend there can be no appeal. On a question which is the best worth having of two pleasures, or which of the two modes of existence is the most grateful to the feelings, apart from its moral attributes and from its consequences, the judgment of these who are qualified by knowledge of both, or, if they differ, that of the majority among them, must be admitted as final. And there needs to be the less hesitation to accept this judgment respecting the quality of pleasures, since there is no other tribunal to be referred to even on the question of quantity. What means are there of determining which is the acutest of two pains, or the intensest of two pleasurable sensations, except the general suffrage of those who are familiar with both? . . .

I must again repeat what the assailants of utilitarianism seldom have the justice to acknowledge, that the happiness which forms the utilitarian standard of what is right in conduct is not the agent's own happiness but that of all concerned. As between his own happiness and that of others, utilitarianism requires him to be as strictly impartial as a disinterested and benevolent spectator. In the golden rule of Jesus of Nazareth, we read the complete spirit of the ethics of utility. "To do as you would be done by," and "to love your neighbor as your self," constitute the ideal perfection of utilitarian morality. As the means of making the nearest approach to this ideal, utility would enjoin, first, that laws and social arrangements should place the happiness or (as, speaking practically, it may be called) the interest of every individual as nearly as possible in harmony with the interest of the whole; and, secondly, that education and opinion, which have so vast a power over human character, should so use that power as to establish in the mind of every individual an indissoluble association between his own happiness and the good of the whole, especially between his own happiness and the practice of such modes of conduct, negative and positive, as regard for the universal happiness prescribes; so that not only he may be unable to conceive the possibility of happiness to himself, consistently with conduct opposed to the general good, but also that a direct impulse to promote the general good may be in every individual one of the habitual motives of action, and the sentiments connected therewith may fill a large and prominent place in every human being's sentient existence. If the impugners of the utilitarian morality represented it to their own minds in this its true character, I know not what recommendation possessed by any other morality they could possibly affirm to be wanting to it; what more beautiful or more exalted developments of human nature any other ethical system can be supposed to foster; or what springs of action, not accessible to the utilitarian, such systems rely on for giving effect to their mandates.

The objectors to utilitarianism cannot always be charged with representing it in a discreditable light. On the contrary, those among them who entertain anything like a just idea of its disinterested character sometimes find fault with its standard as being too high for humanity. They say it is exacting too much to require that people shall always act from the inducement of promoting the general interest of society. But this is to mistake the very meaning of a standard of morals and confound the rule of action with the motive of it. It is the business of ethics to tell us what are our duties, or by what test we may know them; but no system of ethics requires that the sole motive of all we do shall be a feeling of duty; on the contrary, ninety-nine hundredths of all our actions are done from other motives, and rightly so done if the rule of duty does not condemn them. It is the more unjust to utilitarianism that this particular misapprehension should be made a ground of objection to it, inasmuch as utilitarian moralists have gone beyond almost all others in affirming that the motive has nothing to do with the morality of the action, though much with the worth of the agent. He who saves a fellow creature from drowning does what is morally right, whether his motive be duty or the hope of being paid for his trouble; he who betrays the friend that trusts him is guilty of a crime, even if his object be to serve another friend to whom he is under greater obligations. But to speak only of actions done from the motive of duty, and in direct obedience to principle: it is a misapprehension of the utilitarian mode of thought to conceive it as implying that people should fix their minds upon so wide a generality as the world, or society at large. The greatest majority of good actions are intended not for the benefit of the world, but for that of individuals, of which the good of the world is made up; and the thoughts of the most virtuous man need not on these occasions travel beyond the particular persons concerned, except so far as is necessary to assure himself that in benefiting them he is not violating the rights, that is, the legitimate and authorized expectations, of anyone else. The multiplication of happiness is, according to the utilitarian ethics, the object of virtue: the occasions on which any person (except one in a thousand) has it in his power to do this on an extended scale—in other words, to be a public benefactor—are but exceptional; and on these occasions alone is he called on to consider public utility; in every other case, private utility, the interest or happiness of some few persons, is all he has to attend to. Those alone the influence of whose actions extends to society in general need concern themselves habitually about so large an object. In the case of abstinences indeed—of things which people forbear to do from moral considerations, though the consequences in the particular case might be beneficial—it would be unworthy of an intelligent agent not to be consciously aware that the action is of a class which, if practiced generally, would be generally injurious, and that this is the ground of the obligation to abstain from it. The amount of regard for the public interest implied in this recognition is no greater than is demanded by every system of morals, for they all enjoin to abstain from whatever is manifestly pernicious to society. . . .

Of What Sort of Proof the Principle of Utility Is Susceptible

. . . Questions about ends are, in other words, questions about what things are desirable. The utilitarian doctrine is that happiness is desirable and the only thing desirable as an end, all other things being only desirable as means to that end. What ought to be required of the doctrine, what conditions is it requisite that the doctrine should fulfill—to make good its claim to be believed?

The only proof capable of being given that an object is visible is that people actually see it. The only proof that a sound is audible is that people hear it; and so of the other sources of our experience. In like manner, I apprehend, the sole evidence it is possible to produce that anything is desirable is that people do actually desire it. If the end which the utilitarian doctrine proposes to itself were not, in theory and in practice, acknowledged to be an end, nothing could ever convince any person that it was so. No reason can be given why the general happiness is desirable, except that each person, so far as he believes it to be attainable, desires his own happiness. This, however, being a fact, we have not only all the proof which the case admits of, but all which it is possible to require, that happiness is a good, that each person's happiness is a good to that person, and the general happiness, therefore, a good to the aggregate of all persons. Happiness has made out its title as *one* of the ends of conduct and, consequently, one of the criteria of morality.

But it has not, by this alone, proved itself to be the sole criterion. To do that it would seem, by the same rule, necessary to show not only that people desire happiness but that they never desire anything else. Now it is palpable that they do desire things which, in common language, are decidedly distinguished from happiness. They desire, for example, virtue and the absence of vice no less really than pleasure and the absence of pain. The desire of virtue is not as universal, but it is as authentic a fact as the desire of happiness. And hence the opponents of the utilitarian standard deem that they have a right to infer that there are other ends of human action besides happiness, and that happiness is not the standard of approbation and disapprobation.

But does the utilitarian doctrine deny that people desire virtue, or maintain that virtue is not a thing to be desired? The very reverse. It maintains not only that virtue is to be desired, but that it is to be desired disinterestedly, for itself. Whatever may be the opinion of utilitarian moralists as to the original conditions by which virtue is made virtue, however they may believe (as they do) that actions and dispositions are only virtuous because they promote another end than virtue, yet this being granted, and it having been decided, from considerations of this description, what *is* virtuous, they not only place virtue at the very head of the things which are good as means to the ultimate end, but they also recognize as a psychological fact the possibility of its being, to the individual, a good in itself, without looking to any end beyond it; and hold that the mind is not in a right state, not in a state conformable to utility, not in the state most conducive to the general happiness, unless it does love virtue in this manner—as a thing desirable in itself, even although, in the individual instance, it should not produce those other desirable consequences which it tends to produce, and on account of which it is held to be virtue. This opinion is not, in the smallest degree, a departure from the happiness principle. The ingredients of happiness are very various, and each of them is desirable in itself, and not merely when considered as swelling an aggregate. The principle of utility does not mean that any given pleasure, as music, for instance, or any given exemption from pain, as for example health, is to be looked upon as means to a collective something termed happiness, and to be desired on that account. They are desired and desirable in and for themselves; besides being means, they are a part of the end. Virtue, according to the utilitarian doctrine, is not naturally and originally part of the end, but it is capable of becoming so; and in those who live it disinterestedly it has become so, and is desired and cherished, not as a means to happiness, but to a part of their happiness. . . .

It results from the preceding considerations that there is in reality nothing desired except happiness. Whatever is desired otherwise than as a means to some end beyond itself, and ultimately to happiness, is desired as itself a part of happiness, and is not desired for itself until it has become so. Those who desire virtue for its own sake desire it either because the consciousness of it is a pleasure, or because the consciousness of being without it is a pain, or for both reasons united, as in truth the pleasure and pain seldom exist separately, but almost always together—the same person feeling pleasure in the degree of virtue attained, and pain in not having attained more. If one of these gave him no pleasure, and the other no pain, he would not love or desire virtue, or would desire it only for the other benefits which it might produce to himself or to persons whom he cared for.

We have now, then, an answer to the question, of what sort of proof the principle of utility is susceptible.

Study Questions

1. According to Mill, is the agent's own happiness the standard of right conduct?
2. Are some types of pleasure more worthwhile than others?
3. Why does Mill believe lying is wrong?
4. Does Mill believe the principle of utilitarianism can be proved?

CHAPTER 15

Strengths and Weaknesses of Utilitarianism

Louis P. Pojman

Utilitarianism has been subject to a variety of criticisms. Louis P. Pojman (1935–2005), who was Professor of Philosophy at the United States Military Academy, explains the grounds on which utilitarianism has been attacked and the possible responses available to its defenders. Regarding Peter Singer, see chapter 22.

There are two classical types of utilitarianism: act utilitarianism and rule utilitarianism. In applying the principle of utility, act utilitarians . . . say that ideally we ought to apply the principle to all of the alternatives open to us at any given moment. We may define act utilitarianism in this way:

> **act utilitarianism:** An act is right if and only if it results in as much good as any available alternative.

Of course, we cannot do the necessary calculations to determine which act is the correct one in each case, for often we must act spontaneously and quickly. So rules of thumb (for example, "In general don't lie," and "Generally keep your promises") are of practical importance. However, the right act is still that alternative that results in the most utility.

The obvious criticism of act utility is that it seems to fly in the face of fundamental intuitions about minimally correct behavior. Consider Richard Brandt's criticism of act utilitarianism:

It implies that if you have employed a boy to mow your lawn and he has finished the job and asks for his pay, you should pay him what you promised only if you cannot find a better use for your money. It implies that when you bring home your monthly paycheck you should use it to support your family and yourself only if it cannot be used more effectively to supply the needs of others. It implies that if your father is ill and he has no prospect of good in his life, and maintaining him is a drain on the energy and enjoyments of others, then, if you can end his life without provoking any public scandal or setting a bad example, it is your positive duty to take matters into your own hands and bring his life to a close.[1]

Rule utilitarians like Brandt attempt to offer a more credible version of the theory. They state that an act is right if it conforms to a valid rule within a system of rules that, if followed, will result in the best possible state of affairs (or the least bad state of affairs, if it is a question of all the alternatives being bad). We may define rule utilitarianism this way:

> **rule utilitarianism:** An act is right if and only if it is required by a rule that is itself a member of a set of rules whose acceptance would lead to greater utility for society than any available alternative.

Human beings are rule-following creatures. We learn by adhering to the rules of a given subject, whether it is speaking a language, driving a car, dancing, writing an essay, rock climbing, or cooking. We want to have a set of action-guiding rules to live by. The act-utilitarian rule, to do the act that maximizes utility, is too general for most purposes. Often we don't have time to deliberate whether lying will produce more utility than truth telling, so we need a more specific rule prescribing truthfulness, which passes the test of rational scrutiny. Rule utilitarianism asserts that the best chance of maximizing utility is by following the *set of rules* most likely to give us our desired results. . . .

An often-debated question in ethics is whether rule utilitarianism is a consistent version of utilitarianism. . . . [F]or example, we could imagine a situation in which breaking the general rule "Never lie" in order to spare someone's feelings would create more utility . . . than keeping the rule would. It would seem that we could always improve on any version of rule utilitarianism by breaking the set of rules whenever we judge that by so doing we could produce even more utility than by following the set. . . .

Whatever the answers . . . utilitarianism does have two very positive features. It also has several problems. The first attraction or strength is that it is a single principle, an absolute system with a potential answer for every situation. Do what will promote the most utility! It's good to have a simple, action-guiding principle that is applicable to every occasion—even if it may be difficult to apply (life's not simple). Its second strength is that utilitarianism seems to get to the substance of morality. It is not merely a formal system (that is, a system that sets forth broad guidelines for choosing principles but offers no principles; such a guideline would be "Do whatever you can universalize") but rather has a material core: Promote human (and possibly animal) flourishing and ameliorate suffering. The first virtue gives us a clear decision procedure in arriving at our answer about what to do. The second virtue appeals to our sense that morality is made for humans (and other animals?) and that morality is not so much about rules as about helping people and alleviating the suffering in the world. . . .

Opponents raise several . . . objections against utilitarianism. We discuss five of them: (1) the no-rest objection, (2) the absurd-implications objection, (3) the integrity objection, (4) the justice objection, and (5) the publicity objection. . . .

Problem 1: The No-Rest Objection:
According to utilitarianism, one should always do that act that promises to promote the most utility. However, there is usually an infinite set of possible acts to choose from, and even if I can be excused from considering all of them, I can be fairly sure that there is often a preferable act that I could be doing. For example, when I am about to go to the movies with a friend, I should ask myself if helping the homeless in my community wouldn't promote more utility. When I am about to go to sleep, I should ask myself whether I could at that moment be doing something to help save the ozone layer. And why not simply give all my assets (beyond what is absolutely necessary to keep me alive) to the poor in order to promote utility? Following utilitarianism, I should get little or no rest, and, certainly, I have no right to enjoy life when, by sacrificing, I can make others happier. Similar to this point is Peter Singer's contention that middle-class people have a duty to contribute to poor people (especially in undeveloped countries) more than one-third of their income and all of us have a duty to contribute every penny above $30,000 that we possess until we are only marginally better off than the worst-off people on Earth. But, the objection goes, this makes morality too demanding, creates a disincentive to work, and fails to account for differential obligation. So utilitarianism must be a false doctrine.

Response:
The utilitarian responds . . . by insisting that a rule prescribing rest and entertainment is actually the kind of rule that would have a place in a utility-maximizing set of rules. The agent should aim at maximizing his or her own happiness as well as other people's happiness. For the same reason, it is best not to worry much about the needs of those not in our primary circle. Although we should be concerned about the needs of future and distant (especially poor) people, it actually would promote disutility for the average person to become preoccupied with these concerns. Peter Singer represents a radical act-utilitarian position, which fails to give adequate attention to the rules that promote human flourishing, such as the right to own property, educate one's children, and improve one's quality of life, all of which probably costs more than $30,000 per year in many parts of North America. But, the utilitarian would remind us, we can surely do a lot more for suffering humanity than we now are doing—especially if we join together and act cooperatively. And we can simplify our lives, cutting back on conspicuous consumption, while improving our overall quality.

Problem 2: The Absurd-Implications Objection:
W. D. Ross has argued that utilitarianism is to be rejected because it is counterintuitive. If we accept it, we would have to accept an absurd implication. Consider two acts, A and B, that will both result in 100 hedons (units of pleasure of utility). The only difference is that A involves telling a lie and B involves telling the truth. The utilitarian must maintain that the two acts are of equal value. But this seems implausible; truth seems to be an intrinsically good thing. . . .

Response:
. . . [U]tilitarians can agree that there is something counterintuitive in the calculus of equating an act of lying with one of honesty; but, they argue, we must be ready to change our culture-induced moral biases. What is so important about truth telling or so bad about lying? If it turned out that lying really promoted human welfare, we'd have to accept it. But that's not likely. Our happiness is tied up with a need for reliable information (truth) on how to achieve our ends. So truthfulness will be a member of rule utility's set. But when lying will clearly promote utility without undermining the general adherence to the rule, we simply ought to lie. Don't we already accept lying to a gangster or telling white lies to spare people's feelings? . . .

Problem 3: The Integrity Objection:

Bernard Williams argues that utilitarianism violates personal integrity by commanding that we violate our most central and deeply held principles. He illustrates this with the following example:

> Jim finds himself in the central square of a small South American town. Tied up against the wall [is] a row of twenty Indians, most terrified, a few defiant, in front of them several armed men in uniform. A heavy man in a sweat-stained khaki shirt turns out to be the captain in charge and, after a good deal of questioning of Jim which establishes that he got there by accident while on a botanical expedition, explains that the Indians are a random group of inhabitants who, after recent acts of protest against the government, are just about to be killed to remind other possible protesters of the advantages of not protesting. However, since Jim is an honored visitor from another land, the captain is happy to offer him a guest's privilege of killing one of the Indians himself. If Jim accepts, then as a special mark of the occasion, the other Indians will be let off. Of course, if Jim refuses, then there is no special occasion, and Pedro here will do what he was about to do when Jim arrived, and kill them all. Jim, with some desperate recollection of schoolboy fiction, wonders whether if he got hold of a gun, he could hold the captain, Pedro and the rest of the soldiers to threat, but it is quite clear from the set-up that nothing of that kind is going to work: any attempt of that sort of thing will mean that all the Indians will be killed, and himself. The men against the wall, the other villagers, understand the situation, and are obviously begging him to accept. What should he do?[2]

Williams asks rhetorically,

> How can a man, as a utilitarian agent, come to regard as one satisfaction among others, and a dispensable one, a project or attitude round which he has built his life, just because someone else's projects have so structured the causal scene that *that* is how the utilitarian sum comes out?

Williams's conclusion is that utilitarianism leads to personal alienation and so is deeply flawed.

Response:

. . . [T]he utilitarian can argue that (1) some alienation may be necessary for the moral life but (2) the utilitarian (even the act utilitarian) can take this into account in devising strategies of action. That is, integrity is not an absolute that must be adhered to at all costs. Even when it is required that we sacrifice our lives or limit our freedom for others, we may have to limit or sacrifice something of what Williams calls our integrity. We may have to do the "lesser of evils" in many cases. If the utilitarian doctrine of negative responsibility is correct, we need to realize that we are responsible for the evil that we knowingly allow, as well as for the evil we commit.

But . . . a utilitarian may realize that there are important social benefits in having people who are squeamish about committing acts of violence, even those that preliminary utility calculations seem to prescribe. It may be that becoming certain kinds of people (endorsed by utilitarianism) may rule out being able to commit certain kinds of horrors—like Jim's killing of an innocent Indian. That is, utilitarianism recognizes the utility of good character and conscience, which may militate against certain apparently utility-maximizing acts.

Problem 4: The Justice Objection:
Suppose a rape and murder is committed in a racially volatile community. As the sheriff of the town, you have spent a lifetime working for racial harmony. Now, just when your goal is being realized, this incident occurs. The crime is thought to be racially motivated, and a riot is about to break out that will very likely result in the death of several people and create long-lasting racial antagonism. You see that you could frame a derelict for the crime so that a trial will find him guilty and he will be executed. There is every reason to believe that a speedy trial and execution will head off the riot and save community harmony. Only you (and the real criminal, who will keep quiet about it) will know that an innocent man has been tried and executed. What is the morally right thing to do? The utilitarian seems committed to framing the derelict, but many would find this appalling.

Or consider [that you] are a utilitarian physician who has five patients under your care. One needs a heart transplant, two need one lung each, one needs a liver, and the last one needs a kidney. Now into your office comes a healthy bachelor needing an immunization. You judge that he would make a perfect sacrifice for your five patients. Via a utility calculus, you determine that, without doubt, you could do the most good by injecting the healthy man with a fatal drug and then using his organs to save your five patients.

This cavalier view of justice offends us. The very fact that utilitarians even countenance such actions—that they would misuse the legal system or the medical system to carry out their schemes—seems frightening. . . .

Response:

. . . The utilitarian counters that justice is not an absolute—mercy and benevolence and the good of the whole society sometimes should override it; but, the sophisticated utilitarian insists, it makes good utilitarian sense to have a principle of justice that we generally adhere to. It may not be clear what the sheriff should do in the racially torn community. . . . If we could be certain that it would not set a precedent of sacrificing innocent people, it may be right to sacrifice one person for the good of the whole. Wouldn't we all agree, the utilitarian continues, that it would be right to sacrifice one innocent person to prevent a great evil?

Virtually all standard moral systems have a rule against torturing innocent people. But suppose a maniac . . . has a lethal gas that will spread throughout the globe and wipe out all life within a few weeks. His psychiatrist knows the lunatic well and assures us that there is one way to stop him—torture his 10-year-old daughter and televise it. Suppose, for the sake of the argument, there is no way to simulate the torture. Would you not consider torturing the child in this situation?

Is it not right to sacrifice one innocent person to stop a war or to save the human race from destruction? We seem to proceed on this assumption in wartime, in every bombing raid. . . . We seem to be following this rule in our decision to drive automobiles and trucks even though we are fairly certain the practice will result in the death of thousands of innocent people each year.

On the other hand, the sophisticated utilitarian may argue that, in the case of the sheriff framing the innocent derelict, justice should not be overridden by current utility concerns, for human rights themselves are outcomes of utility consideration and should not lightly be violated. That is, because we tend subconsciously to favor our own interests and biases, we institute the principle of rights to protect ourselves and others from capricious and biased acts that would in the long run have great disutility. So we must not undermine institutional rights too easily—we should not kill the bachelor in order to provide a heart, two lungs, a liver, and one kidney to the five other patients—at least not at the present time, given people's expectations of what will happen to them when they enter hospitals. But neither should we worship rights! They are to be taken seriously but not given ultimate authority. The utilitarian cannot foreclose the possibility of sacrificing innocent people for the greater good of humanity. If slavery could be humane and yield great overall utility, utilitarians would accept it. . . .

Problem 5: The Publicity Objection:

It is usually thought that all must know moral principles so that all may freely obey the principles. But utilitarians usually hesitate to recommend that everyone act as a utilitarian, especially an act utilitarian, for it takes a great deal of deliberation to work out the likely consequences of alternative courses of action. . . . So utilitarianism seems to contradict our notion of publicity.

Response:

. . . [U]tilitarians have two responses. First, they can counter that the objection only works against act utilitarianism. Rule utilitarianism can allow for greater publicity, for it is not the individual act that is important but the set of rules that is likely to bring about the most good. But then the act utilitarian may respond that this objection only shows a bias toward publicity (or even democracy). It may well be that publicity is only a rule of thumb to be overridden whenever there is good reason to believe that we can obtain more utility by not publicizing act-utilitarian ideas. Since we need to coordinate our actions with other people, moral rules must be publicly announced, typically through legal statutes. I may profit from cutting across the grass in order to save a few minutes in getting to class, but I also value a beautiful green lawn. We need public rules to ensure the healthy state of the lawn. So we agree on a rule to prohibit walking on the grass—even when it may have a utility function. There are many activities that individually may bring about individual utility advancement or even communal good, which if done regularly, would be disastrous, such as cutting down trees in order to build houses or to make newspaper or paper for books like this one, valuable as it is. We thus regulate the lumber industry so that every tree cut down is replaced with a new one and large forests are kept inviolate. So moral rules must be publicly advertised, often made into laws and enforced.

. . . [O]ne further criticism is that utilitarianism becomes so plastic as to be guilty of becoming a justification for our intuitions. Asked why we support justice . . . it seems too easy to respond, "Well, this principle will likely contribute to the greater utility in the long run." The utilitarian may sometimes become self-serving in such rationalizations. Nevertheless, there may be truth in such a defense.

Notes

1. Richard Brandt, "Towards a Credible Form of Utilitarianism," in *Morality and the Language of Conduct*, ed. H. Castaneda and G. Naknikian (Detroit: Wayne State University Press, 1963), pp. 109–110.
2. Bernard Williams, "A Critique of Utilitarianism," in *Utilitarianism: For and Against*, ed. J. C. C. Smart and Bernard Williams (Cambridge, UK: Cambridge University Press, 1973), p. 98ff.

Study Questions

1. Explain the difference between act utilitarianism and rule utilitarianism.
2. What is the justice objection to utilitarianism?
3. What is the integrity objection to utilitarianism?
4. Does utilitarianism imply that under certain circumstances a physician may be morally justified in killing one patient to save the lives of five others?

CHAPTER 16

The Nature of Virtue

Aristotle

Aristotle (384–322 B.C.E.), a student of Plato, had an enormous impact on the development of Western thought. He grounds morality in human nature, viewing the good as the fulfillment of the human potential to live well. To live well is to live in accordance with virtue. But how does one acquire virtue? Aristotle's answer is that we acquire it by habit; one becomes good by doing good. Repeated acts of justice and self-control result in a just, self-controlled person who not only performs just and self-controlled actions but does so from a fixed character. The virtuous act is a mean between two extremes, which are vices; for example, courage is the mean between rashness and cowardice.

Every art and every inquiry, and similarly every action and pursuit, is thought to aim at some good; and for this reason the good has rightly been declared to be that at which all things aim. . . .

If, then, there is some end of the things we do, which we desire for its own sake (everything else being desired for the sake of this), . . . clearly this must be . . . the chief good. . . .

Now such a thing happiness, above all else, is held to be; for this we choose always for itself and never for the sake of something else. . . .

Presumably, however, to say that happiness is the chief good seems a platitude, and a clearer account of what it is is still desired. This might perhaps be given, if we could first ascertain the function of man. For just as for a flute player, a sculptor, or any artist, and, in general, for all things that have a function or activity, the good and the "well" is thought to reside in the function, so would it seem to be

From Aristotle, *Nicomachean Ethics*, revised edition, edited and translated by David Ross. Copyright © 1998. Reprinted by permission of Oxford University Press.

for man, if he has a function. Have the carpenter, then, and the tanner certain functions or activities, and has man none? Is he born without a function? Or as eye, hand, foot, and in general each of the parts evidently has a function, may one lay it down that man similarly has a function apart from all these? What then can this be? Life seems to belong even to plants, but we are seeking what is peculiar to man. Let us exclude, therefore, the life of nutrition and growth. Next there would be a life of perception, but *it* also seems to be shared even by the horse, the ox, and every animal. There remains, then, an active life of the element that has a rational principle. . . . Now if the function of man is an activity of soul which follows or implies a rational principle, and if . . . any action is well performed when it is performed in accordance with the appropriate excellence . . . human good turns out to be activity of soul exhibiting excellence. . . .

But we must add "in a complete life." For one swallow does not make a summer, nor does one day; and so too one day, or a short time, does not make a man blessed and happy. . . .

Virtue, then, being of two kinds, intellectual and moral, intellectual virtue in the main owes both its birth and its growth to teaching (for which reason it requires experience and time), while moral virtue comes about as a result of habit. . . . From this it is also plain that none of the moral virtues arises in us by nature; for nothing that exists by nature can form a habit contrary to its nature. For instance, the stone which by nature moves downwards cannot be habituated to move upwards, not even if one tries to train it by throwing it up ten thousand times; nor can fire be habituated to move downwards, nor can anything else that by nature behaves in one way be trained to behave in another. Neither by nature, then, nor contrary to nature do the virtues arise in us; rather we are adapted by nature to receive them, and are made perfect by habit.

Again, of all the things that come to us by nature we first acquire the potentiality and later exhibit the activity (this is plain in the case of the senses; for it was not by often seeing or often hearing that we got these senses, but on the contrary we had them before we used them, and did not come to have them by using them); but the virtues we get by first exercising them, as also happens in the case of the arts as well. For the things we have to learn before we can do them, we learn by doing them, e.g., men become builders by building and lyre players by playing the lyre; so too we become just by doing just acts, temperate by doing temperate acts, brave by doing brave acts. . . .

It makes no small difference, then, whether we form habits of one kind or of another from our very youth; it makes a very great difference, or rather *all* the difference.

Since, then, the present inquiry does not aim at theoretical knowledge like the others (for we are inquiring not in order to know what virtue is, but in order to become good, since otherwise our inquiry would have been of no use), we must examine the nature of actions, namely, how we ought to do them; for these determine also the nature of the states of character that are produced, as we have said. . . .

First, then, let us consider this, that it is the nature of such things to be destroyed by defect and excess, as we see in the case of strength and of health (for to gain light on things imperceptible we must use the evidence of sensible things); exercise either excessive or defective destroys the strength, and similarly drink or food which is above or below a certain amount destroys the health, while that which is proportionate both produces and increases and preserves it. So too is it, then, in the case of temperance and courage and the other virtues. For the man who flies from and fears everything and does not stand his ground against anything becomes a coward, and the man who fears nothing at all but goes to meet every danger becomes rash; and similarly the man who indulges in every pleasure and abstains from none becomes self-indulgent, while the man who shuns every pleasure, as boors do, becomes in a way insensible; temperance and courage, then, are destroyed by excess and defect, and preserved by the mean.

But not only are the sources and causes of their origination and growth the same as those of their destruction, but also the sphere of their actualization will be the same; for this is also true of the things which are more evident to sense, e.g., of strength; it is produced by taking much food and undergoing much exertion, and it is the strong man that will be most able to do these things. So too is it with the virtues; by abstaining from pleasures we become temperate, and it is when we have become so that we are most able to abstain from them; and similarly too in the case of courage; for by being habituated to despise things that are fearful and to stand our ground against them we become brave, and it is when we have become so that we shall be most able to stand our ground against them. . . .

The question might be asked what we mean by saying that we must become just by doing just acts, and temperate by doing temperate acts; for if men do just and temperate acts, they are already just and temperate, exactly as if they do what is in accordance with the laws of grammar and of music, they are grammarians and musicians.

Or is this not true even of the arts? It is possible to do something that is in accordance with the laws of grammar, either by chance or under the guidance of another. A man will be a grammarian, then, only when he has both said something grammatical and said it grammatically; and this means doing it in accordance with the grammatical knowledge in himself.

Again, the case of the arts and that of the virtues are not similar; for the products of the arts have their goodness in themselves, so that it is enough that they should have a certain character, but if the acts that are in accordance with the virtues have themselves a certain character it does not follow that they are done justly or temperately. The agent also must be in a certain condition when he does them; in the first place he must have knowledge, secondly he must choose the acts, and choose them for their own sakes, and thirdly his action must proceed from a firm and unchangeable character. These are not reckoned in as conditions of the possession of the arts, except the bare knowledge, but as a condition of the possession of the virtues knowledge has little or no weight, while the other conditions count not for a little but for everything, i.e., the very conditions which result from often doing just and temperate acts.

Actions, then, are called just and temperate when they are such as the just or the temperate man would do; but it is not the man who does these that is just and temperate, but the man who also does them *as* just and temperate men do them. It is well said, then, that it is by doing just acts that the just man is produced, and by doing temperate acts the temperate man; without doing these no one would have even a prospect of becoming good.

But most people do not do these, but take refuge in theory and think they are being philosophers and will become good in this way, behaving somewhat like patients who listen attentively to their doctors, but do none of the things they are ordered to do. As the latter will not be made well in body by such a course of treatment, the former will not be made well in soul by such a course of philosophy. . . .

[E]very virtue or excellence both brings into good condition the thing of which it is the excellence and makes the work of that thing be done well; e.g., the excellence of the eye makes both the eye and its work good; for it is by the excellence of the eye that we see well. Similarly the excellence of the horse makes a horse both good in itself and good at running and at carrying its rider and at awaiting the attack of the enemy. Therefore, if this is true in every case, the virtue of man also will be the state of character which makes a man good and which makes him do his own work well.

How this is to happen we have stated already, but it will be made plain also by the following consideration of the specific nature of virtue. In everything that is continuous and divisible it is possible to take more, less, or an equal amount, and that either in terms of the thing itself or relatively to us; and the equal is an intermediate between excess and defect. By the intermediate in the object I mean that which is equidistant from each of the extremes, which is one and the same for all men; by the intermediate relatively to us that which is neither too much nor too little—and this is not one, nor the same for all. For instance, if ten is many and two is few, six is the intermediate, taken in terms of the object; for it exceeds and is exceeded by an equal amount; this is intermediate according to arithmetical proportion. But the intermediate relatively to us is not to be taken so; if ten pounds are too much for a particular person to eat and two too little, it does not follow that the trainer will order six pounds; for this also is perhaps too much for the person who is to take it, or too little—too little for Milo [a wrestler], too much for the beginner in athletic exercises. The same is true of running and wrestling. Thus a master of any art avoids excess and defect, but seeks the intermediate and chooses this—the intermediate not in the object but relatively to us.

If it is thus, then, that every art does its work well—by looking to the intermediate and judging its works by this standard (so that we often say of good works of art that it is not possible either to take away or to add anything, implying that excess and defect destroy the goodness of works of art, while the mean preserves it; and good artists, as we say, look to this in their work), and if, further, virtue is more exact and better than any art, as nature also is, then virtue must have the quality of aiming at the intermediate. I mean moral virtue; for it is this that is concerned with passions and actions, and in these there is excess, defect, and the intermediate. For instance, both fear and confidence and appetite and anger and pity and in general pleasure and pain may be felt both too much and too little, and in both cases not well; but to feel them at the right times, with reference to the right objects, towards the right people, with the right motive, and in the right way, is what is both intermediate and best, and this is characteristic of virtue. Similarly with regard to actions also there is excess, defect, and the intermediate. Now virtue is concerned with passions and actions, in which excess is a form of failure, and so is defect, while the intermediate is praised and is a form of success; and being praised and being successful are both characteristics of virtue. Therefore virtue is a kind of mean, since, as we have seen, it aims at what is intermediate. . . .

But not every action nor every passion admits of a mean; for some have names that already imply badness, e.g., spite, shamelessness, envy, and in the case of actions adultery, theft, murder; for all of these and suchlike things imply by their names that they are themselves bad, and not the excesses or deficiencies of them. It is not possible, then, ever to be right with regard to them; one must always be wrong. Nor does goodness or badness with regard to such things depend on committing adultery with the right woman, at the right time, and in the right way, but simply to do any of them is to go wrong. . . .

The moral virtue is a mean, then, and in what sense it is so, and that it is a mean between two vices, the one involving excess, the other deficiency, and that it is such because its character is to aim at what is intermediate in passions and in actions, has been sufficiently stated. Hence also it is no easy task to be good. For in everything it is no easy task to find the middle, e.g., to find the middle of a circle is not for everyone but for him who knows; so, too, anyone can get angry—that is easy—or give or spend money; but to do this to the right person, to the right extent, at the right time, with the right motive, and in the right way, *that* is not for everyone, nor is it easy; wherefore goodness is both rare and laudable and noble. . . .

But we must consider the things towards which we ourselves also are easily carried away; for some of us tend to one thing, some to another; and this will be recognizable from the pleasure and the pain we feel. We must drag ourselves away to the contrary extreme; for we shall get into the intermediate state by drawing well away from error. . . .

So much, then, is plain, that the intermediate state is in all things to be praised, but that we must incline sometimes towards the excess, sometimes towards the deficiency; for so shall we most easily hit the mean and what is right.

Study Questions

1. According to Aristotle, what is the function of a human being?
2. How does moral virtue differ from intellectual virtue?
3. How is moral virtue acquired?
4. What is Aristotle's doctrine of the mean?

CHAPTER 17

Virtue Ethics

Julia Driver

In the next selection Julia Driver, whose work we read previously, explains the difference between an ethical theory, like Aristotle's, that focuses on the development of a person's character, and an ethical theory, like that of Kant or Mill, that concentrates on the formulation of rules for right actions. In short, virtue ethics relies on concrete judgments in specific situations rather than abstract principles applicable universally.

Sometimes, in deciding on what we ought to do, we first consider how we ought to be. For example, if faced with a situation that involves social injustice, we might pick someone whom we admired and wanted to be like—Gandhi, let's say, or Mother Teresa—and then ask "What would Gandhi do?" This doesn't give us a rigid formula or decision procedure to employ. Instead, it asks us to consider a virtuous person, to consider his or her virtues, and then ask what behavior people with these good traits and dispositions exemplify. Some writers have thought that a picture like this better reflects how people should go about making their moral decisions. They should do so on the basis of concrete virtue judgments instead of abstract principles, such as "Maximize the good" or "Never treat another person merely as a means," and so forth.

 . . . [V]irtue ethics has actually been around in one form or another for thousands of years. Current virtue ethicists, in fact, tend to take their inspiration from Aristotle, who was a student of Plato, and certainly one of the greatest philosophers in the history of philosophy. Aristotle wrote the *Nicomachean Ethics*, which—as an aid to his son—spelled out the steps to a good life. Of course, "good" is a bit ambiguous—Is that morally good, or prudentially good, or intellectually good, or all of the above? Well, for Aristotle, the good human life had all these ingredients. A good human being was virtuous in the sense that he embodied all the excellences of human character. So, Aristotle is often held up as a paradigmatic virtue ethicist. Again, . . . virtue ethics maintains that character, human excellence, *virtues*, are the basic modes of evaluation in the theory, as opposed to act evaluations such as "right" and "wrong." . . . [A]ct evaluation is to be understood in terms of character evaluation. Virtue is the primary mode of evaluation, and all other modes are understood and defined *in terms of* virtue. . . . Most of the theoretical weight is therefore borne by the account of virtue provided in the theory. . . .

Aristotle famously believed in the claim that virtue is a mean state, that it lies between two opposed vices. This is referred to as the doctrine of the mean. The basic idea is that virtue will tend to lie between two extremes, each of which is a vice. So, bravery lies between cowardice and foolhardiness; temperance lies between gluttony and abstinence; and so forth. Some virtues can be hard to model on this view. Take honesty. Of course, failure to tell the truth—telling a lie—would be one extreme, but is there a vice of telling too much truth? Maybe . . . though I suspect there might be some disagreement over this. Part of the mean state concerned our emotions, however, and not just our actions. The virtuous person not only does the right thing, but he does the right thing in the right way—in the right sort of emotional or psychological state. Our emotions can be excessive or deficient as well. The person who runs into the battle to fight, but who is excessively fearful, is not fully virtuous. The truly well-functioning person is able to control and regulate his feelings and emotions, as well as act rightly.

Aristotle's picture, then, of the virtuous person is the person who functions harmoniously—his desires and emotions do not conflict with what he knows to be right. They go together. This leads him to view a person who acts rightly, but who feels badly about it, as not being virtuous. This person is merely "continent"—this person can control his actions, but needs to work on bringing his emotions in line with what reason tells him is the right and appropriate thing to do. So the excellent human being is not conflicted; he does not suffer inner turmoil and the struggle between reason and passion. . . .

Many challenges have been posed to virtue ethics. . . . One *general* criticism of the whole approach is that it fails to conform to what we know about how best to explain human behavior . . .

For example, John Doris proposes that the globalism of traditional virtue ethics be rejected.[1] There is no one "honesty" trait, for example. Instead, we may have 50 or more "honesties"; that is, narrowly circumscribed traits or dispositions to tell the truth. So, Joe might not have honesty 1, which is the disposition to tell the truth about how well he does on exams, but he might have honesty 34, the disposition to tell the truth about how tall he is. So, Doris thinks that . . . the experimental evidence supports the view that are no robust traits; that is, traits to tell the truth over all or even most contexts or situations. And this is a problem for a virtue ethics that understands virtue as a "stable" or "reliable" character trait.

Another challenge has been that virtue ethics doesn't provide a guide to action. "Be nice, dear"—Well, what is nice, and what are the circumstances under which I should be nice? That's what we really want to know. This shows that it is these other reasons that actually justify our behavior. This has been raised as a very standard problem for the theory, but virtue ethicists have spent a good deal of time trying to show how their theories could be applied. . . .

This challenge can be expanded by noting that virtue ethics has trouble telling us the right thing to do in conflict situations, where two virtues may conflict, and thus the corresponding rules—such as "Be honest" or "Be kind"—may conflict. But some virtue ethicists think that this is simply the way morality is—it is messy, and for any situation there may be more than one right answer. Insisting that morality is neat and tidy is simply to impose a misleading clarity on moral decision-making.

. . . Virtue ethics remains an interesting alternative approach to moral evaluation and moral guidance.

Note

1. John Doris, *Lack of Character: Personality and Moral Behavior* (Cambridge, UK: Cambridge University Press, 2002), p. 31.

Study Questions

1. When you make a moral judgment, which question should you ask yourself: "What should I do?" or "What sort of person should I be?"
2. Should moral decisions always be based on rules?
3. Can findings in psychology be relevant to assessing moral theories?
4. Might a moral question have more than one right answer?

CHAPTER 18

The Ethics of Care

Virginia Held

Virginia Held is Professor Emerita of Philosophy at Hunter College and the Graduate Center of the City University of New York. In the following selection she develops what she terms "the ethics of care," which some philosophers have viewed as one form of virtue ethics. She emphasizes, however, that while the two are in some ways similar, virtue ethics focuses on the character of individuals, whereas the ethics of care is concerned especially with fostering connectedness among people.

I

The ethics of care is only a few decades old. Some theorists do not like the term "care" to designate this approach to moral issues and have tried substituting "the ethic of love," or "relational ethics," but the discourse keeps returning to "care" as the so far more satisfactory of the terms considered, though dissatisfactions with it remain. The concept of care has the advantage of not losing sight of the work involved in caring for people and of not lending itself to the interpretation of morality as ideal but impractical to which advocates of the ethics of care often object. . . .

I think one can discern among various versions of the ethics of care a number of major features.

First, the central focus of the ethics of care is on the compelling moral salience of attending to and meeting the needs of the particular others for whom we take responsibility. Caring for one's child, for instance, may well and defensibly be at the forefront of a person's moral concerns. The ethics of care recognizes that human beings are dependent for many years of their lives, that the moral claims of those dependent on us for the care they need is pressing, and that there are highly important moral aspects in developing the relations of caring that enable human beings to live and progress. All persons need care for at least their early years. Prospects for human progress and flourishing hinge fundamentally on the care that those needing it receive, and the ethics of care stresses the moral force of the responsibility to respond to the needs of the dependent. Many persons will become ill and dependent for some periods of their later lives, including in frail old age, and some who are permanently disabled will need care the whole of their lives. Moralities built on the image of the independent, autonomous, rational individual largely overlook the reality of human dependence and the morality for which it calls. The ethics of care attends to this central concern of human life and delineates the moral values involved. . . .

Second, in the epistemological process of trying to understand what morality would recommend and what it would be morally best for us to do and to be, the ethics of care values emotion rather than rejects it. Not all emotion is valued, of course, but in contrast with the dominant rationalist approaches, such emotions as sympathy, empathy, sensitivity, and responsiveness are seen as the kind of moral emotions that need to be cultivated not only to help in the implementation of the dictates of reason but to better ascertain what morality recommends. Even anger may be a component of the moral indignation that should be felt when people are treated unjustly or inhumanely, and it may contribute to (rather than interfere with) an appropriate interpretation of the moral wrong. This is not to say that raw emotion can be a guide to morality; feelings need to be reflected on and educated. But from the care perspective, moral inquiries that rely entirely on reason and rationalistic deductions or calculations are seen as deficient.

The emotions that are typically considered and rejected in rationalistic moral theories are the egoistic feelings that undermine universal moral norms, the favoritism that interferes with impartiality, and the aggressive and vengeful impulses for which morality is to provide restraints. The ethics of care, in contrast, typically appreciates the emotions and relational capabilities that enable morally concerned persons in actual interpersonal contexts to understand what would be best. Since even the helpful emotions can often become misguided or worse—as when excessive empathy with others leads to a wrongful degree of self-denial or when benevolent concern crosses over into controlling domination—we need an *ethics* of care, not just care itself. The various aspects and expressions of care and caring relations need to be subjected to moral scrutiny and *evaluated*, not just observed and described.

Third, the ethics of care rejects the view of the dominant moral theories that the more abstract the reasoning about a moral problem the better because the more likely to avoid bias and arbitrariness, the more nearly to achieve impartiality. The ethics of care respects rather than removes itself from the claims of particular others with whom we share actual relationships. It calls into question the universalistic and abstract rules of the dominant theories. When the latter consider such actual relations as between a parent and child, if they say anything about them at all, they may see them as permitted and cultivating them a preference that a person may have. Or they may recognize a universal obligation for all parents to care for their children. But they do not permit actual relations ever to take priority over the requirements of impartiality. . . .

The ethics of care may seek to limit the applicability of universal rules to certain domains where they are more appropriate, like the domain of law, and resist their extension to other domains. Such rules may simply be inappropriate in, for instance, the contexts of family and friendship, yet relations in these domains should certainly be *evaluated*, not merely described, hence morality should not be limited to abstract rules. We should be able to give moral guidance concerning actual relations that are trusting, considerate, and caring and concerning those that are not.

Dominant moral theories tend to interpret moral problems as if they were conflicts between egoistic individual interests on the one hand, and universal moral principles on the other. The extremes of "selfish individual" and "humanity" are recognized, but what lies between these is often overlooked. The ethics of care, in contrast, focuses especially on the area between these extremes. Those who conscientiously care for others are not seeking primarily to further their own *individual* interests; their interests are intertwined with the persons they care for. Neither are they acting for the sake of *all others* or *humanity in general*; they seek instead to preserve or promote an actual human relation between themselves and *particular others*. Persons in caring relations are acting for self-and-other together. Their characteristic stance is neither egoistic nor altruistic; these are the options in a conflictual situation, but the well-being of a caring relation involves the cooperative well-being of those in the relation and the well-being of the relation itself. . . .

II

What *is* care? What do we mean by the term "care"? Can we define it in anything like a precise way? There is not yet anything close to agreement among those writing on care on what exactly we should take the meaning of this term to be, but there have been many suggestions, tacit and occasionally explicit.

For over two decades, the concept of care as it figures in the ethics of care has been assumed, explored, elaborated, and employed in the development of theory. But definitions have often been imprecise, or trying to arrive at them has simply been postponed (as in my own case), in the growing discourse. Perhaps this is entirely appropriate for new explorations, but the time may have come to seek greater clarity. Some of those writing on care have attempted to be precise, with mixed results, whereas others have proceeded with the tacit understanding that of course to a considerable extent we know what we are talking about when we speak of taking care of a child or providing care for the ill. But care has many forms, and as the ethics of care evolves, so should our understanding of what care is.

The last words I spoke to my older brother after a brief visit and with special feeling were: "take care." He had not been taking good care of himself, and I hoped he would do better; not many days later he died, of problems quite possibly unrelated to those to which I had been referring. "Take care" was not an expression he and I grew up with. I acquired it over the years in my life in New York City. It may be illuminating to begin thinking about the meaning of "care" with an examination of this expression.

We often say "take care" as routinely as "goodbye" or some abbreviation and with as little emotion. But even then it does convey some sense of connectedness. More often, when said with some feeling, it means something like "take care of yourself because I care about you." Sometimes we say it, especially to children or to someone embarking on a trip or an endeavor, meaning "I care what happens to you, so please don't do anything dangerous or foolish." Or, if we know the danger is inevitable and inescapable, it may be more like a wish that the elements will let the person take care so the worst can be evaded. And sometimes we mean it as a plea: Be careful not to harm yourself or others because our connection will make us feel with and for you. We may be harmed ourselves or partly responsible, or if you do something you will regret we will share that regret.

One way or another, this expression (like many others) illustrates human relatedness and the daily reaffirmations of connection. It is the relatedness of human beings, built and rebuilt, that the ethics of care is being developed to try to understand, evaluate, and guide. The expression has more to do with the feelings and awareness of the persons expressing and the persons receiving such expressions than with the actual tasks and work of "taking care" of a person who is dependent on us, or in need of care, but such attitudes and shared awareness seem at least one important component of care.

A seemingly easy distinction to make is between care as the activity of taking care of someone and the mere "caring about" of how we feel about certain issues. Actually "caring for" a small child or a person who is ill is quite different from merely "caring for" something (or not) in the sense of liking it or not, as in "I don't care for that kind of music." But these distinctions may not be as clear as they appear, since when we take care of a child, for instance, we usually also care about him or her, and although we could take care of a child we do not like, the caring will usually be better care if we care for the child in both senses. If we really do care about world hunger, we will probably be doing something about it, such as at least giving money to alleviate it or to change the conditions that bring it about, and thus establishing some connection between ourselves and the hungry we say we care about. And if we really do care about global climate change and the harm it will bring to future generations, we imagine a connection between ourselves and those future people who will judge our irresponsibility, and we change our consumption practices or political activities to decrease the likely harm. . . .

My own view, then, is that care is both a practice and a value. As a practice, it shows us how to respond to needs and why we should. It builds trust and mutual concern and connectedness between persons. It is not a series of individual actions, but a practice that develops, along with its appropriate attitudes. It has attributes and standards that can be described, but more important that can be recommended and that should be continually improved as adequate care comes closer to being good care. Practices of care should express the caring relations that bring persons together, and they should do so in ways that are progressively more morally satisfactory. Caring practices should gradually transform children and others into human beings who are increasingly morally admirable. . . .

In addition to being a practice, care is also a value. Caring pers~~e~~ and caring attitudes should be valued, and we can organize man~~y~~ evaluations of how persons are interrelated around a constellation of moral considerations associated with care or its absence. For instance, we can ask of a relation whether it is trusting and mutually considerate or hostile and vindictive. We can ask if persons are attentive and responsive to each other's needs or indifferent and self-absorbed. Care is not the same as benevolence, in my view, since it is more the characterization of a social relation than the description of an individual disposition, and social relations are not reducible to individual states. Caring relations ought to be cultivated, between persons in their personal lives and between the members of caring societies. Such relations are often reciprocal over time if not at given times. The values of caring are especially exemplified in caring relations, rather than in persons as individuals.

Study Questions

1. According to Held, what is "the ethics of care"?
2. What does Held mean by her claim that care is both a practice and a value?
3. Is the ethics of care a form of virtue ethics?
4. Does analyzing a moral problem from the perspective of the ethics of care sometimes yield a different result than that obtained by using either a Kantian or utilitarian standard?

CHAPTER 19

The Social Contract

Thomas Hobbes

Thomas Hobbes (1588–1679) was an English philosopher who played a crucial role in the history of social thought. He develops a moral and political theory that views justice and other ethical ideals as resting on an implied agreement among individuals. Hobbes argues that reason requires that we should relinquish the right to do whatever we please in exchange for all others limiting their rights in a similar manner, thus achieving security for all. Outside the social order, each human life is, as Hobbes famously puts it, "solitary, poor, nasty, brutish, and short."

Of the Natural Condition of Mankind as Concerning Their Felicity, and Misery

Nature hath made men so equal in the faculties of body and mind as that, though there be found one man sometimes manifestly stronger in body or of quicker mind than another, yet when all is reckoned together the difference between man and man is not so considerable as that one man can thereupon claim to himself any benefit to which another may not pretend as well as he. For as to the strength of body, the weakest has strength enough to kill the strongest, either by secret machination, or by confederacy with others that are in the same danger with himself.

And as to the faculties of the mind—setting aside the arts grounded upon words, and especially that skill of proceeding upon general, and infallible rules called science (which very few have, and but in few things), as being not a native faculty (born with us), nor attained (as prudence) while we look after someone else—I find yet a greater

From Thomas Hobbes, *Leviathan* (1651). Spelling and punctuation is updated.

equality amongst men than that of strength. For prudence, is but experience; which equal time equally bestows on all men in those things they equally apply themselves unto. That which may perhaps make such equality incredible is but a vain conceit of one's own wisdom, which almost all men think they have in a greater degree than the vulgar, that is, than all men but themselves and a few others whom, by fame or for concurring with themselves, they approve. For such is the nature of men that howsoever they may acknowledge many others to be more witty, or more eloquent, or more learned; yet they will hardly believe there be many so wise as themselves: For they see their own wit at hand, and other men's at a distance. But this proveth rather that men are in that point equal, than unequal. For there is not ordinarily a greater sign of the equal distribution of anything, than that every man is contented with his share.

From this equality of ability ariseth equality of hope in the attaining of our ends. And therefore, if any two men desire the same thing, which nevertheless they cannot both enjoy, they become enemies; and in the way to their end, which is principally their own conservation, and sometimes their delectation only, endeavour to destroy or subdue one another. And from hence it comes to pass that, where an invader hath no more to fear than another man's single power, if one plant, sow, build, or possess a convenient seat, others may probably be expected to come prepared with forces united, to dispossess and deprive him, not only of the fruit of his labour, but also of his life or liberty. And the invader again is in the like danger of another.

And from this diffidence of one another, there is no way for any man to secure himself so reasonable as anticipation, that is, by force or wiles to master the persons of all men he can, so long till he see no other power great enough to endanger him. And this is no more than his own conservation requireth, and is generally allowed. Also, because there be some that taking pleasure in contemplating their own power in the acts of conquest, which they pursue farther than their security requires, if others (that otherwise would be glad to be at ease within modest bounds) should not by invasion increase their power, they would not be able, long time, by standing only on their defence, to subsist. And by consequence, such augmentation of dominion over men being necessary to a man's conservation; it ought to be allowed him.

Again, men have no pleasure, but on the contrary a great deal of grief in keeping company where there is no power able to over-awe them all. For every man looketh that his companion should value him at the same rate he sets upon himself, and upon all signs of contempt, or undervaluing, naturally endeavours, as far as he dares (which amongst them that have no common power to keep them in quiet, is far enough to make them destroy each other), to extort a greater value from his contemners, by damage; and from others, by the example.

So that in the nature of man, we find three principal causes of quarrel. First, competition; secondly, diffidence [distrust]; thirdly, glory.

The first maketh man invade for gain; the second, for safety; and the third, for reputation. The first use violence to make themselves masters of other men's persons, wives, children, and cattle; the second, to defend them; the third, for trifles, as a word, a smile, a different opinion, and any other sign of undervalue, either direct in their persons, or by reflection in their kindred, their friends, their nation, their profession, or their name.

Hereby it is manifest that during the time men live without a common power to keep them all in awe, they are in that condition which is called war, and such a war as is of every man against every man. For WAR consisteth not in battle only, or the act of fighting, but in a tract of time wherein the will to contend by battle is sufficiently known. And therefore, the notion of *time* is to be considered in the nature of war, as it is in the nature of weather. For as the nature of foul weather lieth not in a shower or two of rain, but in an inclination thereto of many days together, so the nature of war consisteth not in actual fighting, but in the known disposition thereto during all the time there is no assurance to the contrary. All other time is PEACE.

Whatsoever therefore is consequent to a time of war, where every man is enemy to every man, the same is consequent to the time wherein men live without other security than what their own strength and their own invention shall furnish them withal. In such condition there is no place for industry, because the fruit thereof is uncertain, and consequently no culture of the earth, no navigation, nor use of the commodities that may be imported by sea, no commodious building, no instruments of moving and removing such things as require much force, no knowledge of the face of the earth, no account of time, no arts, no letters, no society, and which is worst of all, continual fear and danger of violent death, and the life of man, solitary, poor, nasty, brutish, and short.

It may seem strange to some man that has not well weighed these things, that nature should thus dissociate, and render men apt to invade and destroy one another. And he may therefore, not trusting to this inference made from the passions, desire perhaps to have the same confirmed by experience. Let him therefore consider with himself—when taking a journey, he arms himself, and seeks to go well accompanied, when going to sleep, he locks his doors; when even in his house he locks his chests; and this when he knows there be laws, and public officers, armed, to revenge all injuries shall be done him—what opinion he has of his fellow subjects, when he rides armed; of his fellow citizens, when he locks his doors; and of his children and servants, when he locks his chests. Does he not there as much accuse mankind by his actions, as I do by my words? But neither of us accuse man's nature in it. The desires and other passions of man are in themselves no sin. No more are the actions that proceed from those passions, till they know a law that forbids them—which till laws be made they cannot know. Nor can any law be made, till they have agreed upon the person that shall make it.

It may peradventure be thought, there was never such a time nor condition of war as this; and I believe it was never generally so, over all the world. But there are many places where they live so now. For the savage people in many places of *America* (except the government of small families, the concord whereof dependeth on natural lust) have no government at all, and live at this day in that brutish manner as I said before. Howsoever, it may be perceived what manner of life there would be where there were no common power to fear, by the manner of life which men that have formerly lived under a peaceful government use to degenerate into, in a civil war.

But though there had never been any time wherein particular men were in a condition of war one against another, yet in all times kings and persons of sovereign authority, because of their independency, are in continual jealousies and in the state and posture of gladiators, having their weapons pointing and their eyes fixed on one another, that is, their forts, garrisons, and guns upon the frontiers of their kingdoms, and continual spies upon their neighbours; which is a posture of war. But because they uphold thereby the industry of their subjects, there does not follow from it that misery which accompanies the liberty of particular men.

To this war of every man against every man, this also is consequent; that nothing can be unjust. The notions of right and wrong, justice and injustice have there no place. Where there is no common power, there is no law: where no law, no injustice. Force and fraud are in war the two cardinal virtues. Justice, and injustice are none of the faculties neither of the body, nor mind. If they were, they might be in a man that were alone in the world, as well as his senses and passions. They are qualities that relate to men in society, not in solitude. It is consequent also to the same condition that there be no propriety, no dominion, no *mine* and *thine* distinct, but only that to be every man's that he can get, and for so long as he can keep it. And thus much for the ill condition which many by mere nature is actually placed in; though with a possibility to come out of it, consisting partly in the passions, partly in his reason.

The passions that incline men to peace, are fear of death, desire of such things as are necessary to commodious living, and a hope by their industry to obtain them. And reason suggesteth convenient articles of peace, upon which men may be drawn to agreement. These articles are they which otherwise are called the Laws of Nature, whereof I shall speak more particularly in the two following chapters.

Of the First and Second Natural Laws, and of Contracts

The RIGHT OF NATURE, which writers commonly call *jus naturale*, is the liberty each man hath to use his own power, as he will himself, for the preservation of his own nature, that is to say, of his own life, and consequently of doing anything, which in his own judgment, and reason, he shall conceive to be the aptest means thereunto.

By LIBERTY is understood, according to the proper signification of the word, the absence of external impediments, which impediments, may oft take away part of a man's power to do what he would; but cannot hinder him from using the power left him, according as his judgment and reason shall dictate to him.

A LAW OF NATURE, (*lex naturalis*,) is a precept or general rule, found out by reason, by which a man is forbidden to do that, which is destructive of his life or taketh away the means of preserving the same, and to omit that by which he thinketh it may be best preserved. For though they that speak of this subject use to confound *jus* and *lex* (*right* and *law*), yet they ought to be distinguished, because RIGHT consisteth in liberty to do, or to forbear, whereas LAW determineth and bindeth to one of them; so that law, and right differ as much as obligation and liberty, which in one and the same matter are inconsistent.

And because the condition of man (as hath been declared in the precedent chapter) is a condition of war of everyone against everyone (in which case everyone is governed by his own reason and there is nothing he can make use of that may not be a help unto him in preserving his life against his enemies), it followeth that in such a condition every man has a right to everything, even to one another's body. And therefore, as long as this natural right of every man to everything endureth, there can be no security to any man (how strong or wise soever he be,) of living out the time, which nature ordinarily alloweth men to live. And consequently it is a precept, or general rule of reason, *that every man, ought to endeavour peace, as far as he has hope of obtaining it, and when he cannot obtain it, that he may seek and use all helps and advantages of war.* The first branch of which rule containeth the first, and fundamental law of nature, which is *to seek peace, and follow it.* The second, the sum of the right of nature, which is *by all means we can, to defend ourselves.*

From this fundamental law of nature, by which men are commanded to endeavor peace, is derived this second law: *that a man be willing, when others are so too, as far-forth, as for peace and defence of himself he shall think it necessary, to lay down this right to all things; and be contented with so much liberty against other men, as he would allow other men against himself.* For as long as every man holdeth this right of doing anything he liketh, so long are all men in the condition of war. But if other men will not lay down their right as well as he, then there is no reason for anyone to divest himself of his; for that were to expose himself to prey, (which no man is bound to), rather than to dispose himself to peace. This is that law of the Gospel: "whatsoever you require that others should do for you, that do ye to them." . . .

Of Other Laws of Nature

From that law of nature by which we are obliged to transfer to another such rights as, being retained, hinder the peace of mankind, there followeth a third, which is this, *that men perform their covenants made,* without which covenants are in vain, and but empty words; and the right of all men to all things remaining, we are still in the condition of war.

And in this law of nature consisteth the fountain and original of JUSTICE. For where no covenant hath preceded, there hath no right been transferred, and every man has right to every thing; and consequently, no action can be unjust. But when a covenant is made, then to break it is *unjust*; and the definition of INJUSTICE, is no other than *the not performance of covenant.* And whatsoever is not unjust, is *just.*

But because covenants of mutual trust where there is fear of not performance on either part (as hath been said in the former chapter) are invalid, though the original of justice be the making of covenants; yet injustice actually there can be none till the cause of such fear be taken away, which while men are in the natural condition of war, cannot be done. Therefore, before the names of just, and unjust can have place, there must be some coercive power, to compel men equally to the performance of their covenants, by the terror of some punishment greater than the benefit they expect by the breach of their covenant, and to make good that propriety which by mutual contract men acquire, in recompense of the universal right they abandon, and such power there is none before the erection of a commonwealth. And this is also to be gathered out of the ordinary definition of justice in the Schools; for they say that *justice is the constant will of giving to every man his own*. And therefore where there is no *own*, that is, no propriety, there is no injustice; and where there is no coercive power erected, that is, where there is no commonwealth, there is no propriety, all men having right to all things; therefore where there is no commonwealth, there nothing is unjust. So that the nature of justice consisteth in keeping of valid covenants; but the validity of covenants begins not but with the constitution of a civil power sufficient to compel men to keep them; and then it is also that propriety begins.

The fool hath said in his heart; "there is no such thing as justice"; and sometimes also with his tongue, seriously alleging that: "every man's conservation and contentment being committed to his own care, there could be no reason why every man might not do what he thought conduced thereunto, and therefore also to make or not make, keep or not keep, covenants was not against reason, when it conduced to one's benefit." He does not therein deny that there be covenants, and that they are sometimes broken, sometimes kept, and that such breach of them may be called injustice, and the observance of them justice; but he questioneth, whether injustice, taking away the fear of God, (for the same fool hath said in his heart there is no God), may not sometimes stand with that reason which dictateth to every man his own good; and particularly then, when it conduceth to such a benefit as shall put a man in a condition to neglect, not only the dispraise and reviling, but also the power of other men. . . .

This specious reasoning is nevertheless false. . . .

For the question is not of promises mutual where there is no security of performance on either side (as when there is no civil power erected over the parties promising), for such promises are no covenants, but either where one of the parties has performed already, or where there is a power to make him perform, there is the question whether it be against reason, that is, against the benefit of the other to perform or not. And I say it is not against reason. For the manifestation whereof we are to consider: first, that when a man doth a thing which, notwithstanding anything can be foreseen and reckoned on, tendeth to his own destruction (howsoever some accident which he could not expect, arriving may turn it to his benefit), yet such events do not make it reasonably or wisely done. Secondly, that in a condition of war wherein every man to every man (for want of a common power to keep them all in awe) is an enemy, there is no man can hope by his own strength or wit to defend himself from destruction without the help of confederates (where everyone expects the same defence by the confederation that any one else does); and therefore, he which declares he thinks it reason to deceive those that help him can in reason expect no other means of safety than what can be had from his own single power. He therefore that breaketh his covenant, and consequently declareth that he thinks he may with reason do so, cannot be received into any society that unite themselves for peace and defence but by the error of them that receive him; nor when he is received, be retained in it without seeing the danger of their error; which errors a man cannot reasonably reckon upon as the means of his security; and therefore, if he be left or cast out of society, he perisheth, and if he live in society, it is by the errors of other men, which he could not foresee nor reckon upon; and consequently against the reason of his preservation; and so as all men that contribute not to his destruction, forbear him only out of ignorance of what is good for themselves.

Study Questions

1. Without government to enforce laws, would life be, as Hobbes says, "nasty, brutish, and short"?
2. What does Hobbes mean by "the right of nature"?
3. What does he mean by a "law of nature"?
4. Why are we obliged to keep our agreements?

CHAPTER 20

A Theory of Justice

John Rawls

John Rawls (1921–2002) was Professor of Philosophy at Harvard University. He proposes that a just social arrangement is one that would be chosen by the members of society if they did not know either their individual places in that society or their own personal characteristics, such as race, gender, or class. Rawls claims that in "the original position" in which all are behind "a veil of ignorance," the parties would choose two fundamental principles: first, equality of rights and liberties for all; and second, the arrangement of social and economic inequalities so that they are to the greatest benefit of the least advantaged and attached to positions and offices open to all.

The Main Idea of the Theory of Justice

. . . [T]he principles of justice . . . are the principles that free and rational persons concerned to further their own interests would accept in an initial position of equality. . . .

[T]he original position of equality corresponds to the state of nature in the traditional theory of the social contract. This original position is not, of course, thought of as an actual historical state of affairs, much less as a primitive condition of culture. It is understood as a purely hypothetical situation. . . . Among the essential features of this situation is that no one knows his place in society, his class position or social status, nor does any one know his fortune in the distribution of natural assets and abilities, his intelligence, strength, and the like. I shall even assume that the parties do not know their conceptions of the good or their special psychological propensities. The principles of justice are chosen behind a veil of ignorance. This ensures that no one is advantaged or disadvantaged in the choice of principles by the outcome of natural chance or the contingency of social circumstances. Since all are similarly situated and no one is able to design principles to favor his particular condition, the principles of justice are the result of a fair agreement or bargain. For given the circumstances of the original position, the symmetry of everyone's relations to each other, this initial situation is fair between individuals as moral persons, that is, as rational beings with their own ends and capable, I shall assume, of a sense of justice. The original position is, one might say, the appropriate initial status quo, and thus the fundamental agreements reached in it are fair. This explains the propriety of the name "justice as fairness": it conveys the idea that the principles of justice are agreed to in an initial situation that is fair. . . .

I shall maintain . . . that the persons in the initial situation would choose two . . . principles: the first requires equality in the assignment of basic rights and duties, while the second holds that social and economic inequalities, for example inequalities of wealth and authority, are just only if they result in compensating benefits for everyone, and in particular for the least advantaged members of society. These principles rule out justifying institutions on the grounds that the hardships of some are offset by a greater good in the aggregate. It may be expedient but it is not just that some should have less in order that others may prosper. But there is no injustice in the greater benefits earned by a few provided that the situation of persons not so fortunate is thereby improved. The intuitive idea is that since everyone's well-being depends upon a scheme of cooperation without which no one could have a satisfactory life, the division of advantages should be such as to draw forth the willing cooperation of everyone taking part in it, including those less well situated. The two principles mentioned seem to be a fair basis on which those better endowed, or more fortunate in their social position, neither of which we can be said to deserve, could expect the willing cooperation of others when some workable scheme is a necessary condition of the welfare of all. Once we decide to look for a conception of justice that prevents the use of the accidents of natural endowment and the contingencies of social circumstance as counters in a quest of political and economic advantage, we are led to these principles. They express the result of leaving aside those aspects of the social world that seem arbitrary from a moral point of view. . . .

The Original Position and Justification

. . . One should not be misled . . . by the somewhat unusual conditions which characterize the original position. The idea here is simply to make vivid to ourselves the restrictions that it seems reasonable to impose on arguments for principles of justice, and therefore on these principles themselves. Thus it seems reasonable and generally acceptable that no one should be advantaged or disadvantaged by natural fortune or social circumstances in the choice of principles. It also seems widely agreed that it should be impossible to tailor principles to the circumstances of one's own case. We should insure further that particular inclinations and aspirations, and persons' conceptions of their good, do not affect the principles adopted. The aim is to rule out those principles that it would be rational to propose for acceptance, however little the chance of success, only if one knew certain things that are irrelevant from the standpoint of justice. For example, if a man knew that he was wealthy, he might find it rational to advance the principle that various taxes for welfare measures be counted unjust; if he knew that he was poor, he would most likely propose the contrary principle. To represent the desired restrictions one imagines a situation in which everyone is deprived of this sort of information. One excludes the knowledge of those contingencies which sets men at odds and allows them to be guided by their prejudices. In this manner the veil of ignorance is arrived at in a natural way. This concept should cause no difficulty if we keep in mind the constraints on arguments that it is meant to express. At any time we can enter the original position, so to speak, simply by following a certain procedure, namely, by arguing for principles of justice in accordance with these restrictions.

It seems reasonable to suppose that the parties in the original position are equal. That is, all have the same rights in the procedure for choosing principles; each can make proposals, submit reasons for their acceptance, and so on. Obviously the purpose of these conditions is to represent equality between human beings as moral persons, as creatures having a conception of their good and capable of a sense of justice. The basis of equality is taken to be similarity in these two respects. Systems of ends are not ranked in value; and each man is presumed to have the requisite ability to understand and to act upon whatever principles are adopted. Together with the veil of ignorance, these conditions define the principles of justice as those which rational persons concerned to advance their interests would consent to as equals when none are known to be advantaged or disadvantaged by social and natural contingencies. . . .

Two Principles of Justice

I shall now state in a provisional form the two principles of justice that I believe would be chosen in the original position. . . .

The first statement of the two principles reads as follows.

First: each person is to have an equal right to the most extensive scheme of equal basic liberties compatible with a similar scheme of liberties for others.

Second: social and economic inequalities are to be arranged so that they are both (a) reasonably expected to be to everyone's advantage, and (b) attached to positions and offices open to all. . . .

These principles primarily apply . . . to the basic structure of society and govern the assignment of rights and duties and regulate the distribution of social and economic advantages. . . . [I]t is essential to observe that the basic liberties are given by a list of such liberties. Important among these are political liberty (the right to vote and to hold public office) and freedom of speech and assembly; liberty of conscience and freedom of thought; freedom of the person, which includes freedom from psychological oppression and physical assault and dismemberment (integrity of the person); the right to hold personal property and freedom from arbitrary arrest and seizure as defined by the concept of the rule of law. These liberties are to be equal by the first principle.

The second principle applies . . . to the distribution of income and wealth and to the design of organizations that make use of differences in authority and responsibility. While the distributions of wealth and income need not be equal, it must be to everyone's advantage, and at the same time, positions of authority and responsibility must be accessible to all. One applies the second principle by holding positions open, and then, subject to this constraint, arranges social and economic inequalities so that everyone benefits.

These principles are to be arranged in a serial order with the first principle prior to the second. This ordering means that infringements of the basic equal liberties protected by the first principle cannot be justified, or compensated for, by greater social and economic advantages. . . .

[I]n regard to the second principle, the distribution of wealth and income, and positions of authority and responsibility, are to be consistent with both the basic liberties and equality of opportunity. . . .

[T]hese principles are a special case of a more general conception of justice that can be expressed as follows.

> All social values—liberty and opportunity, income and wealth, and the social bases of self-respect—are to be distributed equally unless an unequal distribution of any, or all, of these values is to everyone's advantage.

Injustice, then, is simply inequalities that are not to the benefit of all. . . .

The Veil of Ignorance

. . . The notion of the veil of ignorance raises several difficulties. Some may object that the exclusion of nearly all particular information makes it difficult to grasp what is meant by the original position. Thus it may be helpful to observe that one or more persons can at any time enter this position, or perhaps better, simulate the deliberations of this hypothetical situation, simply by reasoning in accordance with the appropriate restrictions. . . .

It may be protested that the condition of the veil of ignorance is irrational. Surely, some may object, principles should be chosen in the light of all the knowledge available. There are various replies to this contention. . . . To begin with, it is clear that since the differences among the parties are unknown to them, and everyone is equally rational and similarly situated, each is convinced by the same arguments. Therefore, we can view the agreement in the original position from the standpoint of one person selected at random. If anyone after due reflection prefers a conception of justice to another, then they all do, and a unanimous agreement can be reached. We can, to make the circumstances more vivid, imagine that the parties are required to communicate with each other through a referee as intermediary, and that he is to announce which alternatives have been suggested and the reasons offered in their support. He forbids the attempt to form coalitions, and he informs the parties when they have come to an understanding. But such a referee is actually superfluous, assuming that the deliberations of the parties must be similar.

Thus there follows the very important consequence that the parties have no basis for bargaining in the usual sense. No one knows his situation in society nor his natural assets, and therefore no one is in a position to tailor principles to his advantage. We might imagine that one of the contractees threatens to hold out unless the others agree to principles favorable to him. But how does he know which principles are especially in his interests? The same holds for the formation of coalitions: if a group were to decide to band together to the disadvantage of the others, they would not know how to favor themselves in the choice of principles. Even if they could get everyone to agree to their proposal, they would have no assurance that it was to their advantage, since they cannot identify themselves either by name or description. . . .

The restrictions on particular information in the original position are, then, of fundamental importance. Without them we would not be able to work out any definite theory of justice at all. We would have to be content with a vague formula stating that justice is what would be agreed to without being able to say much, if anything, about the substance of the agreement itself. . . . The veil of ignorance makes possible a unanimous choice of a particular conception of justice. Without these limitations on knowledge the bargaining problem of the original position would be hopelessly complicated.

Study Questions

1. What is "the original position"?
2. What is "the veil of ignorance"?
3. According to Rawls, what are the two principles of justice?
4. Do you agree with Rawls that these two principles would be chosen in the original position?

CHAPTER 21

Gender Bias

Cheshire Calhoun

Cheshire Calhoun, Professor of Philosophy at Arizona State University, maintains that philosophical reasoning is shaped by extra-philosophical factors, in particular, gender bias. She suggests, for example, that the role-reversal test, in which you imagine yourself in the place of another in order to help you make a moral decision, may be undermined by a failure to appreciate that socially subordinate individuals may have been socialized to want the things that keep them subordinate.

One concern of moral theory has been with broadening our sensitivities about who has morally considerable rights and interests. The ordinary individual confronts at least two obstacles to taking others' rights and interests seriously. One is his own self-interest, which inclines him to weigh his own rights and interests more heavily; the other is his identification with particular social groups, which inclines him to weigh the rights and interests of co-members more heavily than those of outsiders. . . . Sensitivity to our failure to weigh the rights and interests of all members of the moral community equally led moral theorists to focus, in defining the moral self, on constructing various pictures of the moral self's similarity to other moral selves in an effort to underscore our common humanity and thus our entitlement to equal moral consideration. . . .

Providing us with some way of envisioning our shared humanity, and thus our equal membership in the moral community, is

---

certainly an important thing for moral theory to do. But too much talk about our similarities as moral selves, and too little talk about our differences has its moral dangers. For one, unless we are also quite knowledgeable about the substantial differences between persons, particularly central differences due to gender, race, and class, we may be tempted to slide into supposing that our common humanity includes more substantive similarities than it does in fact. For instance, moral theorists have assumed that moral selves have a prominent interest in property and thus in property rights. But property rights may have loomed large on the moral horizons of past moral theorists partly, or largely, because they were themselves propertied and their activities took place primarily in the public, economic sphere. Historically, women could not share the same interest in property and concern about protecting it, since they were neither legally entitled to hold it nor primary participants in the public, economic world. And arguably, women do not now place the same priority on property. (I have in mind the fact that equal opportunity has had surprisingly little impact on either sex segregation in the workforce or on women's, but not men's, accommodating their work and work schedules to childbearing needs. One explanation is that income matters less to women than other sorts of considerations. The measure of a woman, unlike the measure of a man, is not the size of her paycheck.)

In addition to encouraging us to overlook how our basic interests may differ depending on our social location, the emphasis on common humanity, because it is insensitive to connections between interests, social location, and power, deters questions about the possible malformation of our interests as a result of their development within an inegalitarian social structure. Both dangers plague the role-reversal test, some version of which has been a staple of moral theorizing. Although the point of that test is to eliminate egoistic bias in moral judgments, without a sensitivity to how our (uncommon) humanity is shaped by our social structure, role-reversal tests may simply preserve, rather than eliminate, inequities. This is because role-reversal tests either take individuals' desires as givens, thus ignoring the possibility that socially subordinate individuals have been socialized to want the very things that keep them socially subordinate . . .; or, if they take into account what individuals ought to want, role-reversal tests typically ignore the way that social power structures may have produced an alignment between the concept of a normal, reasonable desire and the desires of the dominant group (so, for example, much of the affirmative action literature takes it for granted that women ought to want traditionally defined male jobs with no consideration of the possibility that women might prefer retailoring those jobs so that they are less competitive, less hierarchical, and more compatible with family responsibilities).

In short, without adequate knowledge of how very different human interests, temperaments, lifestyles, and commitments may be, as well as a knowledge of how those interests may be malformed as a result of power inequities, the very egoism and group bias that the focus on common humanity was designed to eliminate may slip in as a result of that focus.

The objection here is not that a formal, abstract notion of the moral self's common humanity is wrong and ought to be jettisoned. . . . The objection is that repetitive stress on shared humanity creates an ideology of the moral self: the belief that our basic moral interests are not significantly, dissimilarly, and sometimes detrimentally shaped by our social location. Unless moral theory shifts its priority to knowledgeable discussions of human differences—particularly differences tied to gender, race, class, and power—lists and rank orderings of basic human interests and rights as well as the political deployment of those lists are likely to be sexist, racist, and classist. . . .

The call for a shift in theoretical priorities is simultaneously a call for a shift in our methods of evaluating moral theories. Evaluation is not exhausted by carefully scrutinizing individual theories, since in the process of theorizing in a philosophical community we unavoidably contribute to the establishment of a tradition of moral thinking which may implicitly, in virtue of common patterns of talk and silence, endorse views of the moral life which go beyond those of individual contributors. The nonlogical implications of theorizing patterns require evaluation as well.

But, if moral theory suffers from a lopsidedness that produces ideologies of the moral life, why be particularly concerned with eliminating *gender* bias? Would not the more basic, and broader, philosophical task be to eliminate bias in general? Would not a bias sensitive (but gender insensitive) critique do all the work? . . .

Perhaps, but I suspect not. Some moral issues are arguably more critical for women, and thus achieving gender neutrality is partly a matter of prioritizing those issues. But eliminating gender bias cannot be equated (though possibly reducing gender bias can) with simply prioritizing those "women's issues" irrespective of the content of the analysis of those issues. These same issues also have a place in men's moral experience. For that reason, male moral philosophers too may have cause to regret moral theory's neglect of special relations, virtue ethics, compassion and the problem of limiting compassionate impulses; and it is thus no surprise that some of the same critiques of moral theories are coming from both feminist and nonfeminist quarters. But, given that our lives are thoroughly genderized, there is no reason to suppose that gender bias cannot recur in the discussion of these "women's moral issues." Which virtues, after all, will we make focal—intellectual virtues or inter-personal virtues? And what will we say about individual virtues? Will we . . . examine how virtues may undergo deformation in different ways depending on our place in power structures? Which kind of compassion will become paradigmatic: the impersonal, public compassion for strangers and unfortunate populations, or the personal, private compassion felt for friends, children, and neighbors? Will we repeat the same militaristic metaphors of conquest and mastery in describing conflicts between compassion and duty which have dominated descriptions of the moral agent's relation to his self-interest? And, in weighing the value of personal integrity against the moral claims of others, will we take into account the way that gender roles may affect both the value we attach to personal integrity and the weight we attach to others' claims?

The possibility of gender bias recurring in the process of redressing bias in moral theory derives from the fact that philosophical reasoning is shaped by extra-philosophic factors, including the social location of the philosophic reasoner and his audience as well as the contours of the larger social world in which philosophic thought takes place. It is naive to suppose that a reflective, rational, but gender-insensitive critique of moral theory will have the happy outcome of eliminating gender bias. So long as we avoid incorporating gender categories among the tools for philosophical analysis, we will continue running the risks, whether we work within or counter to the tradition, of importing gender bias into our philosophical reflection and of creating an ideology of the moral life.

Study Questions

1. What does Calhoun mean by "gender bias"?
2. According to Calhoun, what dangers plague the role-reversal test?
3. What does Calhoun mean by "the social location of the philosophic reasoner"?
4. In addition to gender, might a source of bias be found in religious affiliation, sexual orientation, military experience, bodily appearance, and a variety of other factors?

PART III

Moral Problems

A. World Hunger

CHAPTER 22

Famine, Affluence, and Morality
Peter Singer

In recent decades philosophers have examined a variety of practical issues involving ethical concerns. For example, what obligations do we have toward those around the globe who are suffering from a lack of food, shelter, or medical care? Does morality permit us to purchase luxuries for ourselves, our families, and our friends, instead of providing needed resources to other people who are suffering in unfortunate circumstances? Peter Singer, who is Ira W. Decamp Professor of Bioethics at the University Center for Human Values at Princeton University, argues that if we can prevent something bad from happening without thereby sacrificing anything of comparable moral importance, we ought to do so. In short, while some view contributing to relief funds as an act of charity, Singer consider such a donation as a moral duty.

As I write this, in November 1971, people are dying in East Bengal from lack of food, shelter, and medical care. The suffering and death that are occurring there now are not inevitable, not unavoidable in any fatalistic sense of the term. Constant poverty, a cyclone, and a civil war have turned at least nine million people into destitute refugees: nevertheless, it is not beyond the capacity of the richer nations to give enough assistance to reduce any further suffering to very small proportions. The decisions and actions of human beings can prevent this kind of suffering. Unfortunately, human beings have not made the necessary decisions. At the individual level, people have, with very few exceptions, not responded to the situation in any significant way. Generally speaking, people have not given large sums to relief funds; they have not written to their parliamentary representatives demanding increased government assistance; they have not demonstrated in the streets, held symbolic fasts, or done anything else directed toward

From Peter Singer, "Famine, Affluence, and Morality," in *Philosophy & Public Affairs*, Vol. 32. Copyright © 1972. Reprinted by permission of Blackwell Publishing Ltd.

providing the refugees with the means to satisfy their essential needs. At the government level, no government has given the sort of massive aid that would enable the refugees to survive for more than a few days. Britain, for instance, has given rather more than most countries. It has, to date, given £14,750,000. For comparative purposes, Britain's share of the nonrecoverable development costs of the Anglo-French Concorde project is already in excess of £275,000,000, and on present estimates will reach £440,000,000. The implication is that the British government values a supersonic transport more than thirty times as highly as it values the lives of the nine million refugees. Australia is another country which, on a per capita basis, is well up in the "aid to Bengal" table. Australia's aid, however, amounts to less than one-twelfth of the cost of Sydney's new opera house. The total amount given, from all sources, now stands at about £65,000,000. The estimated cost of keeping the refugees alive for one year is £464,000,000. Most of the refugees have now been in the camps for more than six months. The World Bank has said that India needs a minimum of £300,000,000 in assistance from other countries before the end of the year. It seems obvious that assistance on this scale will not be forthcoming. India will be forced to choose between letting the refugees starve or diverting funds from her own development program, which will mean that more of her own people will starve in the future.[1]

These are the essential facts about the present situation in Bengal. So far as it concerns us here, there is nothing unique about this situation except its magnitude. The Bengal emergency is just the latest and most acute of a series of major emergencies in various parts of the world, arising both from natural and from man-made causes. There are also many parts of the world in which people die from malnutrition and lack of food independent of any special emergency. I take Bengal as my example only because it is the present concern, and because the size of the problem has ensured that it has been given adequate publicity. Neither individuals nor governments can claim to be unaware of what is happening there.

What are the moral implications of a situation like this? In what follows, I shall argue that the way people in relatively affluent countries react to a situation like that in Bengal cannot be justified; indeed, the whole way we look at moral issues—our moral conceptual scheme—needs to be altered, and with it, the way of life that has come to be taken for granted in our society.

In arguing for this conclusion I will not, of course, claim to be morally neutral. I shall, however, try to argue for the moral position that I take, so that anyone who accepts certain assumptions, to be made explicit, will, I hope, accept my conclusion.

I begin with the assumption that suffering and death from lack of food, shelter, and medical care are bad. I think most people will agree about this, although one may reach the same view by different routes. I shall not argue for this view. People can hold all sorts of eccentric positions, and perhaps from some of them it would not follow that death by starvation is in itself bad. It is difficult, perhaps impossible, to refute such positions, and so for brevity I will henceforth take this assumption as accepted. Those who disagree need read no further.

My next point is this: if it is in our power to prevent something bad from happening, without thereby sacrificing anything of comparable moral importance, we ought, morally, to do it. By "without sacrificing anything of comparable moral importance" I mean without causing anything else comparably bad to happen, or doing something that is wrong in itself, or failing to promote some moral good, comparable in significance to the bad thing that we can prevent. This principle seems almost as uncontroversial as the last one. It requires us only to prevent what is bad, and not to promote what is good, and it requires this of us only when we can do it without sacrificing anything that is, from the moral point of view, comparably important. I could even, as far as the application of my argument to the Bengal emergency is concerned, qualify the point so as to make it: if it is in our power to prevent something very bad from happening, without thereby sacrificing anything morally significant, we ought, morally, to do it. An application of this principle would be as follows: if I am walking past a shallow pond and see a child drowning in it, I ought to wade in and pull the child out. This will mean getting my clothes muddy, but this is insignificant, while the death of the child would presumably be a very bad thing.

The uncontroversial appearance of the principle just stated is deceptive. If it were acted upon, even in its qualified form, our lives, our society, and our world would be fundamentally changed. For the principle takes, firstly, no account of proximity or distance. It makes no moral difference whether the person I can help is a neighbor's child ten yards from me or a Bengali whose name I shall never know, ten thousand miles away. Secondly, the principle makes no distinction between cases in which I am the only person who could possibly do anything and cases in which I am just one among millions in the same position.

I do not think I need to say much in defense of the refusal to take proximity and distance into account. The fact that a person is physically near to us, so that we have personal contact with him, may make it more likely that we *shall* assist him, but this does not show that we *ought* to help him rather than another who happens to be farther away. If we accept any principle of impartiality, universalizability, equality, or whatever, we cannot discriminate against someone merely because he is far away from us (or we are far away from him). Admittedly, it is possible that we are in a better position to judge what needs to be done to help a person near to us than one far away, and perhaps also to provide the assistance we judge to be necessary. If this were the case, it would be a reason for helping those near to us first. This may once have been a justification for being more concerned with the poor in one's own town than with the famine victims in India. Unfortunately for those who like to keep moral responsibilities limited, instant communication and swift transportation have changed the situation. From the moral point of view, the development of the world into a "global village" has made an important, though still unrecognized, difference to our moral situation. Expert observers and supervisors, sent out by famine relief organizations or permanently stationed in famine-prone areas, can direct our aid to a refugee in Bengal almost as effectively as we could get it to someone in our own block. There would seem, therefore, to be no possible justification for discriminating on geographical grounds.

There may be a greater need to defend the second implication of my principle—that the fact that there are millions of other people in the same position, in respect to the Bengali refugees, as I am, does not make the situation significantly different from a situation in which I am the only person who can prevent something very bad from occurring. Again, of course, I admit that there is a psychological difference between the cases; one feels less guilty about doing nothing if one can point to others, similarly placed, who have also done nothing. Yet this can make no real difference to our moral obligations.[2] Should I consider that I am less obliged to pull the drowning child out of the pond if on looking around I see other people, no farther away than I am, who have also noticed the child but are doing nothing? One has only to ask this question to see the absurdity of the view that numbers lessen obligation. It is a view that is an ideal excuse for inactivity; unfortunately most of the major evils—poverty, overpopulation, pollution—are problems in which everyone is almost equally involved.

The view that numbers do make a difference can be made plausible if stated in this way: if everyone in circumstances like mine gave £5 to the Bengal Relief Fund, there would be enough to provide food, shelter, and medical care for the refugees; there is no reason why I should give more than anyone else in the same circumstances as I am; therefore I have no obligation to give more than £5. Each premise in this argument is true, and the argument looks sound. It may convince us, unless we notice that it is based on a hypothetical premise, although the conclusion is not stated hypothetically. The argument would be sound if the conclusion were: if everyone in circumstances like mine were to give £5, I would have no obligation to give more than £5. If the conclusion were so stated, however, it would be obvious that the argument has no bearing on a situation in which it is not the case that everyone else gives £5. This, of course, is the actual situation. It is more or less certain that not everyone in circumstances like mine will give £5. So there will not be enough to provide the needed food, shelter, and medical care. Therefore by giving more than £5 I will prevent more suffering than I would if I gave just £5.

It might be thought that this argument has an absurd consequence. Since the situation appears to be that very few people are likely to give substantial amounts, it follows that I and everyone else in similar circumstances ought to give as much as possible, that is, at least up to the point at which by giving more one would begin to cause serious suffering for oneself and one's dependents—perhaps even beyond this point to the point of marginal utility, at which by giving more one would cause oneself and one's dependents as much suffering as one would prevent in Bengal. If everyone does this, however, there will be more than can be used for the benefit of the refugees, and some of the sacrifice will have been unnecessary. Thus, if everyone does what he ought to do, the result will not be as good as it would be if everyone did a little less than he ought to do, or if only some do all that they ought to do.

The paradox here arises only if we assume that the actions in question—sending money to the relief funds—are performed more or less simultaneously, and are also unexpected. For if it is to be expected that everyone is going to contribute something, then clearly each is not obliged to give as much as he would have been obliged to had others not been giving too. And if everyone is not acting more or less simultaneously, then those giving later will know how much more is needed, and will have no obligation to give more than is necessary to reach this amount. To say this is not to deny the principle that people in the same circumstances have the same obligations, but to point out that the fact that others have given, or may be expected to give, is a relevant circumstance: those giving after it has become known that many others are giving and those giving before are not in the same circumstances. So the seemingly absurd consequence of the principle I have put forward can occur only if people are in error about the actual circumstances—that is, if they think they are giving when others are not, but in fact they are giving when others are. The result of everyone doing what he really ought to do cannot be worse than the result of everyone doing less than he ought to do, although the result of everyone doing what he reasonably believes he ought to do could be.

If my argument so far has been sound, neither our distance from a preventable evil nor the number of other people who, in respect to that evil, are in the same situation as we are, lessens our obligation to mitigate or prevent that evil. I shall therefore take as established the principle I asserted earlier. As I have already said, I need to assert it only in its qualified form: if it is in our power to prevent something very bad from happening, without thereby sacrificing anything else morally significant, we ought, morally, to do it.

The outcome of this argument is that our traditional moral categories are upset. The traditional direction between duty and charity cannot be drawn, or at least, not in the place we normally draw it. Giving money to the Bengal Relief Fund is regarded as an act of charity in our society. The bodies which collect money are known as "charities." These organizations see themselves in this way—if you send them a check, you will be thanked for your "generosity." Because giving money is regarded as an act of charity, it is not thought that there is anything wrong with not giving. The charitable man may be praised, but the man who is not charitable is not condemned. People do not feel in any way ashamed or guilty about spending money on new clothes or a new car instead of giving it to famine relief. (Indeed, the alternative does not occur to them.) This way of looking at the matter cannot be justified. When we buy new clothes not to keep ourselves warm but to look "well-dressed" we are not providing for any important need. We would not be sacrificing anything significant if we were to continue to wear our old clothes, and give the money to famine relief. By doing so, we would be preventing another person from starving. It follows from what I have said earlier that we ought to give money away, rather than spend it on clothes which we do not need to keep us warm. To do so is not charitable, or generous. Nor is it the kind of act which philosophers and theologians have called "supererogatory"—an act which it would be good to do, but not wrong not to do. On the contrary, we ought to give the money away, and it is wrong not to do so.

I am not maintaining that there are no acts which are charitable, or that there are no acts which it would be good to do but not wrong not to do. It may be possible to redraw the distinction between duty and charity in some other place. All I am arguing here is that the present way of drawing the distinction, which makes it an act of charity for a man living at the level of affluence which most people in the "developed nations" enjoy to give money to save someone else from starvation, cannot be supported. It is beyond the scope of my argument to consider whether the distinction should be redrawn or abolished altogether. There would be many other possible ways of drawing the distinction—for instance, one might decide that it is good to make other people as happy as possible, but not wrong not to do so.

Despite the limited nature of the revision in our moral conceptual scheme which I am proposing, the revision would, given the extent of both affluence and famine in the world today, have radical implications. These implications may lead to further objections, distinct from those I have already considered. I shall discuss two of these.

One objection to the position I have taken might be simply that it is too drastic a revision of our moral scheme. People do not ordinarily judge in the way I have suggested they should. Most people reserve their moral condemnation for those who violate some moral norm, such as the norm against taking another person's property. They do not condemn those who indulge in luxury instead of giving to famine relief. But given that I did not set out to present a morally neutral description of the way people make moral judgments, the way people do in fact judge has nothing to do with the validity of my conclusion. My conclusion follows from the principle which I advanced earlier, and unless that principle is rejected, or the arguments shown to be unsound, I think the conclusion must stand, however strange it appears. . . .

The second objection to my attack on the present distinction between duty and charity is one which has from time to time been made against utilitarianism. It follows from some forms of utilitarian theory that we all ought, morally, to be working full time to increase the balance of happiness over misery. The position I have taken here would not lead to this conclusion in all circumstances, for if there were no bad occurrences that we could prevent without sacrificing something of comparable moral importance, my argument would have no application. Given the present conditions in many parts of the world, however, it does follow from my argument that we ought, morally, to be working full time to relieve great suffering of the sort that occurs as a result of famine or other disasters. Of course, mitigating circumstances can be adduced—for instance, that if we wear ourselves out through overwork, we shall be less effective than we would otherwise have been. Nevertheless, when all considerations of this sort have been taken into account, the conclusion remains: we ought to be preventing as much suffering as we can without sacrificing something else of comparable moral importance. This conclusion is one which we may be reluctant to face. I cannot see, though, why it should be regarded as a criticism of the position for which I have argued, rather than a criticism of our ordinary standards of behavior. Since most people are self-interested to some degree, very few of us are likely to do everything that we ought to do. It would, however, hardly be honest to take this as evidence that it is not the case that we ought to do it. . . .

A third point raised by the conclusion reached earlier relates to the question of just how much we all ought to be giving away. One possibility, which has already been mentioned, is that we ought to give until we reach the level of marginal utility—that is, the level at which, by giving more, I would cause as much suffering to myself or my dependents as I would relieve by my gift. This would mean, of course, that one would reduce oneself to very nearly the material circumstances of a Bengali refugee. It will be recalled that earlier I put forward both a strong and a moderate version of the principle of preventing bad occurrences. The strong version, which required us to prevent bad things from happening unless in doing so we would be sacrificing something of comparable moral significance, does seem to require reducing ourselves to the level of marginal utility. I should also say that the strong version seems to me to be the correct one. I proposed the more moderate version—that we should prevent bad occurrences unless, to do so, we had to sacrifice something morally significant— only in order to show that even on this surely undeniable principle a great change in our way of life is required. On the more moderate principle, it may not follow that we ought to reduce ourselves to the level of marginal utility, for one might hold that to reduce oneself and one's family to this level is to cause something significantly bad to happen. Whether this is so I shall not discuss, since, as I have said, I can see no good reason for holding the moderate version of the principle rather than the strong version. Even if we accepted the principle only in its moderate form, however, it should be clear that we would have to give away enough to ensure that the consumer society, dependent as it is on people spending on trivia rather than giving to famine relief, would slow down and perhaps disappear entirely. There are several reasons why this would be desirable in itself. The value and necessity of economic growth are now being questioned not only by conservationists, but by economists as well.[3] There is no doubt, too, that the consumer society has had a distorting effect on the goals and purposes of its members. Yet looking at the matter purely from the point of view of overseas aid, there must be a limit to the extent to which we should deliberately slow down our economy; for it might be the case that if we gave away, say, forty percent of our Gross National Product, we would slow down the economy so much that in absolute terms we would be giving less than if we gave twenty-five percent of the much larger GNP that we would have if we limited our contribution to this smaller percentage.

I mention this only as an indication of the sort of factor that one would have to take into account in working out an ideal. Since Western societies generally consider one percent of the GNP an acceptable level of overseas aid, the matter is entirely academic. Nor does it affect the question of how much an individual should give in a society in which very few are giving substantial amounts.

It is sometimes said, though less often now than it used to be, that philosophers have no special role to play in public affairs, since most public issues depend primarily on an assessment of facts. On questions of fact, it is said, philosophers as such have no special expertise, and so it has been possible to engage in philosophy without committing oneself to any position on major public issues. No doubt there are some issues of social policy and foreign policy about which it can truly be said that a really expert assessment of the facts is required before taking sides or acting, but the issue of famine is surely not one of these. The facts about the existence of suffering are beyond dispute. Nor, I think, is it disputed that we can do something about it, either through orthodox methods of famine relief or through population control or both. This is therefore an issue on which philosophers are competent to take a position. The issue is one which faces everyone who has more money than he needs to support himself and his dependents, or who is in a position to take some sort of political action. These categories must include practically every teacher and student of philosophy in the universities of the Western world. If philosophy is to deal with matters that are relevant to both teachers and students, this is an issue that philosophers should discuss.

Discussion, though, is not enough. What is the point of relating philosophy to public (and personal) affairs if we do not take our conclusions seriously? In this instance, taking our conclusion seriously means acting upon it. The philosopher will not find it any easier than anyone else to alter his attitudes and way of life to the extent that, if I am right, is involved in doing everything that we ought to be doing. At the very least, though, one can make a start. The philosopher who does so will have to sacrifice some of the benefits of the consumer society, but he can find compensation in the satisfaction of a way of life in which theory and practice, if not yet in harmony, are at least coming together.

Notes

1. There was also a third possibility: that India would go to war to enable the refugees to return to their lands. Since I wrote this paper, India has taken this way out. The situation is no longer that described above, but this does not affect my argument, as the next paragraph indicates.
2. In view of the special sense philosophers often give to the term, I should say that I use "obligation" simply as the abstract noun derived from "ought," so that "I have an obligation to" means no more, and no less, than "I ought to." This usage is in accordance with the definition of "ought" given by the *Shorter Oxford English Dictionary*: "the general verb to express duty or obligation." I do not think any issue of substance hangs on the way the term is used; sentences in which I use "obligation" could all be rewritten, although somewhat clumsily, as sentences in which a clause containing "ought" replaces the term "obligation."
3. See, for instance, John Kenneth Galbraith, *The New Industrial State* (Boston, 1967); and E. J. Mishan, *The Costs of Economic Growth* (London, 1967).

Study Questions

1. If you can prevent something bad from happening at a comparatively small cost to yourself, are you obligated to do so?
2. Are you acting immorally by buying a luxury car while others are starving?
3. Are you acting immorally by paying college tuition for your own children while other children have no opportunity for any schooling?
4. Do we have a moral obligation to try to alleviate extreme poverty in our own country before attempting to do so in other countries?

CHAPTER 23

A Reply to Singer

Travis Timmerman

Peter Singer argues that you are obligated to prevent something bad from happening if you can do so without thereby sacrificing something of comparable moral importance. For example, you are morally obligated to save a child from drowning if you can do so without danger to yourself or others. Travis Timmerman, Assistant Professor of Philosophy at Seton Hall University, argues that the strength of your obligation depends on how many children need to be saved. If the number is large, then Singer's line of reasoning would obligate you to spend your entire life saving children. Are you not, however, entitled at some point to pursue your own interests, even if they are not as morally weighty as saving the lives of children?

Peter Singer's "Famine, Affluence, and Morality" is undoubtedly one of the most influential and widely read pieces of contemporary philosophy. Yet, the majority of philosophers (including ethicists) reject Singer's conclusion that we are morally required to donate to aid agencies whenever we can do so without sacrificing anything nearly as important as the good that our donations could bring about. Many ignore Singer's argument simply because they believe morality would just be too demanding if it required people in affluent nations to donate significant sums of money to charity. Of course, merely rejecting Singer's conclusion because it seems absurd does not constitute a refutation of Singer's argument. More importantly, this standard demandingness objection is a particularly inappropriate dialectical move because Singer provides a valid argument for his (demanding) conclusion and, crucially, the argument only consists of ethical

From Travis Timmerman, "Sometimes There Is Nothing Wrong with Letting a Child Drown," *Analysis* 75 (2015). Reprinted by permission of Oxford University Press. Footnotes omitted.

premisses that Singer takes his typical readers to already accept. Singer formulates his argument as follows.

1. Suffering and death from lack of food, shelter and medical care are bad.
2. If it is in your power to prevent something bad from happening, without sacrificing anything nearly as important, it is wrong not to do so.
3. By donating to aid agencies, you can prevent suffering and death from lack of food, shelter and medical care, without sacrificing anything nearly as important.
4. Therefore, if you do not donate to aid agencies, you are doing something wrong.

If it is not true that typical readers' existing ethical commitments entail that they accept premisses one and two, then they should be able to say which premiss(es) they reject and why. Those who believe that Singer's conclusion is too demanding will need to reject premiss two. This requires addressing Singer's infamous *Drowning Child* thought experiment, which elicits a common response that Singer believes demonstrates that his readers are already committed to the truth of premiss two. As such, Singer purports to demonstrate that the ethical commitments his typical readers already accept are demanding enough to require them to donate a substantial portion of their expendable income to aid organizations. . . .

Perhaps premiss two is true, but a proposition with such strong counterintuitive implications requires a strong defence, one that gives us reason to think that certain ordinary moral intuitions are radically misguided. Singer believes he has provided such a defence with *Drowning Child*. Aren't we morally obligated to sacrifice our new clothes to save the child *because* we are obligated to prevent something bad from happening whenever we can do so without sacrificing anything nearly as important? The short answer is 'No.' Here's why. Although Singer's description of *Drowning Child* is ahistorical, the implicit assumption is that *Drowning Child* is an anomalous event. People almost never find themselves in the situation Singer describes, so when they consider their obligations in *Drowning Child*, they implicitly assume that they have not frequently sacrificed their new clothes to save children in the past and will not need to do so frequently in the future.

Giving to aid organizations is, in this respect, unlike *Drowning Child*. Every individual in an affluent nation, so long as they have some expendable income, will always be in a position to save the lives of people living in extreme poverty by donating said income. It may be quite clear that one has a moral obligation to sacrifice $200 worth of new clothing a single time to prevent a child from drowning. It is much less clear that one is morally obligated to spend one's entire life making repeated $200 sacrifices to constantly prevent children from drowning. So, we may be obligated to save the child in *Drowning Child*, but still be disposed to believe that premiss two is false. I will expand on this asymmetry . . . by providing an altered version of Singer's thought experiment that more closely resembles the position those in affluent nations are in with respect to providing aid to those in extreme poverty. I suspect that most people's intuitions in such a case will show that they reject premiss two of Singer's argument.

People almost universally have the intuition that we are morally obligated to rescue the child in *Drowning Child*, but are not morally obligated to donate all their expendable income to aid agencies. Singer attempts to explain away this intuition as a mere psychological difference, a difference that results from our evolutionary history and socialization and not a moral difference. . . . However, there *is* a moral difference between the sacrifice required to save the child in *Drowning Child* (as it is imagined) and the sacrifice Singer believes people in affluent nations are required to make in order to donate the supposed obligatory amount to aid organizations.

This moral difference is easily overlooked because Singer's *Drowning Child* thought experiment is, in a crucial way, under-described. Once the necessary details are filled in, its inability to support premiss two will be made clear. My following *Drowning Children* case is not under-described and gives us reason to believe that there are times at which it is morally permissible to *not* prevent something bad from happening, even when one can do so at a comparably insignificant personal cost.

> **Drowning Children**: Unlucky Lisa gets a call from her 24-hr bank telling her that hackers have accessed her account and are taking $200 out of it every 5 min until Lisa shows up in person to put a hold on her account. Due to some legal loophole, the bank is not required to reimburse Lisa for any of the money she may lose nor will they. In fact, if her account is overdrawn, the bank will seize as much of her assets as is needed to pay the debt created by the hackers.
> Fortunately, for Lisa, the bank is just across the street from her work and she can get there in fewer than 5 min. She was even about to walk to the bank as part of her daily routine. On her way, Lisa notices a vast space of land covered with hundreds of newly formed shallow

ponds, each of which contains a small child who will drown unless someone pulls them to safety. Lisa knows that for each child she rescues, an extra child will live who would have otherwise died. Now, it would take Lisa approximately 5 min to pull each child to safety and, in what can only be the most horrifically surreal day of her life, Lisa has to decide how many children to rescue before entering the bank. Once she enters the bank, all the children who have not yet been rescued will drown.

Things only get worse for poor Lisa. For the remainder of her life, the hackers repeat their actions on a daily basis and, every day, the ponds adjacent to Lisa's bank are filled with drowning children.

The truth of premiss two would entail that Lisa is obligated to rescue children until almost all of her money and assets are gone. It might permit her to close her account before she is unable to rent a studio apartment and eat a healthy diet. However, it would require her to give up her house, her car, her books, her art and anything else not nearly as important as a child's life. That might not seem so counterintuitive if Lisa has to make this monumental sacrifice a single time. But, and here's the rub, premiss two would also prohibit Lisa from ever rebuilding her life. For every day Lisa earns money, she is forced to choose between saving children and letting the hackers steal from her. Lisa would only be permitted to go to the bank each day in time to maintain the things nearly as important as a child's life, which I take to be the basic necessities Lisa needs to lead a healthy life.

I propose that it's a viable option that morality permits Lisa to, *at least* on one day over the course of her entire life, stop the hackers in time to enjoy some good that is not nearly as important as a child's life. Maybe Lisa wants to experience theatre one last time before she spends the remainder of her days pulling children from shallow ponds and stopping hackers. Given the totality of the sacrifice Lisa is making, morality intuitively permits Lisa to indulge in theatre *at least* one time in, let's say, the remaining eighty years of her life. In fact, commonsense morality should permit Lisa to indulge in these comparably morally insignificant goods a non-trivial number of times, though a single instance is all that is required to demonstrate that premiss two is false and, consequently, Singer's argument is unsound. . . .

To sum up, the intuitive pull of premiss two is more apparent than real. . . . How much are we obligated to donate to aid organizations? I am not sure exactly, but it should be the same amount we would be obligated to sacrifice were we to find ourselves in Lisa's position.

Study Questions

1. In *Drowning Child*, is Lisa obligated to continue saving children no matter how many children she has already saved?
2. Are you acting morally if you study philosophy while you could be helping others in need?
3. Are you acting morally if you buy a book for yourself while other people are starving?
4. When, if ever, are you entitled to pursue your own interest while you could, instead, be helping others in need of assistance?

B. Immigration

CHAPTER 24

Immigration: The Case for Limits

David Miller

David Miller, Professor of Political Theory at the University of Oxford, considers three arguments in favor of a right to immigrate but finds none persuasive. He then suggests that safeguarding a state's distinctive culture and controlling its population provide reasons against having open borders. Thus in his view states are justified in not allowing unlimited immigration.

In this chapter, I shall explain why nation-states may be justified in imposing restrictive immigration policies if they so choose. The argument is laid out in three stages. First, I canvass three arguments that purport to justify an unlimited right of migration between states and show why each of them fails. Second, I give two reasons, one having to do with culture, the other with population, that can justify states in limiting immigration. Third, I consider whether states nonetheless have a duty to admit a special class of potential immigrants—namely refugees—and also how far they are allowed to pick and choose among the immigrants they do admit. The third section, in other words, lays down some conditions that an ethical immigration policy must meet. But I begin by showing why there is no general right to choose one's country of residence or citizenship.

Can There Be an Unlimited Right of Migration Between States?

Liberal political philosophers who write about migration usually begin from the premise that people should be allowed to choose

From David Miller, "Immigration: The Case for Limits," in *Contemporary Debates in Applied Ethics*, eds. Andrew I. Cohen and Christopher Heath Wellman (Malden, MA: Blackwell, 2005). Reprinted by permission of the publisher.

where in the world to locate themselves unless it can be shown that allowing an unlimited right of migration would have harmful consequences that outweigh the value of freedom of choice. . . . In other words, the central value appealed to is simply freedom itself. Just as I should be free to decide whom to marry, what job to take, what religion (if any) to profess, so I should be free to decide whether to live in Nigeria, or France, or the USA. Now these philosophers usually concede that in practice some limits may have to be placed on this freedom—for instance, if high rates of migration would result in social chaos or the breakdown of liberal states that could not accommodate so many migrants without losing their liberal character. In these instances, the exercise of free choice would become self-defeating. But the presumption is that people should be free to choose where to live unless there are strong reasons for restricting their choice.

I want to challenge this presumption. Of course there is always *some* value in people having more options to choose between, in this case options as to where to live, but we usually draw a line between *basic* freedoms that people should have as a matter of right and what we might call *bare* freedoms that do not warrant that kind of protection. It would be good from my point of view if I were free to purchase an Aston Martin tomorrow, but that is not going to count as a morally significant freedom—my desire is not one that imposes any kind of obligation on others to meet it. In order to argue against immigration restrictions, therefore, liberal philosophers must do more than show that there is some value to people in being able to migrate, or that they often *want* to migrate (as indeed they do, in increasing numbers). It needs to be demonstrated that this freedom has the kind of weight or significance that could turn it into a right, and that should therefore prohibit states from pursuing immigration policies that limit freedom of movement.

I shall examine three arguments that have been offered to defend a right to migrate. The first starts with the general right to freedom of movement, and claims that this must include the freedom to move into, and take up residence in, states other than one's own. The second begins with a person's right to *exit* from her current state—a right that is widely recognized in international law—and claims that a right of exit is pointless unless it is matched by a right of entry into other states. The third appeals to international distributive justice. Given the huge inequalities in living standards that currently exist between rich and poor states, it is said, people who live in poor states have a claim of justice that can only be met by allowing them to migrate and take advantage of the opportunities that rich states provide.

The idea of a right to freedom of movement is not in itself objectionable. We are talking here about what are usually called basic rights or human rights, and I shall assume (since there is no space to defend the point) that such rights are justified by pointing to the vital interests that they protect. . . . They correspond to conditions in whose absence human beings cannot live decent lives, no matter what particular values and plans of life they choose to pursue. Being able to move freely in physical space is just such a condition, as we can see by thinking about people whose legs are shackled or who are confined in small spaces. A wider freedom of movement can also be justified by thinking about the interests that it serves instrumentally: if I cannot move about over a fairly wide area, it may be impossible for me to find a job, to practice my religion, or to find a suitable marriage partner. Since these all qualify as vital interests, it is fairly clear that freedom of movement qualifies as a basic human right.

What is less clear, however, is the physical extent of that right, in the sense of how much of the earth's surface I must be able to move to in order to say that I enjoy it. Even in liberal societies that make no attempt to confine people within particular geographical areas, freedom of movement is severely restricted in a number of ways. I cannot, in general, move to places that other people's bodies now occupy (I cannot just push them aside). I cannot move on to private property without the consent of its owner, except perhaps in emergencies or where a special right of access exists—and since most land is privately owned, this means that a large proportion of physical space does not fall within the ambit of a *right* to free movement. Even access to public space is heavily regulated: there are traffic laws that tell me where and at what speed I may drive my car, parks have opening and closing hours, the police can control my movements up and down the streets, and so forth. . . . Yet few would argue that because of these limitations, people in these societies are deprived of one of their human rights. . . .

The point here is that liberal societies in general offer their members *sufficient* freedom of movement to protect the interests that the human right to free movement is intended to protect, even though the extent of free movement is very far from absolute. So how could one attempt to show that the right in question must include the right to move to some other country and settle there? What vital interest requires the right to be interpreted in such an extensive way? . . .

[I]t may be true that moving to another country is the only way for an individual to escape persecution, to find work, to obtain necessary medical care, and so forth. In these circumstances the person concerned may have the right to move, not to any state that she chooses, but to *some* state where these interests can be protected. But here the right to move serves only as a remedial right: its existence depends on the fact that the person's vital interests cannot be secured in the country where she currently resides. In a world of decent states— states that were able to secure their citizens' basic rights to security, food, work, medical care, and so forth—the right to move across borders could not be justified in this way.

Our present world is not, of course, a world of decent states, and this gives rise to the issue of refugees, which I shall discuss in the final section of this chapter. But if we leave aside for the moment cases where the right to move freely across borders depends upon the right to avoid persecution, starvation, or other threats to basic interests, how might we try to give it a more general rationale? One reason a person may want to migrate is in order to participate in a culture that does not exist in his native land—for instance he wants to work at an occupation for which there is no demand at home, or to join a religious community which, again, is not represented in the country from which he comes. These might be central components in his plan of life, so he will find it very frustrating if he is not able to move. But does this ground a right to free movement across borders? It seems to me that it does not. What a person can legitimately demand access to is an *adequate* range of options to choose between—a reasonable choice of occupation, religion, cultural activities, marriage partners, and so forth. Adequacy here is defined in terms of generic human interests rather than in terms of the interests of any one person in particular— so, for example, a would-be opera singer living in a society which provides for various forms of musical expression, but not for opera, can have an adequate range of options in this area even though the option she most prefers is not available. So long as they adhere to the standards of decency sketched above, all contemporary states are able to provide such an adequate range internally. So although people certainly have an *interest* in being able to migrate internationally, they do not have a basic interest of the kind that would be required to ground a human right. It is more like my interest in having an Aston Martin than my interest in having access to *some* means of physical mobility.

I turn next to the argument that because people have a right to leave the society they currently belong to, they must also have a right to enter other societies, since the first right is practically meaningless unless the second exists—there is no unoccupied space in the world to exit *to*, so unless the right to leave society A is accompanied by the right to enter societies B, C, D, etc., it has no real force. . . .

The right of exit is certainly an important human right, but once again it is worth examining why it has the significance that it does. Its importance is partly instrumental: knowing that their subjects have the right to leave inhibits states from mistreating them in various ways, so it helps to preserve the conditions of what I earlier called "decency." However, even in the case of decent states the right of exit remains important, and that is because by being deprived of exit rights individuals are forced to remain in association with others whom they may find deeply uncongenial—think of the militant atheist in a society where almost everyone devoutly practices the same religion, or the religious puritan in a society where most people behave like libertines. On the other hand, the right of exit from state A does not appear to entail an unrestricted right to enter any society of the immigrant's choice—indeed, it seems that it can be exercised provided that at least one other society, society B say, is willing to take him in. . . .

It is also important to stress that there are many rights whose exercise is contingent on finding partners who are willing to cooperate in the exercise, and it may be that the right of exit falls into this category. Take the right to marry as an example. This is a right held against the state to allow people to marry the partners of their choice (and perhaps to provide the legal framework within which marriages can be contracted). It is obviously not a right to have a marriage partner provided—whether any given person can exercise the right depends entirely on whether he is able to find someone willing to marry him, and many people are not so lucky. The right of exit is a right held against a person's current state of residence not to prevent her from leaving the state (and perhaps aiding her in that endeavor by, say, providing a passport). But it does not entail an obligation on any other state to let that person in. Obviously, if no state were ever to grant entry rights to people who were not already its citizens, the right of exit would have no value. But suppose states are generally willing to consider entry applications from people who want to migrate, and that most people would get offers from at least one such state: then the position as far as the right of exit goes is pretty much the same as with the right to marry, where by no means everyone is able to wed the partner they would ideally like to have, but most have the opportunity to marry *someone*.

So once the right of exit is properly understood, it does not entail an unlimited right to migrate to the society of one's choice. But now, finally, in this part of the chapter, I want to consider an argument for migration rights that appeals to distributive justice. It begins from the assumption of the fundamental moral equality of human beings. It then points out that, in the world in which we live, a person's life prospects depend heavily on the society into which she happens to be born, so that the only way to achieve equal opportunities is to allow people to move to the places where they can develop and exercise their talents, through employment and in other ways. In other words, there is something fundamentally unfair about a world in which people are condemned to relative poverty through no fault of their own when others have much greater opportunities, whereas if people were free to live and work wherever they wished, then each person could choose whether to stay in the community that had raised him or to look for a better life elsewhere.

The question we must ask here is whether justice demands equality of opportunity at the global level, as the argument I have just sketched assumes, or whether this principle only applies *inside* societies, among those who are already citizens of the same political community. . . . Note to begin with that embracing the moral equality of all human beings—accepting that every human being is equally an object of moral concern—does not yet tell us what we are required to do for them as a result of that equality. One answer *might* be that we should attempt to provide everyone with equal opportunities to pursue their goals in life. But another, equally plausible, answer is that we should play our part in ensuring that their basic rights are respected, where these are understood as rights to a certain minimum level of security, freedom, resources, and so forth—a level adequate to protect their basic interests, as suggested earlier in this chapter. . . .

But what if somebody does fall below this threshold? Does this not give him the right to migrate to a place where the minimum level is guaranteed? Perhaps, but it depends on whether the minimum *could* be provided in the political community he belongs to now, or whether that community is so oppressive, or so dysfunctional, that escape is the only option. So here we encounter again the issue of refugees, to be discussed in my final section. Meanwhile, the lesson for other states, confronted with people whose lives are less than decent, is that they have a choice: they must either ensure that the basic rights of such people are protected in the places where they live—by aid, by intervention, or by some other means—or they must help them to move to other communities where their lives will be better. Simply shutting one's borders and doing nothing else is not a morally defensible option here. People everywhere have a right to a decent life. But before jumping to the conclusion that the way to respond to global injustice is to encourage people whose lives are less than decent to migrate elsewhere, we should consider the fact that this policy will do little to help the very poor, who are unlikely to have the resources to move to a richer country. Indeed, a policy of open migration may make such people worse off still, if it allows doctors, engineers, and other professionals to move from economically undeveloped to economically developed societies in search of higher incomes, thereby depriving their countries of origin of vital skills. Equalizing opportunity for the few may diminish opportunities for the many. Persisting global injustice does impose on rich states the obligation to make a serious contribution to the relief of global poverty, but in most instances they should contribute to improving conditions of life on the ground, as it were, rather than bypassing the problem by allowing (inevitably selective) inward migration.

Justifications for Limiting Immigration

. . . In this section, I shall outline two good reasons that states may have for restricting immigration. One has to do with preserving culture, the other with controlling population. I don't claim that these reasons will apply to every state, but they do apply to many liberal democracies that are currently having to decide how to respond to potentially very large flows of immigrants from less economically developed societies (other states may face larger flows still, but the political issues will be different).

The first reason assumes that the states in question require a common public culture that in part constitutes the political identity of their members, and that serves valuable functions in supporting democracy and other social goals. . . . What I want to do here is to consider how the need to protect the public culture bears upon the issue of immigration. In general terms we can say (a) that immigrants will enter with cultural values, including *political* values, that are more or less different from the public culture of the community they enter; (b) that as a result of living in that community, they will absorb some part of the existing public culture, modifying their own values in the process; and (c) that their presence will also change the public culture in various ways—for instance, a society in which an established religion had formed an important part of national identity will typically exhibit greater religious diversity after accepting immigrants, and as a consequence religion will play a less significant part in defining that identity.

Immigration, in other words, is likely to change a society's public culture rather than destroy it. And since public cultures always change over time, as a result of social factors that are quite independent of immigration (participation in the established religion might have been declining in any case), it doesn't on the face of it seem that states have any good reason to restrict immigration on that basis. They might have reason to limit the *flow* of immigrants, on the grounds that the process of acculturation outlined above may break down if too many come in too quickly. But so long as a viable public culture is maintained, it should not matter that its character changes as a result of taking in people with different cultural values. . . .

What this overlooks, however, is that the public culture of their country is something that people have an interest in controlling: they want to be able to shape the way that their nation develops, including the values that are contained in the public culture. They may not of course succeed: valued cultural features can be eroded by economic and other forces that evade political control. But they may certainly have good reason to try, and in particular to try to maintain cultural continuity over time, so that they can see themselves as the bearers of an identifiable cultural tradition that stretches backward historically. Cultural continuity, it should be stressed, is not the same as cultural rigidity: the most valuable cultures are those that can develop and adapt to new circumstances, including the presence of new subcultures associated with immigrants. . . .

The second reason for states to limit immigration that I want to consider concerns population size. . . .

What we think about this issue may be conditioned to some extent by the population density of the state in which we live. Those of us who live in relatively small and crowded states experience daily the way in which the sheer number of our fellow citizens, with their needs for housing, mobility, recreation, and so forth, impacts on the physical environment, so that it becomes harder to enjoy access to open space, to move from place to place without encountering congestion, to preserve important wildlife habitats, and so on. It's true, of course, that the problems arise not simply from population size, but also from a population that wants to live in a certain way—to move around a lot, to have high levels of consumption, and so on—so we could deal with them by collectively changing the way that we live, rather than by restricting or reducing population size. . . . Perhaps we should. But this, it seems to me, is a matter for political decision: members of a territorial community have the right to decide whether to restrict their numbers, or to live in a more ecologically and humanly sound way, or to do neither and bear the costs of a high-consumption, high-mobility lifestyle in a crowded territory. If restricting numbers is part of the solution, then controlling immigration is a natural corollary.

What I have tried to do in this section is to suggest why states may have good reason to limit immigration. I concede that would-be immigrants may have a strong interest in being admitted—a strong economic interest, for example—but in general they have no obligation-conferring *right* to be admitted, for reasons given in the previous section. On the other side, nation-states have a strong and legitimate interest in determining who comes in and who does not. . . . It remains now to see what conditions an admissions policy must meet if it is to be ethically justified.

Conditions for an Ethical Immigration Policy

I shall consider two issues. The first is the issue of refugees, usually defined as people who have fled their home country as a result of a well-founded fear of persecution or violence. What obligations do states have to admit persons in that category? The second is the issue of discrimination in admissions policy. If a state decides to admit some immigrants (who are not refugees) but refuses entry to others, what criteria can it legitimately use in making its selection?

As I indicated in the first section of this chapter, people whose basic rights are being threatened or violated in their current place of residence clearly do have the right to move to somewhere that offers them greater security. Prima facie, then, states have an obligation to admit refugees, indeed "refugees" defined more broadly than is often the case to include people who are being deprived of rights to subsistence, basic healthcare, etc. . . .

Realistically, . . . states have to be given considerable autonomy to decide on how to respond to particular asylum applications: besides the refugee's own choice, they are entitled to consider the overall number of applications they face, the demands that temporary or longer-term accommodation of refugees will place on existing citizens, and whether there exists any special link between the refugee and the host community—for instance, similarities of language or culture, or a sense of historical responsibility on the part of the receiving state (which might see itself as somehow implicated among the causes of the crisis that has produced the refugees). If states are given this autonomy, there can be no guarantee that every bona fide refugee will find a state willing to take him or her in. Here we simply face a clash between two moral intuitions: on the one hand, every refugee is a person with basic human rights that deserve protection; on the other, the responsibility for insuring this is diffused among states in such a way that we cannot say that any particular state S has an obligation to admit refugee R. Each state is at some point entitled to say that it has done enough to cope with the refugee crisis. So the best we can hope for is that informal mechanisms will continue to evolve which make all refugees the *special* responsibility of one state or another. . . .

The second issue is discrimination among migrants who are not refugees. Currently, states do discriminate on a variety of different grounds, effectively selecting the migrants they want to take in. Can this be justified? Well, given that states are entitled to put a ceiling on the numbers of people they take in, for reasons canvassed in the previous section, they need to select somehow, if only by lottery (as the USA began to do in 1995 for certain categories of immigrant). So what grounds can they legitimately use? It seems to me that receiving states are entitled to consider the benefit they would receive from admitting a would-be migrant as well as the strength of the migrant's own claim to move. So it is acceptable to give precedence to people whose cultural values are closer to those of the existing population—for instance, to those who already speak the native language. This is a direct corollary of the argument in the previous section about cultural self-determination. Next in order of priority come those who possess skills and talents that are needed by the receiving community. Their claim is weakened, as suggested earlier, by the likelihood that in taking them in, the receiving state is also depriving their country of origin of a valuable resource (medical expertise, for example). In such cases, the greater the interest the potential host country has in admitting the would-be migrant, the more likely it is that admitting her will make life worse for those she leaves behind. So although it is reasonable for the receiving state to make decisions based on how much the immigrant can be expected to contribute economically if admitted, this criterion should be used with caution. What cannot be defended in any circumstances is discrimination on grounds of race, sex, or, in most instances, religion—religion could be a relevant criterion only where it continues to form an essential part of the public culture, as in the case of the state of Israel.

If nation-states are allowed to decide how many immigrants to admit in the first place, why can't they pick and choose among potential immigrants on whatever grounds they like—admitting only red-haired women if that is what their current membership prefers? I have tried to hold a balance between the interest that migrants have in entering the country they want to live in, and the interest that political communities having in determining their own character. Although the first of these interests is not strong enough to justify a right of migration, it is still substantial, and so the immigrants who are refused entry are owed an explanation. To be told that they belong to the wrong race, or sex (or have hair of the wrong color) is insulting, given that these features do not connect to anything of real significance to the society they want to join. Even tennis clubs are not entitled to discriminate among applicants on grounds such as these.

Let me conclude by underlining the importance of admitting all long-term immigrants to full and equal citizenship in the receiving society (this does not apply to refugees who are admitted temporarily until it is safe to return to their country of origin, but it does apply to refugees as soon as it becomes clear that return is not a realistic option for them). Controls on immigration must be coupled with active policies to insure that immigrants are brought into the political life of the community, and acquire the linguistic and other skills that they require to function as active citizens. . . . In several states immigrants are now encouraged to take citizenship classes leading up to a formal admissions ceremony, and this is a welcome development insofar as it recognizes that becoming a citizen isn't something that just happens spontaneously. Precisely because they aim to be "communities of character," with distinct public cultures to which new immigrants can contribute, democratic states must bring immigrants into political dialogue with natives. What is unacceptable is the emergence of a permanent class of non-citizens, whether these are guest workers, illegal immigrants, or asylum seekers waiting to have their applications adjudicated. The underlying political philosophy which informs this chapter sees democratic states as political communities formed on the basis of equality among their members, and just as this gives such states the right to exclude, it also imposes the obligation to protect the equal status of all those who live within their borders.

Study Questions

1. What is the difference between *basic* freedoms and *bare* freedoms?
2. Is the right to exit similar to the right to be married?
3. According to Miller, why does preserving culture provide a reason to limit immigration?
4. According to Miller, when should refugees be granted asylum?

CHAPTER 25

Is There a Right to Immigrate?
Michael Huemer

Michael Huemer is Professor of Philosophy at the University of Colorado at Boulder. He argues that closing borders violates the rights of potential immigrants. His view is that everyone has the right to immigrate because all should be free from the threat of physical force, and restrictions on immigration involve harmful coercion.

1. The Immigration Question

Every year, close to one million individuals from foreign nations migrate to the United States legally. But many more are turned away. Individuals seeking to enter without the permission of the U.S. government are regularly barred at the border, and those discovered in the territory without authorization are forcibly removed. The government expels over one million people from the country each year.[1] Hundreds of thousands continue to try to smuggle themselves in, occasionally dying in the attempt. On the face of it, this raises ethical questions. Is it right to forcibly prevent would-be immigrants from living in the United States? Those excluded seem, on the face of it, to suffer a serious harm. Why are we justified in imposing this harm?

Some reason that, just as a private club may exercise its discretion as to whom to admit or exclude, so a nation-state has the right to choose whom to admit or exclude. Some believe that we must exclude most would-be immigrants in order to maintain the integrity of our national culture. Others argue that immigrants cause economic hardship for existing citizens—that they take jobs from American workers, depress wages, and place an undue burden on social services provided by the state. Some go so far as to warn that unchecked immigration would

From Michael Huemer, "Is There a Right to Immigrate?" *Social Theory and Practice* 36 (2010).

bring on environmental, economic, and social catastrophes that would reduce the United States to the status of a Third World country.

Few would question the state's right to exclude at least some potential migrants. For example, the state may deny entry to international terrorists or fugitives from the law. The interesting question concerns the vast majority of other potential immigrants—ordinary people who are simply seeking a new home and a better life. Does the state have the right to exclude these ordinary people?

In the following, I argue that the answer to this question is no. I shall assume that we are considering ordinary, noncriminal migrants who wish to leave their country of origin for morally innocent reasons, whether to escape persecution or economic hardship, or simply to join a society they would prefer to live in. Though I shall conduct the discussion in terms of the situation of the United States, most of my arguments apply equally well to other countries.

My strategy is to argue, first, that immigration restriction is at least a prima facie violation of the rights of potential immigrants. This imposes a burden on advocates of restriction to cite some special conditions that either neutralize or outweigh the relevant prima facie right. I then examine the most popular justifications offered for restricting immigration, finding that none of them offers a credible rationale for claiming either that such restriction does not violate rights or that the rights violation is justified. This leaves immigration restrictions ultimately unjustified. . . .

2. Immigration Restriction as a Prima Facie Rights Violation

In this section, I aim to show that immigration restriction is a prima facie rights violation. A prima facie rights violation is an action of a sort that *normally*—that is, barring any special circumstances—violates someone's rights. For example, killing a human being is a prima facie rights violation: in normal circumstances, to kill someone is to violate his rights. But there are special circumstances that may alter this verdict: euthanasia and self-defense killings do not violate rights, for instance. Furthermore, even when an action violates rights, it may sometimes be justified nevertheless, because the victim's rights may be *outweighed* by competing moral considerations. Thus, killing one innocent person may be justified, though a violation of the victim's right to life, if it is necessary to prevent the deaths of one million others. Or so it seems to me.

The claim that an action is a prima facie rights violation, then, is not a very strong claim. It does not entail that the action is wrong all things considered, for there may be special circumstances that prevent the action from being an actual rights violation, or that render it justified despite its violation of rights. But nor is the claim entirely without force: to accept that an action is a prima facie rights violation has the effect of shifting a normative presumption. It becomes the burden of those who advocate the act in question to identify the special exculpatory or justificatory circumstances that make what tends to be a wrongful rights violation either not a rights violation in this case, or a justified rights violation. Those who oppose the act in question need only rebut such efforts.

Now before we turn to the case of immigration, consider the following scenario. Marvin is in desperate need of food. Perhaps someone has stolen his food, or perhaps a natural disaster destroyed his crops; whatever the reason, Marvin is in danger of starvation. Fortunately, he has a plan to remedy the problem: he will walk to the local marketplace, where he will buy bread. Assume that in the absence of outside interference, this plan would succeed: the marketplace is open, and there are people there who are willing to trade food to Marvin in exchange for something he has. Another individual, Sam, is aware of all this and is watching Marvin. For some reason, Sam decides to detain Marvin on his way to the marketplace, forcibly preventing him from reaching it. As a result, Marvin returns home empty-handed, where he dies of starvation.

What is the proper assessment of Sam's action? Did Sam harm Marvin? Did he violate Marvin's rights? Was Sam's action wrong?

It seems to me that there are clear answers to these questions. Sam's behavior in this scenario was both extremely harmful to Marvin and a severe violation of Marvin's rights. Indeed, if Marvin's death was reasonably foreseeable, then Sam's act was an act of murder. Unless there obtained some unusual circumstances not mentioned in the preceding description, Sam's behavior was extremely wrong.

Intuitively, Sam's behavior would still be wrong if the harm suffered by Marvin were less severe. Suppose that, rather than dying soon after returning home, Marvin foreseeably suffers from serious malnutrition. Again, assume that this misfortune would have been avoided had Marvin been able to trade in the marketplace, but Sam forcibly prevented him from doing so. In this case, again, it seems that Sam violates Marvin's rights and wrongfully harms Marvin.

What do these examples show? I think they show, to begin with, that individuals have a prima facie, negative right not to be subjected to seriously harmful coercion. Sam's behavior in the scenario was, by stipulation, coercive—it involved a use or threat of physical force against Marvin, significantly restricting his freedom of action. It was also extremely harmful, resulting in Marvin's starvation. These facts seem to explain why Sam's action was a violation of Marvin's rights, and why it was wrong.

How do we know that Sam harmed Marvin? A "harm" is commonly understood as a setback to someone's interests. Marvin's death by starvation certainly sets back his interests. Moreover, in my view, no philosophical *theory* of harm is required in this case. Perhaps there are borderline cases in which one would need to appeal to a theory to determine whether an event counted as a harm or not. But the story of starving Marvin presents no such difficult case. Marvin's death is a paradigm case of a harm. . . .

I am not claiming here that all acts of coercion are harmful. Paternalistic coercion, for instance, need not be harmful. Nor are all harmful actions coercive. One might harm a person, for instance, by spreading false rumors about her, without any exercise of physical force. I am only claiming that *this* action, Sam's forcible interference with Marvin's effort to reach the marketplace, was both harmful and coercive. Similarly, I am not claiming that all coercion violates rights, nor that all harmful acts violate rights. I claim only that, when an action is seriously harmful *and* coercive, it tends for that reason to be a rights violation, other things being equal—that is, it is a prima facie rights violation. Sam's behavior in the scenario described violates Marvin's rights, because it is an act of extremely harmful coercion, and there are no relevant extenuating circumstances. Sam's behavior could be justified if, for example, it was necessary to prevent the deaths of a million innocent persons; or, perhaps, if Marvin had for some reason contracted Sam to forcibly prevent Marvin from going to the marketplace. But assume that nothing like that is the case. The case is just as originally described, with no special circumstances. Few would doubt, then, that Sam's behavior is unacceptable.

How does all this relate to U.S. immigration policy? The role of Marvin is played by those potential immigrants who seek escape from oppression or economic hardship. The marketplace is the United States: were they allowed in, most immigrants would succeed in meeting their needs (to a greater extent, at least, than they will if they are not allowed in). The role of Sam is played by the government of the United States, which has adopted severe restrictions on entry. These restrictions are imposed by coercion: armed guards are hired to patrol the borders, physically barring unauthorized entry, and armed officers of the state forcibly detain and expel immigrants who are found residing in the country illegally. As in the case of Sam's detention of Marvin, the U.S. government's exclusion of undocumented immigrants is also very harmful to most of those excluded: many suffer from oppression or poverty that could and would be remedied if only they were able to enter the country of their choice. In view of this, the actions of the U.S. government, prima facie, constitute serious violations of the rights of potential immigrants—specifically, the government violates their prima facie right not to be harmfully coerced. . . .

Sam's action might be justified if there were special circumstances not previously specified, circumstances that either cancelled the right that Marvin normally has not to be harmfully coerced, or that morally outweighed Marvin's rights. Likewise, what we have said so far does not establish that the U.S. government's restrictions on immigration are wrong *tout court* [without qualification], but only that those defending the policy incur a burden of providing a justification for these restrictions. In light of the seriousness of the harms involved in this case, the justification for immigration restrictions must be correspondingly clear and powerful.

3. Reasons for Restriction

Harmful coercion is sometimes justified. It may be justified when necessary to defend an innocent party against harmful coercion. It may be justified when necessary to prevent much worse consequences. It may be justified because of a prior agreement made by the coercee. And there may be other circumstances that justify harmful coercion as well. Some believe, for instance, that harmful coercion may be justified because of a need to rectify severe economic inequality. The latter claim is controversial, as would be many other alleged justifications for harmful coercion. This illustrates one reason why a general theory of the conditions for justified harmful coercion would be difficult to devise and still more difficult to defend.

Fortunately, it may turn out that we do not need any such general theory. Some sorts of reasons . . . are generally accepted as legitimate justifications for harmful coercion. Equally, there are some sorts of reasons that we can see intuitively, even without a general theory, *not* to be legitimate justifications for harmful coercion. For instance, one is not justified in harmfully coercing a person simply because one wants the victim's shoes, or because one hates the race to which the victim belongs, or because one disagrees with the victim's philosophical beliefs. Whatever is the correct theory of justifications for harmful coercion, *those* reasons surely will not qualify. The task at hand is to determine whether there are any circumstances that justify the harmful coercion involved in immigration restrictions. Given that immigration restriction is a prima facie rights violation, the burden of proof falls on advocates of restriction. Thus, we may proceed by considering the reasons they have offered for restricting immigration. If it turns out that all of these reasons fall into the category of things that clearly do not count as valid justifications for harmful coercion, then it is fair to draw the conclusion that immigration restrictions are unjustified.

3.1. Immigration and Employment

In popular discourse, the most common sort of argument for limiting or eliminating immigration is economic. It is said that immigrants take jobs away from American workers, and that they cause a lowering of wage rates due to their willingness to work for lower wages than American workers. At the same time, economists are nearly unanimous in agreeing that the overall economic effects of immigration on existing Americans are positive. These claims are mutually consistent: there are certain industries in which immigrants are disproportionately likely to work. Preexisting workers in those industries are made worse off due to competition with immigrant workers. According to one estimate, immigration during the 1980s may have reduced the wages of native-born workers in the most strongly affected industries by about 1–2% (5% for high school dropouts).[2] At the same time, employers in those industries and customers of their businesses are made better off due to lower production costs, and the economic gains to these latter groups outweigh the economic losses to the workers. Some economists have accused immigration opponents of overlooking the economic benefits of immigration due to a bias against foreigners or members of other races.

Let us leave aside the question of the overall effects of immigration on the economy, and focus instead on the following question. Granted that immigration makes some American workers economically worse off, does this show that immigration restriction does not violate the rights of would-be immigrants, or that if it does, the rights violation is nevertheless justified? More generally, does the following constitute a valid justification for harmful coercion: that the coercive action is necessary to prevent someone else from suffering slight to moderate economic disadvantage through marketplace competition?

It seems to me that it does not. Consider two related examples. In the first example, I am being considered for a particular job, for which I know that Bob is the only other candidate. I also know that Bob is willing to work for a lower salary than the salary that I could obtain if I were the only candidate. On the day Bob is scheduled to have his job interview, I accost him and physically restrain him from going to the interview. When confronted about my seemingly unacceptable conduct, I explain that my action was necessary to protect myself against Bob's taking the job that I would otherwise have, or my being forced to accept a lower salary in order to get the job. Does this provide an adequate justification for my behavior? Does it show that, contrary to initial appearances, my harmful coercion does not really violate Bob's rights? Alternatively, does it show that my action, though a rights violation, was an ethically justified rights violation?

Certainly not. The mere fact that Bob is competing with me for a job that I desire, or that Bob is willing to accept a lower salary than I could obtain if I did not have to compete with him, does not invalidate or suspend Bob's right not to be subjected to harmful coercion. Nor does my interest in having less economic competition *outweigh* Bob's right not to be coercively harmed. If my need for the job in question were very much greater than Bob's need, then some might argue that I would be justified in overriding Bob's rights. We need not decide exactly when a right may be overridden, nor whether a greater economic need could constitute an adequate basis for overriding a competitor's right to be free from harmful coercion; we need not decide these things here, because we can simply stipulate that Bob has at least as much need for the job for which we are competing as I do. In such a case, no one would say that Bob's right to be free from coercive harms is suspended or outweighed.

My second example is a modified version of the story of Sam and Marvin. As before, Marvin plans to walk to the local marketplace to obtain life-sustaining food. Due to his economic circumstances, Marvin will have to buy the cheapest bread available at the market. Sam's daughter, however, also plans to go to the market, slightly later in the day, to buy some of this same bread. This bread is often in short supply, so that the vendor may run out after Marvin's purchase. Sam's daughter could buy more expensive bread, but she would prefer not to. Knowing all this, Sam fears that if Marvin is allowed to go to the market, his daughter will be forced to pay a slightly higher price for bread than she would like. To prevent this from happening, he accosts Marvin on the road and physically restrains him from traveling to the market. Is Sam's action permissible?

Suppose Sam claims that his harmful coercion does not violate Marvin's rights, because it is necessary to protect his daughter from economic disadvantage. Certainly this defense falls flat. A person's right to be free from harmful coercion is not so easily swept aside. Likewise for the suggestion that Sam's action, though a rights violation, is justified because his daughter's interest in saving money outweighs Marvin's rights. No one would accept such feeble justifications.

Yet this seems analogous to the common economic argument for immigration restriction. The claim seems to be that we are justified in forcibly preventing individuals—many of whom are seeking escape from dire economic distress—from entering the American labor market, because American workers would suffer economic disadvantage through price competition. No one claims that American workers would be disadvantaged to anything like the degree that potential immigrants are disadvantaged by being forcibly excluded from the market. Nevertheless, the prospect of a modest lowering of American wages and narrowing of employment opportunities is taken to either suspend or outweigh the rights of needy foreigners. The ethical principle would have to be that a person's right to be free from extremely harmful coercion is sometimes held in abeyance simply by virtue of the fact that such coercion is necessary to protect third parties from modest economic disadvantage resulting from marketplace competition. The implausibility of this principle is shown by the examples of Bob and Marvin above.

3.2. The State's Duty to Its Citizens

Perhaps immigration restriction can be justified by reflection on the special obligations governments owe to their own citizens, as distinct from foreign nationals. Few doubt that there are such duties. States must provide their citizens protection from criminals and hostile foreign governments. A state does not have the same obligation to protect foreign citizens from criminals or other governments. . . .

Perhaps this leads to a rationale for immigration restriction. Perhaps the state has a general duty to serve the interests of its own citizens, including their economic interests, and no such duty, or no duty nearly as strong, to further the interests of foreign nationals. As a result, when the interests of American citizens come into conflict with those of foreigners, the American government must side with its own citizens, even when this results in a lowering of global social utility. Limitations on migration into the United States run contrary to the interests of would-be immigrants, but since those would-be immigrants are not presently U.S. citizens, the U.S. government has either no duty or a much weaker duty to consider their interests, as compared to the interests of its own citizens. Perhaps this gives some traction to the argument that American workers are disadvantaged because of competition with immigrants. Alternatively, one might argue that immigrants impose a financial burden on government providers of social services, such as health care, education, and law enforcement. Since these social programs are financed through revenues collected from existing U.S. citizens, the government's consideration for the interests of its current citizens dictates that it limit the amount of immigration into the country.

Begin with the observation that immigration disadvantages American workers through labor market competition. There are two obstacles to regarding this as a justification for immigration restriction, even if we accept that the state has a much stronger obligation to protect the interests of its own citizens than it has to protect the interests of others. First, only some current citizens would be disadvantaged by increased immigration—those citizens who work in industries that immigrants are disproportionately likely to join. This is a relatively small portion of the population. All other current citizens would either fail to be significantly affected or actually be benefited by increased immigration. As mentioned earlier, most economists believe that the overall economic impact of immigration on current citizens is positive. Thus, if we consider only the interests of current citizens, it is at best unclear that immigration restrictions are beneficial. If we also give *some* weight to the interests of the immigrants themselves, it seems that the case for free immigration is clear.

Second, there are some obligations that any moral agent owes to other persons, merely in virtue of their status as persons. The special obligations that governments owe to their citizens, whatever these obligations may consist of, do not eliminate the obligation to respect the human rights of noncitizens. In particular, the government's duty to give special consideration to its own citizens' interests cannot be taken to imply that the government is entitled to coercively impose grave harms on noncitizens for the sake of securing small economic benefits for citizens.

Consider again the case of starving Marvin. In the last version of the story, Sam coercively prevented Marvin from reaching the local marketplace, on the grounds that doing so was necessary to prevent his daughter from having to pay a higher than normal price for her bread. This action seems unjustified. Would Sam succeed in defending his behavior if he pointed out that, as a father, he has special obligations to his daughter, and that these imply that he must give greater weight to her interests than to the interests of non-family members? Certainly the premise is true—if anything, parents have even stronger and clearer duties to protect the interests of their offspring than a government has to protect its citizens' interests. But this does not negate the rights of non-family members not to be subjected to harmful coercion. One's special duties to one's offspring imply that if one must choose between giving food to one's own child and giving food to a non-family member, one should generally give the food to one's own child. But they do not imply that one may use force to stop non-family members from obtaining food, in order to procure modest economic advantages for one's own children.

Next, consider the charge that immigrants create a fiscal burden due to their consumption of social services. On the whole, immigrants pay slightly less in taxes than the cost of the social services they consume.[3] This is mainly because immigrants tend to have lower-than-average incomes, and thus pay relatively low taxes.[4] Some economists believe, however, that in the long run (over a period of decades), increased immigration would have a net positive fiscal impact.

Assume that immigrants impose a net fiscal burden on government. Would this fact justify forcibly preventing a large number of potential immigrants from entering the country? To answer this, first we must ask whether the state presently has an obligation to provide social services to potential immigrants, even at a net cost to the state. On some theories of distributive justice, it could be argued that the state has such an obligation, even though these potential immigrants are not presently citizens. If so, then the state obviously may not exclude potential immigrants for the purpose of shirking this duty.

Suppose, on the other hand, that the state has no such obligation to provide social services to potential immigrants, at least not without collecting from them sufficient revenues to cover the expenditure. If this is true, the state would perhaps be justified in denying social services to immigrants, raising taxes on immigrants, or charging special fees to immigrants for the use of social services. But it remains implausible that the state would be justified in excluding potential immigrants from the territory entirely. It is not typically a satisfactory defense for a harmful act of coercion to say that because of a policy one has voluntarily adopted, if one did not coerce one's victim in this way, one would instead confer a benefit on the person that one does not wish to confer.

Suppose, for example, that Sam runs a charity organization. He has made a policy of offering free food to all poor people who enter the local marketplace. Unfortunately, the organization is running short on cash, so Sam is looking for ways to cut costs. When he learns that Marvin is heading to the market to buy some food, he decides to save money by forcibly preventing Marvin from reaching the market. Marvin would be better off being allowed into the marketplace, even without free food, since he could still buy some inexpensive food with his limited funds. But Sam has already made a policy of offering free food to all poor people in the marketplace, so he would in fact offer free food to Marvin, were Marvin to make it there. Is it permissible for Sam to coercively inflict a serious harm on Marvin, in order to avoid having to either break his policy or give free food to Marvin?

Surely not. Perhaps Sam would be justified in altering his policy and refusing to give free food to Marvin when he arrives at the marketplace— this would be permissible, provided that Sam has no humanitarian obligation to assist Marvin. But whether or not Sam has any such humanitarian duties, he surely has no right to actively prevent Marvin from getting his own food. If Marvin had been coming to the market to *steal* Sam's food, perhaps then again Sam would be justified in excluding him. Even this claim would be controversial; if Marvin's condition of need were sufficiently urgent, some would say that Sam must let him take the food. But whatever one thinks about that question, surely Sam cannot justify barring Marvin from the opportunity to *buy* food from others, merely on the grounds that if Sam permits him to do so, then Sam will also voluntarily give him some food. . . .

3.4. Cultural Preservation

In the views of some thinkers, states are justified in restricting the flow of immigration into their territories for the purposes of preserving the distinctive cultures of those nations. . . . David Miller argues that existing citizens have an interest in seeking to *control* how their culture does or does not develop, and this requires the ability to limit external influence; thus, again, we have a right to restrict immigration.

To see this as a persuasive reason for restricting American immigration, we must accept two premises, one empirical and the other ethical. The empirical premise is that American culture is in danger of extinction or at least severe alteration if immigration is not restricted. The ethical premise is that the need to preserve one's culture constitutes a legitimate justification for harmful coercion of the sort involved in immigration restrictions.

Both premises are open to question. Empirically, it is doubtful whether apprehensions about the demise of American culture are warranted. Around the world, American culture, and Western culture more generally, have shown a robustness that prompts more concern about the ability of other cultures to survive influence from the West than vice versa. For example, Coca-Cola now sells its products in over 200 countries around the world, with the average human being on Earth drinking 4.8 gallons of Coke per year. McDonald's operates more than 32,000 restaurants in over 100 countries. The three highest grossing movies of all time, worldwide, were *Avatar, Titanic,* and *The Lord of the Rings: The Return of the King.* All three were made by American companies, but 70% of the box office receipts came from outside the United States. The television show *Who Wants to Be a Millionaire?* has been franchised in over 100 countries worldwide, including such diverse places as Japan, Nigeria, Venezuela, and Afghanistan. Whether one sees the phenomenon as desirable, undesirable, or neutral, Western culture has shown a remarkable ability to establish roots in a variety of societies around the world, including societies populated almost entirely by non-Western people. This robustness suggests that American culture is in no danger of being eradicated from America, even if America should drastically increase its rate of immigration. Other societies may have cause to fear the loss of their cultures due to foreign influence, but America does not.

Turning to the ethical premise of the argument for restriction, is the desire to preserve American culture a valid justification for immigration restriction? More generally, can one be justified in harmfully coercing others, solely because doing so is necessary to prevent those others from altering the culture of one's society? Miller is on plausible ground in maintaining that people have a strong interest in controlling their culture. But not everything in which one has an *interest* is something that one may, ethically, secure through harmful coercion of others, even if such coercion is required to protect one's interest. For instance, I have an interest in having my lawn mowed, but I may not force anyone to mow it, even if this is the only method I have available to secure the desired result. Even when one has a *right* to something, it is not always permissible to protect one's enjoyment of the right through coercion. Suppose that I am in need of a liver transplant, but there are no willing donors available. To preserve my life, I must take a liver by force from an unwilling donor. Even though I have both a strong interest in living and a right to life, this does not imply that I may coerce an unwilling donor.

Why, then, should we assume that our admittedly strong interest in preserving our culture entitles us to harmfully coerce others in the name of cultural preservation? Proponents of the cultural preservation argument have neglected this question. Two hypothetical examples, however, may help us to address it.

First, suppose that a number of your neighbors have been converting to Buddhism or selling their homes to Buddhists. Because of this, your neighborhood is in danger of being changed from a Christian to a Buddhist community. The Buddhists do not coercively interfere with your practice of your own religion, nor do they do anything else to violate your rights; still, you object to the transformation, because you would prefer to live among Christians. If you catch on to what is happening in the early stages, are you ethically entitled to use force to stop your neighborhood from becoming Buddhist? Consider a few ways in which you might go about this. You might forcibly interfere with your neighbors' practice of their religion. You could go to their houses, destroy their Buddha statues, and replace them with crucifixes. You could force your neighbors to attend Christian churches. You could forcibly expel all Buddhists from the neighborhood. Or you could forcibly prevent any Buddhists from moving in. All of these actions seem unacceptable. Hardly anyone would accept the suggestion that your interest in preserving a Christian neighborhood either negates or outweighs your neighbors' rights not to be harmfully coerced by you.

A society's dominant religion is an important part of its culture, though not the only important part. But similar intuitions can be elicited with respect to other aspects of culture. You may not forcibly prevent your neighbors from speaking different languages, wearing unusual clothes, listening to unfamiliar music, and so on. This suggests that the protection of one's interest in cultural preservation is not a sufficient justification for harmful coercion against others.

Second, consider another variant of the story of Marvin. Again, imagine that Sam has coercively prevented Marvin from reaching the local marketplace, where he would have bought food needed to sustain his life. His earlier justifications for his behavior having fallen flat, Sam mentions that he had yet another reason. Marvin practices very different traditions from most of the other people in the marketplace. For instance, he wears unusual clothing, belongs to a minority religion, speaks a different language from most others (though he is able to get along well enough to purchase food), and admires very different kinds of art. Sam became concerned that, if Marvin went to the marketplace and interacted with the people gathered there, he might influence the thinking and behavior of others in the marketplace. He might convert others to his religion, for example, or induce more people to speak his language. Because Sam did not want these things to happen, he decided to forcibly prevent Marvin from reaching the marketplace.

Sam had a real interest in preventing the sort of changes that Marvin might have induced. The question is whether this interest is of such a kind that it justifies the use of harmful coercion against innocent others to protect that interest. Intuitively, the answer is no. Sam's desire to be surrounded by people who think and behave in ways similar to himself does not overrule Marvin's right to be free from harmful coercion.

Is this case a fair analogy to the case of immigration restriction? One difference is that Marvin is only one person, and it seems unlikely that he could single-handedly bring about a drastic change in the culture of Sam's society. In contrast, if the United States were to open its borders, *millions* of people would come across, making drastic cultural change a much more realistic possibility.

This difference between the two cases would invalidate my argument, if the reason why Sam's action was impermissible were that Marvin would not in fact have had the effects that Sam feared. But this is not the case. In both of my examples, it should be stipulated that the agent's fears are realistic: in the first example, you have well-founded fears that your neighborhood is becoming Buddhist; in the second example, Sam had well-founded fears that Marvin would have a large impact on the other people in the marketplace. (Perhaps the marketplace is small enough that a single person can significantly influence it.) My contention, with regard to these examples, is not that the cultural change would not happen, but that the avoidance of cultural change does not seem an adequate justification for harmful coercion against innocent others. . . .

5. Conclusion

. . . Literally *millions* of lives are affected in a serious and long-term manner by immigration restrictions. Were these restrictions lifted, millions of people would see greatly expanded opportunities and would take the chance to drastically alter their lives for the better. This makes immigration law a strong candidate for the most harmful body of law in America today. In view of this, it is particularly troubling that these restrictions appear to have so little justification.

Notes

1. U.S. Department of Homeland Security, *Yearbook of Immigration Statistics: 2007*, http://www.dhs.gov/ximgtn/statistics/publications/yearbook. shtm (Washington, D.C.: U.S. Department of Homeland Security, Office of Immigration Statistics, 2008; accessed April 9, 2009), pp. 5, 95.
2. National Research Council, Panel on the Demographic and Economic Impacts of Immigration, *The New Americans: Economic, Demographic, and Fiscal Effects of Immigration*, ed. James P. Smith and Barry Edmonston (Washington, D.C.: National Academies Press, 1997), pp. 6–7.
3. The National Research Council (*The New Americans*, p. 10) estimated that a 10% increase in immigration would impose an increased annual fiscal burden of $15 to $20 per household on existing Americans. As the Congressional Budget Office reports, the most costly government services used by immigrants are public school education, health care, and law enforcement ("The Impact of Unauthorized Immigrants on the Budgets of State and Local Governments," http://www.cbo.gov/doc. cfm?index=8711 (Washington, D.C.: Congressional Budget Office, 2007; accessed April 9, 2009)).
4. National Research Council, *The New Americans*, p. 11.

Study Questions

1. What is a prima facie rights violation?
2. According to Huemer, why is immigration restriction a prima facie rights violation?
3. According to Huemer, are all acts of coercion harmful?
4. Does Huemer agree that a state is justified in restricting the flow of immigration in order to preserve that state's distinctive culture?

C. *Injustice*

CHAPTER 26

Racisms

Kwame Anthony Appiah

Kwame Anthony Appiah, Professor of Philosophy and Law at New York University, distinguishes three doctrines that might be called "racism." The first, which he terms *racialism*, is the view that we can group people according to certain inheritable characteristics, such as skin color. According to Appiah, racialism is morally neutral because it is merely a way to classify people. Nevertheless, racialism can be used to support two pernicious forms of racism, which Appiah terms *extrinsic racism* and *intrinsic racism*. Extrinsic racism holds that different races exhibit different moral traits, such as honesty or dishonesty, whereas intrinsic racism maintains that some races are by nature more valuable than others. Appiah concludes that racialism is false, and that both extrinsic and intrinsic racism are morally objectionable.

Racist Propositions

There are at least three distinct doctrines that might be held to express the theoretical content of what we call "racism." One is the view—which I shall call *racialism*—that there are heritable characteristics, possessed by members of our species, that allow us to divide them into a small set of races, in such a way that all the members of these races share certain traits and tendencies with each other that they do not share with members of any other race. These traits and tendencies characteristic of a race constitute, on the racialist view, a sort of racial essence; and it is part of the content of racialism that the essential heritable characteristics of what the nineteenth century called the "Races of Man" account for more than the visible . . .

From Kwame Anthony Appiah, "Racisms," in *Anatomy of Racism*, ed. David Goldberg (Minneapolis, MN: University of Minnesota Press, 1990).

characteristics—skin color, hair type, facial features—on the basis of which we make our informal classifications. Racialism is at the heart of nineteenth-century Western attempts to develop a science of racial difference. . . .

Racialism is not, in itself, a doctrine that must be dangerous, even if the racial essence is thought to entail moral and intellectual dispositions. Provided positive moral qualities are distributed across the races, each can be respected, can have its "separate but equal" place. Unlike most Western-educated people, I believe . . . that racialism is false; but by itself, it seems to be a cognitive rather than a moral problem. The issue is how the world is, not how we would want it to be.

Racialism is, however, a presupposition of other doctrines that have been called "racism," and these other doctrines have been, in the last few centuries, the basis of a great deal of human suffering and the source of a great deal of moral error.

One such doctrine we might call "extrinsic racism": extrinsic racists make moral distinctions between members of different races because they believe that the racial essence entails certain morally relevant qualities. The basis for the extrinsic racists' discrimination between people is their belief that members of different races differ in respects that *warrant* the differential treatment, respects—such as honesty or courage or intelligence—that are uncontroversially held (at least in most contemporary cultures) to be acceptable as a basis for treating people differently. Evidence that there are no such differences in morally relevant characteristics . . . should thus lead people out of their racism if it is purely extrinsic. As we know, such evidence often fails to change an extrinsic racist's attitudes substantially. . . . But at this point . . . what we have is no longer a false doctrine but a cognitive incapacity, one whose significance I shall discuss later in this essay.

I say that the *sincere* extrinsic racist may suffer from a cognitive incapacity. But some who espouse extrinsic racist doctrines are simply insincere intrinsic racists. For *intrinsic racists*, on my definition, are people who differentiate morally between members of different races because they believe that each race has a different moral status, quite independent of the moral characteristics entailed by its racial essence. Just as, for example, many people assume that the fact that they are biologically related to another person—a brother, an aunt, a cousin—gives them a moral interest in that person, so an intrinsic racist holds that the bare fact of being of the same race is a reason for preferring one person to another. (I shall return to this parallel later as well.)

For an intrinsic racist, no amount of evidence that a member of another race is capable of great moral, intellectual, or cultural achievements, or has characteristics that, in members of one's own race, would make them admirable or attractive, offers any ground for treating that person as he or she would treat similarly endowed members of his or her own race. Just so, some sexists are "intrinsic sexists," holding that the bare fact that someone is a woman (or man) is a reason for treating her (or him) in certain ways. . . .

Racist Dispositions

Most people will want to object already that this discussion of the propositional content of racist moral and factual beliefs misses something absolutely crucial to the character of the psychological and sociological reality of racism, something I touched on when I mentioned that extrinsic racist utterances are often made by people who suffer from what I called a "cognitive incapacity." Part of the standard force of accusations of racism is that their objects are in some way *irrational*. . . .

This cognitive incapacity is not, of course, a rare one. Many of us are unable to give up beliefs that play a part in justifying the special advantages we gain (or hope to gain) from our positions in the social order—in particular, beliefs about the positive characters of the class of people who share that position. Many people who express extrinsic racist beliefs . . . are beneficiaries of social orders that deliver advantages to them by virtue of their "race," so that their disinclination to accept evidence that would deprive them of a justification for those advantages is just an instance of this general phenomenon. . . .

The most interesting cases of this sort of ideological resistance to the truth are not, perhaps, the ones I have just mentioned. On the whole, it is less surprising, once we accept the admittedly problematic notion of self-deception, that people who think that certain attitudes or beliefs advantage them or those they care about should be able, as we say, to "persuade" themselves to ignore evidence that undermines those beliefs or attitudes. What is more interesting is the existence of people who resist the truth of a proposition while thinking that its wider acceptance would in no way disadvantage them or those individuals about whom they care . . . who resist the truth when they recognize that its acceptance would actually advantage them—this might be the case with some black people who have internalized negative racist stereotypes; or who fail, by virtue of their ideological attachments, to recognize what is in their own best interests at all.

My business here is not with the psychological or social processes by which these forms of ideological resistance operate, but it is important, I think, to see the refusal on the part of some extrinsic racists to accept evidence against the beliefs as an instance of a widespread phenomenon in human affairs. It is a plain fact, to which theories of ideology must address themselves, that our species is prone both morally and intellectually to such distortions of judgment, in particular to distortions of judgment that reflect partiality. An inability to change your mind in the face of appropriate evidence is a cognitive incapacity; but it is one that all of us surely suffer from in some areas of belief; especially in areas where our own interests or self-images are (or seem to be) at stake.

It is not, however, as some have held, a tendency that we are powerless to resist. No one, no doubt, can be impartial about everything— even about everything to which the notion of partiality applies; but there is no subject matter about which most sane people cannot, in the end, be persuaded to avoid partiality in judgment. And it may help to shake the convictions of those whose incapacity derives from this sort of ideological defense if we show them how their reaction fits into this general pattern. It is, indeed, because it generally *does* fit this pattern that we call such views "racism"—the suffix "-ism" indicating that what we have in mind is not simply a theory but an ideology. It would be odd to call someone brought up in a remote corner of the world with false and demeaning views about white people a "racist" if that person gave up these beliefs quite easily in the face of appropriate evidence.

Real live racists, then, exhibit a systematically distorted rationality, the kind of systematically distorted rationality that we are likely to call "ideological." And it is a distortion that is especially striking in the cognitive domain: extrinsic racists, as I said earlier, however intelligent or otherwise well informed, often fail to treat evidence against the theoretical propositions of extrinsic racism dispassionately. Like extrinsic racism, intrinsic racism can also often be seen as ideological . . . . What makes intrinsic racism similarly ideological is not so much the failure of inductive or deductive rationality that is so striking in someone . . . but rather the connection that it, like extrinsic racism, has with the interests—real or perceived—of the dominant group.

I propose to use the old-fashioned term "racial prejudice" in the rest of this essay to refer to the deformation of rationality in judgment that characterizes those whose racism is more than a theoretical attachment to certain propositions about race.

Racial Prejudice

It is hardly necessary to raise objections to what I am calling "racial prejudice"; someone who exhibits such deformations of rationality is plainly in trouble. But it is important to remember that propositional racists in a racist culture have false moral beliefs but may not suffer from racial prejudice. Once we show them how society has enforced extrinsic racist stereotypes, once we ask them whether they really believe that race in itself, independently of those extrinsic racist beliefs, justifies differential treatment, many will come to give up racist propositions, although we must remember how powerful a weight of authority our arguments have to overcome. Reasonable people may insist on substantial evidence if they are to give up beliefs that are central to their cultures.

Still in the end, many will resist such reasoning; and to the extent that their prejudices are really not subject to any kind of rational control, we may wonder whether it is right to treat such people as morally responsible for the acts their racial prejudice motivates, or morally reprehensible for holding the views to which their prejudice leads them. It is a bad thing that such people exist; they are, in a certain sense, bad people. But it is not clear to me that they are responsible for the fact that they are bad. Racial prejudice, like prejudice generally, may threaten an agent's autonomy, making it appropriate to treat or train rather than to reason with them.

But once someone has been offered evidence both (1) that their reasoning in a certain domain is distorted by prejudice, and (2) that the distortions conform to a pattern that suggests a lack of impartiality, they ought to take special care in articulating views and proposing policies in that domain. They ought to do so because, as I have already said, the phenomenon of partiality in judgment is well attested in human affairs. Even if you are not immediately persuaded that you are yourself a victim of such a distorted rationality in a certain domain, you should keep in mind always that this is the usual position of those who suffer from such prejudices. To the extent that this line of thought is not one that itself falls within the domain in question, one can be held responsible for not subjecting judgments that *are* within that domain to an especially extended scrutiny; and this is a fortiori [even more so] true if the policies one is recommending are plainly of enormous consequence.

If it is clear that racial prejudice is regrettable, it is also clear in the nature of the case that providing even a superabundance of reasons and evidence will often not be a successful way of removing it. Nevertheless, the racist's prejudice will be articulated through the sorts of theoretical propositions I dubbed extrinsic and intrinsic racism. And we should certainly be able to say something reasonable about why these theoretical propositions should be rejected. . . .

Intrinsic Racism

. . . Intrinsic racism is, in my view, a moral error. Even if racialism were correct, the bare fact that someone was of another race would be no reason to treat them worse—or better—than someone of my race. In our public lives, people are owed treatment independently of their biological characters: if they are to be differently treated there must be some morally relevant difference between them. In our private lives, we are morally free to have aesthetic preferences between people, but once our treatment of people raises moral issues, we may not make arbitrary distinctions. Using race in itself as a morally relevant distinction strikes most of us as obviously arbitrary. Without associated moral characteristics, why should race provide a better basis than hair color or height or timbre of voice? And if two people share all the properties morally relevant to some action we ought to do, it will be an error—a failure to apply the Kantian injunction to universalize our moral judgments—to use the bare facts of race as the basis for treating them differently. No one should deny that a common ancestry might, in particular cases, account for similarities in moral character. But then it would be the moral similarities that justified the different treatment.

It is presumably because most people . . . share the sense that intrinsic racism requires arbitrary distinctions that they are largely unwilling to express it in situations that invite moral criticism. But I do not know how I would argue with someone who was willing to announce an intrinsic racism as a basic moral idea; the best one can do, perhaps, is to provide objections to possible lines of defense of it.

Study Questions

1. According to Appiah, what is racialism?
2. How does Appiah distinguish *extrinsic* and *intrinsic* racism?
3. According to Appiah, why is extrinsic racism unjustifiable?
4. According to Appiah, why is intrinsic racism unjustifiable?

CHAPTER 27

Sexism

Ann E. Cudd and Leslie E. Jones

Ann E. Cudd is Professor of Philosophy at the University of Pittsburgh, and Leslie E. Jones was formerly a doctoral student at the University of Kansas, where he worked with her. Here they explore sexism—that is, the systematic inequality between the sexes. They find it in the rules and norms structuring social institutions, in interactions between persons, and in the beliefs, emotions, and attitudes of individuals. Cudd and Jones conclude that morality demands opposition to sexism in all its manifestations.

What Is Sexism?

[J]ust as racism is most accurately used to refer to various forms of oppression against non-Caucasians (at least in Western societies), . . . "sexism" refers to a historically and globally pervasive form of oppression against women. . . .

[T]here are many parallels between racism and sexism. For one thing, both are pervasive and have a high human cost. But, more importantly, the psychological mechanisms that make sexism and racism possible and desirable are similar: namely, our penchant for categorizing by social group, and making invidious distinctions between in-group and out-group members.[1] Furthermore, the social mechanisms that maintain sexism and racism are similar. Both sexism and racism are maintained through systematic violence and economic disadvantage. Both are difficult to pinpoint, but can be statistically

From Ann E. Cudd and Leslie E. Jones, "Sexism," in *A Companion to Applied Ethics*, eds. R. G. Frey and Christopher Heath Wellman (Malden, MA: Blackwell, 2003). Reprinted by permission of the publisher.

documented and are much more readily perceived by the victims than by the respective dominant social groups. Both sexism and racism can have devastating psychological effects on individuals. And both inspire enormously powerful backlash when they are publicly challenged. . . .

If one holds, as we do, that sexism is pervasive, both historically and globally, then it will be no surprise that its ground will be both wide and deep. Institutions that are sexist will be both causes and effects of sexism. When regarded as a result of past sexism, such institutions will then carry on a tradition of, say, excluding women from available high-paying work. Managers and others who carry on this tradition may, of course, overtly maintain extrinsic sexism. They may sincerely, but falsely, believe women to be incapable of carrying on this work. This *intentional extrinsic sexism* should be distinguished from what might be called *individuated extrinsic sexism*, which maintains that while women (as a group) are capable of carrying on this work, no individual woman is. In either case it will be extremely difficult to persuasively establish such trenchant attitudes as sexist. In the latter case though women in general are held to be able to do this work, the technique of holding that each one now applying cannot do the job will effectively, if unintentionally, maintain the sexist tradition. Within that tradition such judgments are considered to be matters of keeping high standards, not sexism. As this practice requires an increasingly high degree of dubious judgment the longer it continues, over time it becomes correspondingly less reasonable to attribute to managers and others the sincere belief that women (as a group) are equally capable. In the case of intentional extrinsic sexism the fact that there are currently no or few women in the field contributes to the view that women cannot or do not want to do the work. The tradition of excluding women is, in this case, *intentional*. . . .

One important effect of the practice of excluding women in these ways is, of course, that women are made more dependent on others, usually men. By reducing the opportunities women have available to them, women are less able to clearly establish, both to themselves and to others, their general ability to accomplish high-paying (or high-status) tasks. Where these patterns are left unchallenged there is thus little to counter the claim that women are, by nature, more dependent. Moreover, these effects of sexist hiring practices are reinforced in a number of ways. They are reinforced by patterns of language which mark and delimit appropriate activities and attitudes on the basis of sex, and relegate the activities and attitudes of women to a lower status (i.e. sexist language). And they are reinforced by systems of education and enculturation which support, if not create and coerce, discrete proclivities for girls and boys, and relegate the proclivities of girls to a lower status. These social aspects of sexism are further mirrored in psychological dispositions, desires, and self-concepts. Accepting the activities, attitudes, and proclivities which are typically associated with men as "normal" or "standard" for human beings (i.e. the man standard) would render the activities, attitudes, and proclivities which are typically associated with women, when different, abnormal or substandard. For instance, women will appear "highly emotional" or "hysterical" when they display more emotion and concern than men, or "brooding" and "moody" when less. More pertinently, recognition of the man standard enables us to make as much sense as one can of the characterization of pregnancy as a form of illness or a temporary disability. . . .

Levels of Sexism

Sexism can be seen . . . to operate at three levels: institutional sexism, which works on and through the level of social institutions; interpersonal sexism, which works on and through interactions among individuals who are not explicitly mediated by institutional structures; and unconscious sexism, which works at the personal level of the cognitive and affective processes of individuals. It is helpful to sort out these levels in order to explain why some charges of sexism are relatively uncontroversial, while others are difficult to see or evidence conclusively.

Institutional Sexism

Institutional sexism refers to invidious sexual inequalities in the explicit rules and implicit norms governing and structuring social institutions. Religious institutions provide a useful example of how explicit rules and implicit norms structure institutions. In the Catholic Church, for instance, it is an explicit rule that all priests are men and all nuns are women. Only priests can run the church hierarchy, and priests outrank nuns in most decision-making situations. While it is clear how explicit rules can govern and structure institutions, this example can also help us to see that implicit norms also structure Catholic experience and create sexual inequality. While it is no longer widely accepted as an explicit rule that in heterosexual marriage the man is the head of the household and the woman is the helpmeet, it is implied by the relative rank of priests and nuns in the church and by its sacred writings. This implicit norm positions men above women in marriage (as in all other social institutions in which both sexes are present), clearly an invidious sexual inequality. In addition to the more explicitly rule-governed institutions of government, religion, family, health care, and education, there are crucially important informally or implicitly structured institutions prime among them being language, and the sites of cultural and artistic production. . . .

Interpersonal Sexism

Whereas institutional sexism involves the explicit rules and their implicit norms that sustain oppressive social institutions, interpersonal sexism involves interactions between persons that are not governed by explicit rules. Interpersonal sexism comprises actions and other expressions between persons that create, constitute, promote, sustain, and/or exploit invidious sexual inequalities.

The person who is acting in a sexist way or making a sexist expression need not intend sexism; there are intentional and unintentional forms of interpersonal sexism. Here are some examples from our experiences:

- As a child, the girl is not allowed the free play of her brothers; she is prevented by her parents and teachers from engaging in rough-and-tumble play, not included in activities involving building, transportation, etc., not encouraged to try or expected to succeed at sports, mathematics, or leadership activities, and required, unlike her brothers, to do domestic chores.
- In school the teachers require her to speak less and restrain her behavior more than boys. Teachers reward her with better grades for her passivity, but boys exclude her from their games and begin to take the superior attitudes of their fathers.
- In sports she sees males and manhood extolled, females and womanhood ridiculed. Coaches and team-mates insult male athletes by calling them "woman" or "girl," and praise them with the term "man."
- When a man and a woman negotiate a car loan or a home loan, or buy an expensive machine, the salesperson speaks only to the man. Supermarket ads are aimed, meanwhile, at women as housewives.
- In conversations between colleagues men are routinely deferred to while women's remarks are ignored. When a male colleague repeats what a female has said, he is complimented for his good idea.

Sexism is a key motif that unifies this otherwise seemingly disparate set of personal experiences. . . . [S]ociety's ground of legitimacy seems to require that injustice be recognized and socially opposed. Yet the injustice of sexism is built into the very fabric of everyone's everyday experiences from infancy on.

Unconscious Sexism

"Unconscious sexism" refers to the psychological mechanisms and tacit beliefs, emotions, and attitudes that create, constitute, promote, sustain, and/or exploit invidious sexual inequalities. This category will be denied by many as vague, unprovable, or too easily invoked. But there are both conceptual and empirical arguments in favor of its existence. The conceptual argument is that the statistical evidence concerning the lesser lives that women live would be completely puzzling given the legal guarantees of equality for men and women in many countries were it not for the possibility of such unconscious sexism. Institutional and interpersonal sexism cannot alone account for all the data. That implies that there are unconscious attitudes and beliefs that allow persons in positions of power unconsciously to prefer men to women when social rewards are distributed, and yet not to see themselves or be seen as applying sexist standards.

The empirical argument is widely diffused, but accessible. It consists first of all in evidence for the existence of unconscious motivations, which is vast in the psychological literature. Second, there is evidence that when the same work is attributed to a woman it is judged of less value than when attributed to a man.[2] Third, there is evidence that women find it more painful to think of themselves as oppressed, and men find it more painful to think of themselves as the privileged gender. Thus, there is motivation for neither women nor men to think of women as oppressed and men as dominant.[3] Fourth, there is a great deal of evidence from social cognitive psychology to suggest that persons make invidious distinctions among salient social categories, that we tend to amplify them well beyond the real differences between individuals in those categories, and that sex is one of those categories.[4] Now since it surely cannot be argued that men get the worse end of this deal, this fact constitutes evidence for the claim that such cognitive processes tend to create unconscious sexist attitudes and beliefs. There is, no doubt, a great deal more evidence that could be cited, but this much should be sufficient to make the point that unconscious sexism is a real, documented, psychological phenomenon.

Having demonstrated its reality, however, some discussion and examples will be helpful to see how unconscious sexism is manifested and how one might go about discovering it. The key to recognizing unconscious motivations, especially unsavory ones that persons are reluctant to acknowledge in themselves, is to look for decisions or actions that could not be justified by a reasonable assessment of the available evidence. . . . Granting that it is possible that we will not recognize all unconscious (or, indeed, all conscious) sexism, we can still begin by finding the more obvious cases. Consider the following examples:

- A philosophy department is looking to hire a new faculty member. One-third of the applicants are women. One-third of the interview list is made up of women. In the interviews the women are judged as doing worse than the men. The comments afterwards are that they don't seem "as polished" or "professional" as the men. The fact is that the women do not meet the interviewers' expectations of what a philosopher or a faculty member is supposed to look like, a stereotype that includes being a man. . . .
- A drug is being tested for its effectiveness in preventing heart disease. All the research subjects are men. When asked to account for this the research team leader responds that women's hormones would interfere with the study. While it is surely true that the drug could affect women differently from men as a result of female hormones, it is equally true that it could affect men differently from women as a result of male hormones. This symmetry is lost on the research team, who, like most of us, tend to think of women as the ones with the "interfering" or abnormal hormones.

Unconscious sexism often seems to be innocent, in the sense that the beliefs or feelings that make it up are never voiced, and often based on widely shared stereotypes. Whether or not it is innocent surely depends on the degree to which the individual has access to information that counters the unconscious sexist beliefs and attitudes, a condition that depends on larger social factors. Although we do believe that "sexism" names not only a mistake but a prima facie wrong, there are cases where one can commit this wrong and yet not be culpable.

These levels of sexism are, of course, interrelated. Understood as institutional discrimination, sexism concerns the interactions between men and women only as symptoms of a more pervasive problem. Social institutions guide, and on some accounts cause, our interpersonal attitudes. Our self-conceptions and our conception of others are at least partially a product of the social structures through which we interact with one another. . . . Different ways of understanding the interrelations between these levels result in different, and sometimes quite divergent, accounts. Two types of account are prominent in the feminist literature. In the next section we discuss these two types.

Two Feminist Views of Sexism

Though feminists agree that sexism structures our very experience of the world, feminist theories of sexism vary considerably. Nonetheless, they can be very roughly divided into two categories. First, what can be labeled "equality feminism" maintains that social institutions are the primary medium of sexism. Men and women do not differ markedly in their potential capacities, interests, and abilities. Given similar training, men and women would develop fairly similar talents, at least as similar as those between men or between women. Thus if we are to transform society it will require that we resist and undermine those institutions that enforce sex differences and disproportionately deprive women of opportunities to develop highly valued social skills. Equality feminists need not accept what we have above called "the man standard." Rather, most contemporary equality feminists employ measures of social value such as utility, respect for human rights, or hypothetical agreement in order to develop gender-neutral standards by which to judge the opportunities, activities, and proclivities of men and women.

Alternatively, "difference feminists" maintain that unconscious desires are the primary medium of sexism. Accordingly, social institutions are the result, rather than the cause, of sexism. Recently a variety of feminists holding this view have attempted to both articulate the differences between men and women and re-evaluate equality feminism. Some . . . have argued that women's "different voice" involves a greater emphasis on responsiveness, caring, and the maintenance of particular, concrete relationships. This voice is undervalued in society, they argue, because of the dominance of "responsibility"—a notion which involves a strict adherence to principle and which, they argue, typifies the male point of view. Others skeptical of gender neutrality are also skeptical of the idea that caring and relationship maintenance best characterize women's difference. They thus seek to identify a different difference. . . .

Both views aim to transform institutional sexism, interpersonal sexism, and unconscious sexism. They differ, however, over just what form such a transformation would take. For equality feminists the notion that there is a significant difference between men and women, a difference that makes a difference, seems more likely to sustain the global disparity existing between men and women since this disparity has been built on the basis of sex differentiation. For difference feminists, on the other hand, the notion that there is no significant difference between men and women, seems likely to undermine women's emancipation. Since women have been defined and have defined themselves in relation to men, as subordinate to dominant, women's independence depends on discovering, or perhaps imaginatively inventing, a different identity. Importantly, both equality feminists and difference feminists have the same worry. For both, the idea that an attempted transformation of society will result in a mere modification of sexism rather than its elimination is, given its evident though under-acknowledged depth and pervasiveness, a predominant, reasonable, and clearly practical concern. . . .

In conclusion, sexism is alive and well in contemporary Western society, and to an even greater degree in much of the rest of the world. Sexism is a serious form of oppression, and, as such, it is incumbent on decent people to oppose it, though the form that opposition should take remains a serious matter for theorists and activists alike.

Notes

1. A. E. Cudd, "Psychological Explanations of Oppression," in C. Willett, ed., *Theorizing Multiculturalism* (Malden, MA: Blackwell, 1998).
2. V. Valian, *Why So Slow? The Advancement of Women* (Cambridge, MA: MIT Press, 1998).
3. N. Branscombe, "Thinking About One's Gender Group's Privileges or Disadvantages: Consequences for Well-Being in Women and Men," *British Journal of Social Psychology*, 1998, 37:167–84.
4. H. Tajfel, *Human Groups and Social Categories* (Cambridge: Cambridge University Press, 1981).

Study Questions

1. What do Cudd and Jones mean by "sexism"?
2. Does the structure of sexism differ from that of racism?
3. Is sexism implicit in any claim of differences between men and women?
4. How would we know if we were making progress in combating sexism?

D. Prostitution

CHAPTER 28

Value and the Gift of Sexuality

Elizabeth Anderson

Elizabeth Anderson is Professor of Philosophy and Women's Studies at the University of Michigan. She argues against the legalization of prostitution on the grounds that the commodification of sex degrades its value by making it into something impersonal. Sex, instead, should be freely exchanged as a gift based on mutual respect. In response to the claim that people should have the right to enjoy lesser goods in exchange for economic ones, Anderson argues that selling sex in public would lead to the degradation of sex in private.

In legalizing prostitution, the state would accord women property rights in their bodies that they lack at present. This would enable them to legitimately utilize their sexuality for economic gain without being tied to a particular man who provides them with subsistence. This is thought to represent an advance in women's economic freedom over the present situation, which legally permits women only to give away their sexuality, and which enables them to gain subsistence in return only by exclusively committing themselves to one husband or lover at a time.

. . . [P]rostitution is the classic example of how commodification debases a gift value and its giver. The specifically human good of sexual acts exchanged as gifts is founded upon a mutual recognition of the partners as sexually attracted to each other and as affirming an intimate relationship in their mutual offering of themselves to each other. This is a shared good. The couple rejoices in their *union*,

From Elizabeth Anderson, *Value in Ethics and Economics* (Cambridge, MA: Harvard University Press, 1993).

which can be realized only when each partner reciprocates the other's gift *in kind*, offering her own sexuality in the same spirit in which she received the other's—as a genuine offering of the self. The commodification of sexual "services" destroys the kind of reciprocity required to realize human sexuality as a shared good. Each party values the other only instrumentally, not intrinsically. But the nature of the good exchanged implies a particular degradation of the prostitute. The customer's cash payment is impersonal and fully alienable. In paying the prostitute he yields no power over his person to her. The prostitute sells her own sexuality, which is necessarily embodied in her person. In appropriating her sexuality for his own use, the customer expresses a (de)valuation of women as rightfully male sexual property, as objects to be used for men's own sexual purposes, which need not respond to the woman's own personal needs.

This argument shows that commodified sex is degraded and degrading to the prostitute. It does not show that the sale of sexual services should be prohibited. Why shouldn't people have the freedom to enjoy inferior goods? And why shouldn't women have the freedom to get something of economic value from their sexuality? . . . [T]he state has a case for prohibiting or restricting commodification of a good if doing so increases freedom—significant opportunities for people to value different kinds of goods in different ways—or if it increases autonomy; that is, the power of people to value goods in ways they reflectively endorse.

It may appear that commodification promotes . . . freedom. Liberals traditionally address plural and conflicting ideals by giving their adherents private spaces to pursue them, protected from state-sponsored interference by adherents of rival ideals. Let those who value sexuality as a higher good enjoy it in non-commodified personal relations, and those who value it as a commodity exchange it on the market. Feminist theory calls into question the viability of this proposal. Although popular ideology represents present modes of non-commodified sexuality in the sphere of personal relations as independent of and sharply contrasted with its commodified forms, there are deep connections between the ways women's sexuality is valued by men in both spheres. When heterosexual masculine identity is partly defined in terms of the power to have sex with a woman, prostitution and pornography supply the unmet demand for sexual intercourse generated internally in the personal sphere; they also provide techniques and models for sexual gratification that men import back into the sphere of personal relations and make normative for their intimate female partners there. The same "private" masculine gender identity creates a demand for virgins, lovers, wives, and prostitutes alike. Women's sexuality is still valued as male property in both spheres; the only question is how many men have rights to it.

I do not claim that women are treated only as sexual property in the personal sphere. I claim that an aspect of masculine identity imposes an appropriative, unshared dimension on heterosexual intercourse there that contradicts the valuational aspirations of both intimacy and commitment. The same power to appropriate a woman's sexuality that is partly definitive of manhood, the same masculine sexual desire, is gratified in personal and commodified sexual relations. If the state took up this same perspective and recognized women's sexuality as just another kind of property, no social space would be left to affirm women's experiences of rape as a worse crime, a deeper violation of the self, than robbery. . . . If women's sexuality is legally valued as a commodity anywhere in society, it would be even more difficult than it already is to establish insulated social spheres where it can be exclusively and fully valued as a genuinely shared and personal good, where women themselves can be sexually valued in ways fully consonant with their own dignity. The full realization of significant opportunities to value heterosexual relationships as shared and personal goods may therefore require that women's sexuality not be commodified. Pluralistic freedom, as well as the dignity of women, may therefore be enhanced by barriers to commodifying sexuality.

The case against prostitution on grounds of autonomy is clearer. The prostitute, in selling her sexuality to a man, alienates a good necessarily embodied in her person to him and thereby subjects herself to his commands. Her actions under contract express not her own valuations but the will of her customer. Her actions between sales express not her own valuations but the will of her pimp. Prostitution does not enhance women's autonomy over their sexuality—it simply constitutes another mode by which men can appropriate it for their own uses. The realization of women's autonomy requires that some goods embodied in their persons, including their own sexuality, remain market-inalienable.

These arguments establish the legitimacy of a state interest in prohibiting prostitution, but not a conclusive case for prohibition. Given the paucity of economic opportunities available to many women, they may have no alternative to selling their sexual services for money. If the prohibition of prostitution is to serve women's interests in freedom and autonomy, it should not function so as to drive them to starvation. It can serve these interests only where expanded economic opportunities eliminate women's need to resort to prostitution. (These interests already support the prohibition of pimping.) My arguments also do not show that the sale of sexual services cannot have a legitimate place in a just civil society. One could imagine a worthwhile practice of professional sex therapy aimed at helping people liberate themselves from perverse, patriarchal forms of sexuality. Such a practice would not be governed by the market norms that make present forms of prostitution objectionable. Professionals do not alienate control over their actions in selling them, but govern their activity by reflectively endorsed norms internal to the non-market ideals of their professions. The profession envisioned might help men eliminate the ways commodified conceptions of women's sexuality inform their valuations of women in the personal sphere. This possibility illustrates . . . that what confers commodity status on a good is not that people pay for it, but that exclusively market norms govern its production, exchange, and enjoyment. . . .

Study Questions

1. Does prostitution debase sex?
2. Would selling sex in public affect the role of sex in private relationships?
3. Would selling sex in public diminish anyone's freedom?
4. Do Anderson's arguments against the practice of paying women for sex also apply to the practice of paying men for sex?

CHAPTER 29

Taking Money for Bodily Services

Martha C. Nussbaum

Martha C. Nussbaum is Professor of Law and Ethics at the University of Chicago. She maintains that our attitudes toward prostitution reflect prejudice, not reason. In her view, if prostitution were legalized, prostitutes would be better protected.

II

Prostitution ... [is today] ... widely stigmatized. ... Two factors stand out as sources of stigma. One is that prostitution is widely held to be immoral; the other is that prostitution (frequently at least) is bound up with gender hierarchy, with ideas that women and their sexuality are in need of male domination and control, and the related idea that women should be available to men to provide an outlet for their sexual desires. The immorality view would be hard to defend today as a justification for the legal regulation of prostitution, and perhaps even for its moral denunciation. People thought prostitution was immoral because they thought nonreproductive and especially extramarital sex was immoral; the prostitute was seen, typically, as a dangerous figure whose whole career was given over to lust. But female lust was (and still often is) commonly seen as bad and dangerous, so prostitution was seen as bad and dangerous. Some people would still defend these views today, but it seems inconsistent to do so if one is not prepared to repudiate other forms of nonmarital sexual activity on an equal basis. We have to grant, I think, that the most common reason

---

From Martha C. Nussbaum, "Whether from Reason or Prejudice: Taking Money for Bodily Services," *Journal of Legal Services* 27 (1998). Section I is ommitted.

for the stigma attached to prostitution is a weak reason, at least as a public reason: a moralistic view about female sexuality that is rarely consistently applied (to premarital sex, for example) and that seems unable to justify restriction on the activities of citizens who have different views of what is good and proper. At any rate, it seems hard to use the stigma so incurred to justify perpetuating stigma through criminalization, unless one is prepared to accept a wide range of . . . laws that interfere with chosen consensual activities, something that most feminist attackers of prostitution rarely wish to do.

More promising as a source of good moral arguments might be the stigma incurred by the connection of prostitution with gender hierarchy. But what is the connection, and how exactly does gender hierarchy explain pervasive stigma? It is only a small minority of people for whom prostitution is viewed in a negative light because of its collaboration with male supremacy; for only a small minority of people at any time have been reflective feminists, concerned with the eradication of inequality. Such people will view the prostitute as they view veiled women or women in purdah: with sympathetic anger, as victims of an unjust system. This reflective feminist critique, then, does not explain why prostitutes are actually stigmatized, held in disdain—both because it is not pervasive enough and because it leads to sympathy rather than to disdain.

The way that gender hierarchy actually explains stigma is a very different way, a way that turns out in the end to be just another form of the immorality charge. People committed to gender hierarchy, and determined to ensure that the dangerous sexuality of women is controlled by men, frequently have viewed the prostitute, a sexually active woman, as a threat to male control of women. They therefore become determined either to repress the occupation itself by criminalization or, if they also think that male sexuality needs such an outlet and that this outlet ultimately defends marriage by giving male desire a safely debased outlet, to keep it within bounds by close regulation. . . .

In short, sex hierarchy causes stigma, commonly, not through feminist critique but through a far more questionable set of social meanings, meanings that anyone concerned with justice for women should call into question. For it is these same meanings that are also used to justify the seclusion of women, the veiling of women, and the genital mutilation of women. The view boils down to the view that women are essentially immoral and dangerous and will be kept in control by men only if men carefully engineer things so that they do not get out of bounds. The prostitute, being seen as the uncontrolled and sexually free woman, is in this picture seen as particularly dangerous, both necessary to society and in need of constant subjugation. As an honest woman, a woman of dignity, she will wreck society. . . .

It appears, then, that the stigma associated with prostitution has an origin that feminists have good reason to connect with unjust background conditions and to decry as both unequal and irrational, based on a hysterical fear of women's unfettered sexuality. There may be other good arguments against the legality of prostitution, but the existence of widespread stigma all by itself does not appear to be among them. So long as prostitution is stigmatized, people are injured by that stigmatization, and it is a real injury to a person not to have dignity and self-respect in her own society. But that real injury (as with the comparable real injury to the dignity and self-respect of interracial couples or of lesbians and gay men) is not best handled by continued legal strictures against the prostitute and can be better dealt with in other ways: for example, by fighting discrimination against these people and taking measures to promote their dignity. . . .

III

Pervasive stigma itself, then, does not appear to provide a good reason for the continued criminalization of prostitution, any more than it does for the illegality of interracial marriage. Nor does the stigma in question even appear to ground a sound *moral* argument against prostitution. This is not, however, the end of the issue: for there are a number of other significant arguments that have been made to support criminalization. . . . [L]et us now turn to those arguments.

1. *Prostitution Involves Health Risks and Risks of Violence.*   To this we can make two replies. First, insofar as this is true, as it clearly is, the problem is made much worse by the illegality of prostitution, which prevents adequate supervision, encourages the control of pimps, and discourages health checking. . . .

To the extent to which risks remain an inevitable part of the way of life, we must now ask what general view of the legality of risky undertakings we wish to defend. Do we ever want to rule out risky bargains simply because they harm the agent? Or do we require a showing of harm to others (as might be possible in the case of gambling, for example)? Whatever position we take on this complicated question, we will almost certainly be led to conclude that prostitution lies well within the domain of the legally acceptable: for it is probably less risky than boxing, another activity in which working-class people try to survive and flourish by subjecting their bodies to some risk of harm. There is a stronger case for paternalistic regulation of boxing than of prostitution, and externalities (the glorification of violence as example to the young) make boxing at least as morally problematic, probably more so. And yet I would not defend the criminalization of boxing, and I doubt that very many Americans would either. Sensible regulation of both prostitution and boxing, by contrast, seems reasonable and compatible with personal liberty. . . .

2. *The Prostitute Has No Autonomy; Her Activities Are Controlled by Others.* This argument does not serve to distinguish prostitution from very many types of bodily service performed by working-class women. The factory worker does worse on the scale of autonomy, and the domestic servant no better. I think this point expresses a legitimate moral concern: a person's life seems deficient in flourishing if it consists only of a form of work that is totally out of the control and direction of the person herself. . . . It certainly does not help the problem to criminalize prostitution—any more than it would be to criminalize factory work or domestic service. A woman will not exactly achieve more control and "truly human functioning" by becoming unemployed. What we should instead think about are ways to promote more control over choice of activities, more variety, and more general humanity in the types of work that are actually available to people with little education and few options. That would be a lot more helpful than removing one of the options they actually have.

3. *Prostitution Involves the Invasion of One's Intimate Bodily Space.* This argument does not seem to support the legal regulation of prostitution so long as the invasion in question is consensual—that is, that the prostitute is not kidnapped, fraudulently enticed, a child beneath the age of consent, or under duress against leaving if she should choose to leave. . . . The argument does not even appear to support a moral criticism of prostitution, unless one is prepared to make a moral criticism of all sexual contact that does not involve love or marriage.

4. *Prostitution Makes It Harder for People to Form Relationships of Intimacy and Commitment.* This argument is prominently made by Elizabeth Anderson in defense of the criminalization of prostitution. The first question we should ask is, Is this true? People still appear to

fall in love in the Netherlands and Germany and Sweden; they also fell in love in ancient Athens, where prostitution was not only legal but also, probably, publicly subsidized. One type of relationship does not, in fact, appear to remove the need for the other—any more than a Jackie Collins novel removes the desire to read Proust. Proust has a specific type of value that is by no means found in Jackie Collins, so people who want that value will continue to seek out Proust, and there is no reason to think that the presence of Jackie Collins on the bookstand will confuse Proust lovers into thinking that Proust is really like Jackie Collins. So too, one supposes, with love in the Netherlands: people who want relationships of intimacy and commitment continue to seek them out for the special value they provide, and they do not have much trouble telling the difference between one sort of relationship and another, despite the availability of both.

Second, one should ask which women Anderson has in mind. Is she saying that the criminalization of prostitution would facilitate the formation of love relationships on the part of the women who were (or would have been) prostitutes? Or is she saying that the unavailability of prostitution as an option for working-class women would make it easier for romantic middle-class women to have the relationships they desire? The former claim is implausible, since it is hard to see how reinforcing the stigma against prostitutes or preventing some poor women from taking one of the few employment options they might have would be likely to improve their human relations. The latter claim might possibly be true (though it is hardly obvious), but it seems a repugnant idea, which I am sure Anderson would not endorse, that we should make poor women poorer so that middle-class women can find love. Third, one should ask Anderson whether she is prepared to endorse the large number of arguments of this form that might plausibly be made in the realm of popular culture and, if not, whether she has any way of showing how she could reject those as involving an unacceptable infringement of liberty and yet allowing the argument about prostitution that she endorses. For it seems plausible that making rock music illegal would increase the likelihood that people would listen to Mozart and Beethoven, that making Jackie Collins illegal would make it more likely that people would turn to Joyce Carol Oates, that making commercial advertising illegal would make it more likely that we would appraise products with high-minded ideas of value in our minds, and that making television illegal would improve children's reading skills. What is certain, however, is that we would and do utterly reject those ideas (we do not even seriously entertain them) because we do not want to live in Plato's *Republic,* with our cultural options dictated by a group of wise guardians, however genuinely sound their judgments may be.

5. *The Prostitute Alienates Her Sexuality on the Market; She Turns Her Sexual Organs and Acts into Commodities.*   Is this true? It seems implausible to claim that the prostitute alienates her sexuality just on the grounds that she provides sexual services to a client for a fee. . . . The prostitute still has her sexuality; she can use it on her own, apart from the relationship with the client, just as the domestic servant may cook for her family and clean her own house. She can also cease to be a prostitute, and her sexuality will still be with her, and hers, if she does. So she has not even given anyone a monopoly on those services, far less given them over into someone else's hands. The real issue . . . seems to be the degree of choice she exercises over the acts she performs. But is even this a special issue for the prostitute . . . ? Freedom to choose how one works is a luxury, highly desirable indeed, but a feature of few jobs that nonaffluent people perform.

As for the claim that the prostitute turns her sexuality into a commodity, we must ask what that means. If it means only that she accepts a fee for sexual services, then that is obvious; but nothing further has been said that would show us why this is a bad thing. . . .

If, on the other hand, we try to interpret the claim of "commodification" using the narrow technical definition of "commodity" used by the Uniform Commercial Code, the claim is plainly false. For that definition stresses the "fungible" nature of the goods in question, and "fungible" goods are, in turn, defined as goods "of which any unit is, by nature or usage of trade, the equivalent of any other like unit." While we may not think that the soul or inner world of a prostitute is of deep concern to the customer, she is usually not regarded as simply a set of units fully interchangeable with other units. Prostitutes are probably somewhat more fungible than bassoon players, but not totally so. What seems to be the real issue is that the woman is not attended to as an individual, not considered as a special unique being. But that is true of many ways people treat one another in many areas of life, and it seems implausible that we should use that kind of disregard as a basis for criminalization. It may not even be immoral: for surely we cannot deeply know all the people with whom we have dealings in life, and many of those dealings are just fine without deep knowledge. So our moral question boils down to the question, Is sex without deep personal knowledge always immoral? It seems to me officious and presuming to use one's own experience to give an affirmative answer to this question, given that people have such varied experiences of sexuality. . . .

6. *The Prostitute's Activity Is Shaped By, and in Turn Perpetuates, Male Dominance of Women.* The institution of prostitution as it has most often existed is certainly shaped by aspects of male domination of women. As I have argued, it is shaped by the perception that female sexuality is dangerous and needs careful regulation, that male sexuality is rapacious and needs a "safe" outlet, that sex is dirty and degrading, and that only a degraded woman is an appropriate sexual object. Nor have prostitutes standardly been treated with respect or been given the dignity one might think proper to a fellow human being. They share this with working-class people of many types in many ages; but, there is no doubt that there are particular features of the disrespect that derive from male supremacy and the desire to lord it over women—as well as from a tendency to link sex to (female) defilement that is common in the history of Western European culture. . . .

Prostitution is hardly alone in being shaped by, and in reinforcing, male dominance. . . .

[O]ne might argue that the institution of marriage as has most frequently been practiced both expresses and reinforces male dominance. It would be right to use law to change the most iniquitous features of that institution—protecting women from domestic violence and marital rape, giving women equal property and custody rights, and improving their exit options by intelligent shaping of the divorce law. But to rule that marriage as such should be illegal on the grounds that it reinforces male dominance would be an excessive intrusion on liberty, even if one should believe marriage irredeemably unequal. So too, I think, with prostitution: what seems right is to use law to protect the bodily safety of prostitutes from assault, to protect their rights to their incomes against the extortionate behavior of pimps, to protect poor women in developing countries from forced trafficking and fraudulent offers, and to guarantee their full civil rights in the countries where they end up—to make them, in general, equals under the law, both civil and criminal. But the criminalization of prostitution seems to pose a major obstacle to that equality. . . .

7. *Prostitution Is a Trade That People Do Not Enter by Choice; Therefore the Bargains People Make within It Should Not Be Regarded as Real Bargains.* Here we must distinguish three cases. First is the case where the woman's entry into prostitution is caused by some type of conduct that would otherwise be criminal: kidnapping, assault, drugging, rape,

statutory rape, blackmail, a fraudulent offer. Here we may certainly judge that the woman's choice is not a real choice and that the law should take a hand in punishing her coercer. This is a terrible problem currently in developing countries; international human rights organizations are right to make it a major focus. . . .

Different is the case of an adult woman who enters prostitution because of bad economic options: . . . because there is no other employment available to her, and so forth. This too, we should insist, is a case where autonomy has been infringed, but in a different way. . . .

This seems to me the truly important issue raised by prostitution. . . . [I]t is not an option many women choose with alacrity when many other options are on their plate. This might not be so in some hypothetical culture in which prostitutes have legal protection, dignity, and respect and the status of skilled practitioner. . . . But it is true now in most societies, given the reality of the (albeit irrational) stigma attaching to prostitution. But the important thing to realize is that this is not an issue that permits us to focus on prostitution in isolation from the economic situation of women in a society generally. Certainly it will not be ameliorated by the criminalization of prostitution, which reduces poor women's options still further. We may grant that poor women do not have enough options and that society has been unjust to them in not extending more options, while nonetheless respecting and honoring the choices they actually make in reduced circumstances. . . .

IV

The stigma traditionally attached to prostitution is based on a collage of beliefs, most of which are not rationally defensible and which should be especially vehemently rejected by feminists: beliefs about the evil character of female sexuality, the rapacious character of male sexuality, the essentially marital and reproductive character of "good" women and "good" sex. Worries about subordination more recently raised by feminists are much more serious concerns, but they apply to many types of work poor women do. Concerns about force and fraud should be extremely urgent concerns of the international women's movement. Where these conditions do not obtain, feminists should view prostitutes as (usually) poor working women with few options, not as threats to the intimacy and commitment that many women and men (including, no doubt, many prostitutes) seek. This does not mean that we should not be concerned about ways in which prostitution as currently practiced, even in the absence of force and fraud, undermines the dignity of women, just as domestic service in the past undermined the dignity of members of a given race or class. But the correct response to this problem seems to be to work to enhance the economic autonomy and the personal dignity of members of that class, not to rule off-limits an option that may be the only livelihood for many poor women and to further stigmatize women who already make their living this way. . . .

Women in many parts of the world are especially likely to be stuck at a low level of mechanical functioning, whether as agricultural laborers, factory workers, or prostitutes. The real question to be faced is how to expand the options and opportunities such workers face, how to increase the humanity inherent in their work, and how to guarantee that workers of all sorts are treated with dignity. In the further pursuit of these questions, we need, on balance, more studies of women's credit unions and fewer studies of prostitution.

Study Questions

1. How does Nussbaum respond to the claim that prostitutes lack autonomy?
2. How does Nussbaum respond to Anderson's claim that prostitution erodes the value of non-commodified sex?
3. Do you agree with Nussbaum's claim that the institution of marriage as has most frequently been practiced reinforces male dominance?
4. Would the legalization of prostitution be beneficial to prostitutes?

CHAPTER 30

Markets in Women's Sexual Labor

Debra Satz

Debra Satz is Professor of Philosophy at Stanford University. She argues that markets in reproduction are unlike other labor markets in ways that make a moral difference. Of particular relevance is that women form a social and economically disadvantaged group that is viewed as inferior to men. Satz argues that prostitution is morally wrong because it perpetuates this view of women as subordinate. However, the immorality of prostitution on egalitarian grounds does not entail that prostitution should be illegal. Indeed, given that legalization would help undermine the image of the prostitute as of lesser moral status, Satz concludes that, despite being immoral, prostitution should not be banned.

There is a widely shared intuition that markets are inappropriate for some kinds of human endeavor: that some things simply should not be bought and sold. For example, virtually everyone believes that love and friendship should have no price. The sale of other human capacities is disputed, but many people believe that there is something about sexual and reproductive activities that makes their sale inappropriate. I have called the thesis supported by this intuition the asymmetry thesis.[1] Those who hold the asymmetry thesis believe that markets in reproduction and sex are asymmetric to other labor markets. They think that treating sexual and reproductive capacities as commodities, as goods to be developed and exchanged for a price, is worse than treating our other capacities as commodities. They think that there is something wrong with commercial surrogacy and prostitution that is not wrong with teaching and professional sports.

From Debra Satz, "Markets in Women's Sexual Labor," *Ethics* 106 (1995).

The intuition that there is a distinction between markets in different human capacities is a deep one, even among people who ultimately think that the distinction does not justify legally forbidding sales of reproductive capacity and sex. I accept this intuition, which I continue to probe in this article. In particular, I ask: What justifies taking an asymmetric attitude toward markets in our sexual capacities? What, if anything, is problematic about a woman selling her sexual as opposed to her secretarial labor? And, if the apparent asymmetry can be explained and justified, what implications follow for public policy? . . .

Below I survey two types of arguments which can be used to support the asymmetry thesis: (1) essentialist arguments that the sale of sexual labor is intrinsically wrong because it is alienating or contrary to human flourishing and happiness; and (2) my own egalitarian argument that the sale of sex is wrong because, given the background conditions within which it occurs, it tends to reinforce gender inequality. I . . . claim that contemporary prostitution is wrong because it promotes injustice, and not because it makes people less happy.

The Essentialist Approach

. . . [T]he essentialist thesis views the commodification of sex as an assault on personal dignity.[2] Prostitution degrades the prostitute. Elizabeth Anderson, for example, discusses the effect of commodification on the nature of sex as a shared good, based on the recognition of mutual attraction. In commercial sex, each party now values the other only instrumentally, not intrinsically. And, while both parties are thus prevented from enjoying a shared good, it is worse for the prostitute. The customer merely surrenders a certain amount of cash; the prostitute cedes her body: the prostitute is thus degraded to the status of a thing. Call this the degradation objection.

I share the intuition that the failure to treat others as persons is morally significant; it is wrong to treat people as mere things. But I am skeptical as to whether this intuition supports the conclusion that prostitution is wrong. Consider the contrast between slavery and prostitution. Slavery was, in Orlando Patterson's memorable phrase, a form of "social death": it denied to enslaved individuals the ability to press claims, to be—in their own right—sources of value and interest. But the mere sale of the use of someone's capacities does not necessarily involve a failure of this kind, on the part of either the buyer or the seller. Many forms of labor, perhaps most, cede some control

of a person's body to others. Such control can range from requirements to be in a certain place at a certain time (e.g., reporting to the
office), to requirements that a person (e.g., a professional athlete)
eat certain foods and get certain amounts of sleep, or maintain good
humor in the face of the offensive behavior of others (e.g., airline
stewardesses). Some control of our capacities by others does not seem
to be ipso facto destructive of our dignity. Whether the purchase of
a form of human labor power will have this negative consequence
will depend on background social macrolevel and microlevel institutions. Minimum wages, worker participation and control, health
and safety regulations, maternity and paternity leave, restrictions on
specific performance, and the right to "exit" one's job are all features
which attenuate the objectionable aspects of treating people's labor
as a mere economic input. The advocates of prostitution's wrongness
in virtue of its connection to selfhood, flourishing, and degradation have not shown that a system of regulated prostitution would be
unable to respond to their worries. In particular, they have not established that there is something wrong with prostitution irrespective of
its cultural and historical context.

There is, however, another way of interpreting the degradation objection which draws a connection between the current practice of
prostitution and the lesser social status of women. This connection
is not a matter of the logic of prostitution per se but of the fact that
contemporary prostitution degrades women by treating them as the
sexual servants of men. In current prostitution, prostitutes are overwhelmingly women and their clients are almost exclusively men. Prostitution, in conceiving of a class of women as needed to satisfy male
sexual desire, represents women as sexual servants to men. The degradation objection, so understood, can be seen as a way of expressing
an egalitarian concern since there is no reciprocal ideology which
represents men as servicing women's sexual needs. It is to this egalitarian understanding of prostitution's wrongness that I turn in the
next section.

The Egalitarian Approach

While the essentialists rightly call our attention to the different relation we have with our capacities and external things, they overstate
the nature of the difference between our sexual capacities and our
other capacities with respect to our personhood, flourishing, and
dignity. They are also insufficiently attentive to the background

conditions in which commercial sex exchanges take place. [Another] account of prostitution's wrongness stresses its causal relationship to gender inequality. . . .

On my view, there are two important dimensions of gender inequality, often conflated. The first dimension concerns inequalities in the distribution of income, wealth, and opportunity. . . . Inequalities in income and opportunity form an important part of the backdrop against which prostitution must be viewed. While there are many possible routes into prostitution, the largest number of women who participate in it are poor, young, and uneducated. Labor market inequalities will be part of any plausible explanation of why many women "choose" to enter into prostitution.

The second dimension of gender inequality does not concern income and opportunity but status. In many contemporary contexts, women are viewed and treated as inferior to men. . . .

Both forms of inequality—income inequality and status inequality—potentially bear on the question of prostitution's wrongness. Women's decisions to enter into prostitution must be viewed against the background of their unequal life chances and their unequal opportunities for income and rewarding work. The extent to which women face a highly constrained range of options will surely be relevant to whether, and to what degree, we view their choices as autonomous. Some women may actually loathe or judge as inferior the lives of prostitution they "choose." Economic inequality may thus shape prostitution.

We can also ask, Does prostitution itself shape employment inequalities between men and women? In general, whenever there are significant inequalities between groups, those on the disadvantageous side will be disproportionately allocated to subordinate positions. What they do, the positions they occupy, will serve to reinforce negative and disempowering images of themselves. In this sense, prostitution can have an effect on labor-market inequality, associating women with certain stereotypes. For example, images reinforced by prostitution may make it less likely for women to be hired in certain jobs. Admittedly the effect of prostitution on labor-market inequality, if it exists at all, will be small. Other roles which women disproportionately occupy—secretaries, housecleaners, babysitters, waitresses, and saleswomen—will be far more significant in reinforcing (as well as constituting) a gender-segregated division of labor.

I do not think it is plausible to attribute to prostitution a direct causal role in income inequality between men and women. But I believe that it is plausible to maintain that prostitution makes an important and direct contribution to women's inferior social status. Prostitution shapes and is itself shaped by custom and culture, by cultural meanings about the importance of sex, about the nature of women's sexuality and male desire.

If prostitution is wrong it is because of its effects on how men perceive women and on how women perceive themselves. In our society, prostitution represents women as the sexual servants of men. It supports and embodies the widely held belief that men have strong sex drives which must be satisfied—largely through gaining access to some woman's body. This belief underlies the mistaken idea that prostitution is the "oldest" profession, since it is seen as a necessary consequence of human (i.e., male) nature. It also underlies the traditional conception of marriage, in which a man owned not only his wife's property but her body as well. It should not fail to startle us that until recently, most states did not recognize the possibility of "real rape" in marriage.[3]

Why is the idea that women must service men's sexual needs an image of inequality and not mere difference? My argument suggests that there are two primary, contextual reasons:

First, in our culture, there is no reciprocal social practice which represents men as serving women's sexual needs. Men are gigolos and paid escorts—but their sexuality is not seen as an independent capacity whose use women can buy. It is not part of the identity of a class of men that they will service women's sexual desires. Indeed, male prostitutes overwhelmingly service other men and not women. Men are not depicted as fully capable of commercially alienating their sexuality to women; but prostitution depicts women as sexual servants of men.

Second, the idea that prostitution embodies an idea of women as inferior is strongly suggested by the high incidence of rape and violence against prostitutes, as well as the fact that few men seek out or even contemplate prostitutes as potential marriage partners. While all women in our society are potential targets of rape and violence, the mortality rates for women engaged in streetwalking prostitution are roughly forty times higher than that of nonprostitute women.

My suggestion is that prostitution depicts an image of gender inequality, by constituting one class of women as inferior. Prostitution is a "theater" of inequality—it displays for us a practice in which women are subordinated to men. This is especially the case where women are forcibly controlled by their (male) pimps. It follows from my conception of prostitution that it need not have such a negative effect when the prostitute is male.

If, through its negative image of women as sexual servants of men, prostitution reinforces women's inferior status in society, then it is wrong. Even though men can be and are prostitutes, I think that it is unlikely that we will find such negative image effects on men as a group. Individual men may be degraded in individual acts of prostitution: men as a group are not.

Granting all of the above, one objection to the equality approach to prostitution's wrongness remains. Is prostitution's negative image effect greater than that produced by other professions in which women largely service men, for example, secretarial labor? What is special about prostitution?

The negative image effect undoubtedly operates outside the domain of prostitution. But there are two significant differences between prostitution and other gender-segregated professions.

First, most people believe that prostitution, unlike secretarial work, is especially objectionable. Holding such moral views of prostitution constant, if prostitution continues to be primarily a female occupation, then the existence of prostitution will disproportionately fuel negative images of women. Second, and relatedly, the particular image of women in prostitution is more of an image of inferiority than that of a secretary. The image embodies a greater amount of objectification, of representing the prostitute as an object without a will of her own. Prostitutes are far more likely to be victims of violence than are secretaries: the mortality rate of women in prostitution is forty times that of other women. Prostitutes are also far more likely to be raped: a prostitute's "no" does not, to the male she services, mean no.

My claim is that, unless such arguments about prostitution's causal role in sustaining a form of gender inequality can be supported, I am not persuaded that something is morally wrong with markets in sex. In particular, I do not find arguments about the necessary relationship between commercial sex and diminished flourishing and degradation convincing. If prostitution is wrong, it is not because of its effects on happiness or personhood (effects which are shared with other forms of wage-labor); rather, it is because the sale of women's sexual labor may have adverse consequences for achieving a significant form of equality between men and women. My argument for the asymmetry thesis, if correct, connects prostitution to injustice. I now turn to the question of whether, even if we assume that prostitution is wrong under current conditions, it should remain illegal.

Should Prostitution Be Legalized?

It is important to distinguish between prostitution's wrongness and the legal response that we are entitled to make to that wrongness. Even if prostitution is wrong, we may not be justified in prohibiting it if that prohibition makes the facts in virtue of which it is wrong worse, or if its costs are too great for other important values, such as autonomy and privacy. For example, even if someone accepts that the contemporary division of labor in the family is wrong, they may still reasonably object to government surveillance of the family's division of household chores. To determine whether such surveillance is justified, we need to know more about the fundamental interests at stake, the costs of surveillance and the availability of alternative mechanisms for promoting equality in families. While I think that there is no acceptable view which would advocate governmental surveillance of family chores, there remains a range of plausible views about the appropriate scope of state intervention and, indeed, the appropriate scope of equality considerations.

It is also important to keep in mind that in the case of prostitution, as with pornography and hate speech, narrowing the discussion of solutions to the single question of whether to ban or not to ban shows a poverty of imagination. There are many ways of challenging existing cultural values about the appropriate division of labor in the family and the nature of women's sexual and reproductive capacities—for example, education, consciousness-raising groups, changes in employee leave policies, comparable worth programs, etc. The law is not the only way to provide women with incentives to refrain from participating in prostitution. Nonetheless, we do need to decide what the best legal policy toward prostitution should be.

I begin with an assessment of the policy which we now have. The United States is one of the few developed Western countries which criminalizes prostitution. Denmark, the Netherlands, West Germany, Sweden, Switzerland, and Austria all have legalized prostitution, although in some of these countries it is restricted by local ordinances. Where prostitution is permitted, it is closely regulated.

Suppose that we accept that gender equality is a legitimate goal of social policy. The question is whether the current legal prohibition on prostitution in the United States promotes gender equality. The answer I think is that it clearly does not. The current legal policies in the United States arguably exacerbate the factors in virtue of which prostitution is wrong.

The current prohibition on prostitution renders the women who engage in the practice vulnerable. First, the participants in the practice seek assistance from pimps in lieu of the contractual and legal remedies which are denied them. Male pimps may protect women prostitutes from their customers and from the police, but the system of pimp-run prostitution has enormous negative effects on the women at the lowest rungs of prostitution. Second, prohibition of prostitution raises the dilemma of the "double bind": if we prevent prostitution without greater redistribution of income, wealth, and opportunities, we deprive poor women of one way—in some circumstances the only way—of improving their condition. Analogously, we do not solve the problem of homelessness by criminalizing it.

Furthermore, women are disproportionately punished for engaging in commercial sex acts. Many state laws make it a worse crime to sell sex than to buy it. Consequently, pimps and clients ("johns") are rarely prosecuted. In some jurisdictions, patronizing a prostitute is not illegal. The record of arrests and convictions is also highly asymmetric. . . .

There is an additional reason why banning prostitution seems an inadequate response to the problem of gender inequality and which suggests a lack of parallel with the case of commercial surrogacy. Banning prostitution would not by itself—does not—eliminate it. While there is reason to think that making commercial surrogacy arrangements illegal or unenforceable would diminish their occurrence, no such evidence exists about prostitution. No city has eliminated prostitution merely through criminalization. Instead, criminalized prostitution thrives as a black market activity in which pimps substitute for law as the mechanism for enforcing contracts. It thereby makes the lives of prostitutes worse than they might otherwise be and without clearly counteracting prostitution's largely negative image of women. . . .

Conclusion

If the arguments I have offered here are correct, then prostitution is wrong in virtue of its contributions to perpetuating a pervasive form of inequality. In different circumstances, with different assumptions about women and their role in society, I do not think that prostitution would be especially troubling—no more troubling than many other labor markets currently allowed. It follows, then, that in other circumstances, the asymmetry thesis would be denied or less strongly felt. While the idea that prostitution is intrinsically degrading is a powerful intuition . . . I believe that this intuition is itself bound up with well-entrenched views of male gender identity and women's sexual role in the context of that identity. If we are troubled by prostitution, as I think we should be, then we should direct much of our energy to putting forward alternative models of egalitarian relations between men and women.

Notes

1. Debra Satz, "Markets in Women's Reproductive Labor," *Philosophy and Public Affairs* 21 (1992): 107–31.
2. Elizabeth Anderson, *Value in Ethics and Economics* (Cambridge, Mass.: Harvard University Press, 1993), p. 45.
3. Susan Estrich, *Real Rape* (Cambridge, Mass.: Harvard University Press, 1987).

Study Questions

1. How does Satz respond to Anderson's claim that prostitution erodes the value of noncommodified sex?
2. Do you agree that women are economically and socially disadvantaged compared to men?
3. Do the reasons Satz presents against the morality of female prostitution also apply to the morality of male prostitution?
4. Should immoral activity ever be legal?

E. Pornography

CHAPTER 31

Pornography, Oppression, and Freedom

Helen E. Longino

Helen E. Longino is Professor of Philosophy at Stanford University. She argues that the production and distribution of pornography is immoral, because it is harmful to people. Furthermore, legal restrictions on pornography are appropriate and not incompatible with adherence to constitutional rights.

Introduction

. . . One of the beneficial results of the sexual revolution has been a growing acceptance of the distinction between questions of sexual mores and questions of morality. This distinction underlies the old slogan, "Make love, not war," and takes harm to others as the defining characteristic of immorality. What is immoral is behavior which causes injury to or violation of another person or people. Such injury may be physical or it may be psychological. To cause pain to another, to lie to another, to hinder another in the exercise of her or his rights, to exploit another, to degrade another, to misrepresent and slander another are instances of immoral behavior. Masturbation or engaging voluntarily in sexual intercourse with another consenting adult of the same or the other sex, as long as neither injury nor violation of either individual or another is involved, is not immoral. Some sexual behavior is morally objectionable, but not because of its sexual character. Thus, adultery is immoral not because it involves sexual intercourse with someone to whom one is not legally married, but because

---

From *Take Back the Night*, ed. Laura Lederer, New York, William Morrow & Co., 1980. Reprinted by permission of the author.

it involves breaking a promise (of sexual and emotional fidelity to one's spouse). Sadistic, abusive, or forced sex is immoral because it injures and violates another.

The detachment of sexual chastity from moral virtue implies that we cannot condemn forms of sexual behavior merely because they strike us as distasteful or subversive of the Protestant work ethic, or because they depart from standards of behavior we have individually adopted. It has thus seemed to imply that no matter how offensive we might find pornography, we must tolerate it in the name of freedom from illegitimate repression. I wish to argue that this is not so, that pornography is immoral because it is harmful to people.

What Is Pornography?

I define pornography as *verbal or pictorial explicit representations of sexual behavior that*, in the words of the Commission on Obscenity and Pornography, *have as a distinguishing characteristic "the degrading and demeaning portrayal of the role and status of the human female . . . as a mere sexual object to be exploited and manipulated sexually."* In pornographic books, magazines, and films, women are represented as passive and as slavishly dependent upon men. The role of female characters is limited to the provision of sexual services to men. To the extent that women's sexual pleasure is represented at all, it is subordinated to that of men and is never an end in itself as is the sexual pleasure of men. What pleases women is the use of their bodies to satisfy male desires. While the sexual objectification of women is common to pornography, women are the recipients of even worse treatment in violent pornography, in which women characters are killed, tortured, gang-raped, mutilated, bound, and otherwise abused, as a means of providing sexual stimulation or pleasure to the male characters. It is this development which has attracted the attention of feminists and been the stimulus to an analysis of pornography in general.

Not all sexually explicit material is pornography, nor is all material which contains representations of sexual abuse and degradation pornography.

A representation of a sexual encounter between adult persons which is characterized by mutual respect is, once we have disentangled sexuality and morality, not morally objectionable. Such a representation would be one in which the desires and experiences of each participant were regarded by the other participants as having a validity and a subjective importance equal to those of the individual's own

desire and experiences. In such an encounter, each participant acknowledges the other participant's basic human dignity and personhood. Similarly, a representation of a nude human body (in whole or
in part) in such a manner that the person shown maintains
self-respect—e.g., is not portrayed in a degrading position—would
not be morally objectionable. The educational films of the National
Sex Forum, as well as a certain amount of erotic literature and art,
fall into this category. While some erotic materials are beyond the
standards of modesty held by some individuals, they are not for this
reason immoral.

A representation of a sexual encounter which is not characterized
by mutual respect, in which at least one of the parties is treated in a
manner beneath her or his dignity as a human being, is no longer
simple erotica. That a representation is of degrading behavior does
not in itself, however, make it pornographic. Whether or not it is pornographic is a function of contextual features. Books and films may
contain descriptions or representations of a rape in order to explore
the consequences of such an assault upon its victim. What is being
shown is abusive or degrading behavior which attempts to deny the
humanity and dignity of the person assaulted, yet the context surrounding the representation, through its exploration of the consequences of the act, acknowledges and reaffirms her dignity. Such
books and films, far from being pornographic, are (or can be) highly
moral, and fall into the category of moral realism.

What makes a work a work of pornography, then, is not simply its
representation of degrading and abusive sexual encounters, but its
implicit, if not explicit, approval and recommendation of sexual behavior that is immoral, i.e., that physically or psychologically violates
the personhood of one of the participants. Pornography, then, is
verbal or pictorial material which represents or describes sexual behavior that is degrading or abusive to one or more of the participants
in *such a way as to endorse the degradation*. The participants so treated
in virtually all heterosexual pornography are women or children, so
heterosexual pornography is, as a matter of fact, material which endorses sexual behavior that is degrading and/or abusive to women
and children. As I use the term "sexual behavior," this includes sexual
encounters between persons, behavior which produces sexual stimulation or pleasure for one of the participants, and behavior which is
preparatory to or invites sexual activity. Behavior that is degrading or
abusive includes physical harm or abuse, and physical or psychological coercion. In addition, behavior which ignores or devalues the real

interests, desires, and experiences of one or more participants in any way is degrading. Finally, that a person has chosen or consented to be harmed, abused, or subjected to coercion does not alter the degrading character of such behavior.

Pornography communicates its endorsement of the behavior it represents by various features of the pornographic context: the degradation of the female characters is represented as providing pleasure to the participant males and, even worse, to the participant females, and there is no suggestion that this sort of treatment of others is inappropriate to their status as human beings. These two features are together sufficient to constitute endorsement of the represented behavior. The contextual features which make material pornographic are intrinsic to the material. In addition to these, extrinsic features, such as the purpose for which the material is presented—i.e., the sexual arousal/pleasure/satisfaction of its (mostly) male consumers—or an accompanying text, may reinforce or make explicit the endorsement. Representations which in and of themselves do not show or endorse degrading behavior may be put into a pornographic context by juxtaposition with others that are degrading, or by a text which invites or recommends degrading behavior toward the subject represented. In such a case the whole complex—the series of representations or representations with text—is pornographic. . . .

To summarize: Pornography is not just the explicit representation or description of sexual behavior, nor even the explicit representation or description of sexual behavior which is degrading and/or abusive to women. Rather, it is material that explicitly represents or describes degrading and abusive sexual behavior so as to endorse and/or recommend the behavior as described. The contextual features, moreover, which communicate such endorsement are intrinsic to the material; that is, they are features whose removal or alteration would change the representation or description. . . .

Pornography: Lies and Violence Against Women

What is wrong with pornography, then, is its degrading and dehumanizing portrayal of women (and *not* its sexual content). Pornography, by its very nature, requires that women be subordinate to men and mere instruments for the fulfillment of male fantasies. To accomplish this, pornography must lie. Pornography lies when it says that our sexual life is or ought to be subordinate to the service of men, that our pleasure consists in pleasing men and not ourselves, that we are depraved, that we are fit subjects for rape, bondage, torture, and murder. Pornography lies explicitly about women's sexuality, and through such lies fosters more lies about our humanity, our dignity, and our personhood.

Moreover, since nothing is alleged to justify the treatment of the female characters of pornography save their womanhood, pornography depicts all women as fit objects of violence by virtue of their sex alone. Because it is simply being female that, in the pornographic vision, justifies being violated, the lies of pornography are lies about all women. Each work of pornography is on its own libelous and defamatory, yet gains power through being reinforced by every other pornographic work. The sheer number of pornographic productions expands the moral issue to include not only assessing the morality or immorality of individual works, but also the meaning and force of the mass production of pornography.

The pornographic view of women is thoroughly entrenched in a booming portion of the publishing, film, and recording industries, reaching and affecting not only all who look to such sources for sexual stimulation, but also those of us who are forced into an awareness of it as we peruse magazines at newsstands and record albums in record stores, as we check the entertainment sections of city newspapers, or even as we approach a counter to pay for groceries. It is not necessary to spend a great deal of time reading or viewing pornographic material to absorb its male-centered definition of women. No longer confined within plain brown wrappers, it jumps out from billboards that proclaim "Live X-rated Girls!" or "Angels in Pain" or "Hot and Wild," and from magazine covers displaying a woman's genital area being spread open to the viewer by her own fingers. Thus, even men who do not frequent pornographic shops and movie houses are supported in the sexist objectification of women by their environment. Women, too, are crippled by internalizing as self-images those that are presented to us by pornographers. Isolated from one another and with no source of support for an alternative view of female sexuality, we may not always find the strength to resist a message that dominates the common cultural media.

The entrenchment of pornography in our culture also gives it a significance quite beyond its explicit sexual messages. To suggest, as pornography does, that the primary purpose of women is to provide sexual pleasure to men is to deny that women are independently human or have a status equal to that of men. It is, moreover, to deny our equality at one of the most intimate levels of human experience.

This denial is especially powerful in a hierarchical, class society such as ours, in which individuals feel good about themselves by feeling superior to others. Men in our society have a vested interest in maintaining their belief in the inferiority of the female sex, so that no matter how oppressed and exploited by the society in which they live and work, they can feel that they are at least superior to someone or some category of individuals—a woman or women. Pornography, by presenting women as wanton, depraved, and made for the sexual use of men, caters directly to that interest. The very intimate nature of sexuality which makes pornography so corrosive also protects it from explicit public discussion. The consequent lack of any explicit social disavowal of the pornographic image of women enables this image to continue fostering sexist attitudes even as the society publicly proclaims its (as yet timid) commitment to sexual equality.

In addition to finding a connection between the pornographic view of women and the denial to us of our full human rights, women are beginning to connect the consumption of pornography with committing rape and other acts of sexual violence against women. Contrary to the findings of the Commission on Obscenity and Pornography a growing body of research is documenting (1) a correlation between exposure to representations of violence and the committing of violent acts generally, and (2) a correlation between exposure to pornographic materials and the committing of sexually abusive or violent acts against women. While more study is needed to establish precisely what the causal relations are, clearly so-called hard-core pornography is not innocent.

From "snuff" films and miserable magazines in pornographic stores to *Hustler*, to phonograph album covers and advertisements, to *Vogue*, pornography has come to occupy its own niche in the communications and entertainment media and to acquire a quasi-institutional character (signaled by the use of diminutives such as "porn" or "porno" to refer to pornographic material, as though such familiar naming could take the hurt out). Its acceptance by the mass media, whatever the motivation, means a cultural endorsement of its message. As much as the materials themselves, the social tolerance of these degrading and distorted images of women in such quantities is harmful to us, since it indicates a general willingness to see women in ways incompatible with our fundamental human dignity and thus to justify treating us in those ways. The tolerance of pornographic representations of the rape, bondage, and torture of women helps to create and maintain a climate more tolerant of the actual physical abuse of women. The tendency on the part of the legal system to view the victim of a rape as responsible for the crime against her is but one manifestation of this.

In sum, pornography is injurious to women in at least three distinct ways:

1. Pornography, especially violent pornography, is implicated in the committing of crimes of violence against women.
2. Pornography is the vehicle for the dissemination of a deep and vicious lie about women. It is defamatory and libelous.
3. The diffusion of such a distorted view of women's nature in our society as it exists today supports sexist (i.e., male-centered) attitudes, and thus reinforces the oppression and exploitation of women.

Society's tolerance of pornography, especially pornography on the contemporary massive scale, reinforces each of these modes of injury: By not disavowing the lie, it supports the male-centered myth that women are inferior and subordinate creatures. Thus, it contributes to the maintenance of a climate tolerant of both psychological and physical violence against women.

Pornography and the Law

Congress shall make no law respecting the establishment of religion, or prohibiting the free exercise thereof; or abridging the freedom of speech, or of the press; or the right of the people peaceably to assemble, and to petition the Government for a redress of grievances.

—First Amendment, Bill of Rights
of the United States Constitution

Pornography is clearly a threat to women. Each of the modes of injury cited above offers sufficient reason at least to consider proposals for the social and legal control of pornography. The almost universal response from progressives to such proposals is that constitutional guarantees of freedom of speech and privacy preclude recourse to law. While I am concerned about the erosion of constitutional rights and also think for many reasons that great caution must be exercised before undertaking a legal campaign against pornography, I find objections to such a campaign that are based on appeals to the First Amendment or to a right to privacy ultimately unconvincing.

Much of the defense of the pornographer's right to publish seems to assume that, while pornography may be tasteless and vulgar, it is basically an entertainment that harms no one but its consumers, who may at worst suffer from the debasement of their taste; and that therefore those who argue for its control are demanding an unjustifiable abridgment of the rights to freedom of speech of those who make and distribute pornographic materials and of the rights to privacy of their customers. The account of pornography given above shows that the assumptions of this position are false. Nevertheless, even some who acknowledge its harmful character feel that it is granted immunity from social control by the First Amendment, or that the harm that would ensue from its control outweighs the harm prevented by its control.

There are three ways of arguing that control of pornography is incompatible with adherence to constitutional rights. The first argument claims that regulating pornography involves an unjustifiable interference in the private lives of individuals. The second argument takes the First Amendment as a basic principle constitutive of our form of government, and claims that the production and distribution of pornographic material, as a form of speech, is an activity protected by that amendment. The third argument claims not that the pornographer's rights are violated, but that others' rights will be if controls against pornography are instituted.

The privacy argument is the easiest to dispose of. Since the open commerce in pornographic materials is an activity carried out in the public sphere, the publication and distribution of such materials, unlike their use by individuals, is not protected by rights to privacy. The distinction between the private consumption of pornographic material and the production and distribution of, or open commerce in it, is sometimes blurred by defenders of pornography. But I may entertain, in the privacy of my mind, defamatory opinions about another person, even though I may not broadcast them. So one might create without restraint—as long as no one were harmed in the course of preparing them—pornographic materials for one's personal use, but be restrained from reproducing and distributing them. In both cases what one is doing—in the privacy of one's mind or basement—may indeed be deplorable, but immune from legal proscription. Once the activity becomes public, however—i.e., once it involves others—it is no longer protected by the same rights that protect activities in the private sphere.

In considering the second argument (that control of pornography, private or public, is wrong in principle), it seems important to determine whether we consider the right to freedom of speech to be absolute and unqualified. If it is, then obviously all speech, including pornography, is entitled to protection. But the right is, in the first place, not an unqualified right: There are several kinds of speech not protected by the First Amendment, including the incitement to violence in volatile circumstances, the solicitation of crimes, perjury and misrepresentation, slander, libel, and false advertising. That there are forms of proscribed speech shows that we accept limitations on the right to freedom of speech if such speech, as do the forms listed, impinges on other rights. The manufacture and distribution of material which defames and threatens all members of a class by its recommendation of abusive and degrading behavior toward some members of that class simply in virtue of their membership in it seems a clear candidate for inclusion on the list. The right is therefore not an unqualified one.

Nor is it an absolute or fundamental right, underived from any other right: If it were there would not be exceptions or limitations. The first ten amendments were added to the Constitution as a way of guaranteeing the "blessings of liberty" mentioned in its preamble, to protect citizens against the unreasonable usurpation of power by the state. The specific rights mentioned in the First Amendments—those of religion, speech, assembly, press, petition—reflect the recent experiences of the makers of the Constitution under colonial government as well as a sense of what was and is required generally to secure liberty. . . .

The right to freedom of speech is not a fundamental, absolute right, but one derivative from, possessed in virtue of, the more basic right to independence. Taking this view of liberty requires providing arguments showing that the more specific rights we claim are necessary to guarantee our status as persons "independent and equal rather than subservient." In the context of government, we understand independence to be the freedom of each individual to participate as an equal among equals in the determination of how she or he is to be governed. Freedom of speech in this context means that an individual may not only entertain beliefs concerning government privately, but may express them publicly. We express our opinions about taxes, disarmament, wars, social-welfare programs, the function of the police, civil rights, and so on. Our right to freedom of speech includes the right to criticize the government and to protest against various forms of injustice and the abuse of power. What we wish to protect is the free expression of ideas even when they are unpopular. What we do not always remember is that speech has functions other than the expression of ideas.

Regarding the relationship between a right to freedom of speech and the publication and distribution of pornographic materials, there are two points to be made. In the first place, the latter activity is hardly an exercise of the right to the free expression of ideas as understood above. In the second place, to the degree that the tolerance of material degrading to women supports and reinforces the attitude that women are not fit to participate as equals among equals in the political life of their communities, and that the prevalence of such an attitude effectively prevents women from so participating, the absolute and fundamental right of women to liberty (political independence) is violated.

This second argument against the suppression of pornographic material, then, rests on a premise that must be rejected, namely, that the right to freedom of speech is a right to utter anything one wants. It thus fails to show that the production and distribution of such material is an activity protected by the First Amendment. Furthermore, an examination of the issues involved leads to the conclusion that tolerance of this activity violates the rights of women to political independence.

The third argument (which expresses concern that curbs on pornography are the first step toward political censorship) runs into the same ambiguity that besets the arguments based on principle. These arguments generally have as an underlying assumption that the maximization of freedom is a worthy social goal. Control of pornography diminishes freedom—directly the freedom of pornographers, indirectly that of all of us. But again, what is meant by "freedom"? It cannot be that what is to be maximized is license—as the goal of a social group whose members probably have at least some incompatible interests, such a goal would be internally inconsistent. If, on the other hand, the maximization of political independence is the goal, then that is in no way enhanced by, and may be endangered by, the tolerance of pornography. To argue that the control of pornography would create a precedent for suppressing political speech is thus to confuse license with political independence. In addition, it ignores a crucial basis for the control of pornography, i.e., its character as libelous speech. The prohibition of such speech is justified by the need for protection from the injury (psychological as well as physical or economic) that results from libel. A very different kind of argument would be required to justify curtailing the right to speak our minds about the institutions which govern us. As long as such distinctions are insisted upon, there is little danger of the government's using the control of pornography as precedent for curtailing political speech.

In summary, neither as a matter of principle nor in the interests of maximizing liberty can it be supposed that there is an intrinsic right to manufacture and distribute pornographic material.

The only other conceivable source of protection for pornography would be a general right to do what we please as long as the rights of others are respected. Since the production and distribution of pornography violates the rights of women—to respect and to freedom from defamation, among others—this protection is not available.

Conclusion

I have defined pornography in such a way as to distinguish it from erotica and from moral realism, and have argued that it is defamatory and libelous toward women, that it condones crimes against women, and that it invites tolerance of the social, economic, and cultural oppression of women. The production and distribution of pornographic material is thus a social and moral wrong. Contrasting both the current volume of pornographic production and its growing infiltration of the communications media with the status of women in this culture makes clear the necessity for its control. Since the goal of controlling pornography does not conflict with constitutional rights, a common obstacle to action is removed.

Study Questions

1. According to Longino, what is pornography?
2. Why does Longino believe that pornography is immoral?
3. Should all immoral activity be illegal?
4. Does Longino's case against heterosexual pornography apply to homosexual pornography?

CHAPTER 32

The Case Against Pornography: An Assessment

Joel Feinberg

Joel Feinberg (1926–2004) was Professor of Philosophy at the University of Arizona. He argues that the law cannot legitimately be used to restrict the liberty of those who distribute or purchase erotic materials that are violently abusive of women.

May the law legitimately be used to restrict the liberty of pornographers to produce and distribute, and their customers to purchase and use, erotic materials that are violently abusive of women? (I am assuming that no strong case can be made for the proscription of materials that are merely degrading in one of the relatively subtle and nonviolent ways.) Many . . . answer, often with reluctance, in the affirmative. Their arguments can be divided into two general classes. Some simply invoke the harm principle. Violent pornography wrongs and harms women, according to these arguments, either by defaming them as a group, or (more importantly) by inciting males to violent crimes against them or creating a cultural climate in which such crimes are likely to become more frequent. The two traditional legal categories involved in these harm-principle arguments, then, are *defamation* and *incitement*. The other class of arguments invoke the offense principle, not in order to prevent mere "nuisances," but to prevent profound offense analogous to that of the Jews in Skokie or the blacks in a town where the K.K.K. rallies.

I shall not spend much time on the claim that violent and other extremely degrading pornography should be banned on the ground that it *defames* women. In a skeptical spirit, I can begin by pointing out that there are immense difficulties in applying the civil law of libel and slander as it is presently constituted in such a way as not to violate freedom of expression. Problems with *criminal* libel and slander would be even more unmanageable, and *group* defamation, whether civil or criminal, would multiply the problems still further. The argument on the other side is that pornography is essentially propaganda—propaganda against women. It does not slander women in the technical legal sense by asserting damaging falsehoods about them, because it *asserts* nothing at all. But it spreads an image of women as mindless playthings or "objects," inferior beings fit only to be used and abused for the pleasure of men, whether they like it or not, but often to their own secret pleasure. This picture lowers the esteem men have for women, and for that reason (if defamation is the basis of the argument) is sufficient ground for proscription even in the absence of any evidence of tangible harm to women caused by the behavior of misled and deluded men.

If degrading pornography defames (libels or slanders) women, it must be in virtue of some beliefs about women—false beliefs—that it conveys, so that in virtue of those newly acquired or reenforced false beliefs, consumers lower their esteem for women in general. If a work of pornography, for example, shows a woman (or group of women) in exclusively subservient or domestic roles, that may lead the consumer to *believe* that women, in virtue of some inherent female characteristics, are only fit for such roles. There is no doubt that much pornography does portray women in subservient positions, but if that is defamatory to women in anything like the legal sense, then so are soap commercials on TV. So are many novels, even some good ones. (A good novel may yet be about some degraded characters.) That some groups are portrayed in unflattering roles has not hitherto been a ground for the censorship of fiction or advertising. Besides, it is not clearly the *group* that is portrayed at all in such works, but only one individual (or small set of individuals) and fictitious ones at that. Are fat men defamed by Shakespeare's picture of Falstaff? Are Jews defamed by the characterization of Shylock? Could any writer today even hope to write a novel partly about a fawning corrupted black, under group defamation laws, without risking censorship or worse? The chilling effect on the practice of fiction-writing would amount to a near freeze.

Moreover, . . . the degrading images and defamatory beliefs pornographic works are alleged to cause are not produced in the consumer by explicit statements asserted with the intent to convince the reader or auditor of their truth. Rather they are caused by the stimulus of the work, in the context, on the expectations, attitudes, and beliefs the viewer brings with him to the work. That is quite other than believing an assertion on the authority or argument of the party making the assertion, or understanding the assertion in the first place in virtue of fixed conventions of language use and meaning. Without those fixed conventions of language, the work has to be interpreted in order for any message to be extracted from it, and the process of interpretation. . . . What looks like sexual subservience to some looks like liberation from sexual repression to others. It is hard to imagine how a court could provide a workable, much less fair, test of whether a given work has sufficiently damaged male esteem toward women for it to be judged criminally defamatory, when so much of the viewer's reaction he brings on himself, and viewer reactions are so widely variable. . . .

The major argument for repression of violent pornography under the harm principle is that it promotes rape and physical violence. In the United States there is a plenitude both of sexual violence against women and of violent pornography. . . . This has suggested to some writers that there must be a direct causal link between violent pornography and sexual violence against women; but causal relationships between pornography and rape, if they exist, must be more complicated than that. The suspicion of direct connection is dissipated, as Aryeh Neier points out,

> . . . when one looks at the situation in other countries. For example, violence against women is common in . . . Ireland and South Africa, but pornography is unavailable in those countries. By contrast violence against women is relatively uncommon in Denmark, Sweden, and the Netherlands, even though pornography seems to be even more plentifully available than in the United States. To be sure, this proves little or nothing except that more evidence is needed to establish a causal connection between pornography and violence against women beyond the fact that both may exist at the same time. But this evidence . . . simply does not exist.[1]

On the other hand, there is evidence that novel ways of committing crimes are often suggested (usually inadvertently) by bizarre tales in films or TV . . . , and even factual newspaper reports of crimes can trigger the well-known "copy-cat crime" phenomenon. But if the possibility of copy-cat cases, by itself, justified censorship or punishment, we would have grounds for supressing films of *The Brothers Karamozov* and the TV series *Roots* (both of which have been cited as influences on imitative crimes). "There would be few books left on our library shelves and few films that could be shown if every one that had at some time 'provoked' bizarre behavior were censored." A violent episode in a pornographic work may indeed be a causally necessary condition for the commission of some specific crime by a specific perpetrator on a specific victim at some specific time and place. But for his reading or viewing that episode, the perpetrator may not have done precisely what he did in just the time, place, and manner that he did it. But so large a part of the full causal explanation of his act concerns his own psychological character and predispositions, that it is likely that some similar crime would have suggested itself to him in due time. It is not likely that non-rapists are converted into rapists *simply* by reading and viewing pornography. If pornography has a serious causal bearing on the occurence of rape (as opposed to the trivial copy-cat effect) it must be in virtue of its role (still to be established) in implanting the appropriate cruel dispositions in the first place.

Rape is such a complex social phenomenon that there is probably no one simple generalization to account for it. Some rapes are no doubt ineliminable, no matter how we design our institutions. Many of these are the product of deep individual psychological problems, transferred rages, and the like. But for others, perhaps the preponderant number, the major part of the explanation is sociological, not psychological. In these cases the rapist is a psychologically normal person well adjusted to his particular subculture, acting calmly and deliberately rather than in a rage, and doing what he thinks is expected of him by his peers, what he must do to acquire or preserve standing in his group. His otherwise inexplicable violence is best explained as a consequence of the peculiar form of his socialization among his peers, his pursuit of a prevailing ideal of manliness, what the Mexicans have long called *machismo*, but which exists to some degree or other among men in most countries, certainly in our own.

The macho male wins the esteem of his associates by being tough, fearless, reckless, wild, unsentimental, hard-boiled, hard drinking, disrespectful, profane, willing to fight whenever his honor is impugned, and fight without fear of consequences no matter how extreme. He is a sexual athlete who must be utterly dominant over "his" females, who are expected to be slavishly devoted to him even though he lacks gentleness with them and shows his regard only by displaying them like trophies. . . .

Would it significantly reduce sexual violence if violent pornography were effectively banned? No one can know for sure, but if the cult of macho is the main source of such violence, as I suspect, then repression of violent pornography, whose function is to pander to the macho values already deeply rooted in society, may have little effect. Pornography does not cause normal decent chaps, through a single exposure, to metamorphoze into rapists. Pornography-reading machos commit rape, but that is because they already have macho values, not because they read the violent pornography that panders to them. Perhaps then *constant* exposure to violent porn might turn a decent person into a violence-prone macho. But that does not seem likely either, since the repugnant violence of the materials could not have any appeal in the first place to one who did not already have some strong macho predispositions, so "constant exposure" could not begin to become established. Clearly, other causes, and more foundational ones, must be at work, if violent porn is to have any initial purchase. Violent pornography is more a symptom of *machismo* than a cause of it, and treating symptoms merely is not a way to offer protection to potential victims of rapists. At most, I think there may be a small spill-over effect of violent porn on actual violence. . . .

How then can we hope to weaken and then extirpate the cultish values at the root of our problem? The criminal law is a singularly ill-adapted tool for that kind of job. We might just as well legislate against entrepreneurship on the grounds that capitalism engenders "acquisitive personalities," or against the military on the grounds that it produces "authoritarian personalities," or against certain religious sects on the ground that they foster puritanism, as criminalize practices and institutions on the grounds that they contribute to *machismo*. But macho values are culturally, not instinctively, transmitted, and the behavior that expresses them is learned, not inherited, behavior. What is learned can be unlearned. Schools should play a role. Surely, learning to see through machismo and avoid its traps should be as important a part of a child's preparation for citizenship as the acquisition of patriotism and piety. To be effective, such teaching should be frank and direct, not totally reliant on general moral platitudes. It should talk about the genesis of children's attitudes toward the other sex, and invite discussion of male insecurity, resentment of women, cruelty, and even specific odious examples. Advertising firms and film companies should be asked (at first), then pressured (if necessary) to cooperate, as they did in the successful campaign to deglamorize cigarette smoking. Fewer exploitation films should be made. . . . Materials (especially films) should be made available to clergymen as well as teachers, youth counselors, and parole officers. A strong part of the emphasis of these materials should be on the harm that bondage to the cult of macho does to men too, and how treacherous a trap *machismo* can be. The new moral education must be careful, of course, not to preach dull prudence as a preferred style for youthful living. A zest for excitement, adventure, even danger, cannot be artificially removed from adolescent nature. Moreover, teamwork, camaraderie, and toughness of character need not be denigrated. But the cult of macho corrupts and distorts these values in ways that can be made clear to youths. The mistreatment of women, when its motivation is clearly revealed and understood, should be a sure way of eliciting the contempt of the group, not a means to greater prestige within it.

Note

1. Aryeh Neier, "Expurgating the First Amendment," *The Nation*, June 21, 1980, p. 754.

Study Questions

1. How does Feinberg differentiate the "harm principle" and the "offense principle"?
2. What difficulties does Feinberg find in applying to pornography the civil law of libel and slander?
3. Can a good novel be pornographic?
4. Do you agree with Feinberg that the criminal law is ill-adapted to weaken macho values?

F. Animals

CHAPTER 33

Equality for Animals?
Peter Singer

Does the principle of equality extend to nonhuman animals? Peter Singer, whose work we read previously, maintains that it does. He argues that to think otherwise is to be what he calls a "speciesist," engaging in the same kind of prejudicial thinking as racists or sexists. See whether you accept his reasoning and its consequences for changing the food we eat, the farming methods we use, the experimental procedures we adopt, and the approach we take toward activities such as hunting or fishing and establishments such as circuses, rodeos, and zoos.

Racism and Speciesism

. . . [T]he fundamental principle of equality, on which the idea that humans are equal rests, is the principle of equal consideration of interests. Only a basic moral principle of this kind can allow us to defend a form of equality that embraces almost all human beings, despite the differences that exist between them. . . . Although the principle of equal consideration of interests provides the best possible basis for human equality, its scope is not limited to humans. When we accept the principle of equality for humans, we are also committed to accepting that it extends to some nonhuman animals. . . .

The argument for extending the principle of equality beyond our own species is simple. It amounts to no more than a clear understanding of the principle of equal consideration of interests. . . . [T]his principle implies that our concern for others ought not to depend on what they are like or what abilities they possess (although precisely

---

From Peter Singer, *Practical Ethics*, 3rd Edition (Cambridge: Cambridge University Press, 2011). Reprinted by permission of the publisher.

what this concern requires us to do may vary according to the characteristics of those affected by what we do). It is on this basis that we are able to say that the fact that some people are not members of our race does not entitle us to exploit them, and the fact that some people are less intelligent than others does not mean that their interests may be discounted or disregarded. The principle also implies that the fact that beings are not members of our species does not entitle us to exploit them, and it similarly implies that the fact that other animals are less intelligent than we are does not mean that their interests may be discounted or disregarded. . . .

[M]any philosophers have advocated equal consideration of interests, in some form or another, as a basic moral principle. Few recognized that the principle has applications beyond our own species. One of those few was Jeremy Bentham, the founding father of modern utilitarianism. In a forward-looking passage, . . . Bentham wrote:

> The day may come when the rest of the animal creation may acquire those rights which never could have been withholden from them but by the hand of tyranny. . . . [A] full-grown horse or dog is beyond comparison a more rational, as well as a more conversable animal, than an infant of a day, or a week, or even a month, old. But suppose they were otherwise, what would it avail? The question is not, Can they *reason*? nor Can they *talk*? but, *Can they suffer*?

In this passage, Bentham points to the capacity for suffering as the vital characteristic that entitles a being to equal consideration. The capacity for suffering—or more strictly, for suffering and/or enjoyment or happiness—is not just another characteristic like the capacity for language or for higher mathematics. . . . The capacity for suffering and enjoying things is a prerequisite for having interests at all, a condition that must be satisfied before we can speak of interests in any meaningful way. It would be nonsense to say that it was not in the interests of a stone to be kicked along the road by a child. A stone does not have interests because it cannot suffer. Nothing that we can do to it could possibly make any difference to its welfare. A mouse, on the other hand, does have an interest in not being tormented, because mice will suffer if they are treated in this way.

If a being suffers, there can be no moral justification for refusing to take that suffering into consideration. No matter what the nature of the being, the principle of equality requires that the suffering be counted equally with the like suffering—in so far as rough comparisons can be made—of any other being. If a being is not capable of suffering, or of experiencing enjoyment or happiness, there is nothing to be taken into account. This is why the limit of sentience (using the term as convenient, if not strictly accurate, shorthand for the capacity to suffer or experience enjoyment or happiness) is the only defensible boundary of concern for the interests of others. To mark this boundary by some characteristic like intelligence or rationality would be to mark it in an arbitrary way. Why not choose some other characteristic, like skin colour?

Racists violate the principle of equality by giving greater weight to the interests of members of their own race when there is a clash between their interests and the interests of those of another race. The white racists who supported slavery typically did not give the suffering of Africans as much weight as they gave to the suffering of Europeans. Similarly, speciesists give greater weight to the interests of members of their own species when there is a clash between their interests and the interests of those of other species. Human speciesists do not accept that pain is as bad when it is felt by pigs or mice as when it is felt by humans.

That, then, is really the whole of the argument for extending the principle of equality to nonhuman animals, but there may be some doubts about what this equality amounts to in practice. In particular, the last sentence of the previous paragraph may prompt some people to reply: 'Surely pain felt by a mouse just is not as bad as pain felt by a human. Humans have much greater awareness of what is happening to them, and this makes their suffering worse. You can't equate the suffering of, say, a person dying slowly from cancer and a laboratory mouse undergoing the same fate.'

I fully accept that in the case described, the human cancer victim normally suffers more than the nonhuman cancer victim. This in no way undermines the extension of equal consideration of interests to nonhumans. It means, rather, that we must take care when we compare the interests of different species. In some situations, a member of one species will suffer more than a member of another species. In this case, we should still apply the principle of equal consideration of interests but the result of so doing is, of course, to give priority to relieving the greater suffering. A simpler case may help to make this clear.

If I give a horse a hard slap across its rump with my open hand, the horse may start, but it presumably feels little pain. Its skin is thick enough to protect it against a mere slap. If I slap a baby in the same way, however, the baby will cry and presumably does feel pain, for the baby's skin is more sensitive. So it is worse to slap a baby than a horse, if both slaps are administered with equal force. But there must be some kind of blow—I don't know exactly what it would be, but perhaps a blow with a heavy stick—that would cause the horse as much pain as we cause a baby by a simple slap. That is what I mean by 'the same amount of pain', and if we consider it wrong to inflict that much pain on a baby for no good reason then we must, unless we are speciesists, consider it equally wrong to inflict the same amount of pain on a horse for no good reason.

There are other differences between humans and animals that cause other complications. Normal adult human beings have mental capacities that will, in certain circumstances, lead them to suffer more than animals would in the same circumstances. If, for instance, we decided to perform extremely painful or lethal scientific experiments on normal adult humans, kidnapped at random from public parks for this purpose, adults who entered parks would become fearful that they would be kidnapped. The resultant terror would be a form of suffering additional to the pain of the experiment. The same experiments performed on non-human animals would cause less suffering because the animals would not have the anticipatory dread of being kidnapped and experimented on. This does not mean, of course, that it would be *right* to perform the experiment on animals, but only that there is a reason, and one that is not speciesist, for preferring to use animals rather than normal adult humans, if the experiment is to be done at all. Note, however, that this same argument gives us a reason for preferring to use human infants—orphans perhaps—or severely intellectually disabled humans for experiments, rather than adults, because infants and severely intellectually disabled humans would also have no idea of what was going to happen to them. So far as this argument is concerned, nonhuman animals and infants and severely intellectually disabled humans are in the same category; and if we use this argument to justify experiments on nonhuman animals, we have to ask ourselves whether we are also prepared to allow experiments on human infants and severely intellectually disabled adults. If we make a distinction between animals and these humans, how can we do it, other than on the basis of a morally indefensible preference for members of our own species?

There are many areas in which the superior mental powers of normal adult humans make a difference: anticipation, more detailed memory, greater knowledge of what is happening and so on. These differences explain why a human dying from cancer is likely to suffer more than a mouse. It is the mental anguish that makes the human's position so much harder to bear. Yet these differences do not all point to greater suffering on the part of the normal human being. Sometimes animals may suffer more because of their more limited understanding. If, for instance, we are taking prisoners in wartime, we can explain to them that although they must submit to capture, search and confinement, they will not otherwise be harmed and will be set free at the conclusion of hostilities. If we capture wild animals, however, we cannot explain that we are not threatening their lives. Animals cannot distinguish attempts to overpower and confine from attempts to kill them; the one causes as much terror as the other.

It may be objected that comparisons of the sufferings of different species are impossible to make, and that for this reason when the interests of animals and humans clash, the principle of equality gives no guidance. It is true that comparisons of suffering between members of different species cannot be made precisely. Nor, for that matter, can comparisons of suffering between different human beings be made precisely. Precision is not essential. As we shall see shortly, even if we were to prevent the infliction of suffering on animals only when the interests of humans will not be affected to anything like the extent that animals are affected, we would be forced to make radical changes in our treatment of animals that would involve the food we eat, the farming methods we use, experimental procedures in many fields of science, our approach to wildlife and to hunting, trapping and the wearing of furs, and areas of entertainment like circuses, rodeos and zoos. As a result, the total quantity of suffering we cause would be hugely reduced. . . .

Speciesism in Practice

Animals as Food

For most people in modern, urbanized societies, the principal form of contact with nonhuman animals is at meal times. The use of animals for food is probably the oldest and the most widespread form of animal use. There is also a sense in which it is the most basic form of animal use, the foundation stone of an ethic that sees animals as things for us to use to meet our needs and interests.

If animals count in their own right, our use of animals for food becomes questionable. Inuit living a traditional lifestyle in the far north where they must eat animals or starve can reasonably claim that their interest in surviving overrides that of the animals they kill. Most of us cannot defend our diet in this way. People living in industrialized societies can easily obtain an adequate diet without the use of animal flesh. Meat is not necessary for good health or longevity. . . .

Nor is animal production in industrialized societies an efficient way of producing food, because most of the animals consumed have been fattened on grains and other foods that we could have eaten directly. When we feed these grains to animals, only about one-quarter—and in some cases, as little as one-tenth—of the nutritional value remains as meat for human consumption. So, with the exception of animals raised entirely on grazing land unsuitable for crops, animals are eaten neither for health nor to increase our food supply. Their flesh is a luxury, consumed because people like its taste. . . .

In considering the ethics of the use of animal products for human food in industrialized societies, we are considering a situation in which a relatively minor human interest must be balanced against the lives and welfare of the animals involved. The principle of equal consideration of interests does not allow major interests to be sacrificed for minor interests.

The case against using animals for food is at its strongest when animals are made to lead miserable lives so that their flesh can be made available to humans at the lowest possible cost. Modern forms of intensive farming apply science and technology to the attitude that animals are objects for us to use. Competition in the marketplace forces meat producers to copy rivals who are prepared to cut costs by giving animals more miserable lives. In buying the meat, eggs or milk produced in these ways, we tolerate methods of meat production that confine sentient animals in cramped, unsuitable conditions for the entire duration of their lives. They are treated like machines that convert fodder into flesh, and any innovation that results in a higher 'conversion ratio' is liable to be adopted. As one authority on the subject has said, 'cruelty is acknowledged only when profitability ceases'. To avoid speciesism, we must stop these practices. . . .

Experimenting on Animals

Perhaps the area in which speciesism can most clearly be observed is the use of animals in experiments. Here the issue stands out starkly, because experimenters often seek to justify experimenting on animals by claiming that the experiments lead us to discoveries about humans; if this is so, the experimenter must agree that human and nonhuman animals are similar in crucial respects. For instance, if forcing a rat to choose between starving to death and crossing an electrified grid to obtain food tells us anything about the reactions of humans to stress, we must assume that the rat feels stress in this kind of situation. . . .

In the past, argument about animal experimentation . . . has been put in absolutist terms: would the opponent of experimentation be prepared to let thousands die from a terrible disease that could be cured only by experimenting on one animal? This is a purely hypothetical question, because no experiment could ever be predicted to have such dramatic results, but so long as its hypothetical nature is clear . . . [I]f one, or even a dozen animals had to suffer experiments in order to save thousands, I would think it right and in accordance with equal consideration of interests that they should do so.

To the hypothetical question about saving thousands of people through experiments on limited number of animals, opponents of speciesism can reply with a hypothetical question of their own: would experimenters be prepared to perform their experiments on orphaned humans with severe and irreversible brain damage if that were the only way to save thousands? (I say 'orphaned' in order to avoid the complication of the feelings of the human parents.) If experimenters are not prepared to use orphaned humans with severe and irreversible brain damage, their readiness to use nonhuman animals seems to discriminate on the basis of species alone, because apes, monkeys, dogs, cats and even mice and rats are more intelligent, more aware of what is happening to them, more sensitive to pain and so on than many severely brain-damaged humans barely surviving in hospital wards and other institutions. There seems to be no morally relevant characteristic that such humans have that nonhuman animals lack. Experimenters, then, show bias in favour of their own species whenever they carry out experiments on nonhuman animals for purposes that they would not think justified them in using human beings at an equal or lower level of sentience, awareness, sensitivity and so on. If this bias were eliminated, the number of experiments performed on animals would be greatly reduced. . . .

Some Objections

In this final section of the chapter, I shall attempt to answer the most important . . . objections.

How Do We Know That Animals Can Feel Pain?

We can never directly experience the pain of another being, whether that being is human or not. When I see a child fall and scrape her knee, I know that she feels pain because of the way she behaves—she cries, she tells me her knee hurts, she rubs the sore spot and so on. I know that I myself behave in a somewhat similar—if more inhibited— way when I feel pain, and so I accept that the child feels something like what I feel when I scrape my knee.

The basis of my belief that animals can feel pain is similar to the basis of my belief that children can feel pain. Animals in pain behave in much the same way as humans do, and their behaviour is sufficient justification for the belief that they feel pain. It is true that, with the exception of a few animals who have learned to communicate with us in a human language, they cannot actually say that they are feeling pain—but babies and toddlers cannot talk either. They find other ways to make their inner states apparent, however, demonstrating that we can be sure that a being is feeling pain even if the being cannot use language.

To back up our inference from animal behaviour, we can point to the fact that the nervous systems of all vertebrates, and especially of birds and mammals, are fundamentally similar. Those parts of the human nervous system that are concerned with feeling pain are rela- tively old, in evolutionary terms. Unlike the cerebral cortex, which developed only after our ancestors diverged from other mammals, the basic nervous system evolved in more distant ancestors and so is common to all of the other 'higher' animals, including humans. This anatomical parallel makes it likely that the capacity of vertebrate ani- mals to feel is similar to our own.

The nervous systems of invertebrates are less like our own, and perhaps for that reason we are not justified in having quite the same confidence that they can feel pain. In the case of bivalves like oysters, mussels and clams, a capacity for pain or any other form of conscious- ness seems unlikely, and if that is so, the principle of equal consider- ation of interests will not apply to them. On the other hand, scientists studying the responses of crabs and prawns to stimuli like electric shock or a pinch on an antenna have found evidence that does sug- gest pain. Moreover, the behaviour of some invertebrates—especially the octopus, who can learn to solve novel problems like opening a screw-top glass jar to get at a tasty morsel inside—is difficult to ex- plain without accepting that consciousness has also evolved in at least some invertebrates.

It is significant that none of the grounds we have for believing that animals feel pain hold for plants. We cannot observe behaviour suggest- ing pain—sensational claims to have detected feelings in plants by attaching lie detectors to them proved impossible to replicate—and plants do not have a centrally organized nervous system like ours.

Animals Eat Each Other, So Why Shouldn't We Eat Them?

This might be called the Benjamin Franklin Objection because Franklin recounts in his *Autobiography* that he was for a time a vegetarian, but his abstinence from animal flesh came to an end when he was watching some friends prepare to fry a fish they had just caught. When the fish was cut open, it was found to have a smaller fish in its stomach. 'Well', Franklin said to himself, 'if you eat one another, I don't see why we may not eat you', and he proceeded to do so.

Franklin was at least honest. In telling this story, he confesses that he convinced himself of the validity of the objection only after the fish was already in the frying pan and smelling 'admirably well'; and he remarks that one of the advantages of being a 'reasonable creature' is that one can find a reason for whatever one wants to do. The replies that can be made to this objection are so obvious that Franklin's acceptance of it does testify more to his hunger on that occasion than to his powers of reason. For a start, most animals who kill for food would not be able to survive if they did not, whereas we have no need to eat animal flesh. Next, it is odd that humans, who normally think of the behaviour of animals as 'beastly' should, when it suits them, use an argument that implies that we ought to look to animals for moral guidance. The most decisive point, however, is that nonhuman animals are not capable of considering the alternatives open to them or of reflecting on the ethics of their diet. Hence, it is impossible to hold the animals responsible for what they do or to judge that because of their killing they 'deserve' to be treated in a similar way. Those who read these lines, on the other hand, must consider the justifiability of their dietary habits. You cannot evade responsibility by imitating beings who are incapable of making this choice.

Sometimes people draw a slightly different conclusion from the fact that animals eat each other. This suggests, they think, not that animals deserve to be eaten, but rather that there is a natural law according to which the stronger prey on the weaker, a kind of Darwinian 'survival of the fittest' in which by eating animals we are merely playing our part.

This interpretation of the objection makes two basic mistakes, one of fact and the other of reasoning. The factual mistake lies in the assumption that our own consumption of animals is part of some natural evolutionary process. This might be true of those who still hunt for food, but it has nothing to do with the mass production of domestic animals in factory farms.

Suppose that we did hunt for our food, though, and this was part of some natural evolutionary process. There would still be an error of reasoning in the assumption that because this process is natural it is right. It is, no doubt, 'natural' for women to produce an infant every year or two from puberty to menopause, but this does not mean that it is wrong to interfere with this process. We need to understand nature and develop the best theories we can to explain why things are as they are, because only in that way can we work out what the consequences our actions are likely to be; but it would be a serious mistake to assume that natural ways of doing things are incapable of improvement. . . .

Differences Between Humans and Animals

That humans and animals are utterly different *kinds* of beings was unquestioned for most of the course of Western civilization. The basis of this assumption was undermined by Darwin's discovery of our origins and the associated decline in the credibility of the story of our divine creation in the image of God. Darwin himself argued that the difference between us and animals is one of degree, rather than of kind—a view that even today, some find difficult to accept. They have searched for ways of drawing a line between humans and animals. To date, these boundaries have been short-lived. For instance, it used to be said that only humans used tools. Then it was observed that the Galapagos woodpecker used a cactus thorn to dig insects out of crevices in trees. Next, it was suggested that even if other animals *used* tools, humans are the only animals who *make* tools. Then Jane Goodall found that chimpanzees in the jungles of Tanzania chewed up leaves to make a sponge for sopping up water and trimmed the leaves from branches to make tools for catching insects. The use of language was another boundary line—but now chimpanzees, bonobos, gorillas and orangutans have learnt to sign in the language used in America by people who are deaf, and parrots have learned to speak—and not merely parrot—English.

Even if these attempts to draw the line between humans and animals had fitted the facts, they would still not carry the moral weight required to justify our treatment of animals. As Bentham pointed out, the fact that an animal does not use language is no reason for ignoring its suffering, and neither is the fact that she does not use tools.

Some philosophers have claimed that there is a more profound difference between humans and animals. They have claimed that animals cannot think or reason, and that accordingly, they have no conception of themselves, no self-awareness. They live from instant to instant and do not see themselves as distinct entities with a past and a future. Nor do they have autonomy, the ability to choose how to live one's life. It has been suggested that autonomous, self-aware beings are in some way much more morally significant than beings who live from moment to moment, without the capacity to see themselves as distinct beings with a past and a future. . . . [D]oes the fact that a being is self-aware entitle that being to some kind of priority of consideration?

The claim that self-aware beings are entitled to more consideration than other beings is compatible with the principle of equal consideration of interests if it amounts to no more than the claim that something that happens to self-aware beings can be contrary to their interests, whereas similar occurrences would not be contrary to the interests of beings who are not self-aware. This might be because the self-aware creature can fit the event into the overall framework of a longer time period, has different desires and so on. This, however, is a point I granted at the start of this chapter, and provided that it is not carried to ludicrous extremes—like insisting that if I am self-aware and a veal calf is not, depriving me of veal causes more suffering than depriving the calf of his freedom to walk, stretch and eat grass—it is not denied by the criticisms I made of animal experimentation and factory farming.

It would be a different matter if it were claimed that, even when a self-aware being did not suffer more than a being that was merely sentient, the suffering of the self-aware being is more important because these are inherently more valuable beings. . . .

[W]e are entitled to ask *why* self-aware beings should be considered more valuable and in particular why the alleged greater value of a self-aware being should result in preferring the lesser interests of a self-aware being to the greater interests of a merely sentient being, even where the self-awareness of the former being is not itself at stake. This last point is an important one, for we are not now considering cases in which the lives of self-aware beings are at risk but cases in which self-aware beings will go on living, their faculties intact, whatever we decide. In these cases, if the existence of self-awareness does not mean that the interests of the self-aware being really are greater, and more adversely affected, than the interests of the non-self-aware being, it is not clear why we should bring self-awareness into the discussion at all, any more than we should bring species, race or sex into similar discussions.

There is another possible reply to the claim that self-awareness, or autonomy or some similar characteristic, can serve to distinguish human from nonhuman animals. Recall that there are intellectually disabled humans who have less claim to be regarded as self-aware or autonomous than many nonhuman animals. If we use these characteristics to place a gulf between humans and other animals, we place these less able humans on the other side of the gulf; and if the gulf is taken to mark a difference in moral status, then these humans would have the moral status of animals rather than humans. . . .

Defending Speciesism

When faced with the objection that their position implies that we would be entitled to treat profoundly intellectually disabled humans as we now treat nonhuman animals, some philosophers fall back on defending speciesism, either because of its instrumental value, or, more boldly, on the grounds that species membership is itself morally significant.

The instrumental defence of speciesism invokes the widely used 'slippery slope' argument. The claim is that a first step in a certain direction will put us on a slippery slope, and we shall not be able to stop sliding into a moral abyss. In the present context, the argument is used to suggest that we need a clear line to divide those beings we can experiment on, or fatten for dinner, from those we cannot. The species boundary makes a nice sharp dividing line, whereas levels of self-awareness, autonomy or sentience do not. Once we allow that any human being, no matter how profoundly intellectually disabled, has no higher moral status than an animal, the argument goes, we have begun to slide down a slope, the next level of which is denying rights to social misfits, and the bottom of which is classifying anyone we do not like as sub-human and eliminating them.

In response to this slippery slope argument, it is important to remember that the aim of my argument is to elevate the status of animals rather than to lower the status of any humans. I do not wish to suggest that intellectually disabled humans should be force-fed with food colourings until they get ill or die—although this would certainly give us a more accurate indication of whether the substance was safe for humans than doing this to rabbits or dogs. I would like our conviction that it would be wrong to treat intellectually disabled humans in this way to be transferred to nonhuman animals at similar levels of self-awareness and with similar capacities for suffering. It is excessively pessimistic to refrain from trying to alter the way we treat animals on the grounds that we might start treating intellectually disabled humans with the same lack of concern we now have for animals, rather than give animals the greater concern that we now have for intellectually disabled humans. If we really are convinced of the dangers of the slippery slope, we can avoid it by insisting that all sentient beings, whether self-aware or not, should have basic rights.

Study Questions

1. According to Singer, what is the fundamental principle of equality?
2. Is considering human interests more morally important than animal interests merely a prejudice?
3. Under what circumstances, if any, are zoos morally acceptable?
4. Of birds, fish, reptiles, and insects, which have interests deserving of equal consideration?

CHAPTER 34

Speciesism and the Idea of Equality

Bonnie Steinbock

Bonnie Steinbock is Professor Emerita of Philosophy at the University of Albany, State University of New York. She maintains that because human beings can be held morally responsible, their interests should be given extra weight. In response to the objection that some humans lack intelligence, she replies that we can look on all other members of the human species and think, "That could be me." By contrast, we cannot have this thought about nonhuman animals.

Most of us believe that we are entitled to treat members of other species in ways which would be considered wrong if inflicted on members of our own species. We kill them for food, keep them confined, use them in painful experiments. The moral philosopher has to ask what relevant difference justifies this difference in treatment. A look at this question will lead us to reexamine the distinctions which we have assumed make a moral difference.

It has been suggested by Peter Singer[1] that our current attitudes are "speciesist," a word intended to make one think of "racist" or "sexist." The idea is that membership in a species is in itself not relevant to moral treatment, and that much of our behaviour and attitudes toward nonhuman animals [are] based simply on this irrelevant fact.

There is, however, an important difference between racism or sexism and "speciesism." We do not subject animals to different moral treatment simply because they have fur and feathers but because they are in fact different from human beings in ways that could be morally relevant. It is false that women are incapable of being benefited by education, and therefore that claim cannot serve to justify preventing

From Bonnie Steinbock, "Speciesism and the Idea of Equality," *Philosophy* 53 (1978).

them from attending school. But this is not false of cows and dogs, even chimpanzees. Intelligence is thought to be a morally relevant capacity because of its relation to the capacity for moral responsibility.

What is Singer's response? He agrees that nonhuman animals lack certain capacities that human animals possess and that this may justify different *treatment*. But it does not justify giving less consideration to their needs and interests. According to Singer, the moral mistake which the racist or sexist makes is not essentially the factual error of thinking that blacks or women are inferior to white men. For even if there were no factual error, even if it were true that blacks and women are less intelligent and responsible than whites and men, this would not justify giving less consideration to their needs and interests. It is important to note that the term "speciesism" is in one way like, and in another way unlike, the terms "racism" and "sexism." What the term "speciesism" has in common with these terms is the reference to focusing on a characteristic which is, in itself, irrelevant to moral treatment. And it is worth reminding us of this. But Singer's real aim is to bring us to a new understanding of the idea of equality. The question is, On what do claims to equality rest? The demand for *human* equality is a demand that the interests of all human beings be considered equally unless there is a moral justification for not doing so. But why should the interests of all human beings be considered equally? In order to answer this question, we have to give some sense to the phrase, "All men (human beings) are created equal." Human beings are manifestly *not* equal, differing greatly in intelligence, virtue, and capacities. In virtue of what can the claim to equality be made?

It is Singer's contention that claims to equality do not rest on factual equality. Not only do human beings differ in their capacities, but it might even turn out that intelligence, the capacity for virtue, etc., are not distributed evenly among the races and sexes:

> The appropriate response to those who claim to have found evidence of genetically based differences in ability between the races or sexes is not to stick to the belief that the genetic explanation must be wrong, whatever evidence to the contrary may turn up; instead we should make it quite clear that the claim to equality does not depend on intelligence, moral capacity, physical strength, or similar matters of fact. Equality is a moral ideal, not a simple assertion of fact. There is no logically compelling reason for assuming that a factual difference in ability between two people justifies any difference in the amount of consideration we give to satisfying their needs and interests. The principle of equality of human beings is not a description of an alleged

actual equality among humans: it is a prescription of how we should treat humans.[2]

. . . Singer says, quite rightly I think, "If a being suffers, there can be no moral justification for refusing to take that suffering into consideration."[3] But he thinks that the principle of equality requires that no matter what the nature of the being, its suffering be counted equally with the like suffering of any other being. In other words, sentience does not simply provide us with reasons for acting; it is the only relevant consideration for equal consideration of interests. It is this view that I wish to challenge.

I want to challenge it partly because it has such counterintuitive results. It means, for example, that feeding starving children before feeding starving dogs is just like a Catholic charity's feeding hungry Catholics before feeding hungry non-Catholics. It is simply a matter of taking care of one's own, something which is usually morally permissible. But whereas we would admire the Catholic agency which did not discriminate, but fed all children, first come, first served, we would feel quite differently about someone who had this policy for dogs and children. Nor is this, it seems to me, simply a matter of a sentimental preference for our own species. I might feel much more love for my dog than for a strange child—and yet I might feel morally obliged to feed the child before I fed my dog. If I gave in to the feelings of love and fed my dog and let the child go hungry, I would probably feel guilty. This is not to say that we can simply rely on such feelings. Huck Finn felt guilty at helping Jim escape, which he viewed as stealing from a woman who had never done him any harm. But while the existence of such feelings does not settle the morality of an issue, it is not clear to me that they can be explained away. In any event, their existence can serve as a motivation for trying to find a rational justification for considering human interests above nonhuman ones. . . .

I think we do have to justify counting our interests more heavily than those of animals. But how? Singer is right, I think, to point out that it will not do to refer vaguely to the greater value of human life, to human worth and dignity:

> Faced with a situation in which they see a need for some basis for the moral gulf that is commonly thought to separate humans and animals, but can find no concrete difference that will do this without undermining the equality of humans, philosophers tend to waffle. They resort to high-sounding phrases like "the intrinsic dignity of the human individual." They talk of "the intrinsic worth of all men" as if men

had some worth that other beings do not have or they say that human beings, and only human beings, are "ends in themselves," while "everything other than a person can only have value for a person." . . . Why should we not attribute "intrinsic dignity" or "intrinsic worth" to ourselves? Why should we not say that we are the only things in the universe that have intrinsic value? Our fellow human beings are unlikely to reject the accolades we so generously bestow upon them and those to whom we deny the honour are unable to object.[4]

Singer is right to be skeptical of terms like "intrinsic dignity" and "intrinsic worth." These phrases are no substitute for a moral argument. But they may point to one. In trying to understand what is meant by these phrases, we may find a difference or differences between human beings and nonhuman animals that will justify different treatment while not undermining claims for human equality. While we are not compelled to discriminate among people because of different capacities, if we can find a significant difference in capacities between human and nonhuman animals, this could serve to justify regarding human interests as primary.

It is not arbitrary or smug, I think, to maintain that human beings have a different moral status from members of other species because of certain capacities which are characteristic of being human. We may not all be equal in these capacities, but all human beings possess them to some measure, and nonhuman animals do not. For example, human beings are normally held to be responsible for what they do. In recognizing that someone is responsible for his or her actions, you accord that person a respect which is reserved for those possessed of moral autonomy or capable of achieving such autonomy.

Secondly, human beings can be expected to reciprocate in a way that nonhuman animals cannot. Nonhuman animals cannot be motivated by altruistic or moral reasons; they cannot treat you fairly or unfairly. This does not rule out the possibility of an animal being motivated by sympathy or pity. It does rule out altruistic motivation in the sense of motivation due to the recognition that the needs and interests of others provide one with certain reasons for acting. Human beings are capable of altruistic motivation in this sense. We are sometimes motivated simply by the recognition that someone else is in pain and that pain is a bad thing, no matter who suffers it. It is this sort of reason that I claim cannot motivate an animal or any entity not possessed of fairly abstract concepts. (If some nonhuman animals do possess the requisite concepts— perhaps chimpanzees who have learned a language—they might well be capable of altruistic motivation.) This means that our moral dealings with animals are necessarily much more limited than our dealings with other human beings. If rats invade our houses, carrying disease and biting our children, we cannot reason with them, hoping to persuade them of the injustice they do us. We can only attempt to get rid of them. And it is this that makes it reasonable for us to accord them a separate and not equal moral status, even though their capacity to suffer provides us with some reason to kill them painlessly, if this can be done without too much sacrifice of human interests.

Thirdly, . . . there is the ["desire for self-respect"]. . . . Some animals may have some form of this desire, and to the extent that they do, we ought to consider their interest in freedom and self-determination. (Such considerations might affect our attitudes toward zoos and circuses.) But the desire for self-respect *per se* requires the intellectual capacities of human beings, and this desire provides us with special reasons not to treat human beings in certain ways. It is an affront to the dignity of a human being to be a slave (even if a well-treated one); this cannot be true for a horse or a cow. To point this out is of course only to say that the justification for the treatment of an entity will depend on the sort of entity in question. In our treatment of other entities, we must consider the desire for autonomy, dignity, and respect, but only where such a desire exists. Recognition of different desires and interests will often require different treatment, a point Singer himself makes.

But is the issue simply one of different desires and interests justifying and requiring different treatment? I would like to make a stronger claim, namely, that certain capacities, which seem to be unique to human beings, entitle their possessors to a privileged position in the moral community. Both rats and human beings dislike pain, and so we have a *prima facie* reason not to inflict pain on either. But if we can free human beings from crippling diseases, pain, and death through experimentation which involves making animals suffer, and if this is the only way to achieve such results, then I think that such experimentation is justified because human lives are more valuable than animal lives. And this is because of certain capacities and abilities that normal human beings have which animals apparently do not and which human beings cannot exercise if they are devastated by pain or disease.

My point is not that the lack of the sorts of capacities I have been discussing gives us a justification for treating animals just as we like, but rather that it is these differences between human beings and non-human animals which provide a rational basis for different moral treatment and consideration. Singer focuses on sentience alone as the basis of equality, but we can justify the belief that human beings have a moral worth that nonhuman animals do not, in virtue of specific capacities and without resorting to "high-sounding phrases."

Singer thinks that intelligence, the capacity for moral responsibility, for virtue, etc., are irrelevant to equality, because we would not accept a hierarchy based on intelligence any more than one based on race. We do not think that those with greater capacities ought to have their interests weighed more heavily than those with lesser capacities, and this, he thinks, shows that differences in such capacities are irrelevant to equality. But it does not show this at all. . . . [W]hat entitles us human beings to a privileged position in the moral community is a certain minimal level of intelligence, which is a prerequisite for morally relevant capacities. The fact that we would reject a hierarchical society based on degree of intelligence does not show that a minimal level of intelligence cannot be used as a cut-off point justifying giving greater consideration to the interests of those entities which meet this standard.

Interestingly enough, Singer concedes the rationality of valuing the lives of normal human beings over the lives of nonhuman animals.[5] We are not required to value equally the life of a normal human being and the life of an animal, he thinks, but only their suffering. But I doubt that the value of an entity's life can be separated from the value of its suffering in this way. If we value the lives of human beings more than the lives of animals, this is because we value certain capacities that human beings have and animals do not. But freedom from suffering is, in general, a minimal condition for exercising these capacities, for living a fully human life. So valuing human life more involves regarding human interests as counting for more. That is why we regard human suffering as more deplorable than comparable animal suffering.

But there is one point of Singer's which I have not yet met. Some human beings (if only a very few) are less intelligent than some nonhuman animals. Some have less capacity for moral choice and responsibility. What status in the moral community are these members of our species to occupy? Are their interests to be considered equally with ours? Is experimenting on them permissible where such experiments are painful or injurious but somehow necessary for human well-being? If it is certain of our capacities which entitle us to a privileged position, it looks as if those lacking those capacities are not entitled to a privileged position. To think it is justifiable to experiment on an adult chimpanzee but not on a severely mentally incapacitated human being seems to be focusing on membership in a species where that has no moral relevance. (It is being "speciesist" in a perfectly reasonable use of the word.) How are we to meet this challenge? . . .

I doubt that anyone will be able to come up with a concrete and morally relevant difference that would justify, say, using a chimpanzee in an experiment rather than a human being with less capacity for reasoning, moral responsibility, etc. Should we then experiment on the severely retarded? . . . [W]e feel a special obligation to care for the handicapped members of our own species, who cannot survive in this world without such care. Nonhuman animals manage very well, despite their "lower intelligence" and lesser capacities; most of them do not require special care from us. This does not, of course, justify experimenting on them. However, to subject to experimentation those people who depend on us seems even worse than subjecting members of other species to it. In addition, when we consider the severely retarded, we think, "That could be me." It makes sense to think that one might have been born retarded but not to think that one might have been born a monkey. And so, although one can imagine one's self in the monkey's place, one feels a closer identification with the severely retarded human being.

Here we are getting away from such things as "morally relevant differences" and talking about something much more difficult to articulate, namely, the role of feeling and sentiment in moral thinking. We would be horrified by the use of the retarded in medical research. But what are we to make of this horror? Has it moral significance or is it "mere" sentiment, of no more importance than the sentiment of whites against blacks? It is terribly difficult to know how to evaluate such feelings.

I am not going to say more about this, because I think that the treatment of severely incapacitated human beings does not pose an insurmountable objection to the privileged-status principle. I am willing to admit that my horror at the thought of experiments being performed on severely mentally incapacitated human beings in cases in which I would find it justifiable and preferable to perform the same experiments on nonhuman animals (capable of similar suffering) may not be a moral emotion. But it is certainly not wrong of us to extend special care to members of our own species, motivated by feelings of sympathy, protectiveness, etc. If this is speciesism, it is stripped of its tone of moral condemnation. It is not racist to provide special care to members of your own race; it is racist to fall below your moral obligation to a person because of his or her race.

I have been arguing that we are morally obliged to consider the interests of all sentient creatures but not to consider those interests equally with human interests. Nevertheless, even this recognition will mean some radical changes in our attitude toward and treatment of other species.

Notes

1. Peter Singer, *Animal Liberation* (New York: Avon Books, 1977).
2. Singer, *Animal Liberation*, p. 5.
3. Singer, *Animal Liberation*, p. 9.
4. Singer, *Animal Liberation*, pp. 266–67.
5. Singer, *Animal Liberation*, p. 22.

Study Questions

1. According to Steinbock, why should we count human interests more heavily than those of nonhuman animals?
2. According to Steinbock, how should we weight the interests of human beings who lack the capacities required for moral responsibility?
3. Do you agree with Steinbock that a human being cannot look at any nonhuman animal in pain and think, "That could be me"?
4. If, as Steinbock asserts, we are morally obliged to consider the interests of all sentient creatures, would doing so, as she says, "mean radical changes in our attitude toward and treatment of other species"?

CHAPTER 35

Getting Animals in View

Christine Korsgaard

Christine Korsgaard is Professor of Philosophy at Harvard University. She maintains that, like human beings, nonhuman animals are ends in themselves, because they pursue the things that are important to them. In short, all creatures display, in her words, "the essentially self-affirming nature of life itself." In her discussion Korsgaard refers to George Eliot, the remarkably gifted Englishwoman, born Mary Ann or Marion Evans (1819–1880), who adopted a pseudonym to aid publication of her work. She was an accomplished philosopher and towering literary figure, whose output included one of the greatest of all novels, *Middlemarch.*

What sorts of philosophical problems do we face because of the existence of non-human animals? Most humane people would agree that their existence presents us with some moral and legal quandaries. And recently, but only recently, philosophers have taken a serious interest in the character of animal minds. But I have come to think that animals present us with a philosophical problem deeper than either of those—that the existence of non-human animals is the source of a profound disturbance in the way that human beings conceptualize the world. It is almost as if we—I'm using "we" to mean "us human beings" here—are unable to get them firmly into view, to see them for what they really are.

Many people, to take one small example, find nothing odd about the sentence, "I live alone with a cat." Okay, granted, someone might also say, "I live alone with a child," at least so long as the child was a

Christine Korsgaard, "Getting Animals in View," *The Point Magazine,* issue 6. Reprinted by permission of the journal.

very small one.[1] But "I live alone with four children" would be starting to put the language under stress, even if they were all toddlers, while "I live alone with four cats" would not. Here's another example: People wondering about whether there might be life on other planets sometimes ask, "Are we alone in the universe?" Just look around!

Well, you may reply, they mean to ask whether there is any other *intelligent* life in the universe. Right. Just look around! Animals also seem to pop in and out of our moral view. Most people would agree that it is wrong to hurt or kill a non-human animal without a good reason, but then it turns out that any reason, short of malicious pleasure, is reason enough. We want to eat the animal, and to raise her cheaply for that purpose; we can learn from doing experiments on her; we can make useful or attractive products out of her; she is interfering with our agriculture or gardening; or maybe we just don't feel comfortable having her come so near. Her interests have weight, we insist—but never weight enough to outweigh our own.

Then there is the disturbing use of the phrase "treated like an animal." People whose rights are violated, people whose interests are ignored or overridden, people who are used, harmed, neglected, starved or unjustly imprisoned standardly complain that they are being treated like animals, or protest that after all they are not just animals. Of course, rhetorically, complaining that you are being treated like an animal is more effective than complaining that you are being treated like a thing or an object or a stone, for a thing or an object or a stone has no interests that can be ignored or overridden. In the sense intended, an object *can't* be treated badly, while an animal can. But then the curious implication seems to be that animals are the beings that it's all right to treat badly, and the complainant is saying that he is not one of *those*.

Do we need that contrast, between the beings it is *all right* to treat badly and the ones it is not? My otherwise favorite philosopher, Immanuel Kant, seemed to think so. In his essay "Conjectures on the Beginning of Human History," Kant traces the development of reason through a series of steps, the last of which is this:

> The fourth and last step which reason took, thereby raising man completely above animal society, was his . . . realization that he is the true *end of nature*. . . . When he first said to the sheep "the pelt which you wear was given to you by nature not for your own use, but for mine" and took it from the sheep to wear it himself, he became aware of a prerogative which . . . he enjoyed over all the animals; and he now no longer regarded them as fellow creatures, but as means and

instruments to be used at will for the attainment of whatever ends he pleased. This notion implies . . . an awareness of the following distinction: man should not address other *human beings* in the same way as animals, but should regard them as having an equal share in the gifts of nature. . . . Thus man had attained a position of *equality with all rational beings*, because he could claim *to be an end in himself* . . . and not to be used by anyone else as a mere means to other ends.

Non-human animals, on this showing, are the ultimate and final Other. They are the beings we can still use as mere means once we have given up the idea that other human beings are there for our purposes—once we've rejected the ideas that women are *for* housework and childcare, that girls are *for* sex, that boys are *for* fighting wars that serve older men's interests, and that people of color are *for* harvesting the fields and doing the menial jobs that all of us hate. Is that . . . what animals are for? Are they there so that there will be someone we can still use as mere means to our ends?

Not being what Kant called a "mere means" is not a privative condition—a way of being useless, say. It's a positive condition, which Kant calls being an "end in yourself." For a human being, it means that your choices should be respected and your ends promoted, that you have rights that the community should be prepared to uphold, that your happiness is valuable and your suffering should be cured or mitigated or met with tenderness when it is beyond cure. "Morality" is our name for demanding this kind of treatment from one another, and for meeting that demand. When we do use others to serve our own purposes—for of course we do—it must be done in a way that is consistent with all this, and then we are not treating them as "mere means," but at the same time as ends in themselves. But why shouldn't the other animals also be treated as ends in themselves?

I'll come back to that question. But first, let me respond to those readers who are now tempted to protest that there are plenty of people who *do* treat the other animals as ends in themselves. After all, it is notorious these days that more people than ever not only live with companion animals, but treat them like human children, keeping them in the house, providing them with toys and furniture, buying them medical insurance, bribing their affection with treats and burying them in graveyards when they die. Of course it's also true that in tough economic times when there is no longer money for such indulgences, these companion animals are turned loose onto the streets and into shelters in a way that human children ordinarily are not. But even those of us who are convinced that *we* would never treat our beloved pets in this way should remember that keeping an animal for affection and companionship is also a way of *using* the animal. Is it using the animal as a "mere means"?

It could be. Even among people, of course, it is possible to use someone for affection and companionship without keeping her existence and value as an independent being firmly in view. In *Middlemarch*, George Eliot tells the story of Dorothea, an idealistic young woman hungry to do some good in the world, who marries an older man whom she conceives to be a scholar engaged in a great work. Eliot writes:

> We are all of us born in moral stupidity, taking the world as an udder to feed our supreme selves: Dorothea had early begun to emerge from that stupidity, but yet it had been easier to her to imagine how she would devote herself to Mr. Casaubon, and become wise and strong in his strength and wisdom, than to conceive with that distinctness which is no longer reflection but feeling—an idea wrought back to the directness of sense, like the solidity of objects—that he had an equivalent center of self, whence the lights and shadows must always fall with a certain difference.

Eliot's purpose, at the particular moment at which this passage occurs, is to emphasize that Dorothea has failed to understand Casaubon's feelings. She has not quite managed to get his "center of self" into her view. But the moment is also one of moral revelation, a moment in which Dorothea grasps that "there is as great a need on his side as on her own" and so acquires "a new motive." Eliot is accusing her heroine, just a little, of having used Casaubon as a mere means to give significance and purpose to her own life. How much easier, then, to do something like that to a creature whose "center of self" you may not—rightly or wrongly—grant to be the "equivalent" of your own.

Is it because the other animals have lesser "centers of self" that so many people suppose they are not entitled to be treated as ends in themselves? In his Tanner Lectures, written as a work of fiction called *The Lives of Animals,* J. M. Coetzee imagines a professional philosopher who says: "It is licit to kill animals because their lives are not as important to them as ours are to us." George Eliot reminds us how hard it is to keep in view—not just to tell yourself, but to feel with "the directness of sense"—that other *people's* lives are as just important to them as yours is to you. But we are at least theoretically committed to the importance, and the equal importance, of every human life. Many of our religious and philosophical traditions try to explain this equal importance. We, these traditions assert—we human beings, that is—are all God's children, or have some special sort of intrinsic value that the other animals lack. But what makes it possible to believe such things at all is probably the thing that Coetzee puts in his philosopher's mouth: the passionate sense of importance that each of us attaches to himself or herself. After all, every human being pursues the things that are important to himself and to those whom he loves as if they were important *absolutely*, important in deadly earnest—for what else can we do? And just by doing that, we claim our own standing as ends in ourselves. For when we claim that the things that are important to us should be treated as important absolutely, just because they are important to us, we also claim that we are important ourselves.[2] But the other animals also pursue the things that are important to them and their loved ones as if they were important in deadly earnest. Why then should we think they must be less important to themselves than we are to ourselves?

Some of the philosophical views about the nature of animal minds are, among other things, attempts to answer that question. The other animals are not conscious at all, some people argue, or their consciousness is so fleeting and ephemeral that it just does not add up to the consciousness of a self, so nothing really could matter to them in quite the same that way it does to us. A less extreme version of that last view—one that even many defenders of the moral claims of animals, such as Peter Singer, endorse—is that animals live so thoroughly in the moment that their deaths are not regrettable, although their suffering is.

That might seem puzzling. After all, when we consider our fellow human beings, we often regard a capacity for living in the moment as a good thing. The human mind can be so cluttered and overshadowed with worries about the future and regrets about the past that we fail to enjoy the present—the only thing, after all, that is real. So why would the fact that the other animals live in the moment, supposing it is a fact, make their deaths less regrettable? Jeff MacMahan offers this explanation:

> . . . the lives of persons typically have a narrative structure that may demand completion in a certain way. People autonomously establish purposes for their lives, form patterns of structured relations with others, and thereby create expectations and dependencies that require fulfillment. The importance of later events in a typical human life may thus be greatly magnified by their relation to ambitions formed and activities engaged in earlier . . . In the lives of animals,

however, this potential for complex narrative unity is entirely absent. There are no projects that require completion, mistakes that demand rectification, or personal relations that promise to ripen or mature. Rather, as Aldous Huxley once put it, "the dumb creation lives a life made up of discreet and mutually irrelevant episodes." And each day is merely more of the same.

According to this argument, to deprive a human being of life is worse than to deprive another animal of life, because you are depriving the non-human animal only of "more of the same," while you may be disrupting the narrative unity of the human being's life.

I have mixed reactions to this kind of argument. On the one hand, animal lives are not the same every day—rather, at least for many of them, they have a rhythm that is set by the seasons of the year, and by the age of breeding, and may involve the raising of families, migrations, the building of homes, preparation for the winter and so on. Many mother animals raise new young every year or so, and most of those die and presumably are forgotten, but in some social animals, the bonds that result from family ties are permanent and important. Relationships, families and larger social groups persist over time. For some animals there is even a narrative structure to the course of an individual life that *we* can recognize and describe—even if they cannot. Among social animals, for instance, certain male individuals rise to positions of power and leadership in middle age, only to be deposed by younger members when they are older. Females move through a distinct set of roles in family life as daughters, then mothers, then grandmothers in much the same way that, in many cultures, human females do.

Which brings me to the other side of what bothers me about this—that human lives also have established rhythms set by the seasons of the year and the age of breeding, and that many human lives, especially when you look at the species historically, or at less developed nations, have been pretty much the same every day. You get up, do some work, eat breakfast, then do some more work. You tend the children and prepare the food, or you feed the animals, or you hoe the fields, or you go to the factory, depending on when and where your life takes place, but you go to work, and then you have supper, and then go to bed and start over. Each day is merely more of the same. Perhaps it is exactly those lives that most challenge the ability of the more privileged members of developed nations to feel with "the directness of sense" that every person's life is just as important to her as ours are to us.

Yet there is clearly something right about MacMahan's picture. I think it is this: we human beings, unlike the other animals, think of ourselves and our lives in normative terms. We are governed not merely by instinctive likes and dislikes, attractions and aversions, enjoyment and suffering, but by values. Being reflective animals, we endorse or reject our likes and dislikes, attractions and aversions, pleasures or pains, declaring them to be good or bad. Each of us identifies himself in terms of certain roles, relationships, occupations and causes, all of them governed by normative standards, which it is then the business of our lives to live up to. And so we come to think of ourselves as worthy or unworthy, lovable or unlovely, good or bad.

Philosophers disagree about what exactly it is about our nature that makes us like this— whether it is rationality, or a special kind of sentiment, or something else. However that may be, this kind of evaluative self-conception is a condition that gives a strange extra dimension to human life, both a special source of pride and interest, and a profound cause of suffering. It is not that nothing is important to the other animals, for instinctive desire and aversion have an imperative character all their own. But that does not seem to suffuse whatever sense of their own being the other animals have. Some of the other animals seem to have moments of pride, but they don't seem in general to think of themselves as worthy or unworthy beings. Some of them certainly want to be loved, but they don't seem to worry about being lovable. Thinking of yourself as having a kind of identity that is at once up to you and subject to normative assessment is a distinctive feature of being human. It gives a human being's life, in his own eyes, the character of a *project,* of something at which he can succeed or fail. That possibility of success or failure is what gives human life the kind of narrative structure that MacMahan describes.

If this is right, it shows that human lives are important to human beings in *a way* that the lives of the other animals are not important to them. But it does not show that our lives are *more* important than theirs. It is not that our lives have a kind of importance that the lives of the other animals lack. It is rather that our lives have a kind of importance *for us* that the other animals' lives do not have *for them.* And I am prepared to make a further claim here: that there is nothing that is therefore *missing* from the lives of the other animals.

This is where things start to get a little bit dizzying, conceptually speaking. The difficulty is that everything that is important must be important because it is important *to* someone: to some person or animal. What makes it important to that person or animal is that it satisfies some desire or conforms to some standard that applies to that person or animal. But the standard of normative success and failure, which goes with the project of making yourself into a worthy or an unworthy being, does not apply to the other animals. There is nothing missing from the lives of the other animals because they fail to see themselves as good or bad, successes or failures. The standards that we use when we measure ourselves in these ways apply to us in virtue of something about our nature, and do not apply to them.

Perhaps a comparison will help. John Stuart Mill famously claimed that it is better to be Socrates dissatisfied than a pig satisfied.[3] Mill believed this because he held that human beings have access to what he called "higher pleasures"—for instance, the pleasures of poetry. But for whom is it better? Would it be better *for the pig* if he were Socrates? Temple Grandin, in her book *Animals Make Us Human,* reports that there is nothing pigs love more than rooting around in straw. Poetry is not good for a pig, so it is not something valuable that is missing from the pig's life, something he would get access to if he were changed into Socrates, any more than rooting around in straw is something valuable that is missing from your life, something you would get access to if you were changed into a pig. But isn't poetry a higher pleasure than rooting around in straw? If what makes a pleasure "higher" is, as Kant and others have suggested, that it cultivates our capacity for even deeper and greater pleasures of the very same kind, then we must have that capacity before the pleasure can be judged a higher one for us. Since the pig lacks that capacity, poetry is not a higher pleasure for a pig. Of course, we might try the argument that, so far as we can tell, none of the pig's pleasures are "higher" in this sense. But then perhaps it is only for us jaded human beings that the lower pleasures seem to grow stale. So long as the straw itself is fresh, pigs apparently *never* lose their enthusiasm for rooting around in straw.

There's a notorious philosophical problem about thoughts that begin, "if I were you . . ." When I tell you what I would do if I were you, I must bring something of myself with me, usually some standard for the assessment of actions that also applies to you, or a superior ability to apply some standard that we already share. Otherwise it's a foregone conclusion that whatever *you* would do if I weren't offering you advice is exactly what I would do if I were you. But the standard I bring with me may be one that does not apply to you or that you do not share. David Hume reminds us of the famous story of the advice Parmenio gave to Alexander the Great. *"Were I Alexander,* said Parmenio, *I would accept of these offers made by Darius. So would I too,* replied Alexander, *were I Parmenio."* This problem pervades our efforts to think about the other animals, for when we try to think about what it is like to be another animal, we bring our human standards with us, and then the other animals seem to us like lesser beings. A human being who lives a life governed only by desires and instincts, not by values, would certainly be a lesser being. But that doesn't mean that the other animals are lesser beings. They are simply beings of a different kind. When we look at the other animals through the lens of our own standards, just as when we look at them through the lens of our own interests, we cannot get them properly in view.

We are all born, as Eliot says, in moral stupidity, unable to see others except through the lens of our own interests and standards. Kant suggested that it took four steps for us to emerge from this moral stupidity, but perhaps there is a fifth step we have yet to take. That is to try to look at the other animals and their lives unhindered by our own interests and specifically human standards, and to see them for what they really are. What is important about the other animals is what we have in common: that they, like us, are the kinds of beings to whom things *can* be important. Like us, they pursue the things that are important *to* them as if they were important *absolutely,* important in deadly earnest—for, like us, what else can they do? When we do this, we claim our own standing as ends in ourselves. But our only reason for doing that is that it is essential to the kinds of beings we are, beings who take their own concerns to be important. The claim of the other animals to the standing of ends in themselves has same ultimate foundation as our own—the essentially self-affirming nature of life itself.

Notes

1. There's interference here from another use of "I live alone with" in which it means, "I have sole charge of": "I can't go out whenever I please; I live alone with an autistic child." That's obviously not what is meant by "I live alone with a cat," but it might be what's meant by "I live alone with a child." But notice that very small babies, like animals, get called "it." It's tempting to speculate that this practice dates from the days when human infant mortality rates were higher and babies, like non-human animals, were regarded as fungible.

2. These remarks are a loose reading of Kant's claim that "representing" ourselves as ends in ourselves is a subjective principle of human action. See *Groundwork of the Metaphysics of Morals,* 4:429.

3. Actually Mill claims, on p. 10 of *Utilitarianism*, that it is better to be a human being dissatisfied than a pig satisfied, and better to be Socrates dissatisfied than a fool satisfied, so I am merging his claims by taking Socrates as the exemplar of humanity here.

Study Questions

1. According to Korsgaard, what sorts of philosophical problems do we face because of the existence of nonhuman animals?
2. What use does Korsgaard make of Kant's idea of an "end in yourself"?
3. What use does Korsgaard make of the story of Dorothea in George Eliot's *Middlemarch*?
4. Do any implications for eating animals or using them in experimentation follow from Korsgaard's conclusion that they are ends in themselves?

CHAPTER 36

Speaking of Animal Rights

Mary Anne Warren

Mary Anne Warren (1942–2010) was Professor of Philosophy at San Francisco State University. She believes that animals have rights, although not rights as strong as human rights. But on what basis can we justify regarding the rights of persons as stronger than those of animals who are not persons? Warren's answer is that people, unlike nonhuman animals, are sometimes capable of being moved to action or inaction by the force of reasoning.

Why Are Animal Rights Weaker than Human Rights?

How can we justify regarding the rights of persons as generally stronger than those of sentient beings which are not persons? There are a plethora of bad justifications, based on religious premises or false or unprovable claims about the differences between human and nonhuman nature. But there is one difference which has a clear moral relevance: people are at least sometimes capable of being moved to action or inaction by the force of reasoned argument. . . .

Why is rationality morally relevant? It does not make us "better" than other animals or more "perfect." It does not even automatically make us more intelligent. (Bad reasoning reduces our effective intelligence rather than increasing it.) But it is morally relevant insofar as it provides greater possibilities for cooperation and for the nonviolent resolution of problems. It also makes us more dangerous than

From Mary Anne Warren, "Difficulties with the Strong Rights Position," *Between the Species* 4 (1987).

non-rational beings can ever be. Because we are potentially more dangerous and less predictable than wolves, we need an articulated system of morality to regulate our conduct. Any human morality, to be workable in the long run, must recognize the equal moral status of all persons, whether through the postulate of equal basic moral rights or in some other way. The recognition of the moral equality of other persons is the price we must each pay for their recognition of our moral equality. Without this mutual recognition of moral equality, human society can exist only in a state of chronic and bitter conflict. The war between the sexes will persist so long as there is sexism and male domination; racial conflict will never be eliminated so long as there are racist laws and practices. But, to the extent that we achieve a mutual recognition of equality, we can hope to live together, perhaps as peacefully as wolves, achieving (in part) through explicit moral principles what they do not seem to need explicit moral principles to achieve.

Why not extend this recognition of moral equality to other creatures, even though they cannot do the same for us? The answer is that we cannot. Because we cannot reason with most non-human animals, we cannot always solve the problems which they may cause without harming them—although we are always obligated to try. We cannot negotiate a treaty with the feral cats and foxes, requiring them to stop preying on endangered native species in return for suitable concessions on our part.

> If rats invade our houses . . . we cannot reason with them, hoping to persuade them of the injustice they do us. We can only attempt to get rid of them.[1]

Aristotle was not wrong in claiming that the capacity to alter one's behavior on the basis of reasoned argument is relevant to the full moral status which he accorded to free men. Of course, he was wrong in his other premise, that women and slaves by their nature cannot reason well enough to function as autonomous moral agents. Had that premise been true, so would his conclusion that women and slaves are not quite the moral equals of free men. In the case of most non-human animals, the corresponding premise is true. If, on the other hand, there are animals with whom we can (learn to) reason, then we are obligated to do this and to regard them as our moral equals. . . .

But what about people who are clearly not rational? It is often argued that sophisticated mental capacities such as rationality cannot be essential for the possession of equal basic moral rights, since nearly everyone agrees that human infants and mentally incompetent persons have such rights, even though they may lack those sophisticated mental capacities. But this argument is inconclusive, because there are powerful practical and emotional reasons for protecting non-rational human beings, reasons which are absent in the case of most non-human animals. Infancy and mental incompetence are human conditions which all of us either have experienced or are likely to experience at some time. We also protect babies and mentally incompetent people because we care for them. We don't normally care for animals in the same way, and when we do—e.g., in the case of much-loved pets—we may regard them as having special rights by virtue of their relationship to us. We protect them not only for their sake but also for our own, lest we be hurt by harm done to them. . . .

Why Speak of "Animal Rights" at All?

If, as I have argued, reality precludes our treating all animals as our moral equals, then why should we still ascribe rights to them? Everyone agrees that animals are entitled to some protection against human abuse, but why speak of animal *rights* if we are not prepared to accept most animals as our moral equals? . . .

The most plausible alternative to the view that animals have moral rights is that, while they do not have *rights*, we are, nevertheless, obligated not to be cruel to them. . . . Cruelty is inflicting pain or suffering and either taking pleasure in that pain or suffering or being more or less indifferent to it. Thus, to express the demand for the decent treatment of animals in terms of the rejection of cruelty is to invite the too easy response that those who subject animals to suffering are not being cruel because they regret the suffering they cause but sincerely believe that what they do is justified. The injunction to avoid cruelty is also inadequate in that it does not preclude the killing of animals—for any reason, however trivial—so long as it is done relatively painlessly.

The inadequacy of the anti-cruelty view provides one practical reason for speaking of animal rights. Another practical reason is that this is an age in which nearly all significant moral claims tend to be expressed in terms of rights. Thus, the denial that animals have rights, however carefully qualified, is likely to be taken to mean that we may do whatever we like to them, provided that we do not violate any human rights. In such a context, speaking of the rights of animals may be the only way to persuade many people to take seriously protests against the abuse of animals.

Why not extend this line of argument and speak of the rights of trees, mountains, oceans, or anything else which we may wish to see protected from destruction? Some environmentalists have not hesitated to speak in this way, and, given the importance of protecting such elements of the natural world, they cannot be blamed for using this rhetorical device. But, I would argue that moral rights can meaningfully be ascribed only to entities which have some capacity for sentience. This is because moral rights are protections designed to protect rights holders from harms or to provide them with benefits which matter *to them*. Only beings capable of sentience can be harmed or benefited in ways which matter to them, for only such beings can like or dislike what happens to them or prefer some conditions to others. Thus, sentient animals, unlike mountains, rivers, or species, are at least logically possible candidates for moral rights. This fact, together with the need to end current abuses of animals, . . . provides a plausible case for speaking of animal rights.

Note

1. Bonnie Steinbock, "Speciesism and the Idea of Equality," *Philosophy* 53 (1978): 253.

Study Questions

1. Do all human beings deserve the same rights?
2. Do all nonhuman animals deserve the same rights?
3. According to Warren, do mountains have rights?
4. According to Warren, why do people who are not rational have rights?

G. The Environment

CHAPTER 37

Philosophical Problems for Environmentalism

Elliott Sober

Should species and ecosystems be preserved for reasons beyond their value as resources for human use? Environmentalists believe so, but what compelling arguments can they offer to support their view? Elliott Sober, Professor of Philosophy at the University of Wisconsin–Madison, maintains that environmental values are analogous to aesthetic ones. Thus, if a striking rock formulation were found next to the ruins of a Greek temple, both would be equally valuable and worthy of preservation.

I. Introduction

A number of philosophers have recognized that the environmental movement, whatever its practical political effectiveness, faces considerable theoretical difficulties in justification.[1] It has been recognized that traditional moral theories do not provide natural underpinnings for policy objectives and this has led some to skepticism about the claims of environmentalists, and others to the view that a revolutionary reassessment of ethical norms is needed. In this chapter, I will try to summarize the difficulties that confront a philosophical defense of environmentalism. I also will suggest a way of making sense of some environmental concerns that does not require the wholesale jettisoning of certain familiar moral judgments. . . .

From Elliott Sober, "Philosophical Problems for Environmentalism," in *The Preservation of Species*, ed. Bryan G. Norton (Princeton, NJ: Princeton University Press, 1986).

The problem for environmentalism stems from the idea that species and ecosystems ought to be preserved for reasons additional to their known value as resources for human use. The feeling is that even when we cannot say what nutritional, medicinal, or recreational benefit the preservation provides, there still is a value in preservation. It is the search for a rationale for this feeling that constitutes the main conceptual problem for environmentalism.

The problem is especially difficult in view of the holistic (as opposed to individualistic) character of the things being assigned value. Put simply, what is special about environmentalism is that it values the preservation of species, communities, or ecosystems, rather than the individual organisms of which they are composed. "Animal liberationists" have urged that we should take the suffering of sentient animals into account in ethical deliberation.[2] Such beasts are not mere things to be used as cruelly as we like no matter how trivial the benefit we derive. But in "widening the ethical circle," we are simply including in the community more individual organisms whose costs and benefits we compare. Animal liberationists are extending an old and familiar ethical doctrine—namely, utilitarianism—to take account of the welfare of other individuals. Although the practical consequences of this point of view may be revolutionary, the theoretical perspective is not at all novel. If suffering is bad, then it is bad for any individual who suffers. Animal liberationists merely remind us of the consequences of familiar principles.

But trees, mountains, and salt marshes do not suffer. They do not experience pleasure and pain, because, evidently, they do not have experiences at all. The same is true of species. Granted, individual organisms may have mental states; but the species—taken to be a population of organisms connected by certain sorts of interactions (preeminently, that of exchanging genetic material in reproduction)—does not. Or put more carefully, we might say that the only sense in which species have experiences is that their member organisms do: the attribution at the population level, if true, is true simply in virtue of its being true at the individual level. Here is a case where reductionism is correct.

So perhaps it is true in this reductive sense that some species experience pain. But the values that environmentalists attach to preserving species do not reduce to any value of preserving organisms. It is in this sense that environmentalists espouse a holistic value system. Environmentalists care about entities that by no stretch of the imagination have experiences (e.g., mountains). What is more, their position does not force them to care if individual organisms suffer pain, so long as the species is preserved. Steel traps may outrage an animal liberationist because of the suffering they inflict, but an environmentalist aiming just at the preservation of a balanced ecosystem might see here no cause for complaint. Similarly, environmentalists think that the distinction between wild and domesticated organisms is important, in that it is the preservation of "natural" (i.e., not created by the "artificial interference" of human beings) objects that matters, whereas animal liberationists see the main problem in terms of the suffering of any organism—domesticated or not. And finally, environmentalists and animal liberationists diverge on what might be called the $n + m$ *question*. If two species—say blue and sperm whales—have roughly comparable capacities for experiencing pain, an animal liberationist might tend to think of the preservation of a sperm whale as wholly on an ethical par with the preservation of a blue whale. The fact that one organism is part of an endangered species while the other is not does not make the rare individual more intrinsically important. But for an environmentalist, this holistic property—membership in an endangered species—makes all the difference in the world: a world with n sperm and m blue whales is far better than a world with $n + m$ sperm and 0 blue whales. Here we have a stark contrast between an ethic in which it is the life situation of individuals that matters, and an ethic in which the stability and diversity of populations of individuals are what matter.[3]

Both animal liberationists and environmentalists wish to broaden our ethical horizons—to make us realize that it is not just human welfare that counts. But they do this in very different, often conflicting, ways. It is no accident that at the level of practical politics the two points of view increasingly find themselves at loggerheads. This practical conflict is the expression of a deep theoretical divide.

II.   The Ignorance Argument

"Although we might not now know what use a particular endangered species might be to us, allowing it to go extinct forever closes off the possibility of discovering and exploiting a future use." According to this point of view, our ignorance of value is turned into a reason for action. The scenario envisaged in this environmentalist argument is not without precedent; who could have guessed that penicillin would be good for something other than turning out cheese? But there is a fatal defect in such arguments, which we might summarize with the phrase *out of nothing, nothing comes:* rational decisions require assumptions about what is true and what is valuable. . . . If you are completely ignorant of values, then you are incapable of making a rational decision, either for or against preserving some species. The fact that you do not know the value of a species, by itself, cannot count as a reason for wanting one thing rather than another to happen to it.

And there are so many species. How many geese that lay golden eggs are there apt to be in that number? It is hard to assign probabilities and utilities precisely here, but an analogy will perhaps reveal the problem confronting this environmentalist argument. Most of us willingly fly on airplanes, when safer (but less convenient) alternative forms of transportation are available. Is this rational? Suppose it were argued that there is a small probability that the next flight you take will crash. This would be very bad for you. Is it not crazy for you to risk this, given that the only gain to you is that you can reduce your travel time by a few hours (by not going by train, say)? Those of us who not only fly, but congratulate ourselves for being rational in doing so, reject this argument. We are prepared to accept a small chance of a great disaster in return for the high probability of a rather modest benefit. If this is rational, no wonder that we might consistently be willing to allow a species to go extinct in order to build a hydroelectric plant.

That the argument from ignorance is no argument at all can be seen from another angle. If we literally do not know what consequences the extinction of this or that species may bring, then we should take seriously the possibility that the extinction may be beneficial as well as the possibility that it may be deleterious. It may sound deep to insist that we preserve endangered species precisely because we do not know why they are valuable. But ignorance on a scale like this cannot provide the basis for any rational action.

Rather than invoke some unspecified future benefit, an environmentalist may argue that the species in question plays a crucial role in stabilizing the ecosystem of which it is a part. This will undoubtedly be true for carefully chosen species and ecosystems, but one should not generalize this argument into a global claim to the effect that *every* species is crucial to a balanced ecosystem. Although ecologists used to agree that the complexity of an ecosystem stabilizes it, this hypothesis has been subject to a number of criticisms and qualifications, both from a theoretical and an empirical perspective.[4] And for certain kinds of species (those which occupy a rather small area and whose normal population is small) we can argue that extinction would probably not disrupt the community. However fragile the biosphere may be, the extreme view that everything is crucial is almost certainly not true.

But, of course, environmentalists are often concerned by the fact that extinctions are occurring now at a rate much higher than in earlier times. It is mass extinction that threatens the biosphere, they say, and this claim avoids the spurious assertion that communities are so fragile that even one extinction will cause a crash. However, if the point is to avoid a mass extinction of species, how does this provide a rationale for preserving a species of the kind just described, of which we rationally believe that its passing will not destabilize the ecosystem? And, more generally, if mass extinction is known to be a danger to us, how does this translate into a value for preserving any particular species? Notice that we have now passed beyond the confines of the argument from ignorance; we are taking as a premise the idea that mass extinction would be a catastrophe (since it would destroy the ecosystem on which we depend). But how should that premise affect our valuing the California condor, the blue whale, or the snail darter?

III.   The Slippery Slope Argument

Environmentalists sometimes find themselves asked to explain why each species matters so much to them, when there are, after all, so many. We may know of special reasons for valuing particular species, but how can we justify thinking that each and every species is important? "Each extinction impoverishes the biosphere" is often the answer given, but it really fails to resolve the issue. Granted, each extinction impoverishes, but it only impoverishes a little bit. So if it is the *wholesale* impoverishment of the biosphere that matters, one would apparently have to concede that each extinction matters a little, but only a little. But environmentalists may be loathe to concede this, for if they concede that each species matters only a little, they seem to be inviting the wholesale impoverishment that would be an unambiguous disaster. So they dig in their heels and insist that each species matters a lot. But to take this line, one must find some other rationale than the idea that mass extinction would be a great harm. Some of these alternative rationales we will examine later. For now, let us take a closer look at the train of thought involved here.

Slippery slopes are curious things: if you take even one step onto them, you inevitably slide all the way to the bottom. So if you want to avoid finding yourself at the bottom, you must avoid stepping onto them at all. To mix metaphors, stepping onto a slippery slope is to invite being nickeled and dimed to death. . . .

Starting with 10 million extant species, and valuing overall diversity, the environmentalist does not want to grant that each species matters only a little. For having granted this, commercial expansion and other causes will reduce the tally to 9,999,999. And then the argument is repeated, with each species valued only a little, and diversity declines another notch. And so we are well on our way to a considerably impoverished biosphere, a little at a time. Better to reject the starting premise—namely, that each species matters only a little—so that the slippery slope can be avoided.

Slippery slopes should hold no terror for environmentalists, because it is often a mistake to demand that a line be drawn. Let me illustrate by an example. What is the difference between being bald and not? Presumably, the difference concerns the number of hairs you have on your head. But what is the precise number of hairs marking the boundary between baldness and not being bald? There is no such number. Yet, it would be a fallacy to conclude that there is no difference between baldness and hairiness. The fact that you cannot draw a line does not force you to say that the two alleged categories collapse into one. . . . [M]y point is just that differences in degree do not demolish the possibility of there being real moral differences.

In the environmental case, if one places a value on diversity, then each species becomes more valuable as the overall diversity declines. If we begin with 10 million species, each may matter little, but as extinctions continue, the remaining ones matter more and more. According to this outlook, a better and better reason would be demanded for allowing yet another species to go extinct. Perhaps certain sorts of economic development would justify the extinction of a species at one time. But granting this does not oblige one to conclude that the same sort of decision would have to be made further down the road. This means that one can value diversity without being obliged to take the somewhat exaggerated position that each species, no matter how many there are, is terribly precious in virtue of its contribution to that diversity.

Yet, one can understand that environmentalists might be reluctant to concede this point. They may fear that if one now allows that most species contribute only a little to overall diversity, one will set in motion a political process that cannot correct itself later. The worry is that even when the overall diversity has been drastically reduced, our ecological sensitivities will have been so coarsened that we will no longer be in a position to realize (or to implement policies fostering) the preciousness of what is left. This fear may be quite justified, but it is important to realize that it does not conflict with what was argued above. The political utility of making an argument should not be confused with the argument's soundness.

The fact that you are on a slippery slope, by itself, does not tell you whether you are near the beginning, in the middle, or at the end. If species diversity is a matter of degree, where do we currently find ourselves—on the verge of catastrophe, well on our way in that direction, or at some distance from a global crash? Environmentalists often urge that we are fast approaching a precipice; if we are, then the reduction in diversity that every succeeding extinction engenders should be all we need to justify species preservation.

Sometimes, however, environmentalists advance a kind of argument not predicated on the idea of fast approaching doom. The goal is to show that there is something wrong with allowing a species to go extinct (or with causing it to go extinct), even if overall diversity is not affected much. I now turn to one argument of this kind.

IV. Appeals to What Is Natural

I noted earlier that environmentalists and animal liberationists disagree over the significance of the distinction between wild and domesticated animals. Since both types of organisms can experience pain, animal liberationists will think of each as meriting ethical consideration. But environmentalists will typically not put wild and domesticated organisms on a par. Environmentalists typically are interested in preserving what is natural, be it a species living in the wild or a wilderness ecosystem. If a kind of domesticated chicken were threatened with extinction, I doubt that environmental groups would be up in arms. And if certain unique types of human environments—say urban slums in the United States—were "endangered," it is similarly unlikely that environmentalists would view this process as a deplorable impoverishment of the biosphere.

The environmentalist's lack of concern for humanly created organisms and environments may be practical rather than principled. It may be that at the level of values, no such bifurcation is legitimate, but that from the point of view of practical political action, it makes sense to put one's energies into saving items that exist in the wild. This subject has not been discussed much in the literature, so it is

hard to tell. But I sense that the distinction between wild and domesticated has a certain theoretical importance to many environmentalists. They perhaps think that the difference is that we created
domesticated organisms which would otherwise not exist, and so are
entitled to use them solely for our own interests. But we did not create
wild organisms and environments, so it is the height of presumption
to expropriate them for our benefit. A more fitting posture would be
one of "stewardship": we have come on the scene and found a treasure not of our making. Given this, we ought to preserve this treasure
in its natural state.

I do not wish to contest the appropriateness of "stewardship." It is
the dichotomy between artificial (domesticated) and natural (wild)
that strikes me as wrong-headed. I want to suggest that to the degree
that "natural" means anything biologically, it means very little ethically. And, conversely, to the degree that "natural" is understood as a
normative concept, it has very little to do with biology.

Environmentalists often express regret that we human beings find
it so hard to remember that we are part of nature—one species
among many others—rather than something standing outside of
nature. I will not consider here whether this attitude is cause for complaint; the important point is that seeing us as part of nature rules
out the environmentalist's use of the distinction between artificial-
domesticated and natural-wild described above. *If we are part of nature,
then everything we do is part of nature, and is natural in that primary sense.*
When we domesticate organisms and bring them into a state of dependence on us, this is simply an example of one species exerting a
selection pressure on another. If one calls this "unnatural," one might
just as well say the same of parasitism or symbiosis (compare human
domestication of animals and plants and "slave-making" in the social
insects).

The concept of naturalness is subject to the same abuses as the
concept of normalcy. *Normal* can mean *usual* or it can mean *desirable.*
Although only the total pessimist will think that the two concepts are
mutually exclusive, it is generally recognized that the mere fact that
something is common does not by itself count as a reason for thinking that it is desirable. This distinction is quite familiar now in popular discussions of mental health, for example. Yet, when it comes to
environmental issues, the concept of naturalness continues to live a
double life. The destruction of wilderness areas by increased indus-
trialization is bad because it is unnatural. And it is unnatural because
it involves transforming a natural into an artificial habitat. Or one

might hear that although extinction is a natural process, the kind of mass extinction currently being precipitated by our species is unprecedented, and so is unnatural. Environmentalists should look elsewhere for a defense of their policies, lest conservation simply become a variant of uncritical conservatism in which the axiom "Whatever is, is right" is modified to read "Whatever is (before human beings come on the scene), is right." . . .

V.   Appeals to Needs and Interests

The version of utilitarianism considered earlier (according to which something merits ethical consideration if it can experience pleasure and/or pain) leaves the environmentalist in the lurch. But there is an alternative to Bentham's hedonistic utilitarianism that has been thought by some to be a foundation for environmentalism. Preference utilitarianism says that an object's having interests, needs, or preferences gives it ethical status. . . .

If one does not require of an object that it have a mind for it to have wants or needs, what is required for the possession of these ethically relevant properties? Suppose one says that an object needs something if it will cease to exist if it does not get it. Then species, plants, and mountain ranges have needs, but only in the sense that automobiles, garbage dumps, and buildings do too. If everything has needs, the advice to take needs into account in ethical deliberation is empty, unless it is supplemented by some technique for weighing and comparing the needs of different objects. A corporation will go bankrupt unless a highway is built. But the swamp will cease to exist if the highway is built. Perhaps one should take into account all relevant needs, but the question is how to do this in the event that needs conflict.

Although the concept of need can be provided with a permissive, all-inclusive definition, it is less easy to see how to do this with the concept of want. Why think that a mountain range "wants" to retain its unspoiled appearance, rather than house a new amusement park?[5] Needs are not at issue here, since in either case, the mountain continues to exist. One might be tempted to think that natural objects like mountains and species have "natural tendencies," and that the concept of want should be liberalized so as to mean that natural objects "want" to persist in their natural states. . . . Granted, a commercially undeveloped mountain will persist in this state, unless it is commercially developed. But it is equally true that a commercially untouched hill will become commercially developed, unless something causes this not to happen. I see no hope for extending the concept of wants to the full range of objects valued by environmentalists.

The same problems emerge when we try to apply the concepts of needs and wants to species. A species may need various resources, in the sense that these are necessary for its continued existence. But what do species want? Do they want to remain stable in numbers, neither growing nor shrinking? Or since most species have gone extinct, perhaps what species really want is to go extinct, and it is human meddlesomeness that frustrates this natural tendency? Preference utilitarianism is no more likely than hedonistic utilitarianism to secure autonomous ethical status for endangered species. . . .

VI.   Granting Wholes Autonomous Value

A number of environmentalists have asserted that environmental values cannot be grounded in values based on regard for individual welfare. . . . The point of view . . . isn't that preserving the integrity of ecosystems has autonomous value, to be taken into account just as the quite distinct value of individual human welfare is. Rather, the idea is that the only value is the holistic one of maintaining ecological balance and diversity. Here we have a view that is just as monolithic as the most single-minded individualism; the difference is that the unit of value is thought to exist at a higher level of organization.

It is hard to know what to say to someone who would save a mosquito, just because it is rare, rather than a human being, if there were a choice. In ethics, as in any other subject, rationally persuading another person requires the existence of shared assumptions. If this monolithic environmentalist view is based on the notion that ecosystems have needs and interests, and that these take total precedence over the rights and interests of individual human beings, then the discussion of the previous sections is relevant. And even supposing that these higher-level entities have needs and wants, what reason is there to suppose that these matter and that the wants and needs of individuals matter not at all? But if this source of defense is jettisoned, and it is merely asserted that only ecosystems have value, with no substantive defense being offered, one must begin by requesting an argument: *why* is ecosystem stability and diversity the only value? . . .

VII.   The Demarcation Problem

Perhaps the most fundamental theoretical problem confronting an environmentalist who wishes to claim that species and ecosystems have autonomous value is what I will call the *problem of demarcation*. Every ethical theory must provide principles that describe which objects matter for their own sakes and which do not. Besides marking the boundary between these two classes by enumerating a set of ethically relevant properties, an ethical theory must say why the properties named, rather than others, are the ones that count. Thus, for example, hedonistic utilitarianism cites the capacity to experience pleasure and/or pain as the decisive criterion; preference utilitarianism cites the having of preferences (or wants, or interests) as the decisive property. And a Kantian ethical theory will include an individual in the ethical community only if it is capable of rational reflection and autonomy. Not that justifying these various proposed solutions to the demarcation problem is easy; indeed, since this issue is so fundamental, it will be very difficult to justify one proposal as opposed to another. Still, a substantive ethical theory is obliged to try.

Environmentalists, wishing to avoid the allegedly distorting perspective of individualism, frequently want to claim autonomous value for wholes. This may take the form of a monolithic doctrine according to which the only thing that matters is the stability of the ecosystem. Or it may embody a pluralistic outlook according to which ecosystem stability and species preservation have an importance additional to the welfare of individual organisms. But an environmentalist theory shares with all ethical theories an interest in not saying that everything has autonomous value. The reason this position is proscribed is that it makes the adjudication of ethical conflict very difficult indeed. . . .

Environmentalists, as we have seen, may think of natural objects, like mountains, species, and ecosystems, as mattering for their own sake, but of artificial objects, like highway systems and domesticated animals, as having only instrumental value. If a mountain and a highway are both made of rock, it seems unlikely that the difference between them arises from the fact that mountains have wants, interests, and preferences, but highway systems do not. But perhaps the place to look for the relevant difference is not in their present physical composition, but in the historical fact of how each came into existence. Mountains were created by natural processes, whereas highways are humanly constructed. But once we realize that organisms construct their environments in nature, this contrast begins to cloud. Organisms do not passively reside in an environment whose properties are independently determined. Organisms transform their environments by physically interacting with them. An anthill is an artifact just as a highway is. Granted, a difference obtains at the level of whether conscious deliberation played a role, but can one take seriously the view that artifacts produced by conscious planning are thereby *less* valuable than ones that arise without the intervention of mentality. As we have noted before, although environmentalists often accuse their critics of failing to think in a biologically realistic way, their use of the distinction between "natural" and "artificial" is just the sort of idea that stands in need of a more realistic biological perspective.

My suspicion is that the distinction between natural and artificial is not the crucial one. On the contrary, certain features of environmental concerns imply that natural objects are exactly on a par with certain artificial ones. Here the intended comparison is not between mountains and highways, but between mountains and works of art. My goal in what follows is not to sketch a substantive conception of what determines the value of objects in these two domains, but to motivate an analogy.

For both natural objects and works of art, our values extend beyond the concerns we have for experiencing pleasure. Most of us value seeing an original painting more than we value seeing a copy, even when we could not tell the difference. When we experience works of art, often what we value is not just the kinds of experiences we have, but, in addition, the connections we usually have with certain real objects. . . . Nor is this fact about our valuation limited to such aesthetic and environmentalist contexts. We love various people in our lives. If a molecule-for-molecule replica of a beloved person were created, you would not love that individual, but would continue to love the individual to whom you actually were historically related. Here again, our attachments are to objects and people as they really are, and not just to the experiences that they facilitate.

Another parallel between environmentalist concerns and aesthetic values concerns the issue of context. Although environmentalists often stress the importance of preserving endangered species, they would not be completely satisfied if an endangered species were preserved by putting a number of specimens in a zoo or in a humanly constructed preserve. What is taken to be important is preserving the species in its natural habitat. This leads to the more holistic position that preserving ecosystems, and not simply preserving certain member species, is of primary importance. Aesthetic concerns often lead in the same direction. It was not merely saving a fresco or an altar piece that motivated art historians after the most recent flood in Florence. Rather, they wanted to save these works of art in their original ("natural") settings. Not just the painting, but the church that housed it; not just the church, but the city itself. The idea of objects residing in a "fitting" environment plays a powerful role in both domains.

Environmentalism and aesthetics both see value in rarity. Of two whales, why should one be more worthy of aid than another, just because one belongs to an endangered species? Here we have the $n + m$ question mentioned in Section I. As an ethical concern, rarity is difficult to understand. Perhaps this is because our ethical ideas concerning justice and equity (note the word) are saturated with individualism. But in the context of aesthetics, the concept of rarity is far from alien. A work of art may have enhanced value simply because there are very few other works by the same artist, or from the same historical period, or in the same style. It isn't that the price of the item may go up with rarity; I am talking about aesthetic value, not monetary worth. Viewed as valuable aesthetic objects, rare organisms may be valuable because they are rare.

A disanalogy may suggest itself. It may be objected that works of art are of instrumental value only, but that species and ecosystems have intrinsic value. Perhaps it is true, as claimed before, that our attachment to works of art, to nature, and to our loved ones extends beyond the experiences they allow us to have. But it may be argued that what is valuable in the aesthetic case is always the relation of a valuer to a valued object. When we experience a work of art, the value is not simply in the experience, but in the composite fact that we and the work of art are related in certain ways. This immediately suggests that if there were no valuers in the world, nothing would have value, since such relational facts could no longer obtain. So . . . it would seem that if an ecological crisis precipitated a collapse of the world system, the last human being (whom we may assume for the purposes of this example to be the last valuer) could set about destroying all works of art, and there would be nothing wrong in this. That is, if aesthetic objects are valuable only in so far as valuers can stand in certain relations to them, then when valuers disappear, so does the possibility of aesthetic value. This would deny, in one sense, that aesthetic objects are intrinsically valuable: it isn't they, in themselves, but rather the relational facts that they are part of, that are valuable.

In contrast, it has been claimed that the "last man" would be wrong to destroy natural objects such as mountains, salt marshes, and species. . . . If the last man ought to preserve these natural objects, then these objects appear to have a kind of autonomous value; their value would extend beyond their possible relations to valuers. If all this were true, we would have here a contrast between aesthetic and natural objects, one that implies that natural objects are more valuable than works of art. . . .

I find the example more puzzling than decisive. But, in the present context, . . . [w]e only have to decide whether this imagined situation brings out any relevant difference between aesthetic and environmental values. Were the last man to look up on a certain hillside, he would see a striking rock formation next to the ruins of a Greek temple. Long ago the temple was built from some of the very rocks that still stud the slope. Both promontory and temple have a history, and both have been transformed by the biotic and the abiotic environments. I myself find it impossible to advise the last man that the peak matters more than the temple. I do not see a relevant difference. Environmentalists, if they hold that the solution to the problem of demarcation is to be found in the distinction between natural and artificial, will have to find such a distinction. But if environmental values are aesthetic, no difference need be discovered.

Environmentalists may be reluctant to classify their concern as aesthetic. Perhaps they will feel that aesthetic concerns are frivolous. Perhaps they will feel that the aesthetic regard for artifacts that has been made possible by culture is antithetical to a proper regard for wilderness. But such contrasts are illusory. Concern for environmental values does not require a stripping away of the perspective afforded by civilization; to value the wild, one does not have to "become wild" oneself (whatever that may mean). Rather, it is the material comforts of civilization that make possible a serious concern for both aesthetic and environmental values. These are concerns that can become pressing in developed nations in part because the populations of those countries now enjoy a certain substantial level of prosperity. It would be the height of condescension to expect a nation experiencing hunger and chronic disease to be inordinately concerned with the autonomous value of ecosystems or with creating and preserving works of art. Such values are not frivolous, but they can become important to us only after certain fundamental human needs are satisfied. Instead of radically jettisoning individualist ethics, environmentalists may find a more hospitable home for their values in a category of value that has existed all along.

Notes

1. Mark Sagoff, "On Preserving the Natural Environment," *Yale Law Review* 84 (1974): 205–38; J. Baird Callicott, "Animal Liberation: A Triangular Affair," *Environmental Ethics* 2 (1980): 311–38; and Bryan Norton, "Environmental Ethics and Nonhuman Rights," *Environmental Ethics* 4 (1982): 17–36.

2. Peter Singer, *Animal Liberation* (New York: Random House, 1975), has elaborated a position of this sort.

3. A parallel with a quite different moral problem will perhaps make it clearer how the environmentalist's holism conflicts with some fundamental ethical ideas. When we consider the rights of individuals to receive compensation for harm, we generally expect that the individuals compensated must be one and the same as the individuals harmed. . . .

4. David Ehrenfeld, "The Conservation of Non-Resources," *American Scientist* 64 (1976): 648–56. For a theoretical discussion see Robert M. May, *Stability and Complexity in Model Ecosystems* (Princeton: Princeton University Press, 1973).

5. The example is Sagoff's, "Natural Environment," pp. 220–24.

Study Questions

1. What does Sober mean by "a holistic value system"?
2. What different meanings can be given to the term "natural"?
3. According to Sober, what is "the demarcation problem"?
4. In what ways, if any, is the extinction of a species akin to the destruction of a work of art?

CHAPTER 38

Ethics and Global Change

Dale Jamieson

Dale Jamieson is Professor of Environmental Studies and Philosophy at New York University. He argues that global warming requires us to alter our current value system. After all, if the environment were destroyed, no single individual would be found responsible. In the face of the challenge posed by climate change, he urges emphasis on such virtues as humility, courage, and moderation.

There are many uncertainties concerning climate change, but an international consensus has emerged that we are likely to see a 1.1 to 6.4 centigrade increase in the earth's mean surface temperature by the end of this century. Such a warming would have diverse impacts on human activities and would likely be catastrophic for many plants and nonhuman animals. My claim is that the problems engendered by the possibility of climate change are not purely scientific but also concern how we ought to live and how humans should relate to each other and to the rest of nature, and these are problems of ethics. . . .

Our current value system presupposes that harms and their causes are individual, that they can readily be identified, and that they are local in space and time. It is these aspects of our conception of responsibility on which I want to focus.

Consider an example of the sort of case with which our value system deals best. Jones breaks into Smith's house and steals Smith's television set. Jones's intent is clear: she wants Smith's television set. Smith suffers a clear harm; he is made worse off by having lost the

Dale Jamieson, "Ethics, Public Policy, and Global Warming," *Science, Technology, and Human Values*, 17, no. 2 (1992). Copyright © 1992 by Sage Publications and reprinted with its permission. Revised in 2010. Notes and references omitted.

television set. Jones is responsible for Smith's loss, for she was the cause of the harm and no one else was involved.

What we have in this case is a clear, self-contained story about Smith's loss. We know how to identify the harms and how to assign responsibility. We respond to this breech of our norms by punishing Jones in order to prevent her from doing it again and to deter others from such acts, or we require compensation from Jones so that Smith may be restored to his former position.

It is my contention that this paradigm collapses when we try to apply it to global environmental problems, such as those associated with human-induced global climate change. It is for this reason that we are often left feeling confused about how to think about these problems.

There are three important dimensions along which global environmental problems such as those involved with climate change vary from the paradigm: Apparently innocent acts can have devastating consequences, causes and harms may be diffuse, and causes and harms may be remote in space and time.

Consider an example. Some projections suggest that one effect of greenhouse warming may be to shift the Southern Hemisphere cyclone belt to the south. If this occurs the frequency of cyclones in Sydney, Australia, will increase enormously, resulting in great death and destruction. The causes of this death and destruction will be diffuse. There is no one whom we can identify as the cause of destruction in the way in which we can identify Jones as the cause of Smith's loss. Instead of a single cause, millions of people will have made tiny, almost imperceptible causal contributions—by driving cars, cutting trees, using electricity, and so on. They will have made these contributions in the course of their daily lives performing apparently "innocent" acts, without intending to bring about this harm. Moreover, most of these people will be geographically remote from Sydney, Australia. (Many of them will have no idea where Sydney, Australia, is.) Further, some people who are harmed will be remote in time from those who have harmed them. Sydney may suffer in the twenty-first century in part because of people's behavior in the nineteenth and twentieth centuries. Many small people doing small things over a long period of time together will cause unimaginable harms.

Despite the fact that serious, clearly identifiable harms will have occurred because of human agency, conventional morality would have trouble finding anyone to blame. For no one intended the bad outcome or brought it about or even was able to foresee it.

Today we face the possibility that the global environment may be destroyed, yet no one will be responsible. This is a new problem. It takes a great many people and a high level of consumption and production to change the earth's climate. It could not have been done in low-density, low-technology societies. Nor could it have been done in societies like ours until recently. London could be polluted by its inhabitants in the eighteenth century, but its reach was limited. Today no part of the planet is safe. Unless we develop new values and conceptions of responsibility, we will have enormous difficulty in motivating people to respond to this problem. . . .

In this essay I cannot hope to say what new values are needed or to provide a recipe for how to bring them about. Values are collectively created rather than individually dictated, and the dominance of economic models has meant that the study of values and value change has been neglected. However, I do have one positive suggestion: We should focus more on character and less on calculating probable outcomes. Focusing on outcomes has made us cynical calculators and has institutionalized hypocrisy. We can each reason: Since my contribution is small, outcomes are likely to be determined by the behavior of others. Reasoning in this way we can each justify driving cars while advocating bicycles or using fireplaces while favoring regulations against them. . . .

Calculating probable outcomes leads to unraveling the patterns of collective behavior that are needed in order to respond successfully to many of the global environmental problems that we face. When we "economize" our behavior in the way that is required for calculating, we systematically neglect the subtle and indirect effects of our actions, and for this reason we see individual action as inefficacious. For social change to occur it is important that there be people of integrity and character who act on the basis of principles and ideals.

The content of our principles and ideals is, of course, important. Principles and ideals can be eccentric or even demented. In my opinion, in order to address such problems as global climate change, we need to nurture and give new content to some old virtues such as humility, courage, and moderation and perhaps develop such new virtues as those of simplicity and conservatism. But whatever the best candidates are for twenty-first century virtues, what is important to recognize is the importance and centrality of the virtues in bringing about value change.

Study Questions

1. According to Jamieson, does global warming calls for new values?
2. Do you agree with Jamieson that global warming calls for new values?
3. Which values does he suggest?
4. Are the values he suggests new?

H. Abortion

CHAPTER 39

A Defense of Abortion

Judith Jarvis Thomson

Consider the argument that because a fetus is an innocent human being, and killing an innocent human being is always wrong, abortion is always wrong. Some would respond by denying that the earliest embryo is a human person, but putting that issue aside, is killing an innocent human being always wrong? In an article that has given rise to much discussion, Judith Jarvis Thomson, Professor Emerita at the Massachusetts Institute of Technology, argues that while people have a right not to be killed unjustly, they do not have an unqualified right to life. Hence even if the human fetus is a person, abortion may be morally permissible.

Most opposition to abortion relies on the premise that the fetus is a human being, a person, from the moment of conception. The premise is argued for, but, as I think, not well. Take, for example, the most common argument. We are asked to notice that the development of a human being from conception through birth into childhood is continuous; then it is said that to draw a line, to choose a point in this development and say "before this point the thing is not a person, after this point it is a person" is to make an arbitrary choice, a choice for which in the nature of things no good reason can be given. It is concluded that the fetus is, or anyway that we had better say it is, a person from the moment of conception. But this conclusion does not follow. Similar things might be said about the development of an acorn into an oak tree, and it does not follow that acorns are oak trees, or that we had better say they are. Arguments of this form are sometimes called "slippery slope arguments"— the phrase is perhaps self-explanatory—and it is dismaying that opponents of abortion rely on them so heavily and uncritically.

From *Philosophy & Public Affairs*, Vol. 1. Copyright © 1971. Reprinted by permission of Blackwell Publishing Ltd.

I am inclined to agree, however, that the prospects for "drawing a line" in the development of the fetus look dim. I am inclined to think also that we shall probably have to agree that the fetus has already become a human person well before birth. Indeed, it comes as a surprise when one first learns how early in its life it begins to acquire human characteristics. By the tenth week, for example, it already has a face, arms and legs, fingers and toes; it has internal organs, and brain activity is detectable. On the other hand, I think that the premise is false, that the fetus is not a person from the moment of conception. A newly fertilized ovum, a newly implanted clump of cells, is no more a person than an acorn is an oak tree. But I shall not discuss any of this. For it seems to me to be of great interest to ask what happens if, for the sake of argument, we allow the premise. How, precisely, are we supposed to get from there to the conclusion that abortion is morally impermissible? Opponents of abortion commonly spend most of their time establishing that the fetus is a person, and hardly any time explaining the step from there to the impermissibility of abortion. Perhaps they think the step too simple and obvious to require much comment. Or perhaps instead they are simply being economical in argument. Many of those who defend abortion rely on the premise that the fetus is not a person, but only a bit of tissue that will become a person at birth; and why pay out more arguments than you have to? Whatever the explanation, I suggest that the step they take is neither easy nor obvious, that it calls for closer examination than it is commonly given, and that when we do give it this closer examination we shall feel inclined to reject it.

I propose, then, that we grant that the fetus is a person from the moment of conception. How does the argument go from here? Something like this, I take it. Every person has a right to life. So the fetus has a right to life. No doubt the mother has a right to decide what shall happen in and to her body; everyone would grant that. But surely a person's right to life is stronger and more stringent than the mother's right to decide what happens in and to her body, and so outweighs it. So the fetus may not be killed; an abortion may not be performed.

It sounds plausible. But now let me ask you to imagine this. You wake up in the morning and find yourself back to back in bed with an unconscious violinist. A famous unconscious violinist. He has been found to have a fatal kidney ailment, and the Society of Music Lovers has canvassed all the available medical records and found that you alone have the right blood type to help. They have therefore kidnapped you, and last night the violinist's circulatory system was plugged into yours, so that your kidneys can be used to extract poisons from his blood as well as your own. The director of the hospital now tells you, "Look, we're sorry the Society of Music Lovers did this to you—we would never have permitted it if we had known. But still, they did it, and the violinist now is plugged into you. To unplug you would be to kill him. But never mind, it's only for nine months. By then he will have recovered from his ailment, and can safely be unplugged from you." Is it morally incumbent on you to accede to this situation? No doubt it would be very nice of you if you did, a great kindness. But do you *have* to accede to it? What if it were not nine months, but nine years? Or longer still? What if the director of the hospital says, "Tough luck, I agree, but you've now got to stay in bed, with the violinist plugged into you, for the rest of your life. Because remember this. All persons have a right to life, and violinists are persons. Granted you have a right to decide what happens in and to your body, but a person's right to life outweighs your right to decide what happens in and to your body. So you cannot ever be unplugged from him." I imagine you would regard this as outrageous, which suggests that something really is wrong with that plausible-sounding argument I mentioned a moment ago.

In this case, of course, you were kidnapped; you didn't volunteer for the operation that plugged the violinist into your kidneys. Can those who oppose abortion on the ground I mentioned make an exception for a pregnancy due to rape? Certainly. They can say that persons have a right to life only if they didn't come into existence because of rape; or they can say that all persons have a right to life, but that some have less of a right to life than others, in particular, that those who came into existence because of rape have less. But these statements have a rather unpleasant sound. Surely the question of whether you have a right to life at all, or how much of it you have, shouldn't turn on the question of whether or not you are the product of a rape. And in fact the people who oppose abortion on the ground I mentioned do not make this distinction, and hence do not make an exception in case of rape.

Nor do they make an exception for a case in which the mother has to spend the nine months of her pregnancy in bed. They would agree that would be a great pity, and hard on the mother; but all the same, all persons have a right to life, the fetus is a person, and so on. I suspect, in fact, that they would not make an exception for a case in which, miraculously enough, the pregnancy went on for nine years, or even the rest of the mother's life.

Some won't even make an exception for a case in which continuation of the pregnancy is likely to shorten the mother's life; they regard abortion as impermissible even to save the mother's life. Such cases are nowadays very rare, and many opponents of abortion do not accept this extreme view. All the same, it is a good place to begin: a number of points of interest come out in respect to it.

1. Let us call the view that abortion is impermissible even to save the mother's life "the extreme view." I want to suggest first that it does not issue from the argument I mentioned earlier without the addition of some fairly powerful premises. Suppose a woman has become pregnant, and now learns that she has a cardiac condition such that she will die if she carries the baby to term. What may be done for her? The fetus, being a person, has a right to life, but as the mother is a person too, so has she a right to life. Presumably they have an equal right to life. How is it supposed to come out that an abortion may not be performed? If mother and child have an equal right to life, shouldn't we perhaps flip a coin? Or should we add to the mother's right to life her right to decide what happens in and to her body, which everybody seems to be ready to grant—the sum of her rights now outweighing the fetus' right to life?

The most familiar argument here is the following: We are told that performing the abortion would be directly killing[1] the child, whereas doing nothing would not be killing the mother, but only letting her die. Moreover, in killing the child, one would be killing an innocent person, for the child has committed no crime, and is not aiming at his mother's death. And then there are a variety of ways in which this might be continued. (1) But as directly killing an innocent person is always and absolutely impermissible, an abortion may not be performed. Or, (2) as directly killing an innocent person is murder, and murder is always and absolutely impermissible, an abortion may not be performed. Or, (3) as one's duty to refrain from directly killing an innocent person is more stringent than one's duty to keep a person from dying, an abortion may not be performed. Or, (4) if one's only options are directly killing an innocent person or letting a person die, one must prefer letting the person die, and thus an abortion may not be performed.[2]

Some people seem to have thought that these are not further premises which must be added if the conclusion is to be reached, but that they follow from the very fact that an innocent person has a right to life. But this seems to me to be a mistake, and perhaps the simplest way to show this is to bring out that while we must certainly grant that innocent persons have a right to life, the theses in (1) through (4) are all false. Take (2), for example. If directly killing an innocent person is murder, and thus is impermissible, then the mother's directly killing the innocent person inside her is murder, and thus is impermissible. But it cannot seriously be thought to be murder if the mother performs an abortion on herself to save her life. It cannot seriously be said that she *must* refrain, that she *must* sit passively by and wait for her death. Let us look again at the case of you and the violinist. There you are, in bed with the violinist, and the director of the hospital says to you, "It's all most distressing, and I deeply sympathize, but you see this is putting an additional strain on your kidneys, and you'll be dead within the month. But you *have* to stay where you are all the same. Because unplugging you would be directly killing an innocent violinist, and that's murder, and that's impermissible." If anything in the world is true, it is that you do not commit murder, you do not do what is impermissible, if you reach around to your back and unplug yourself from that violinist to save your life.

The main focus of attention in writings on abortion has been on what a third party may or may not do in answer to a request from a woman for an abortion. This is in a way understandable. Things being as they are, there isn't much a woman can safely do to abort herself. So the question asked is what a third party may do, and what the mother may do, if it is mentioned at all, is deduced, almost as an afterthought, from what it is concluded that third parties may do. But it seems to me that to treat the matter in this way is to refuse to grant to the mother that very status of person which is so firmly insisted on for the fetus. For we cannot simply read off what a person may do from what a third party may do. Suppose you find yourself trapped in a tiny house with a growing child. I mean a very tiny house, and a rapidly growing child—you are already up against the wall of the house and in a few minutes you'll be crushed to death. The child on the other hand won't be crushed to death; if nothing is done to stop him from growing he'll be hurt, but in the end he'll simply burst open the house and walk out a free man. Now I could well understand it if a bystander were to say, "There's nothing we can do for you. We cannot choose between your life and his, we cannot be the ones to decide who is to live, we cannot intervene." But it cannot be concluded that you too can do nothing, that you cannot attack it to save your life. However innocent the child may be, you do not have to wait passively while it crushes you to death. Perhaps a pregnant woman is vaguely felt to have the status of house, to which we don't allow the right of self-defense. But if the woman houses the child, it should be remembered that she is a person who houses it.

I should perhaps stop to say explicitly that I am not claiming that people have a right to do anything whatever to save their lives. I think, rather, that there are drastic limits to the right of self-defense. If someone threatens you with death unless you torture someone else to death, I think you have not the right, even to save your life, to do so. But the case under consideration here is very different. In our case there are only two people involved, one whose life is threatened, and one who threatens it. Both are innocent: the one who is threatened is not threatened because of any fault, the one who threatens does not threaten because of any fault. For this reason we may feel that we bystanders cannot intervene. But the person threatened can.

In sum, a woman surely can defend her life against the threat to it posed by the unborn child, even if doing so involves its death. And this shows not merely that the theses in (1) through (4) are false; it shows also that the extreme view of abortion is false, and so we need not canvass any other possible ways of arriving at it from the argument I mentioned at the outset.

2. The extreme view could of course be weakened to say that while abortion is permissible to save the mother's life, it may not be performed by a third party, but only by the mother herself. But this cannot be right either. For what we have to keep in mind is that the mother and the unborn child are not like two tenants in a small house which has, by an unfortunate mistake, been rented to both: the mother *owns* the house. The fact that she does adds to the offensiveness of deducing that the mother can do nothing from the supposition that third parties can do nothing. But it does more than this: it casts a bright light on the supposition that third parties can do nothing. Certainly it lets us see that a third party who says "I cannot choose between you" is fooling himself if he thinks this is impartiality. If Jones has found and fastened on a certain coat, which he needs to keep him from freezing, but which Smith also needs to keep him from freezing, then it is not impartiality that says "I cannot choose between you" when Smith owns the coat. Women have said again and again, "This body is *my* body!" and they have reason to feel angry, reason to feel that it has been like shouting into the wind. Smith, after all, is hardly likely to bless us if we say to him, "Of course it's your coat, anybody would grant that it is. But no one may choose between you and Jones who is to have it."

We should really ask what it is that says "no one may choose" in the face of the fact that the body that houses the child is the mother's body. It may be simply a failure to appreciate this fact. But it may be something more interesting, namely, the sense that one has a right to refuse to lay hands on people, even where it would be just and fair to do so, even where justice seems to require that somebody do so. Thus justice might call for somebody to get Smith's coat back from Jones, and yet you have a right to refuse to be the one to lay hands on Jones, a right to refuse to do physical violence to him. This, I think, must be granted. But then what should be said is not "no one may choose," but only "*I* cannot choose," and indeed not even this, but "*I* will not *act*," leaving it open that somebody else can or should, and in particular that anyone in a position of authority, with the job of securing people's rights, both can and should. So this is no difficulty. I have not been arguing that any given third party must accede to the mother's request that he perform an abortion to save her life, but only that he may.

I suppose that in some views of human life the mother's body is only on loan to her, the loan not being one which gives her any prior claim to it. One who held this view might well think it impartiality to say "I cannot choose." But I shall simply ignore this possibility. My own view is that if a human being has any just, prior claim to anything at all, he has a just, prior claim to his own body. And perhaps this needn't be argued for here anyway, since, as I mentioned, the arguments against abortion we are looking at do grant that the woman has a right to decide what happens in and to her body.

But although they do grant it, I have tried to show that they do not take seriously what is done in granting it. I suggest the same thing will reappear even more clearly when we turn away from cases in which the mother's life is at stake, and attend, as I propose we now do, to the vastly more common cases in which a woman wants an abortion for some less weighty reason than preserving her own life.

3. Where the mother's life is not at stake, the argument I mentioned at the outset seems to have a much stronger pull. "Everyone has a right to life, so the unborn person has a right to life." And isn't the child's right to life weightier than anything other than the mother's own right to life, which she might put forward as ground for an abortion?

This argument treats the right to life as if it were unproblematic. It is not, and this seems to me to be precisely the source of the mistake.

For we should now, at long last, ask what it comes to, to have a right to life. In some views having a right to life includes having a right to be given at least the bare minimum one needs for continued life. But suppose that what in fact *is* the bare minimum a man needs for continued life is something he has no right at all to be given. If I am sick unto death, and the only thing that will save my life is the touch of Henry Fonda's cool hand on my fevered brow, then all the same, I have no right to be given the touch of Henry Fonda's cool hand on my fevered brow. It would be frightfully nice of him to fly in from the West Coast to provide it. It would be less nice, though no doubt well meant, if my friends flew out to the West Coast and carried Henry Fonda back with them. But I have no right at all against anybody that he should do this for me. Or again, to return to the story I told earlier, the fact that for continued life that violinist needs the continued use of your kidneys does not establish that he has a right to be given the continued use of your kidneys. He certainly has no right against you that *you* should give him continued use of your kidneys. For nobody has any right to use your kidneys unless you give him such a right; and nobody has the right against you that you shall give him this right—if you do allow him to go on using your kidneys, this is a kindness on your part, and not something he can claim from you as his due. Nor has he any right against anybody else that *they* should give him continued use of your kidneys. Certainly he had no right against the Society of Music Lovers that they should plug him into you in the first place. And if you now start to unplug yourself, having learned that you will otherwise have to spend nine years in bed with him, there is nobody in the world who must try to prevent you, in order to see to it that he is given something he has a right to be given.

Some people are rather stricter about the right to life. In their view, it does not include the right to be given anything, but amounts to, and only to, the right not to be killed by anybody. But here a related difficulty arises. If everybody is to refrain from killing that violinist, then everybody must refrain from doing a great many different sorts of things. Everybody must refrain from slitting his throat, everybody must refrain from shooting him—and everybody must refrain from unplugging you from him. But does he have a right against everybody that they shall refrain from unplugging you from him? To refrain from doing this is to allow him to continue to use your kidneys. It could be argued that he has a right against us that *we* should allow him to continue to use your kidneys. That is, while he had no right against us that we should give him the use of your kidneys, it might be argued that he anyway has a right against us that we shall not now intervene and deprive him of the use of your kidneys. I shall come back to third-party interventions later. But certainly the violinist has no right against you that *you* shall allow him to continue to use your kidneys. As I said, if you do allow him to continue to use them, it is a kindness on your part, and not something you owe him.

The difficulty I point to here is not peculiar to the right to life. It reappears in connection with all the other natural rights; and it is something which an adequate account of rights must deal with. For present purposes it is enough just to draw attention to it. But I would stress that I am not arguing that people do not have a right to life—quite to the contrary, it seems to me that the primary control we must place on the acceptability of an account of rights is that it should turn out in that account to be a truth that all persons have a right to life. I am arguing only that having a right to life does not guarantee having either a right to be given the use of or a right to be allowed continued use of another person's body—even if one needs it for life itself. So the right to life will not serve the opponents of abortion in the very simple and clear way in which they seem to have thought it would.

4. There is another way to bring out the difficulty. In the most ordinary sort of case, to deprive someone of what he has a right to is to treat him unjustly. Suppose a boy and his small brother are jointly given a box of chocolates for Christmas. If the older boy takes the box and refuses to give his brother any of the chocolates, he is unjust to him, for the brother has been given a right to half of them. But suppose that, having learned that otherwise it means nine years in bed with that violinist, you unplug yourself from him. You surely are not being unjust to him, for you gave him no right to use your kidneys, and no one else can have given him any such right. But we have to notice that in unplugging yourself, you are killing him; and violinists, like everybody else, have a right to life, and thus in the view we were considering just now, the right not to be killed. So here you do what he supposedly has a right you shall not do, but you do not act unjustly to him in doing it.

The emendation which may be made at this point is this: the right to life consists not in the right not to be killed, but rather in the right not to be killed unjustly. This runs a risk of circularity, but never mind: it would enable us to square the fact that the violinist has a right to life with the fact that you do not act unjustly toward him in unplugging yourself, thereby killing him. For if you do not kill him unjustly, you do not violate his right to life, and so it is no wonder you do him no injustice.

But if this emendation is accepted, the gap in the argument against abortion stares us plainly in the face: it is by no means enough to show that the fetus is a person, and to remind us that all persons have a right to life—we need to be shown also that killing the fetus violates its right to life, i.e., that abortion is unjust killing. And is it?

I suppose we may take it as a datum that in a case of pregnancy due to rape the mother has not given the unborn person a right to the use of her body for food and shelter. Indeed, in what pregnancy could it be supposed that the mother has given the unborn person such a right? It is not as if there were unborn persons drifting about the world, to whom a woman who wants a child says, "I invite you in."

But it might be argued that there are other ways one can have acquired a right to the use of another person's body than by having been invited to use it by that person. Suppose a woman voluntarily indulges in intercourse, knowing of the chance it will issue in pregnancy, and then she does become pregnant; is she not in part responsible for the presence, in fact the very existence, of the unborn person inside her? No doubt she did not invite it in. But doesn't her partial responsibility for its being there itself give it a right to the use of her body? If so, then her aborting it would be more like the boy's taking away the chocolates, and less like your unplugging yourself from the violinist—doing so would be depriving it of what it does have a right to, and thus would be doing it an injustice.

And then, too, it might be asked whether or not she can kill it even to save her own life: If she voluntarily called it into existence, how can she now kill it, even in self-defense?

The first thing to be said about this is that it is something new. Opponents of abortion have been so concerned to make out the independence of the fetus, in order to establish that it has a right to life, just as its mother does, that they have tended to overlook the possible support they might gain from making out that the fetus is *dependent* on the mother, in order to establish that she has a special kind of responsibility for it, a responsibility that gives it rights against her which are not possessed by any independent person—such as an ailing violinist who is a stranger to her.

On the other hand, this argument would give the unborn person a right to its mother's body only if her pregnancy resulted from a voluntary act, undertaken in full knowledge of the chance a pregnancy might result from it. It would leave out entirely the unborn person whose existence is due to rape. Pending the availability of some further argument, then, we would be left with the conclusion that unborn persons whose existence is due to rape have no right to the use of their mothers' bodies, and thus that aborting them is not depriving them of anything they have a right to and hence is not unjust killing.

And we should also notice that it is not at all plain that this argument really does go even as far as it purports to. For there are cases and cases, and the details make a difference. If the room is stuffy, and I therefore open a window to air it, and a burglar climbs in, it would be absurd to say, "Ah, now he can stay, she's given him a right to the use of her house—for she is partially responsible for his presence there, having voluntarily done what enabled him to get in, in full knowledge that there are such things as burglars, and that burglars burgle." It would be still more absurd to say this if I had had bars installed outside my windows, precisely to prevent burglars from getting in, and a burglar got in only because of a defect in the bars. It remains equally absurd if we imagine it is not a burglar who climbs in, but an innocent person who blunders or falls in. Again, suppose it were like this: people-seeds drift about in the air like pollen, and if you open your windows, one may drift in and take root in your carpets or upholstery. You don't want children, so you fix up your windows with fine mesh screens, the very best you can buy. As can happen, however, and on very, very rare occasions does happen, one of the screens is defective; and a seed drifts in and takes root. Does the person-plant who now develops have a right to the use of your house? Surely not—despite the fact that you voluntarily opened your windows, you knowingly kept carpets and upholstered furniture, and you knew that screens were sometimes defective. Someone may argue that you are responsible for its rooting, that it does have a right to your house, because after all you *could* have lived out your life with bare floors and furniture, or with sealed windows and doors. But this won't do—for by the same token anyone can avoid a pregnancy due to rape by having a hysterectomy, or anyway by never leaving home without a (reliable!) army.

It seems to me that the argument we are looking at can establish at most that there are *some* cases in which the unborn person has a right to the use of its mother's body, and therefore *some* cases in which abortion is unjust killing. There is room for much discussion and argument as to precisely which, if any. But I think we should sidestep this issue and leave it open, for at any rate the argument certainly does not establish that all abortion is unjust killing.

5. There is room for yet another argument here, however. We surely must all grant that there may be cases in which it would be morally indecent to detach a person from your body at the cost of his life. Suppose you learn that what the violinist needs is not nine years of your life, but only one hour: all you need do to save his life is to spend one hour in that bed with him. Suppose also that letting him use your kidneys for that one hour would not affect your health in the slightest. Admittedly you were kidnapped. Admittedly you did not give anyone permission to plug him into you. Nevertheless it seems to me plain you *ought* to allow him to use your kidneys for that hour—it would be indecent to refuse.

Again, suppose pregnancy lasted only an hour, and constituted no threat to life or health. And suppose that a woman becomes pregnant as a result of rape. Admittedly she did not voluntarily do anything to bring about the existence of a child. Admittedly she did nothing at all which would give the unborn person a right to the use of her body. All the same it might well be said, as in the newly emended violinist story, that she *ought* to allow it to remain for that hour—that it would be indecent of her to refuse.

Now some people are inclined to use the term "right" in such a way that it follows from the fact that you ought to allow a person to use your body for the hour he needs, that he has a right to use your body for the hour he needs, even though he has not been given that right by any person or act. They may say that it follows also that if you refuse, you act unjustly toward him. This use of the term is perhaps so common that it cannot be called wrong; nevertheless it seems to me to be an unfortunate loosening of what we would do better to keep a tight rein on. Suppose that box of chocolates I mentioned earlier had not been given to both boys jointly, but was given only to the older boy. There he sits, stolidly eating his way through the box, his small brother watching enviously. Here we are likely to say, "You ought not to be so mean. You ought to give your brother some of those chocolates." My own view is that it just does not follow from the truth of this that the brother has any right to any of the chocolates. If the boy refuses to give his brother any, he is greedy, stingy, callous—but not unjust. I suppose that the people I have in mind will say it does follow that the brother has a right to some of the chocolates, and thus that the boy does act unjustly if he refuses to give his brother any. But the effect of saying this is to obscure what we should keep distinct, namely, the difference between the boy's refusal in this case and the boy's refusal in the earlier case, in which the box was given to both boys jointly, and in which the small brother thus had what was from any point of view clear title to half.

A further objection to so using the term "right" that from the fact that A ought to do a thing for B, it follows that B has a right against A that A do it for him, is that it is going to make the question of whether or not a man has a right to a thing turn on how easy it is to provide him with it; and this seems not merely unfortunate, but morally unacceptable. Take the case of Henry Fonda again. I said earlier that I had no right to the touch of his cool hand on my fevered brow, even though I needed it to save my life. I said it would be frightfully nice of him to fly in from the West Coast to provide me with it, but that I had no right against him that he should do so. But suppose he isn't on the West Coast. Suppose he has only to walk across the room, place a hand briefly on my brow—and lo, my life is saved. Then surely he ought to do it, it would be indecent to refuse. Is it to be said, "Ah, well, it follows that in this case she has a right to the touch of his hand on her brow, and so it would be an injustice in him to refuse"? So that I have a right to it when it is easy for him to provide it, though no right when it's hard? It's rather a shocking idea that anyone's rights should fade away and disappear as it gets harder and harder to accord them to him.

So my own view is that even though you ought to let the violinist use your kidneys for the one hour he needs, we should not conclude that he has a right to do so—we should say that if you refuse, you are, like the boy who owns all the chocolates and will give none away, self-centered and callous, indecent in fact, but not unjust. And similarly, that even supposing a case in which a woman pregnant due to rape ought to allow the unborn person to use her body for the hour he needs, we should not conclude that he has a right to do so; we should conclude that she is self-centered, callous, indecent, but not unjust, if she refuses. The complaints are no less grave; they are just different. However, there is no need to insist on this point. If anyone does wish to deduce "he has a right" from "you ought," then all the same he must surely grant that there are cases in which it is not morally required of you that you allow that violinist to use your kidneys, and in which he does not have a right to use them, and in which you do not do him an injustice if you refuse. And so also for mother and unborn child. Except in such cases as the unborn person has a right to demand it—and we were leaving open the possibility that there may be such cases—nobody is morally *required* to make large sacrifices, of health, of all other interests and concerns, of all other duties and commitments, for nine years, or even for nine months, in order to keep another person alive.

6. We have in fact to distinguish between two kinds of Samaritan: the Good Samaritan and what we might call the Minimally Decent Samaritan. The story of the Good Samaritan, you will remember, goes like this:

> A certain man went down from Jerusalem to Jericho, and fell among thieves, which stripped him of his raiment, and wounded him, and departed, leaving him half dead.
>
> And by chance there came down a certain priest that way; and when he saw him, he passed by on the other side.
>
> And likewise a Levite, when he was at the place, came and looked on him, and passed by on the other side.
>
> But a certain Samaritan, as he journeyed, came where he was; and when he saw him he had compassion on him.
>
> And went to him, and bound up his wounds, pouring in oil and wine, and set him on his own beast, and brought him to an inn, and took care of him.
>
> And on the morrow, when he departed, he took out two pence, and gave them to the host, and said unto him, "Take care of him; and whatsoever thou spendest more, when I come again, I will repay thee."
>
> —(Luke 10:30–35)

The Good Samaritan went out of his way, at some cost to himself, to help one in need of it. We are not told what the options were, that is, whether or not the priest and the Levite could have helped by doing less than the Good Samaritan did, but assuming they could have, then the fact they did nothing at all shows they were not even Minimally Decent Samaritans, not because they were not Samaritans, but because they were not even minimally decent. . . .

After telling the story of the Good Samaritan, Jesus said, "Go, and do thou likewise." Perhaps he meant that we are morally required to act as the Good Samaritan did. Perhaps he was urging people to do more than is morally required of them. At all events it seems plain that . . . it is not morally required of anyone that he give long stretches of his life—nine years or nine months—to sustaining the life of a person who has no special right (we were leaving open the possibility of this) to demand it. . . .

We have . . . to look now at third-party interventions. I have been arguing that no person is morally required to make large sacrifices to sustain the life of another who has no right to demand them, and this even where the sacrifices do not include life itself; we are not morally required to be Good Samaritans or anyway Very Good Samaritans to one another. But what if a man cannot extricate himself from such a situation? What if he appeals to us to extricate him? It seems to me plain that there are cases in which we can, cases in which a Good Samaritan would extricate him. There you are, you were kidnapped, and nine years in bed with that violinist lie ahead of you. You have your own life to lead. You are sorry, but you simply cannot see giving up so much of your life to the sustaining of his. You cannot extricate yourself, and ask us to do so. I should have thought that—in light of his having no right to the use of your body—it was obvious that we do not have to accede to your being forced to give up so much. We can do what you ask. There is no injustice to the violinist in our doing so.

7. Following the lead of the opponents of abortion, I have through-out been speaking of the fetus merely as a person, and what I have been asking is whether or not the argument we began with, which proceeds only from the fetus' being a person, really does establish its conclusion. I have argued that it does not.

But of course there are arguments and arguments, and it may be said that I have simply fastened on the wrong one. It may be said that what is important is not merely the fact that the fetus is a person, but that it is a person for whom the woman has a special kind of respon-sibility issuing from the fact that she is its mother. And it might be argued that all my analogies are therefore irrelevant—for you do not have that special kind of responsibility for that violinist, Henry Fonda does not have that special kind of responsibility for me. And our attention might be drawn to the fact that men and women both *are* compelled by law to provide support for their children.

I have in effect dealt (briefly) with this argument in section 4 above; but a (still briefer) recapitulation now may be in order. Surely we do not have any such "special responsibility" for a person unless we have assumed it, explicitly or implicitly. If a set of parents do not try to prevent pregnancy, do not obtain an abortion, and then at the time of birth of the child do not put it out for adoption, but rather take it home with them, then they have assumed responsibility for it, they have given it rights, and they cannot *now* withdraw support from it at the cost of its life because they now find it difficult to go on pro-viding for it. But if they have taken all reasonable precautions against having a child, they do not simply by virtue of their biological rela-tionship to the child who comes into existence have a special respon-sibility for it. They may wish to assume responsibility for it, or they may not wish to. And I am suggesting that if assuming responsibility for it would require large sacrifices, then they may refuse. A Good Samaritan would not refuse—or anyway, a Splendid Samaritan, if the sacrifices that had to be made were enormous. But then so would a Good Samaritan assume responsibility for that violinist; so would Henry Fonda, if he is a Good Samaritan, fly in from the West Coast and assume responsibility for me.

8. My argument will be found unsatisfactory on two counts by many of those who want to regard abortion as morally permissible. First, while I do argue that abortion is not impermissible, I do not argue that it is always permissible. There may well be cases in which carrying the child to term requires only Minimally Decent Samaritanism of the mother, and this is a standard we must not fall below. I am inclined to think it a merit of my account precisely that it does *not* give a general yes or a general no. It allows for and supports our sense that, for example, a sick and desperately frightened fourteen-year-old schoolgirl, pregnant due to rape, may *of course* choose abortion, and that any law which rules this out is an insane law. And it also allows for and supports our sense that in other cases resort to abortion is even positively indecent. It would be indecent in the woman to request an abortion, and indecent in the doctor to perform it, if she is in her seventh month, and wants the abortion just to avoid the nuisance of postponing a trip abroad. The very fact that the arguments I have been drawing attention to treat all cases of abortion, or even all cases of abortion in which the mother's life is not at stake, as morally on a par ought to have made them suspect at the outset.

Secondly, while I am arguing for the permissibility of abortion in some cases, I am not arguing for the right to secure the death of the unborn child. It is easy to confuse these two things in that up to a certain point in the life of the fetus it is not able to survive outside the mother's body; hence removing it from her body guarantees its death. But they are importantly different. I have argued that you are not morally required to spend nine months in bed, sustaining the life of that violinist; but to say this is by no means to say that if, when you unplug yourself, there is a miracle and he survives, you then have a right to turn round and slit his throat. You may detach yourself even if this costs him his life; you have no right to be guaranteed his death, by some other means, if unplugging yourself does not kill him. There are some people who will feel dissatisfied by this feature of my argument. A woman may be utterly devastated by the thought of a child, a bit of herself, put out for adoption and never seen or heard of again.

She may therefore want not merely that the child be detached from her, but more, that it die. Some opponents of abortion are inclined to regard this as beneath contempt—thereby showing insensitivity to what is surely a powerful source of despair. All the same, I agree that the desire for the child's death is not one which anybody may gratify, should it turn out to be possible to detach the child alive.

At this place, however, it should be remembered that we have only been pretending throughout that the fetus is a human being from the moment of conception. A very early abortion is surely not the killing of a person, and so is not dealt with by anything I have said here.

Notes

1. The term "direct" in the arguments I refer to is a technical one. Roughly, what is meant by "direct killing" is either killing as an end in itself, or killing as a means to some end, for example, the end of saving someone else's life. . . .
2. The thesis in (4) is in an interesting way weaker than those in (1), (2), and (3): they rule out abortion even in cases in which both mother *and* child will die if the abortion is not performed. By contrast, one who held the view expressed in (4) could consistently say that one needn't prefer letting two persons die to killing one.

Study Questions

1. What are the main points Thomson seeks to make by the example of the unconscious violinist?
2. Does the morality of aborting a fetus depend on the conditions surrounding its conception?
3. If abortion is murder, who is the murderer, and what is the appropriate punishment?
4. If the abortion controversy is described as a debate between those who believe in a right to life and those who affirm a woman's right to choose, on which side is Thomson?

CHAPTER 40

On the Moral and Legal Status of Abortion

Mary Anne Warren

Mary Anne Warren, whose work we read previously, argues that among the characteristics central to personhood are the capacity to experience pain and pleasure, feel happy or sad, solve complex problems, communicate messages on a variety of topics, have a concept of oneself as a member of a social group, and regulate one's own action through moral principles. Warren maintains that a fetus, lacking these traits, is not a person, and hence women's rights override whatever right to life a fetus may possess.

For our purposes, abortion may be defined as the act a woman performs in deliberately terminating her pregnancy before it comes to term, or in allowing another person to terminate it. Abortion usually entails the death of a fetus. Nevertheless, I will argue that it is morally permissible, and should be neither legally prohibited nor made needlessly difficult to obtain, e.g., by obstructive legal regulations.

Some philosophers have argued that the moral status of abortion cannot be resolved by rational means. If this is so then liberty should prevail; for it is not a proper function of the law to enforce prohibitions upon personal behavior that cannot clearly be shown to be morally objectionable, and seriously so. But the advocates of prohibition believe that their position is objectively correct, and not merely a result of religious beliefs or personal prejudices. They argue that the humanity of the fetus is a matter of scientific fact, and that abortion is therefore the moral equivalent of murder, and must be prohibited in all or most cases. (Some would make an exception when the woman's life is in danger, or when the pregnancy is due to rape or incest; others would prohibit abortion even in these cases.)

In response, advocates of a right to choose abortion point to the terrible consequences of prohibiting it, especially while contraception is still unreliable, and is financially beyond the reach of much of the world's population. Worldwide, hundreds of thousands of women die each year from illegal abortions, and many more suffer from complications that may leave them injured or infertile. Women who are poor, underage, disabled, or otherwise vulnerable, suffer most from the absence of safe and legal abortion. Advocates of choice also argue that to deny a woman access to abortion is to deprive her of the right to control her own body—a right so fundamental that without it other rights are often all but meaningless.

These arguments do not convince abortion opponents. The tragic consequences of prohibition leave them unmoved, because they regard the deliberate killing of fetuses as even more tragic. Nor do appeals to the right to control one's own body impress them, since they deny that this right includes the right to destroy a fetus. We cannot hope to persuade those who equate abortion with murder that they are mistaken, unless we can refute the standard anti-abortion argument: that because fetuses are human beings, they have a right to life equal to that of any other human being. Unfortunately, confusion has prevailed with respect to the two important questions which that argument raises: (1) Is a human fetus really a human being at all stages of prenatal development? and (2) If so, what (if anything) follows about the moral and legal status of abortion? . . .

My . . . inquiry will . . . have two stages. In Section I, I consider whether abortion can be shown to be morally permissible even on the assumption that a fetus is a human being with a strong right to life. I argue that this cannot be established, except in special cases. Consequently, we cannot avoid facing the question of whether or not a fetus has the same right to life as any human being.

In Section II, I propose an answer to this question, namely, that a fetus is not a member of the moral community—the set of beings with full and equal moral rights. The reason that a fetus is not a member of the moral community is that it is not yet a person, nor is it enough like a person in the morally relevant respects to be regarded the equal of those human beings who are persons. I argue that it is personhood, and not genetic humanity, which is the fundamental basis for membership in the moral community. A fetus, especially in the early stages of its development, satisfies none of the criteria of personhood. Consequently, it makes no sense to grant it moral rights strong enough to override the woman's moral rights to liberty, bodily integrity, and sometimes life itself. Unlike an infant who has already been born, a fetus cannot be granted full and equal moral rights without severely threatening the rights and well-being of women. Nor, as we will see, is a fetus's *potential* personhood a threat to the moral permissibility of abortion, since merely potential persons do not have a moral right to become actual—or none that is strong enough to override the fundamental moral rights of actual persons.

I

Judith Thomson argues that, even if a fetus has a right to life, abortion is often morally permissible. Her argument is based upon an imaginative analogy. She asks you to picture yourself waking up one day, in bed with a famous violinist, who is a stranger to you. Imagine that you have been kidnapped, and your bloodstream connected to that of the violinist, who has an ailment that will kill him unless he is permitted to share your kidneys for nine months. No one else can save him, since you alone have the right type of blood. Consequently, the Society of Music Lovers has arranged for you to be kidnapped and hooked up. If you unhook yourself, he will die. But if you remain in bed with him, then after nine months he will be cured and able to survive without further assistance from you.

Now, Thomson asks, what are your obligations in this situation? To be consistent, the anti-abortionist must say that you are obliged to stay in bed with the violinist: for violinists are human beings, and all human beings have a right to life. But this is outrageous; thus, there must be something very wrong with the same argument when it is applied to abortion. It would be extremely generous of you to agree to stay in bed with the violinist; but it is absurd to suggest that your refusal to do so would be the moral equivalent of murder. The violinist's right to life does not oblige you to do whatever is required to keep him alive; still less does it justify anyone else in forcing you to do so. A law which required you to stay in bed with the violinist would be an unjust law, since unwilling persons ought not to be required to be Extremely Good Samaritans, i.e., to make enormous personal sacrifices for the sake of other individuals toward whom they have no special prior obligation.

Thomson concludes that we can grant the anti-abortionist his claim that a fetus is a human being with a right to life, and still hold that a pregnant woman is morally entitled to refuse to be an Extremely Good Samaritan toward the fetus. For there is a great gap between the claim that a human being has a right to life, and the claim that other human beings are morally obligated to do whatever is necessary to keep him alive. One has no duty to keep another human being alive *at a great personal cost*, unless one has somehow contracted a special obligation toward that individual; and a woman who is pregnant may have done nothing that morally obliges her to make the burdensome personal sacrifices necessary to preserve the life of the fetus.

This argument is plausible, and in the case of pregnancy due to rape it is probably conclusive. Difficulties arise, however, when we attempt to specify the larger range of cases in which abortion can be justified on the basis of this argument. Thomson considers it a virtue of her argument that it does not imply that abortion is *always* morally permissible. It would, she says, be indecent for a woman in her seventh month of pregnancy to have an abortion in order to embark on a trip to Europe. On the other hand, the violinist analogy shows that, "a sick and desperately frightened fourteen-year-old schoolgirl, pregnant due to rape, may *of course* choose abortion, and that any law which rules this out is an insane law." So far, so good; but what are we to say about the woman who becomes pregnant not through rape but because she and her partner did not use available forms of contraception, or because their attempts at contraception failed? What about a woman who becomes pregnant intentionally, but then re-evaluates the wisdom of having a child? In such cases, the violinist analogy is considerably less useful to advocates of the right to choose abortion.

It is perhaps only when a woman's pregnancy is due to rape, or some other form of coercion, that the situation is sufficiently analogous to the violinist case for our moral intuitions to transfer convincingly from the one case to the other. One difference between a pregnancy caused by rape and most unwanted pregnancies is that only in the former case is it perfectly clear that the woman is in no way responsible for her predicament. In the other cases, she *might* have been able to avoid becoming pregnant, e.g., by taking birth control pills (more faithfully), or insisting upon the use of high-quality condoms, or even avoiding heterosexual intercourse altogether throughout her fertile years. In contrast, if you are suddenly kidnapped by strange music lovers and hooked up to a sick violinist, then you are in no way responsible for your situation, which you could not have foreseen or prevented. And responsibility does seem to matter here. If a person behaves in a way which she could have avoided, and which she knows might bring into existence a human being who will depend upon her for survival, then it is not entirely clear that if and when that happens she may rightly refuse to do what she must in order to keep that human being alive.

This argument shows that the violinist analogy provides a persuasive defense of a woman's right to choose abortion only in cases where she is in no way morally responsible for her own pregnancy. In all other cases, the assumption that a fetus has a strong right to life makes it necessary to look carefully at the particular circumstances in order to determine the extent of the woman's responsibility, and hence the extent of her obligation. This outcome is unsatisfactory to advocates of the right to choose abortion, because it suggests that the decision should not be left in the woman's own hands, but should be supervised by other persons, who will inquire into the most intimate aspects of her personal life in order to determine whether or not she is entitled to choose abortion.

A supporter of the violinist analogy might reply that it is absurd to suggest that forgetting her pill one day might be sufficient to morally oblige a woman to complete an unwanted pregnancy. And indeed it is absurd to suggest this. As we will see, a woman's moral right to choose abortion does not depend upon the extent to which she might be thought to be morally responsible for her own pregnancy. But once we allow the assumption that a fetus has a strong right to life, we cannot avoid taking this absurd suggestion seriously. On this assumption, it is a vexing question whether and when abortion is morally justifiable. The violinist analogy can at best show that aborting a pregnancy is a deeply tragic act, though one that is sometimes morally justified.

My conviction is that an abortion is not always this deeply tragic, because a fetus is not yet a person, and therefore does not yet have a strong moral right to life. Although the truth of this conviction may not be self-evident, it does, I believe, follow from some highly plausible claims about the appropriate grounds for ascribing moral rights. It is worth examining these grounds, since this has not been adequately done before.

II

The question we must answer in order to determine the moral status of abortion is, How are we to define the moral community, the set of

beings with full and equal moral rights? What sort of entity has the in-
alienable moral rights to life, liberty, and the pursuit of happiness? . . .

On the Definition of "Human"

The term "human being" has two distinct, but not often distinguished, senses. This results in a slide of meaning, which serves to
conceal the fallacy in the traditional argument that, since (1) it is
wrong to kill innocent human beings, and (2) fetuses are innocent
human beings, therefore (3) it is wrong to kill fetuses. For if "human
being" is used in the same sense in both (1) and (2), then whichever
of the two senses is meant, one of these premises is question-begging.
And if it is used in different senses then the conclusion does not
follow.

Thus, (1) is a generally accepted moral truth,[1] and one that does
not beg the question about abortion, only if "human being" is used to
mean something like "a full-fledged member of the moral community, who is also a member of the human species." I will call this the
moral sense of "human being." It is not to be confused with what I will
call the *genetic* sense, i.e., the sense in which any individual entity that
belongs to the human species is a human being, regardless of whether
or not it is rightly considered to be an equal member of the moral
community. Premise (1) avoids begging the question only if the moral
sense is intended, while premise (2) avoids it only if what is intended
is the genetic sense. . . .

Defining the Moral Community

Is genetic humanity sufficient for moral humanity? There are good
reasons for not defining the moral community in this way. I would
suggest that the moral community consists, in the first instance, of all
persons, rather than all genetically human entities.[2] It is persons who
invent moral rights, and who are (sometimes) capable of respecting
them. It does not follow from this that only persons can have moral
rights. However, persons are wise not to ascribe to entities that clearly
are not persons moral rights that cannot in practice be respected
without severely undercutting the fundamental moral rights of those
who clearly are.

What characteristics entitle an entity to be considered a person?
This is not the place to attempt a complete analysis of the concept
of personhood; but we do not need such an analysis to explain why

a fetus is not a person. All we need is an approximate list of the most basic criteria of personhood. In searching for these criteria, it is useful to look beyond the set of people with whom we are acquainted, all of whom are human. Imagine, then, a space traveler who lands on a new planet, and encounters organisms unlike any she has ever seen or heard of. If she wants to behave morally toward these organisms, she has somehow to determine whether they are people and thus have full moral rights, or whether they are things that she need not feel guilty about treating, for instance, as a source of food.

How should she go about making this determination? If she has some anthropological background, she might look for signs of religion, art, and the manufacturing of tools, weapons, or shelters, since these cultural traits have frequently been used to distinguish our human ancestors from prehuman beings, in what seems to be closer to the moral than the genetic sense of "human being." She would be right to take the presence of such traits as evidence that the extraterrestrials were persons. It would, however, be anthropocentric of her to take the absence of these traits as proof that they were not, since they could be people who have progressed beyond, or who have never needed, these particular cultural traits.

I suggest that among the characteristics which are central to the concept of personhood are the following:

1. *sentience*—the capacity to have conscious experiences, usually including the capacity to experience pain and pleasure;
2. *emotionality*—the capacity to feel happy, sad, angry, loving, etc.;
3. *reason*—the capacity to solve new and relatively complex problems;
4. *the capacity to communicate*, by whatever means, messages of an indefinite variety of types; that is, not just with an indefinite number of possible contents, but on indefinitely many possible topics;
5. *self-awareness*—having a concept of oneself as an individual and/or as a member of a social group; and finally
6. *moral agency*—the capacity to regulate one's own actions through moral principles or ideals.

It is difficult to produce precise definitions of these traits, let alone to specify universally valid behavioral indications that these traits are present. But let us assume that our explorer knows approximately what these six characteristics mean, and that she is able to observe whether or not the extraterrestrials possess these mental and behavioral capacities. How should she use her findings to decide whether or not they are persons?

An entity need not have *all* of these attributes to be a person. And perhaps none of them is absolutely necessary. For instance, the absence of emotion would not disqualify a being that was person-like in all other ways. Think, for instance, of two of the *Star Trek* characters, Mr. Spock (who is half human and half alien), and Data (who is an android). Both are depicted as lacking the capacity to feel emotion; yet both are sentient, reasoning, communicative, self-aware moral agents, and unquestionably persons. Some people are unemotional; some cannot communicate well; some lack self-awareness; and some are not moral agents. It should not surprise us that many people do not meet all of the criteria of personhood. Criteria for the applicability of complex concepts are often like this: none may be logically necessary, but the more criteria that are satisfied, the more confident we are that the concept is applicable. Conversely, the fewer criteria are satisfied, the less plausible it is to hold that the concept applies. And if none of the relevant criteria are met, then we may be confident that it does not.

Thus, to demonstrate that a fetus is not a person, all I need to claim is that an entity that has *none* of these six characteristics is not a person. Sentience is the most basic mental capacity, and the one that may have the best claim to being a necessary (though not sufficient) condition for personhood. Sentience can establish a claim to moral considerability, since sentient beings can be harmed in ways that matter to them; for instance, they can be caused to feel pain, or deprived of the continuation of a life that is pleasant to them. It is unlikely that an entirely insentient organism could develop the other mental behavioral capacities that are characteristic of persons. Consequently, it is odd to claim that an entity that is not sentient, and that has never been sentient, is nevertheless a person. Persons who have permanently and irreparably lost all capacity for sentience, but who remain biologically alive, arguably still have strong moral rights by virtue of what they have been in the past. But small fetuses, which have not yet begun to have experiences, are not persons yet and do not have the rights that persons do.

The presumption that all persons have full and equal basic moral rights may be part of the very concept of a person. If this is so, then the concept of a person is in part a moral one; once we have admitted that X is a person, we have implicitly committed ourselves to recognizing X's right to be treated as a member of the moral community.

The claim that X is a *human being* may also be voiced as an appeal to treat X decently; but this is usually either because "human being" is used in the moral sense, or because of a confusion between genetic and moral humanity.

If (1)–(6) are the primary criteria of personhood, then genetic humanity is neither necessary nor sufficient for personhood. Some genetically human entities are not persons, and there may be persons who belong to other species. A man or woman whose consciousness has been permanently obliterated but who remains biologically alive is a human entity who may no longer be a person; and some unfortunate humans, who have never had any sensory or cognitive capacities at all, may not be people either. Similarly, an early fetus is a human entity which is not yet a person. It is not even minimally sentient, let alone capable of emotion, reason, sophisticated communication, self-awareness, or moral agency.[3] Thus, while it may be greatly valued as a future child, it does not yet have the claim to moral consideration that it may come to have later.

Moral agency matters to moral status, because it is moral agents who invent moral rights, and who can be obliged to respect them. Human beings have become moral agents from social necessity. Most social animals exist well enough, with no evident notion of a moral right. But human beings need moral rights, because we are not only highly social, but also sufficiently clever and self-interested to be capable of undermining our societies through violence and duplicity. For human persons, moral rights are essential for peaceful and mutually beneficial social life. So long as some moral agents are denied basic rights, peaceful existence is difficult, since moral agents justly resent being treated as something less. If animals of some terrestrial species are found to be persons, or if alien persons come from other worlds, or if human beings someday invent machines whose mental and behavioral capacities make them persons, then we will be morally obliged to respect the moral rights of these nonhuman persons—at least to the extent that they are willing and able to respect ours in turn.

Although only those persons who are moral agents can participate directly in the shaping and enforcement of moral rights, they need not and usually do not ascribe moral rights only to themselves and other moral agents. Human beings are social creatures who naturally care for small children, and other members of the social community who are not currently capable of moral agency. Moreover, we are all vulnerable to the temporary or permanent loss of the mental capacities necessary for moral agency. Thus, we have self-interested as well as altruistic reasons for extending basic moral rights to infants and other sentient human beings who have already been born, but who currently lack some of these other mental capacities. These human beings, despite their current disabilities, are persons and members of the moral community.

But in extending moral rights to beings (human or otherwise) that have few or none of the morally significant characteristics of persons, we need to be careful not to burden human moral agents with obligations that they cannot possibly fulfill, except at unacceptably great cost to their own well-being and that of those they care about. Women often cannot complete unwanted pregnancies, except at intolerable mental, physical, and economic cost to themselves and their families. And heterosexual intercourse is too important a part of the social lives of most men and women to be reserved for times when pregnancy is an acceptable outcome. . . . If fetuses were persons, then they would have rights that must be respected, even at great social or personal cost. But given that early fetuses, at least, are unlike persons in the morally relevant respects, it is unreasonable to insist that they be accorded exactly the same moral and legal status.

Fetal Development and the Right to Life

Two questions arise regarding the application of these suggestions to the moral status of the fetus. First, if indeed fetuses are not yet persons, then might they nevertheless have strong moral rights based upon the degree to which they *resemble* persons? Secondly, to what extent, if any, does a fetus's potential to *become* a person imply that we ought to accord to it some of the same moral rights? Each of these questions requires comment.

It is reasonable to suggest that the more like a person something is—the more it appears to meet at least some of the criteria of personhood—the stronger is the case for according it a right to life, and perhaps the stronger its right to life is. That being the case, perhaps the fetus gradually gains a stronger right to life as it develops. We should take seriously the suggestion that, just as "the human individual develops biologically in a continuous fashion, the rights of a human person . . . develop in the same way."[4] A seven-month fetus can apparently feel pain, and can respond to such stimuli as light and sound. Thus, it may have a rudimentary form of consciousness.

Nevertheless, it is probably not as conscious, or as capable of emotion, as even a very young infant is; and it has as yet little or no capacity for reason, sophisticated intentional communication, or self-awareness. In these respects, even a late-term fetus is arguably less like a person than are many nonhuman animals. Many animals (e.g., large-brained mammals such as elephants, cetaceans, or apes) are not only sentient, but clearly possessed of a degree of reason, and perhaps even of self-awareness. Thus, on the basis of its resemblance to a person, even a late-term fetus can have no more right to life than do these animals.

Animals may, indeed, plausibly be held to have some moral rights, and perhaps rather strong ones. But it is impossible in practice to accord full and equal moral rights to all animals. When an animal poses a serious threat to the life or well-being of a person, we do not, as a rule, greatly blame the person for killing it; and there are good reasons for this species-based discrimination. Animals, however intelligent in their own domains, are generally not beings with whom we can reason; we cannot persuade mice not to invade our dwellings or consume our food. That is why their rights are necessarily weaker than those of a being who can understand and respect the rights of other beings.

But the probable sentience of late-term fetuses is not the only argument in favor of treating late abortion as a morally more serious matter than early abortion. Many—perhaps most—people are repulsed by the thought of needlessly aborting a late-term fetus. The late-term fetus has features which cause it to arouse in us almost the same powerful protective instinct as does a small infant.

This response needs to be taken seriously. If it were impossible to perform abortions early in pregnancy, then we might have to tolerate the mental and physical trauma that would be occasioned by the routine resort to late abortion. But where early abortion is safe, legal, and readily available to all women, it is not unreasonable to expect most women who wish to end a pregnancy to do so prior to the third trimester. Most women strongly prefer early to late abortion, because it is far less physically painful and emotionally traumatic. Other things being equal, it is better for all concerned that pregnancies that are not to be completed should be ended as early as possible. Few women would consider ending a pregnancy in the seventh month in order to take a trip to Europe. If, however, a woman's own life or health is at stake, or if the fetus has been found to be so severely abnormal as to be unlikely to survive or to have a life worth living, then late abortion may be the morally best choice. For even a late-term fetus is not a person yet, and its rights must yield to those of the woman whenever it is impossible for both to be respected.

Potential Personhood and the Right to Life

We have seen that a presentient fetus does not yet resemble a person in ways which support the claim that it has strong moral rights. But what about its *potential*, the fact that if nurtured and allowed to develop it may eventually become a person? Doesn't that potential give it at least some right to life? The fact that something is a potential person may be a reason for not destroying it; but we need not conclude from this that potential people have a strong right to life. It may be that the feeling that it is better not to destroy a potential person is largely due to the fact that potential people are felt to be an invaluable resource, not to be lightly squandered. If every speck of dust were a potential person, we would be less apt to suppose that all potential persons have a right to become actual.

We do not need to insist that a potential person has no right to life whatever. There may be something immoral, and not just imprudent, about wantonly destroying potential people, when doing so isn't necessary. But even if a potential person does have some right to life, that right could not outweigh the right of a woman to obtain an abortion; for the basic moral rights of an actual person outweigh the rights of a merely potential person, whenever the two conflict. Since this may not be immediately obvious in the case of a human fetus, let us look at another case.

Suppose that our space explorer falls into the hands of an extraterrestrial civilization, whose scientists decide to create a few thousand new human beings by killing her and using some of her cells to create clones. We may imagine that each of these newly created women will have all of the original woman's abilities, skills, knowledge, and so on, and will also have an individual self-concept; in short, that each of them will be a bona fide (though not genetically unique) person. Imagine, further, that our explorer knows all of this, and knows that these people will be treated kindly and fairly. I maintain that in such a situation she would have the right to escape if she could, thus depriving all of the potential people of their potential lives. For her right to life outweighs all of theirs put together, even though they are not genetically human, and have a high probability of becoming people, if only she refrains from acting.

Indeed, I think that our space traveler would have a right to escape even if it were not her life which the aliens planned to take, but only a year of her freedom, or only a day. She would not be obliged to stay, even if she had been captured because of her own lack of caution—or even if she had done so deliberately, knowing the possible consequences. Regardless of why she was captured, she is not obliged to remain in captivity for *any* period of time in order to permit merely potential people to become actual people. By the same token, a woman's rights to liberty and the control of her own body outweigh whatever right a fetus may have merely by virtue of its potential personhood.

The Objection from Infanticide

One objection to my argument is that it appears to justify not only abortion, but also infanticide. A newborn infant is not much more personlike than a nine-month fetus, and thus it might appear that if late-term abortion is sometimes justified then infanticide must also sometimes be justified. Yet most people believe that infanticide is a form of murder, and virtually never justified.

This objection is less telling than it may seem. There are many reasons why infanticide is more difficult to justify than abortion, even though neither fetuses nor newborn infants are clearly persons. In this period of history, the deliberate killing of newborns is virtually never justified. This is in part because newborns are so close to being persons that to kill them requires a very strong moral justification— as does the killing of dolphins, chimpanzees, and other highly person-like creatures. It is certainly wrong to kill such beings for the sake of convenience, or financial profit, or "sport." Only the most vital human needs, such as the need to defend one's own life and physical integrity, can provide a plausible justification for killing such beings.

In the case of an infant, there is no such vital need, since in the contemporary world there are usually other people who are eager to provide a good home for an infant whose own parents are unable or unwilling to care for it. Many people wait years for the opportunity to adopt a child, and some are unable to do so, even though there is every reason to believe that they would be good parents. The needless destruction of a viable infant not only deprives a sentient human being of life, but also deprives other persons of a source of great satisfaction, perhaps severely impoverishing *their* lives.

Even if an infant is unadoptable (e.g., because of some severe physical disability), it is still wrong to kill it. For most of us value the lives of infants, and would greatly prefer to pay taxes to support foster care and state institutions for disabled children, rather than to allow them to be killed or abandoned. So long as most people feel this way, and so long as it is possible to provide care for infants who are unwanted, or who have special needs that their parents cannot meet without assistance, it is wrong to let any infant die who has a chance of living a reasonably good life.

If these arguments show that infanticide is wrong, at least in today's world, then why don't they also show that late-term abortion is always wrong? After all, third-trimester fetuses are almost as personlike as infants, and many people value them and would prefer that they be preserved. As a potential source of pleasure to some family, a fetus is just as valuable as an infant. But there is an important difference between these two cases: once the infant is born, its continued life cannot pose any serious threat to the woman's life or health, since she is free to put it up for adoption or to place it in foster care. While she might, in rare cases, prefer that the child die rather than being raised by others, such a preference would not establish a right on her part.

In contrast, a pregnant woman's right to protect her own life and health outweighs other people's desire that the fetus be preserved— just as, when a person's desire for life or health is threatened by an animal, and when the threat cannot be removed without killing the animal, that person's right to self-defense outweighs the desires of those who would prefer that the animal not be killed. Thus, while the moment of birth may mark no sharp discontinuity in the degree to which an infant resembles a person, it does mark the end of the mother's right to determine its fate. Indeed, if a late abortion can be safely performed without harming the fetus, the mother has in most cases no right to insist upon its death, for the same reason that she has no right to insist that a viable infant be killed or allowed to die.

It remains true that, on my view, neither abortion nor the killing of newborns is obviously a form of murder. Perhaps our legal system is correct in its classification of infanticide as murder, since no other legal category adequately expresses the force of our disapproval of this action. But some moral distinction remains, and it has important consequences. When a society cannot possibly care for all of the children who are born, without endangering the survival of adults and older children, allowing some infants to die may be the best of a bad set of options. Throughout history, most societies—from those that lived by gathering and hunting to the highly civilized Chinese, Japanese, Greeks, and Romans—have permitted infanticide under such unfortunate circumstances, regarding it as a necessary evil. It shows a lack of understanding to condemn these societies as morally benighted for this reason alone, since in the absence of safe and effective means of contraception and abortion, parents must sometimes have had no morally better options.

Conclusion

I have argued that fetuses are neither persons nor members of the moral community. Furthermore, neither a fetus's resemblance to a person, nor its potential for becoming a person, provides an adequate basis for the claim that it has a full and equal right to life. At the same time, there are medical as well as moral reasons for preferring early to late abortion when the pregnancy is unwanted.

Women, unlike fetuses, are undeniably persons and members of the human moral community. If unwanted or medically dangerous pregnancies never occurred, then it might be possible to respect women's basic moral rights, while at the same time extending the same basic rights to fetuses. But in the real world such pregnancies do occur—often despite the woman's best efforts to prevent them. Even if the perfect contraceptive were universally available, the continued occurrence of rape and incest would make access to abortion a vital human need. Because women are persons, and fetuses are not, women's rights to life, liberty, and physical integrity morally override whatever right to life it may be appropriate to ascribe to a fetus. Consequently, laws that deny women the right to obtain abortions, or that make safe early abortions difficult or impossible for some women to obtain, are an unjustified violation of basic moral and constitutional rights.

Notes

1. The principle that it is always wrong to kill innocent human beings may be in need of other modifications, e.g., that it may be permissible to kill innocent human beings in order to save a larger number of equally innocent human beings; but we may ignore these complications here.
2. From here on, I will use "human" to mean "genetically human," since the moral sense of the term seems closely connected to, and perhaps derived from, the assumption that genetic humanity is both necessary and sufficient for membership in the moral community.
3. Fetal sentience is impossible prior to the development of neurological connections between the sense organs and the brain, and between the

various parts of the brain involved in the processing of conscious experience. This stage of neurological development is currently thought to occur at some point in the late second or early third trimester.
4. Thomas L. Hayes, "A Biological View," *Commonweal* 85 (March 17, 1967): pp. 677–78; cited by Daniel Callahan in *Abortion: Law, Choice, and Morality* (London: Macmillan, 1970).

Study Questions

1. What characteristics entitle an entity to be considered a person?
2. Is infanticide more difficult to justify than abortion?
3. If a fetus is a human being, is abortion ever morally permissible?
4. If a fetus is not a human being, is abortion ever morally wrong?

CHAPTER 41

Why Abortion Is Immoral

Don Marquis

Don Marquis, Professor of Philosophy at the University of Kansas, argues that, with rare exceptions, abortion is immoral. He bases his argument not on the claim that the fetus is a person, but rather on the view that an aborted fetus loses the future goods of consciousness, such as the pursuit of goals, completion of projects, aesthetic enjoyment, friendships, intellectual pursuits, and various physical pleasures. In short, premature death deprives individuals of a future of value.

The view that abortion is, with rare exceptions, seriously immoral has received little support in the recent philosophical literature. No doubt most philosophers affiliated with secular institutions of higher education believe that the anti-abortion position is either a symptom of irrational religious dogma or a conclusion generated by seriously confused philosophical argument. The purpose of this essay is to undermine this general belief. This essay sets out an argument that purports to show, as well as any argument in ethics can show, that abortion is, except possibly in rare cases, seriously immoral, that it is in the same moral category as killing an innocent adult human being. . . .

II

. . . [W]e can start from the following unproblematic assumption concerning our own case: it is wrong to kill *us*. Why is it wrong? Some answers can be easily eliminated. It might be said that what makes killing us wrong is that a killing brutalizes the one who kills. But the

From Don Marquis, "Why Abortion Is Immoral," in *The Journal of Philosophy*, Vol. 86. Copyright © 1989. Reprinted by permission of the author and *The Journal of Philosophy*.

brutalization consists of being inured to the performance of an act that is hideously immoral; hence, the brutalization does not explain the immorality. It might be said that what makes killing us wrong is the great loss others would experience due to our absence. Although such hubris is understandable, such an explanation does not account for the wrongness of killing hermits, or those whose lives are relatively independent and whose friends find it easy to make new friends.

A more obvious answer is better. What primarily makes killing wrong is neither its effect on the murderer nor its effect on the victim's friends and relatives, but its effect on the victim. The loss of one's life is one of the greatest losses one can suffer. The loss of one's life deprives one of all the experiences, activities, projects, and enjoyments that would otherwise have constituted one's future. Therefore, killing someone is wrong, primarily because the killing inflicts (one of) the greatest possible losses on the victim. To describe this as the loss of life can be misleading, however. The change in my biological state does not by itself make killing me wrong. The effect of the loss of my biological life is the loss to me of all those activities, projects, experiences, and enjoyments which would otherwise have constituted my future personal life. These activities, projects, experiences, and enjoyments are either valuable for their own sakes or are means to something else that is valuable for its own sake. Some parts of my future are not valued by me now, but will come to be valued by me as I grow older and as my values and capacities change. When I am killed, I am deprived both of what I now value which would have been part of my future personal life, but also what I would come to value. Therefore, when I die, I am deprived of all of the value of my future. Inflicting this loss on me is ultimately what makes killing me wrong. This being the case, it would seem that what makes killing *any* adult human being prima facie seriously wrong is the loss of his or her future.[1]

How should this rudimentary theory of the wrongness of killing be evaluated? It cannot be faulted for deriving an "ought" from an "is," for it does not. The analysis assumes that killing me (or you, reader) is prima facie seriously wrong. The point of the analysis is to establish which natural property ultimately explains the wrongness of the killing, given that it is wrong. A natural property will ultimately explain the wrongness of killing, only if (1) the explanation fits with our intuitions about the matter and (2) there is no other natural property that provides the basis for a better explanation of the wrongness of killing. This analysis rests on the intuition that what makes killing a particular human or animal wrong is what it does to that particular human or animal. What makes killing wrong is some natural effect or other of the killing. Some would deny this. For instance, a divine command theorist in ethics would deny it. Surely this denial is, however, one of those features of divine command theory which renders it so implausible.

The claim that what makes killing wrong is the loss of the victim's future is directly supported by two considerations. In the first place, this theory explains why we regard killing as one of the worst of crimes. Killing is especially wrong, because it deprives the victim of more than perhaps any other crime. In the second place, people with AIDS or cancer who know they are dying believe, of course, that dying is a very bad thing for them. They believe that the loss of a future to them that they would otherwise have experienced is what makes their premature death a very bad thing for them. A better theory of the wrongness of killing would require a different natural property associated with killing which better fits with the attitudes of the dying. What could it be?

The view that what makes killing wrong is the loss to the victim of the value of the victim's future gains additional support when some of its implications are examined. In the first place, it is incompatible with the view that it is wrong to kill only beings who are biologically human. It is possible that there exists a different species from another planet whose members have a future like ours. Since having a future like that is what makes killing someone wrong, this theory entails that it would be wrong to kill members of such a species. Hence, this theory is opposed to the claim that only life that is biologically human has great moral worth, a claim which many anti-abortionists have seemed to adopt. This opposition, . . . seems to be a merit of the theory.

In the second place, the claim that the loss of one's future is the wrong-making feature of one's being killed entails the possibility that the futures of some actual nonhuman mammals on our own planet are sufficiently like ours that it is seriously wrong to kill them also. Whether some animals do have the same right to life as human beings depends on adding to the account of the wrongness of killing some additional account of just what it is about my future or the futures of other adult human beings which makes it wrong to kill us. No such additional account will be offered in this essay. Undoubtedly, the provision of such an account would be a very difficult matter. Undoubtedly, any such account would be quite controversial. Hence, it surely should not reflect badly on this sketch of an elementary theory of the wrongness of killing that it is indeterminate with respect to some very difficult issues regarding animal rights.

In the third place, the claim that the loss of one's future is the wrong-making feature of one's being killed does not entail, as sanctity of human life theories do, that active euthanasia is wrong. Persons who are severely and incurably ill, who face a future of pain and despair, and who wish to die will not have suffered a loss if they are killed. It is, strictly speaking, the value of a human's future which makes killing wrong in this theory. This being so, killing does not necessarily wrong some persons who are sick and dying. Of course, there may be other reasons for a prohibition of active euthanasia, but that is another matter. Sanctity-of-human-life theories seem to hold that active euthanasia is seriously wrong even in an individual case where there seems to be good reason for it independently of public policy considerations. This consequence is most implausible, and it is a plus for the claim that the loss of a future of value is what makes killing wrong that it does not share this consequence.

In the fourth place, the account of the wrongness of killing defended in this essay does straightforwardly entail that it is prima facie seriously wrong to kill children and infants, for we do presume that they have futures of value. Since we do believe that it is wrong to kill defenseless . . . babies, it is important that a theory of the wrongness of killing easily account for this. Personhood theories of the wrongness of killing, on the other hand, cannot straightforwardly account for the wrongness of killing infants and young children. Hence, such theories must add special ad hoc accounts of the wrongness of killing the young. The plausibility of such ad hoc theories seems to be a function of how desperately one wants such theories to work. The claim that the primary wrong-making feature of a killing is the loss to the victim of the value of its future accounts for the wrongness of killing young children and infants directly; it makes the wrongness of such acts as obvious as we actually think it is. This is a further merit of this theory. Accordingly, it seems that this value of a future-like-ours theory of the wrongness of killing shares strengths of both sanctity-of-life and personhood accounts while avoiding weaknesses of both. In addition, it meshes with a central institution concerning what makes killing wrong.

The claim that the primary wrong-making feature of a killing is the loss to the victim of the value of its future has obvious consequences for the ethics of abortion. The future of a standard fetus includes a set of experiences, projects, activities, and such which are identical with the futures of adult human beings and are identical with the futures of young children. Since the reason that is sufficient to explain why it is wrong to kill human beings after the time of birth is a reason that also applies to fetuses, it follows that abortion is prima facie seriously morally wrong.

This argument does not rely on the invalid inference that, since it is wrong to kill persons, it is wrong to kill potential persons also. The category that is morally central to this analysis is the category of having a valuable future like ours; it is not the category of person-hood. The argument to the conclusion that abortion is prima facie seriously morally wrong proceeded independently of the notion of person or potential person or any equivalent. Someone may wish to start with this analysis in terms of the value of a human future, con-clude that abortion is, except perhaps in rare circumstances, seri-ously morally wrong, infer that fetuses have the right to life, and then call fetuses "persons" as a result of their having the right to life. Clearly, in this case, the category of person is being used to state the *conclusion* of the analysis rather than to generate the *argument* of the analysis. . . .

Of course, this value of a future-like-ours argument, if sound, shows only that abortion is prima facie wrong, not that it is wrong in any and all circumstances. Since the loss of the future to a standard fetus, if killed, is, however, at least as great a loss as the loss of the future to a standard adult human being who is killed, abortion, like ordinary killing, could be justified only by the most compelling rea-sons. The loss of one's life is almost the greatest misfortune that can happen to one. Presumably abortion could be justified in some cir-cumstances, only if the loss consequent on failing to abort would be at least as great. Accordingly, morally permissible abortions will be rare indeed unless, perhaps, they occur so early in pregnancy that a fetus is not yet definitely an individual. Hence, this argument should be taken as showing that abortion is presumptively very seriously wrong, where the presumption is very strong—as strong as the pre-sumption that killing another adult human being is wrong. . . .

V

In this essay, it has been argued that the correct ethic of the wrong-ness of killing can be extended to fetal life and used to show that there is a strong presumption that any abortion is morally impermissible. If the ethic of killing adopted here entails, however, that contraception is also seriously immoral, then there would appear to be a difficulty with the analysis of this assay.

But this analysis does not entail that contraception is wrong. Of course, contraception prevents the actualization of a possible future of value. Hence, it follows from the claim that futures of value should be maximized that contraception is prima facie immoral. This obligation to maximize does not exist, however; furthermore, nothing in the ethics of killing in this paper entails that it does. The ethics of killing in this essay would entail that contraception is wrong only if something were denied a human future of value by contraception. Nothing at all is denied such a future by contraception, however.

Candidates for a subject of harm by contraception fall into four categories: (1) some sperm or other, (2) some ovum or other, (3) a sperm and an ovum separately, and (4) a sperm and an ovum together. Assigning the harm to some sperm is utterly arbitrary, for no reason can be given for making a sperm the subject of harm rather than an ovum. Assigning the harm to some ovum is utterly arbitrary, for no reason can be given for making an ovum the subject of harm rather than a sperm. One might attempt to avoid these problems by insisting that contraception deprives both the sperm and the ovum separately of a valuable future like ours. On this alternative, too many futures are lost. Contraception was supposed to be wrong, because it deprived us of one future of value, not two. One might attempt to avoid this problem by holding that contraception deprives the combination of sperm and ovum of a valuable future like ours. But here the definite article misleads. At the time of contraception, there are hundreds of millions of sperm, one (released) ovum and millions of possible combinations of all of these. There is no actual combination at all. Is the subject of the loss to be a merely possible combination? Which one? This alternative does not yield an actual subject of harm either. Accordingly, the immorality of contraception is not entailed by the loss of a future-like-ours argument simply because there is no nonarbitrarily identifiable subject of the loss in the case of contraception.

VI

The purpose of this essay has been to set out an argument for the serious presumptive wrongness of abortion subject to the assumption that the moral permissibility of abortion stands or falls on the moral status of the fetus. Since a fetus possesses a property, the possession of which in adult human beings is sufficient to make killing an adult human being wrong, abortion is wrong. This way of dealing with the problem of abortion seems superior to other approaches to the ethics of abortion, because it rests on an ethics of killing which is close to self-evident, because the crucial morally relevant property clearly applies to fetuses, and because the argument avoids the usual equivocations of "human life," "human being," or "person." . . . Its soundness is compatible with the moral permissibility of euthanasia and contraception. It deals with our intuitions concerning young children.

Finally, this analysis can be viewed as resolving a standard problem—indeed, *the* standard problem—concerning the ethics of abortion. Clearly, it is wrong to kill adult human beings. Clearly, it is not wrong to end the life of some arbitrarily chosen single human cell. Fetuses seem to be like arbitrarily chosen human cells in some respects and like adult humans in other respects. The problem of the ethics of abortion is the problem of determining the fetal property that settles this moral controversy. The thesis of this essay is that the problem of the ethics of abortion, so understood, is solvable.

Note

1. I have been most influenced on this matter by Jonathan Glover, *Causing Death and Saving Lives* (New York: Penguin, 1977), chap. 3; and Robert Young, "What Is So Wrong with Killing People?" *Philosophy* LIV, 210 (1979), pp. 518–28.

Study Questions

1. Is the loss of one's future as devastating for a fetus as for a child?
2. Does Marquis's argument that abortion is immoral depend on religious considerations?
3. Does Marquis accept the argument that because killing persons is wrong, killing potential persons is also wrong?
4. According to Marquis, in what circumstances is abortion not wrong?

CHAPTER 42

Virtue Theory and Abortion

Rosalind Hursthouse

Rosalind Hursthouse is Professor of Philosophy at the University of Auckland in New Zealand. She demonstrates how virtue theory can be applied to the issue of abortion. The term "deontological" that she uses refers to an ethical theory, such as Kant's, based on fulfilling duties, as opposed to a consequentialist theory, such as utilitarianism, that appeals to achieving good states of affairs.

The sort of ethical theory derived from Aristotle, variously described as virtue ethics, virtue-based ethics, or neo-Aristotelianism, is becoming better known, and is now quite widely recognized as at least a possible rival to deontological and utilitarian theories. . . . I aim to deepen that understanding . . . by illustrating what the theory looks like when it is applied to a particular issue, in this case, abortion. . . .

As everyone knows, the morality of abortion is commonly discussed in relation to just two considerations: first, and predominantly, the status of the fetus and whether or not it is the sort of thing that may or may not be innocuously or justifiably killed; and second, and less predominantly (when, that is, the discussion concerns the *morality* of abortion rather than the question of permissible legislation in a just society), women's rights. If one thinks within this familiar framework, one may well be puzzled about what virtue theory, as such, could contribute. Some people assume the discussion will be conducted solely in terms of what the virtuous agent would or would not do. . . . Others assume that only justice, or at most justice and charity, will be applied to the issue, generating a discussion very similar to Judith Jarvis Thomson's.[1]

From *Philosophy & Public Affairs*, 20 (1991), by permission of Blackwell Publishing.

Now if this is the way the virtue theorist's discussion of abortion is imagined to be, no wonder people think little of it. It seems obvious in advance that in any such discussion there must be either a great deal of extremely tendentious application of the virtue terms *just*, *charitable*, and so on or a lot of rhetorical appeal to "this is what only the virtuous agent knows." But these are caricatures; they fail to appreciate the way in which virtue theory quite transforms the discussion of abortion by dismissing the two familiar dominating considerations as, in a way, fundamentally irrelevant. In what way or ways, I hope to make both clear and plausible.

Let us first consider women's rights. Let me emphasize again that we are discussing the *morality* of abortion, not the rights and wrongs of laws prohibiting or permitting it. If we suppose that women do have a moral right to do as they choose with their own bodies, or, more particularly, to terminate their pregnancies, then it may well follow that a *law* forbidding abortion would be unjust. Indeed, even if they have no such right, such a law might be, as things stand at the moment, unjust, or impractical, or inhumane: on this issue I have nothing to say in this article. But, putting all questions about the justice or injustice of laws to one side, and supposing only that women have such a moral right, *nothing* follows from this supposition about the morality of abortion, according to virtue theory, once it is noted (quite generally, not with particular reference to abortion) that in exercising a moral right I can do something cruel, or callous, or selfish, light-minded, self-righteous, stupid, inconsiderate, disloyal, dishonest—that is act viciously.[2] Love and friendship do not survive their parties constantly insisting on their rights, nor do people live well when they think that getting what they have a right to is of preeminent importance; they harm others, and they harm themselves. So whether women have a moral right to terminate their pregnancies is irrelevant within virtue theory, for it is irrelevant to the question "In having an abortion in these circumstances, would the agent be acting virtuously or viciously or neither?"

What about the consideration of the status of the fetus—what can virtue theory say about that? One might say that this issue is not in the province of *any* moral theory; it is a metaphysical question, and an extremely difficult one at that. Must virtue theory then wait upon metaphysics to come up with the answer?

At first sight it might seem so. For virtue is said to involve knowledge, and part of this knowledge consists in having the *right* attitude to things. "Right" here does not just mean "morally right" or "proper" or "nice" in the modern sense; it means "accurate, true." One cannot have the right or correct attitude to something if the attitude is based on or involves false beliefs. And this suggests that if the status of the fetus is relevant to the rightness or wrongness of abortion, its status must be known, as a truth, to the fully wise and virtuous person.

But the sort of wisdom that the fully virtuous person has is not supposed to be recondite; it does not call for fancy philosophical sophistication, and it does not depend upon, let alone wait upon, the discoveries of academic philosophers.[3] And this entails the following, rather startling, conclusion: that the status of the fetus—that issue over which so much ink has been spilt—is, according to virtue theory, simply not relevant to the rightness or wrongness of abortion (within, that is, a secular morality).

Or rather, since that is clearly too radical a conclusion, it is in a sense relevant, but only in the sense that the familiar biological facts are relevant. By "the familiar biological facts" I mean the facts that most human societies are and have been familiar with—that, standardly (but not invariably), pregnancy occurs as the result of sexual intercourse, that it lasts about nine months, during which time the fetus grows and develops, that standardly it terminates in the birth of a living baby, and that this is how we all come to be.

It might be thought that this distinction—between the familiar biological facts and the status of the fetus—is a distinction without a difference. But this is not so. To attach relevance to the status of the fetus, in the sense in which virtue theory claims it is not relevant, is to be gripped by the conviction that we must go beyond the familiar biological facts, deriving some sort of conclusion from them, such as that the fetus has rights, or is not a person, or something similar. It is also to believe that this exhausts the relevance of the familiar biological facts, that all they are relevant to is the status of the fetus and whether or not it is the sort of thing that may or may not be killed.

These convictions, I suspect, are rooted in the desire to solve the problem of abortion by getting it to fall under some general rule such as "You ought not to kill anything with the right to life but may kill anything else." But they have resulted in what should surely strike any nonphilosopher as a most bizarre aspect of nearly all the current philosophical literature on abortion, namely, that, far from treating abortion as a unique moral problem, markedly unlike any other, nearly everything written on the status of the fetus and its bearing on the abortion issue would be consistent with the human reproductive facts' (to say nothing of family life) being totally different from what they are. Imagine that you are an alien extraterrestrial anthropologist who does not know that the human race is roughly 50 percent female and 50 percent male, or that our only (natural) form of reproduction involves heterosexual intercourse, viviparous birth, and the female's (and only the female's) being pregnant for nine months, or that females are capable of childbearing from late childhood to late middle age, or that childbearing is painful, dangerous, and emotionally charged—do you think you would pick up these facts from the hundreds of articles written on the status of the fetus? I am quite sure you would not. And that, I think, shows that the current philosophical literature on abortion has got badly out of touch with reality.

Now if we are using virtue theory, our first question is not "What do the familiar biological facts show—what can be derived from them about the status of the fetus?" but "How do these facts figure in the practical reasoning, actions and passions, thoughts and reactions, of the virtuous and the nonvirtuous? What is the mark of having the right attitude to these facts and what manifests having the wrong attitude to them?" This immediately makes essentially relevant not only all the facts about human reproduction I mentioned above, but a whole range of facts about our emotions in relation to them as well. I mean such facts as that human parents, both male and female, tend to care passionately about their offspring, and that family relationships are among the deepest and strongest in our lives—and, significantly, among the longest-lasting.

These facts make it obvious that pregnancy is not just one among many other physical conditions; and hence that anyone who genuinely believes that an abortion is comparable to a haircut or an appendectomy is mistaken.[4] The fact that the premature termination of a pregnancy is, in some sense, the cutting off of a new human life, and thereby, like the procreation of a new human life, connects with all our thoughts about human life and death, parenthood, and family relationships, must make it a serious matter. To disregard this fact about it, to think of abortion as nothing but the killing of something that does not matter, or as nothing but the exercise of some right or rights one has, or as the incidental means to some desirable state of affairs, is to do something callous and light-minded, the sort of thing that no virtuous and wise person would do. It is to have the wrong attitude not only to fetuses, but more generally to human life and death, parenthood, and family relationships.

Although I say that the facts make this obvious, I know that this is one of my tendentious points. In partial support of it I note that even the most dedicated proponents of the view that deliberate abortion is just like an appendectomy or haircut rarely hold the same view of spontaneous abortion, that is, miscarriage. It is not so tendentious of me to claim that to react to people's grief over miscarriage by saying, or even thinking, "What a fuss about nothing!" would be callous and light-minded, whereas to try to laugh someone out of grief over an appendectomy scar or a botched haircut would not be. It is hard to give this point due prominence within act-centered theories, for the inconsistency is an inconsistency in attitude about the seriousness of loss of life, not in beliefs about which acts are right or wrong. Moreover, an act-centered theorist may say, "Well, there is nothing wrong with *thinking* 'What a fuss about nothing!' as long as you do not say it and hurt the person who is grieving. And besides, we cannot be held responsible for our thoughts, only for the intentional actions they give rise to." But the character traits that virtue theory emphasizes are not simply dispositions to intentional actions, but a seamless disposition to certain actions and passions, thoughts and reactions.

To say that the cutting off of a human life is always a matter of some seriousness, at any stage, is not to deny the relevance of gradual fetal development. Notwithstanding the well-worn point that clear boundary lines cannot be drawn, our emotions and attitudes regarding the fetus do change as it develops, and again when it is born, and indeed further as the baby grows. Abortion for shallow reasons in the later stages is much more shocking than abortion for the same reasons in the early stages in a way that matches the fact that deep grief over miscarriage in the later stages is more appropriate than it is over miscarriage in the earlier stages (when, that is, the grief is solely about the loss of *this* child, not about, as might be the case, the loss of one's only hope of having a child or of having one's husband's child). Imagine (or recall) a woman who already has children; she had not intended to have more, but finds herself unexpectedly pregnant. Though contrary to her plans, the pregnancy, once established as a fact, is welcomed—and then she loses the embryo almost immediately. If this were bemoaned as a tragedy, it would, I think, be a misapplication of the concept of what is tragic. But it may still properly be mourned as a loss. The grief is expressed in such terms as "I shall always wonder how she or he would have turned out" or "When I look at the others, I shall think, 'How different their lives would have been if this other one had been part of them.'" It would, I take it, be callous and light-minded to say, or think, "Well, she has already *got* four children; what's the problem?"; it would be neither, nor arrogantly intrusive in the case of a close friend, to try to correct prolonged mourning by saying, "I know it's sad, but it's not a tragedy; rejoice in the ones you have." The application of *tragic* becomes more appropriate as the fetus grows, for the mere fact that one has lived with it for longer, conscious of its existence, makes a difference. To shrug off an early abortion is understandable just because it is very hard to be fully conscious of the fetus's existence in the early stages and hence hard to appreciate that an early abortion is the destruction of life. It is particularly hard for the young and inexperienced to appreciate this, because appreciation of it usually comes only with experience.

I do not mean "with the experience of having an abortion" (though that may be part of it) but, quite generally, "with the experience of life." Many women who have borne children contrast their later pregnancies with their first successful one, saying that in the later ones they were conscious of a new life growing in them from very early on. And, more generally, as one reaches the age at which the next generation is coming up close behind one, the counterfactuals "If I, or she, had had an abortion, Alice, or Bob, would not have been born" acquire a significant application, which casts a new light on the conditionals "If I or Alice have an abortion then some Caroline or Bill will not be born."

The fact that pregnancy is not just one among many physical conditions does not mean that one can never regard it in that light without manifesting a vice. When women are in very poor physical health, or worn out from childbearing, or forced to do very physically demanding jobs, then they cannot be described as self-indulgent, callous, irresponsible, or light-minded if they seek abortions mainly with a view to avoiding pregnancy as the physical condition that it is. To go through with a pregnancy when one is utterly exhausted, or when one's job consists of crawling along tunnels hauling coal, as many women in the nineteenth century were obliged to do, is perhaps heroic, but people who do not achieve heroism are not necessarily vicious. That they can view the pregnancy only as eight months of misery, followed by hours if not days of agony and exhaustion, and abortion only as the blessed escape from this prospect, is entirely understandable and does not manifest any lack of serious respect for human life or a shallow attitude to motherhood. What it does show is that something is terribly amiss in the conditions of their lives, which make it so hard to recognize pregnancy and childbearing as the good that they can be.

In relation to this last point I should draw attention to the way in which virtue theory has a sort of built-in indexicality. Philosophers arguing against anything remotely resembling a belief in the sanctity of life (which the above claims clearly embody) frequently appeal to the existence of other communities in which abortion and infanticide are practiced. We should not automatically assume that it is impossible that some other communities could be morally inferior to our own; maybe some are, or have been, precisely insofar as their members are, typically, callous or light-minded or unjust. But in communities in which life is a great deal tougher for everyone than it is in ours, having the right attitude to human life and death, parenthood, and family relationships might well manifest itself in ways that are unlike ours. When it is essential to survival that most members of the community fend for themselves at a very young age or work during most of their waking hours, selective abortion or infanticide might be practiced either as a form of genuine euthanasia or for the sake of the community and not, I think, be thought callous or light-minded. But this does not make everything all right; as before, it shows that there is something amiss with the conditions of their lives, which are making it impossible for them to live really well.

The foregoing discussion, insofar as it emphasizes the right attitude to human life and death, parallels to a certain extent those standard discussions of abortion that concentrate on it solely as an issue of killing. But it does not, as those discussions do, gloss over the fact, emphasized by those who discuss the morality of abortion in terms of women's rights, that abortion, wildly unlike any other form of killing, is the termination of a pregnancy, which is a condition of a woman's body and results in *her* having a child if it is not aborted. This fact is given due recognition not by appeal to women's rights but by emphasizing the relevance of the familiar biological and psychological facts and their connection with having the right attitude to parenthood and family relationships. But it may well be thought that failing to bring in women's rights still leaves some important aspects of the problem of abortion untouched.

Speaking in terms of women's rights, people sometimes say things like, "Well, it's her life you're talking about too, you know; she's got a right to her own life, her own happiness." And the discussion stops there. But in the context of virtue theory, given that we are particularly concerned with what constitutes a good human life, with what true happiness or *eudaimonia* is, this is no place to stop. We go on to ask, "And is this life of hers a good one? Is she living well?"

If we are to go on to talk about good human lives, in the context of abortion, we have to bring in our thoughts about the value of love and family life, and our proper emotional development through a natural life cycle. The familiar facts support the view that parenthood in general, and motherhood and childbearing in particular, are intrinsically worthwhile, are among the things that can be correctly thought to be partially constitutive of a flourishing human life.[5] If this is right, then a woman who opts for not being a mother (at all, or again, or now) by opting for abortion may thereby be manifesting a flawed grasp of what her life should be, and be about—a grasp that is childish, or grossly materialistic, or short-sighted, or shallow.

I said "*may* thereby"; this *need* not be so. Consider, for instance, a woman who has already had several children and fears that to have another will seriously affect her capacity to be a good mother to the ones she has—she does not show a lack of appreciation of the intrinsic value of being a parent by opting for abortion. Nor does a woman who has been a good mother and is approaching the age at which she may be looking forward to being a good grandmother. Nor does a woman who discovers that her pregnancy may well kill her, and opts for abortion and adoption. Nor, necessarily, does a woman who has decided to lead a life centered around some other worthwhile activity or activities with which motherhood would compete.

People who are childless by choice are sometimes described as "irresponsible," or "selfish," or "refusing to grow up," or "not knowing what life is about." But one can hold that having children is intrinsically worthwhile without endorsing this, for we are, after all, in the happy position of there being more worthwhile things to do than can be fitted into one lifetime. Parenthood, and motherhood in particular, even if granted to be intrinsically worthwhile, undoubtedly take up a lot of one's adult life, leaving no room for some other worthwhile pursuits. But some women who choose abortion rather than have their first child, and some men who encourage their partners to choose abortion, are not avoiding parenthood for the sake of other worthwhile pursuits, but for the worthless one of "having a good time," or for the pursuit of some false vision of the ideals of freedom or self-realization. And some others who say "I am not ready for parenthood yet" are making some sort of mistake about the extent to which one can manipulate the circumstances of one's life so as to make it fulfill some dream that one has. Perhaps one's dream is to have two perfect children, a girl and a boy, within a perfect marriage, in financially secure circumstances, with an interesting job of one's own. But to care too much about that dream, to demand of life that it give it to one and act accordingly, may be both greedy and foolish, and is to run the risk of missing out on happiness entirely. Not only may fate make the dream impossible, or destroy it, but one's own attachment to it may make it impossible. Good marriages, and the most promising children, can be destroyed by just one adult's excessive demand for perfection.

Once again, this is not to deny that girls may quite properly say "I am not ready for motherhood yet," especially in our society, and, far from manifesting irresponsibility or light-mindedness, show an appropriate modesty or humility, or a fearfulness that does not amount to cowardice. However, even when the decision to have an abortion is the right decision—one that does not itself fall under a vice-related term and thereby one that the perfectly virtuous could recommend— it does not follow that there is no sense in which having the abortion is wrong, or guilt inappropriate. For, by virtue of the fact that a human life has been cut short, some evil has probably been brought about,[6] and that circumstances make the decision to bring about some evil the right decision will be a ground for guilt if getting into those circumstances in the first place itself manifested a flaw in character.

What "gets one into those circumstances" in the case of abortion is, except in the case of rape, one's sexual activity and one's choices, or the lack of them, about one's sexual partner and about contraception. The virtuous woman (which here of course does not mean simply "chaste woman" but "woman with the virtues") has such character traits as strength, independence, resoluteness, decisiveness, self-confidence, responsibility, serious-mindedness, and self-determination—and no one, I think, could deny that many women become pregnant in circumstances in which they cannot welcome or cannot face the thought of having *this* child precisely because they lack one or some of these character traits. So even in the cases where the decision to have an abortion is the right one, it can still be the reflection of a moral failing—not because the decision itself is weak or cowardly or irresolute or irresponsible or light-minded, but because lack of the requisite opposite of these failings landed one in the circumstances in the first place. Hence the common universalized claim that guilt and remorse are never appropriate emotions about an abortion is denied. They may be appropriate, and appropriately inculcated, even when the decision was the right one.

Another motivation for bringing women's rights into the discussion may be to attempt to correct the implication, carried by the killing-centered approach, that insofar as abortion is wrong, it is a wrong that only women do, or at least (given the preponderance of male doctors) that only women instigate. I do not myself believe that we can thus escape the fact that nature bears harder on women than it does on men,[7] but virtue theory can certainly correct many of the injustices that the emphasis on women's rights is rightly concerned about. With very little amendment, everything that has been said above applies to boys and men too. Although the abortion decision is, in a natural sense, the woman's decision, proper to her, boys and men are often party to it, for well or ill, and even when they are not, they are bound to have been party to the circumstances that brought it up. No less than girls and women, boys and men can, in their actions, manifest self-centeredness, callousness, and light-mindedness about life and parenthood in relation to abortion. They can be self-centered or courageous about the possibility of disability in their offspring; they need to reflect on their sexual activity and their choices, or the lack of them, about their sexual partner and contraception; they need to grow up and take responsibility for their own actions and life in relation to fatherhood. If it is true, as I maintain, that insofar as motherhood is intrinsically worthwhile, being a mother is an important purpose in women's lives, being a father (rather than a mere generator) is an important purpose in men's lives as well, and it is adolescent of men to turn a blind eye to this and pretend that they have many more important things to do.

Much more might be said, but I shall end the actual discussion of the problem of abortion here, and conclude by highlighting what I take to be its significant features. . . .

The discussion does not proceed simply by our trying to answer the question "Would a perfectly virtuous agent ever have an abortion and, if so, when?"; virtue theory is not limited to considering "Would Socrates have had an abortion if he were a raped, pregnant fifteen-year-old?" nor automatically stumped when we are considering circumstances into which no virtuous agent would have got herself. Instead, much of the discussion proceeds in the virtue- and vice-related terms whose application, in several cases, yields practical conclusions. . . . These terms are difficult to apply correctly, and anyone might challenge my application of any one of them. So, for example, I have claimed that some abortions, done for certain reasons, would be callous or light-minded; that others might indicate an appropriate modesty or humility; that others would reflect a greedy and foolish attitude to what one could expect out of life. Any of these examples may be disputed, but what is at issue is, should these difficult terms be there, or should the discussion be couched in terms that all clever adolescents can apply correctly? . . .

Proceeding as it does in the virtue- and vice-related terms, the discussion thereby, inevitably, also contains claims about what is worthwhile, serious and important, good and evil, in our lives. So, for example, I claimed that parenthood is intrinsically worthwhile, and that having a good time was a worthless end (in life, not on individual occasions); that losing a fetus is always a serious matter (albeit not a tragedy in itself in the first trimester) whereas acquiring an appendectomy scar is a trivial one; that (human) death is an evil. Once again, these are difficult matters, and anyone might challenge any one of my claims. But what is at issue is, as before, should those difficult claims be there or can one reach practical conclusions about real moral issues that are in no way determined by premises about such matters? . . .

The discussion also thereby, inevitably, contains claims about what life is like (e.g., my claim that love and friendship do not survive their parties' constantly insisting on their rights; or the claim that to demand perfection of life is to run the risk of missing out on happiness entirely). What is at issue is, should those disputable claims be there, or is our knowledge (or are our false opinions) about what life is like irrelevant to our understanding of real moral issues? . . .

Naturally, my own view is that all these concepts should be there in any discussion of real moral issues and that virtue theory, which uses all of them, is the right theory to apply to them. I do not pretend to have shown this. I realize that proponents of rival theories may say that, now that they have understood how virtue theory uses the range of concepts it draws on, they are more convinced than ever that such concepts should not figure in an adequate normative theory, because they are sectarian, or vague or too particular, or improperly anthropocentric. . . . Or, finding many of the details of the discussion appropriate, they may agree that many, perhaps even all, of the concepts should figure, but argue that virtue theory gives an inaccurate account of the way the concepts fit together (and indeed of the concepts themselves) and that another theory provides a better account; that would be interesting to see.

Notes

1. Judith Jarvis Thomson, "A Defense of Abortion," *Philosophy & Public Affairs* 1, no. 1 (Fall 1971): 47–66. One could indeed regard this article as proto-virtue theory (no doubt to the surprise of the author) if the concepts of callousness and kindness were allowed more weight.

2. One possible qualification: if one ties the concept of justice very closely to rights, then if women do have a moral right to terminate their pregnancies it *may* follow that in doing so they do not act unjustly. (Cf. Thomson, "A Defense of Abortion.") But it is debatable whether even that much follows.

3. This is an assumption of virtue theory, and I do not attempt to defend it here. An adequate discussion of it would require a separate article, since, although most moral philosophers would be chary of claiming that intellectual sophistication is a necessary condition of moral wisdom or virtue, most of us, from Plato onward, tend to write as if this were so. Sorting out which claims about moral knowledge are committed to this kind of elitism and which can, albeit with difficulty, be reconciled with the idea that moral knowledge can be acquired by anyone who really wants it would be a major task.

4. Mary Anne Warren, in "On the Moral and Legal Status of Abortion," *Monist* 57 (1973), sec. 1, says of the opponents of restrictive laws governing abortion that "their conviction (for the most part) is that abortion is not a *morally* serious and extremely unfortunate, even though sometimes justified, act, comparable to killing in self-defense or to letting the violinist die, but rather is closer to being a *morally neutral* act, like cutting one's hair" (italics mine). I would like to think that no one *genuinely* believes this. But certainly in discussion, particularly when arguing against restrictive laws or the suggestion that remorse over abortion might be appropriate, I have found that some people *say* they believe it. . . . Those who allow that it is morally serious, and far from morally neutral, have to argue against restrictive laws, or the appropriateness of remorse, on a very different ground from that laid down by the premise "The fetus is just part of the woman's body (and she has a right to determine what happens to her body and should not feel guilt about anything she does to it)."

5. I take this as a premise here, but argue for it in some detail in my *Beginning Lives* (Oxford: Basil Blackwell, 1987). In this connection I also discuss adoption and the sense in which it may be regarded as "second best," and the difficult question of whether the good of parenthood may properly be sought, or indeed bought, by surrogacy.

6. I say "some evil has probably been brought about" on the ground that (human) life is (usually) a good and hence (human) death usually an evil. The exceptions would be (*a*) where death is actually a good or a benefit, because the baby that would come to be if the life were not cut

short would be better off dead than alive, and (*b*) where death, though not a good, is not an evil either, because the life that would be led (e.g., in a state of permanent coma) would not be a good.

7. I discuss this point at greater length in *Beginning Lives*.

Study Questions

1. According to Hursthouse, is the status of the fetus relevant to the rightness or wrongness of abortion?
2. According to Hursthouse, do women's rights have anything to do with the morality of abortion?
3. What connections does Hursthouse draw between good human lives and a decision about abortion?
4. Do you agree with Hursthouse that simply "having a good time" is a "worthless" pursuit?

I. Euthanasia

CHAPTER 43

Active and Passive Euthanasia

James Rachels

The American Medical Association takes the position that while at a patient's request a physician may withhold extraordinary means of prolonging the patient's life, a physician may not take steps, even if requested by the patient, to terminate that life intentionally. James Rachels, whose work we read previously, argues that killing is not in itself any worse than letting die, and therefore no moral difference between active and passive euthanasia is defensible.

The distinction between active and passive euthanasia is thought to be crucial for medical ethics. The idea is that it is permissible, at least in some cases, to withhold treatment and allow a patient to die, but it is never permissible to take any direct action designed to kill the patient. This doctrine seems to be accepted by most doctors, and it is endorsed in a statement adopted by the House of Delegates of the American Medical Association on 4 December 1973:

> The intentional termination of the life of one human being by another—mercy killing—is contrary to that for which the medical profession stands and is contrary to the policy of the American Medical Association.
>
> The cessation of the employment of extraordinary means to prolong the life of the body when there is irrefutable evidence that biological death is imminent is the decision of the patient and/or his immediate family. The advice and judgement of the physician should be freely available to the patient and/or his immediate family.

From James Rachels, "Active and Passive Euthanasia," *New England Journal of Medicine* 292 (1975).

However, a strong case can be made against this doctrine. In what follows I will set out some of the relevant arguments, and urge doctors to reconsider their views on this matter.

To begin with a familiar type of situation, a patient who is dying of incurable cancer of the throat is in terrible pain, which can no longer be satisfactorily alleviated. He is certain to die within a few days, even if present treatment is continued, but he does not want to go on living for those days since the pain is unbearable. So he asks the doctor for an end to it, and his family joins in the request.

Suppose the doctor agrees to withhold treatment, as the conventional doctrine says he may. The justification for his doing so is that the patient is in terrible agony, and since he is going to die anyway, it would be wrong to prolong his suffering needlessly. But now notice this. If one simply withholds treatment, it may take the patient longer to die, and so he may suffer more than he would if more direct action were taken and a lethal injection given. This fact provides strong reason for thinking that, once the initial decision not to prolong his agony has been made, active euthanasia is actually preferable to passive euthanasia, rather than the reverse. To say otherwise is to endorse the opinion that leads to more suffering rather than less, and is contrary to the humanitarian impulse that prompts the decision not to prolong his life in the first place.

Part of my point is that the process of being "allowed to die" can be relatively slow and painful, whereas being given a lethal injection is relatively quick and painless. Let me give a different sort of example. In the United States about one in 600 babies is born with Down's syndrome. Most of these babies are otherwise healthy—that is, with only the usual pediatric care, they will proceed to an otherwise normal infancy. Some, however, are born with congenital defects such as intestinal obstructions that require operations if they are to live. Sometimes, the parents and the doctor will decide not to operate, and let the infant die. Anthony Shaw describes what happens then:

> When surgery is denied [the doctor] must try to keep the infant from suffering while natural forces sap the baby's life away. As a surgeon whose natural inclination is to use the scalpel to fight off death, standing by and watching a salvageable baby die is the most emotionally exhausting experience I know. It is easy at a conference, in a theoretical discussion to decide that such infants should be allowed to die. It is altogether different to stand by in the nursery and watch as dehydration and infection wither a tiny being over hours and days. This is a terrible ordeal for me and the hospital staff—much more so than for the parents who never set foot in the nursery.[1]

I can understand why some people are opposed to all euthanasia, and insist that such infants must be allowed to live. I think I can also understand why other people favour destroying these babies quickly and painlessly. But why should anyone favour letting "dehydration and infection wither a tiny being over hours and days"? The doctrine that says a baby may be allowed to dehydrate and wither, but may not be given an injection that would end its life without suffering, seems so patently cruel as to require no further refutation. The strong language is not intended to offend, but only to put the point in the clearest possible way.

My second argument is that the conventional doctrine leads to decisions concerning life and death made on irrelevant grounds.

Consider again the case of the infants with Down's syndrome who need operations for congenital defects unrelated to the syndrome to live. Sometimes, there is no operation, and the baby dies, but when there is no such defect, the baby lives on. Now, an operation such as that to remove an intestinal obstruction is not prohibitively difficult. The reason why such operations are not performed in these cases is, clearly, that the child has Down's syndrome and the parents and the doctor judge that because of that fact it is better for the child to die.

But notice that this situation is absurd, no matter what view one takes of the lives and potentials of such babies. If the life of such an infant is worth preserving, what does it matter if it needs a simple operation? Or, if one thinks it better that such a baby should not live on, what difference does it make that it happens to have an unobstructed intestinal tract? In either case, the matter of life and death is being decided on irrelevant grounds. It is the Down's syndrome, and not the intestines, that is the issue. The matter should be decided, if at all, on that basis, and not be allowed to depend on the essentially irrelevant question of whether the intestinal tract is blocked.

What makes this situation possible, of course, is the idea that when there is an intestinal blockage, one can "let the baby die," but when there is no such defect there is nothing that can be done, for one must not "kill" it. The fact that this idea leads to such results as deciding life or death on irrelevant grounds is another good reason why the doctrine would be rejected.

One reason why so many people think that there is an important moral difference between active and passive euthanasia is that they think killing someone is morally worse than letting someone die. But is it? Is killing, in itself, worse than letting die? To investigate this issue, two cases may be considered that are exactly alike except that one involves killing whereas the other involves letting someone die. Then, it can be asked whether this difference makes any difference to the moral assessments. It is important that the cases be exactly alike, except for this one difference, since otherwise one cannot be confident that it is this difference and not some other that accounts for any variation in the assessments of the two cases. So, let us consider this pair of cases:

In the first, Smith stands to gain a large inheritance if anything should happen to his six-year-old cousin. One evening while the child is taking his bath, Smith sneaks into the bathroom and drowns the child, and then arranges things so that it will look like an accident.

In the second, Jones also stands to gain if anything should happen to his six-year-old cousin. Like Smith, Jones sneaks in planning to drown the child in his bath. However, just as he enters the bathroom Jones sees the child slip and hit his head, and fall facedown in the water. Jones is delighted; he stands by, ready to push the child's head back under if it is necessary, but it is not necessary. With only a little thrashing about, the child drowns all by himself, "accidentally," as Jones watches and does nothing.

Now Smith killed the child, whereas Jones "merely" let the child die. That is the only difference between them. Did either man behave better, from a moral point of view? If the difference between killing and letting die were in itself a morally important matter, one should say that Jones's behaviour was less reprehensible than Smith's. But does one really want to say that? I think not. In the first place, both men acted from the same motive, personal gain, and both had exactly the same end in view when they acted. It may be inferred from Smith's conduct that he is a bad man, although that judgement may be withdrawn or modified if certain further facts are learned about him—for example, that he is mentally deranged. But would not the very same thing be inferred about Jones from his conduct? And would not the same further considerations also be relevant to any modification of this judgement? Moreover, suppose Jones pleaded, in his own defence, "After all, I didn't do anything except just stand there and watch the child drown. I didn't kill him; I only let him die." Again, if letting die were in itself less bad than killing, this defence should have at least some weight. But it does not. Such a "defence" can only be regarded as a grotesque perversion of moral reasoning. Morally speaking, it is no defence at all.

Now, it may be pointed out, quite properly, that the cases of euthanasia with which doctors are concerned are not like this at all. They do not involve personal gain or the destruction of normal, healthy children. Doctors are concerned only with cases in which the patient's life is of no further use to him, or in which the patient's life has become or will soon become a terrible burden. However, the point is the same in these cases: the bare difference between killing and letting die does not, in itself, make a moral difference. If a doctor lets a patient die, for humane reasons, he is in the same moral position as if he had given the patient a lethal injection for humane reasons. If his decision was wrong—if, for example, the patient's illness was in fact curable—the decision would be equally regrettable no matter which method was used to carry it out. And if the doctor's decision was the right one, the method used is not in itself important.

The AMA policy statement isolates the crucial issue very well; the crucial issue is "the intentional termination of the life of one human being by another." But after identifying this issue, and forbidding "mercy killing," the statement goes on to deny that the cessation of treatment is the intentional termination of a life. This is where the mistake comes in, for what is the cessation of treatment, in these circumstances, if it is not "the intentional termination of the life of one human being by another"? Of course it is exactly that, and if it were not, there would be no point to it.

Many people will find this judgement hard to accept. One reason, I think, is that it is very easy to conflate the question of whether killing is, in itself, worse than letting die, with the very different question of whether most actual cases of killing are more reprehensible than most actual cases of letting die. Most actual cases of killing are clearly terrible (think, for example, of all the murders reported in the newspapers), and one hears of such cases every day. On the other hand, one hardly ever hears of a case of letting die, except for the actions of doctors who are motivated by humanitarian reasons. So one learns to think of killing in a much worse light than of letting die. But this does not mean that there is something about killing that makes it in itself worse than letting die, for it is not the bare difference between killing and letting die that makes the difference in these cases. Rather, the other factors—the murderer's motive of personal gain, for example, contrasted with the doctor's humanitarian motivation—account for different reactions to the different cases.

I have argued that killing is not in itself any worse than letting die; if my contention is right, it follows that active euthanasia is not any worse than passive euthanasia. What arguments can be given on the other side? The most common, I believe, is the following:

> The important difference between active and passive euthanasia is that, in passive euthanasia, the doctor does not do anything to bring about the patient's death. The doctor does nothing, and the patient

dies of whatever ills already afflict him. In active euthanasia, however, the doctor does something to bring about the patient's death: he kills him. The doctor who gives the patient with cancer a lethal injection has himself caused his patient's death; whereas if he merely ceases treatment, the cancer is the cause of the death.

A number of points need to be made here. The first is that it is not exactly correct to say that in passive euthanasia the doctor does nothing, for he does do one thing that is very important: he lets the patient die. "Letting someone die" is certainly different, in some respects, from other types of action—mainly in that it is a kind of action that one may perform by way of not performing certain other actions. For example, one may let a patient die by way of not giving medication, just as one may insult someone by way of not shaking his hand. But for any purpose of moral assessment, it is a type of action nonetheless. The decision to let a patient die is subject to moral appraisal in the same way that a decision to kill him would be subject to moral appraisal: it may be assessed as wise or unwise, compassionate or sadistic, right or wrong. If a doctor deliberately let a patient die who was suffering from a routinely curable illness, the doctor would certainly be to blame for what he had done, just as he would be to blame if he had needlessly killed the patient. Charges against him would then be appropriate. If so, it would be no defence at all for him to insist that he didn't "do anything." He would have done something very serious indeed, for he let his patient die.

Fixing the cause of death may be very important from a legal point of view, for it may determine whether criminal charges are brought against the doctor. But I do not think that this notion can be used to show a moral difference between active and passive euthanasia. The reason why it is considered bad to be the cause of someone's death is that death is regarded as a great evil—and so it is. However, if it has been decided that euthanasia—even passive euthanasia—is desirable in a given case, it has also been decided that in this instance death is no greater an evil than the patient's continued existence. And if this is true, the usual reason for not wanting to be the cause of someone's death simply does not apply.

Finally, doctors may think that all of this is only of academic interest—the sort of thing that philosophers may worry about but that has no practical bearing on their own work. After all, doctors must be concerned about the legal consequences of what they do, and active euthanasia is clearly forbidden by the law. But even so, doctors should also be concerned with the fact that the law is forcing upon them a moral doctrine that may be indefensible, and has a considerable effect on their practices. Of course, most doctors are not now in the position of being coerced in this matter, for they do not regard themselves as merely going along with what the law requires. Rather, in statements such as the AMA policy statement that I have quoted, they are endorsing this doctrine as a central point of medical ethics. In that statement, active euthanasia is condemned not merely as illegal but as "contrary to that for which the medical profession stands," whereas passive euthanasia is approved. However, the preceding considerations suggest that there is really no moral difference between the two, considered in themselves (there may be important moral differences in some cases in their *consequences*, but, as I pointed out, these differences may make active euthanasia, and not passive euthanasia, the morally preferable option). So, whereas doctors may have to discriminate between active and passive euthanasia to satisfy the law, they should not do any more than that. In particular, they should not give the distinction any added authority and weight by writing it into official statements of medical ethics.

Note

1. Anthony Shaw, "Doctor, Do We Have a Choice?" *New York Times Magazine*, 30 January 1972, p. 54.

Study Questions

1. According to Rachels, in passive euthanasia does the physician do anything?
2. According to Rachels, under what circumstances is active euthanasia morally preferable to passive euthanasia?
3. Is someone who allows another person to drown morally guilty of killing the person?
4. Should the punishment be the same whether you drown someone or allow someone to drown?

CHAPTER 44

The Intentional Termination of Life

Bonnie Steinbock

> Bonnie Steinbock, whose work we read previously, wrote the follow-
> ing essay responding to the previous article by James Rachels. Who
> has the better of the argument? That question is for each reader to
> answer.

According to James Steinbock, ... a common mistake in medical ethics
is the belief that there is a moral difference between active and passive euthanasia. This is a mistake, [he argues], because the rationale
underlying the distinction between active and passive euthanasia is
the idea that there is a significant moral difference between intentionally killing and intentionally letting die. . . .

Whether . . . there is a significant moral difference . . . is not my
concern here. For it is far from clear that this distinction *is* the
basis of the doctrine of the American Medical Association which
Rachels attacks. And if the killing/letting die distinction is not the
basis of the AMA doctrine, then arguments showing that the distinction has no moral force do not, in themselves, reveal in the
doctrine's adherents either "confused thinking" or "a moral point
of view unrelated to the interests of individuals." Indeed, as we examine the AMA doctrine, I think it will become clear that it appeals to and makes use of a number of overlapping distinctions,
which may have moral significance in particular cases, such as the
distinction between intending and foreseeing, or between ordinary
and extraordinary care. Let us then turn to the 1973 statement,

Bonnie Steinbock, "The Intentional Termination of Life," *Social Science & Medicine*, Vol. 6,
No. 1, 1979, pp. 59–64. Reprinted by permission of the journal. The footnotes were edited.

from the House of Delegates of the American Medical Association, which Rachels cites:

> The intentional termination of the life of one human being by another—mercy killing—is contrary to that for which the medical profession stands and is contrary to the policy of the American Medical Association.
>
> The cessation of the employment of extraordinary means to prolong the life of the body when there is irrefutable evidence that biological death is imminent is the decision of the patient and/or his immediate family. The advice and judgment of the physician should be freely available to the patient and/or his immediate family.

Rachels attacks this statement because he believes that it contains a moral distinction between active and passive euthanasia. . . .

[He takes] the AMA position to prohibit active euthanasia, while allowing, under certain conditions, passive euthanasia.

I intend to show that the AMA statement does not imply support of the active/passive euthanasia distinction. In forbidding the intentional termination of life, the statement rejects both active and passive euthanasia. It does allow for "the cessation of the employment of extraordinary means" to prolong life. The mistake Rachels . . . make[s] is in identifying the cessation of life-prolonging treatment with passive euthanasia, or intentionally letting die. If it were right to equate the two, then the AMA statement would be self-contradictory, for it would begin by condemning, and end by allowing, the intentional termination of life. But if the cessation of life-prolonging treatment is not always or necessarily passive euthanasia, then there is no confusion and no contradiction.

Why does Rachels think that the cessation of life-prolonging treatment is the intentional termination of life? He says:

> The AMA policy statement isolates the crucial issue very well: the crucial issue is "the intentional termination of the life of one human being by another." But after identifying this issue, and forbidding "mercy killing," the statement goes on to deny that the cessation of treatment is the intentional termination of a life. This is where the mistake comes in, for what is the cessation of treatment, in these circumstances, if it is not "the intentional termination of the life of one human being by another"? Of course it is exactly that, and if it were not, there would be no point to it.

However, there *can* be a point (to the cessation of life-prolonging treatment) other than an endeavor to bring about the patient's death, and so the blanket identification of cessation of treatment with the intentional termination of a life is inaccurate. There are at least two situations in which the termination of life-prolonging treatment cannot be identified with the intentional termination of the life of one human being by another.

The first situation concerns the patient's right to refuse treatment. . . . Rachels give[s] the example of a patient dying of an incurable disease, accompanied by unrelievable pain, who wants to end the treatment which cannot cure him but can only prolong his miserable existence. Why, they ask, may a doctor accede to the patient's request to stop treatment, but not provide a patient in a similar situation with a lethal dose? The answer lies in the patient's right to refuse treatment. In general, a competent adult has the right to refuse treatment, even where such treatment is necessary to prolong life. Indeed, the right to refuse treatment has been upheld even when the patient's reason for refusing treatment is generally agreed to be inadequate.[1] This right can be overridden (if, for example, the patient has dependent children) but, in general, no one may legally compel you to undergo treatment to which you have not consented. "Historically, surgical intrusion has always been considered a technical battery upon the person and one to be excused or justified by consent of the patient or justified by necessity created by the circumstances of the moment. . . ."[2]

At this point, an objection might be raised that if one has the right to refuse life-prolonging treatment, then consistency demands that one have the right to decide to end his or her life, and to obtain help in doing so. The idea is that the right to refuse treatment somehow implies a right to voluntary euthanasia, and we need to see why someone might think this. The right to refuse treatment has been considered by legal writers as an example of the right to privacy or, better, the right to bodily self-determination. You have the right to decide what happens to your own body, and the right to refuse treatment is an instance of that right. But if you have the right to determine what happens to your own body, then should you not have the right to choose to end your life, and even a right to get help in doing so?

However, it is important to see that the right to refuse treatment is not the same as, nor does it entail, a right to voluntary euthanasia, even if both can be derived from the right to bodily self-determination. The right to refuse treatment is not itself a "right to die"; that one may choose to exercise this right even at the risk of death, or even *in order to die*, is irrelevant. The purpose of the right to refuse medical treatment is not to give persons a right to decide whether to live or die, but to protect them from the unwanted interferences of others. Perhaps we ought to interpret the right to bodily self-determination more broadly, so as to include a right to die; but this would be a substantial extension of our present understanding of the right to bodily self-determination, and not a consequence of it. If we were to recognize a right to voluntary euthanasia, we would have to agree that people have the right not merely to be left alone but also the right to be killed. I leave to one side that substantive moral issue. My claim is simply that there can be a reason for terminating life-prolonging treatment other than "to bring about the patient's death."

The second case in which termination of treatment cannot be identified with intentional termination of life is where continued treatment has little chance of improving the patient's condition and brings greater discomfort than relief.

The question here is what treatment is appropriate to the particular case. A cancer specialist describes it in this way:

> My general rule is to administer therapy as long as a patient responds well and has the potential for a reasonably good quality of life. But when all feasible therapies have been administered and a patient shows signs of rapid deterioration, the continuation of therapy can cause more discomfort than the cancer. From that time I recommend surgery, radiotherapy, or chemotherapy only as a means of relieving pain. But if a patient's condition should once again stabilize after the withdrawal of active therapy and if it should appear that he could still gain some good time, I would immediately reinstitute active therapy. The decision to cease anticancer treatment is never irrevocable, and often the desire to live will push a patient to try for another remission, or even a few more days of life.[3]

The decision here to cease anticancer treatment cannot be construed as a decision that the patient die, or as the intentional termination of life. It is a decision to provide the most appropriate treatment for that patient at that time. Rachels suggests that the point of the cessation of treatment is the intentional termination of life. But here the point of discontinuing treatment is not to bring about the patient's death but to avoid treatment that will cause more discomfort than the cancer and has little hope of benefiting the patient. Treatment that meets this description is often called "extraordinary."[4] The concept is flexible, and what might be considered "extraordinary" in one situation might be ordinary in another. The use of a respirator to sustain a patient through a severe bout with a respiratory disease would be considered ordinary; its use to sustain the life of a severely brain-damaged person in an irreversible coma would be considered extraordinary.

Contrasted with extraordinary treatment is ordinary treatment, the care a doctor would normally be expected to provide. Failure to provide ordinary care constitutes neglect, and can even be construed as the intentional infliction of harm, where there is a legal obligation to provide care. The importance of the ordinary/extraordinary care distinction lies partly in its connection to the doctor's intention. The withholding of extraordinary care should be seen as a decision not to inflict painful treatment on a patient without reasonable hope of success. The withholding of ordinary care, by contrast, must be seen as neglect. Thus, one doctor says, "We have to draw a distinction between ordinary and extraordinary means. We never withdraw what's needed to make a baby comfortable, we would never withdraw the care a parent would provide. We never kill a baby. . . . But we may decide certain heroic intervention is not worthwhile."[5]

We should keep in mind the ordinary/extraordinary care distinction when considering an example given by . . . Rachels to show the irrationality of the active/passive distinction with regard to infanticide. The example is this: a child is born with [Down] syndrome and also has an intestinal obstruction that requires corrective surgery. If the surgery is not performed, the infant will starve to death, since it cannot take food orally. This may take days or even weeks, as dehydration and infection set in. Commenting on this situation in his article in this book, Rachels says:

> I can understand why some people are opposed to all euthanasia, and insist that such infants must be allowed to live. I think I can also understand why other people favor destroying these babies quickly and painlessly. But why should anyone favor letting "dehydration and infection wither a tiny being over hours and days"? The doctrine that says that a baby may be allowed to dehydrate and wither, but may not be given an injection that would end its life without suffering, seems so patently cruel as to require no further refutation.

Such a doctrine perhaps does not need further refutation; but this is not the AMA doctrine. The AMA statement criticized by Rachels allows only for the cessation of extraordinary means to prolong life when death is imminent. Neither of these conditions is satisfied in this example. Death is not imminent in this situation, any more than it would be if a normal child had an attack of appendicitis. Neither the corrective surgery to remove the intestinal obstruction nor the intravenous feeding required to keep the infant alive until such surgery is performed can be regarded as extraordinary means, for neither is particularly expensive, nor does either place an overwhelming burden on the patient or others. (The continued existence of the child might be thought to place an overwhelming burden on its parents, but that has nothing to do with the characterization of the means to prolong its life as extraordinary. If it had, then *feeding* a severely defective child who required a great deal of care could be regarded as extraordinary.) The chances of success if the operation is undertaken are quite good, though there is always a risk in operating on infants. Though the [Down] syndrome will not be alleviated, the child will proceed to an otherwise normal infancy.

It cannot be argued that the treatment is withheld for the infant's sake, unless one is prepared to argue that all mentally retarded babies are better off dead. This is particularly implausible in the case of [Down] syndrome babies, who generally do not suffer and are capable of giving and receiving love, of learning and playing, to varying degrees.

In a film on this subject entitled, "Who Should Survive?" a doctor defended a decision not to operate, saying that since the parents did not consent to the operation, the doctor's hands were tied. As we have seen, surgical intrusion requires consent, and in the case of infants, consent would normally come from the parents. But, as legal guardians, parents are required to provide medical care for their children, and failure to do so can constitute criminal neglect or even homicide. In general, courts have been understandably reluctant to recognize a parental right to terminate life-prolonging treatment.[6] Although prosecution is unlikely, physicians who comply with invalid instructions from the parents and permit the infant's death could be liable for aiding and abetting, failure to report child neglect, or even homicide. So it is not true that, in this situation, doctors are legally bound to do as the parents wish.

To sum up, I think that Rachels is right to regard the decision not to operate in the [Down] syndrome example as the intentional termination of life. But there is no reason to believe that either the law or the AMA would regard it otherwise. Certainly the decision to withhold treatment is not justified by the AMA statement. That such infants have been allowed to die cannot be denied; but this, I think, is the result of doctors misunderstanding the law and the AMA position.

Withholding treatment in this case is the intentional termination of life because the infant is deliberately allowed to die; that is the point of not operating. But there are other cases in which that is not the point. If the point is to avoid inflicting painful treatment on a patient with little or no reasonable hope of success, this is not the intentional termination of life. The permissibility of such withholding of treatment, then, would have no implications for the permissibility of euthanasia, active or passive.

The decision whether or not to operate, or to institute vigorous treatment, is particularly agonizing in the case of children born with spina bifida, an opening in the base of the spine usually accompanied by hydrocephalus and mental retardation. If left unoperated, these children usually die of meningitis or kidney failure within the first few years of life. Even if they survive, all affected children face a lifetime of illness, operations, and varying degrees of disability. The policy used to be to save as many as possible, but the trend now is toward selective treatment, based on the physician's estimate of the chances of success. If operating is not likely to improve significantly the child's condition, parents and doctors may agree not to operate. This is not the intentional termination of life, for again the purpose is not the termination of the child's life but the avoidance of painful and pointless treatment. Thus, the fact that withholding treatment is justified does not imply that killing the child would be equally justified.

Throughout the discussion, I have claimed that intentionally ceasing life-prolonging treatment is not the intentional termination of life unless the doctor has, as his or her purpose in stopping treatment, the patient's death.

It may be objected that I have incorrectly characterized the conditions for the intentional termination of life. Perhaps it is enough that the doctor intentionally ceases treatment, foreseeing that the patient will die.

In many cases, if one acts intentionally, foreseeing that a particular result will occur, one can be said to have brought about that result intentionally. Indeed, this is the general legal rule. Why, then, am I not willing to call the cessation of life-prolonging treatment, in compliance with the patient's right to refuse treatment, the intentional termination of life? It is not because such an *identification* is necessarily opprobrious; for we could go on to *discuss* whether such cessation of treatment is a *justifiable* intentional termination of life. Even in the law, some cases of homicide are justifiable; e.g., homicide in self-defense.

However, the cessation of life-prolonging treatment, in the cases which I have discussed, is not regarded in law as being justifiable homicide, because it is not homicide at all. Why is this? Is it because the doctor "doesn't do anything," and so cannot be guilty of homicide? Surely not, since, as I have indicated, the law sometimes treats an omission as the cause of death. A better explanation, I think, has to do with the fact that in the context of the patient's right to refuse treatment, a doctor is not at liberty to continue treatment. It seems a necessary ingredient of intentionally letting die that one could have done something to prevent the death. In this situation, of course the doctor can physically prevent the patient's death, but since we do not regard the doctor as *free* to continue treatment, we say that there is "nothing he can do." Therefore he does not intentionally let the patient die.

To discuss this suggestion fully, I would need to present a full-scale theory of intentional action. However, at least I have shown, through the discussion of the above examples, that such a theory will be very complex, and that one of the complexities concerns the agent's reason for acting. The reason why an agent acted (or failed to act) may affect the characterization of what he did intentionally. The mere fact that he did *something* intentionally, foreseeing a certain result, does not necessarily mean that he brought about that *result* intentionally.

In order to show that the cessation of life-prolonging treatment, in the cases I've discussed, is the intentional termination of life, one would either have to show that treatment was stopped in order to bring about the patient's death, or provide a theory of intentional action according to which the reason for ceasing treatment is irrelevant to its characterization as the intentional termination of life. I find this suggestion implausible, but am willing to consider arguments for it. Rachels has provided no such arguments: indeed, he apparently shares my view about the intentional termination of life. For when he claims that the cessation of life-prolonging treatment is the intentional termination of life, his reason for making the claim is that "if it were not, there would be no point to it." Rachels believes that the point of ceasing treatment, "in these cases," is to bring about the patient's death. If that were not the point, he suggests, why would the doctor cease treatment? I have shown, however, that there can be a point to ceasing treatment which is not the death of the patient. In showing this, I have refuted Rachels' reason for identifying the cessation of life-prolonging treatment with the intentional termination of life, and thus his argument against the AMA doctrine.

Here someone might say: Even if the withholding of treatment is not the intentional termination of life, does that make a difference, morally speaking? If life-prolonging treatment may be withheld, for the sake of the child, may not an easy death be provided, for the sake of the child, as well? The unoperated child with spina bifida may take months or even years to die. Distressed by the spectacle of children "lying around, waiting to die," one doctor has written, "It is time that society and medicine stopped perpetuating the fiction that withholding treatment is ethically different from terminating a life. It is time that society began to discuss mechanisms by which we can alleviate the pain and suffering for those individuals whom we cannot help."[7]

I do not deny that there may be cases in which death is in the best interests of the patient. In such cases, a quick and painless death may be the best thing. However, I do not think that, once active or vigorous treatment is stopped, a quick death is always preferable to a lingering one. We must be cautious about attributing to defective children *our* distress at seeing them linger. Waiting for them to die may be tough on parents, doctors, and nurses—it isn't necessarily tough on the child. The decision not to operate need not mean a decision to neglect, and it may be possible to make the remaining months of the child's life comfortable, pleasant, and filled with love. If this alternative is possible, surely it is more decent and humane than killing the child. In such a situation, withholding treatment, foreseeing the child's death, is not ethically equivalent to killing the child, and we cannot move from the permissibility of the former to that of the latter. I am worried that there will be a tendency to do precisely that if active euthanasia is regarded as morally equivalent to the withholding of life-prolonging treatment.

Conclusion

The AMA statement does not make the distinction Rachels . . . wish[es] to attack, that between active and passive euthanasia. Instead, the statement draws a distinction between the intentional termination of life, on the one hand, and the cessation of the employment of extraordinary means to prolong life, on the other. Nothing said by Rachels . . . shows that this distinction is confused. It may be that doctors have misinterpreted the AMA statement, and that this has led, for example, to decisions to allow defective infants to starve slowly to death. I quite agree with Rachels . . . that the decisions to which they allude were cruel and made on irrelevant grounds. Certainly it is worth pointing out that allowing someone to die *can* be the intentional termination of life, and that it can be just as bad as, or worse than, killing someone. However, the withholding of life-prolonging treatment is not necessarily the intentional termination of life, so that if it is permissible to withhold life-prolonging treatment it does not follow that, other things being equal, it is permissible to kill. Furthermore, most of the time, other things are not equal. In many of the cases in which it would be right to cease treatment, I do not think that it would also be right to kill.

Notes

1. For example, *In re Yetter,* 62 Pa. D & C. 2d 619 (C.P., Northampton County Ct. 1974).
2. David W. Meyers, "Legal Aspects of Voluntary Euthanasia," in *Dilemmas of Euthanasia,* ed. John Behnke and Sissela Bok (New York: Anchor Books, 1975), p. 56.
3. Ernest H. Rosenbaum, M.D., *Living With Cancer* (New York: Praeger, 1975), p. 27.
4. See Tristram Engelhardt, Jr.; "Ethical Issues in Aiding the Death of Young Children," in *Beneficent Euthanasia,* ed. Marvin Kohl (Buffalo, N.Y.: Prometheus Books, 1975). . . .
5. B. D. Colen, *Karen Ann Quinlan: Living and Dying in the Age of Eternal Life* (Los Angeles: Nash, 1976), p. 115.
6. See Norman L. Cantor, "Law and the Termination of an Incompetent Patient's Life-Preserving Care," in *Dilemmas of Euthanasia,* pp. 69–105.
7. John Freeman, "Is There a Right to Die—Quickly?," *Journal of Pediatrics,* 80, no. 5 (1972), 904–905.

Study Questions

1. Is killing someone always worse than letting the person die?
2. Is the physician's intention crucial to assessing the morality of the means used to bring about death?
3. Are we ever justified in performing actions with unfortunate consequences in an effort to achieve other purposes?
4. What should a physician do if a paralyzed patient on life support asks to be euthanized?

J. Death

CHAPTER 45

Death

Thomas Nagel

Having explored a variety of practical problems ranging from world hunger to euthanasia, we turn in the next two sections to the overarching issues of death and the meaning of life. As to death, it looms for all. But is it an evil? Thomas Nagel, whose work we read previously, concludes that if life without limit is good, then a bad end is in store for everyone.

If death is the unequivocal and permanent end of our existence, the question arises whether it is a bad thing to die.

There is conspicuous disagreement about the matter: some people think death is dreadful; others have no objection to death *per se*, though they hope their own will be neither premature nor painful. Those in the former category tend to think those in the latter are blind to the obvious, while the latter suppose the former to be prey to some sort of confusion. On the one hand it can be said that life is all we have and the loss of it is the greatest loss we can sustain. On the other hand it may be objected that death deprives this supposed loss of its subject, and that if we realize that death is not an unimaginable condition of the persisting person, but a mere blank, we will see that it can have no value whatever, positive or negative.

Since I want to leave aside the question whether we are, or might be, immortal in some form, I shall simply use the word "death" and its cognates in this discussion to mean *permanent* death, unsupplemented by any form of conscious survival. I want to ask whether death is in itself an evil; and how great an evil, and of what kind, it might be. The question should be of interest even to those who believe in some form of immortality, for one's attitude toward immortality must depend in part on one's attitude toward death.

If death is an evil at all, it cannot be because of its positive features, but only because of what it deprives us of. I shall try to deal with the difficulties surrounding the natural view that death is an evil because it brings to an end all the goods that life contains. We need not give an account of these goods here, except to observe that some of them, like perception, desire, activity, and thought, are so general as to be constitutive of human life. They are widely regarded as formidable benefits in themselves, despite the fact that they are conditions of misery as well as of happiness, and that a sufficient quantity of more particular evils can perhaps outweigh them. That is what is meant, I think, by the allegation that it is good simply to be alive, even if one is undergoing terrible experiences. The situation is roughly this: There are elements which, if added to one's experience, make life better; there are other elements which, if added to one's experience, make life worse. But what remains when these are set aside is not merely *neutral*: it is emphatically positive. Therefore life is worth living even when the bad elements of experience are plentiful, and the good ones too meager to outweigh the bad ones on their own. The additional positive weight is supplied by experience itself, rather than by any of its contents.

I shall not discuss the value that one person's life or death may have for others, or its objective value, but only the value it has for the person who is its subject. That seems to me the primary case, and the case which presents the greatest difficulties. Let me add only two observations. First, the value of life and its contents does not attach to mere organic survival: almost everyone would be indifferent (other things equal) between immediate death and immediate coma followed by death twenty years later without reawakening. And second, like most goods, this can be multiplied by time: more is better than less. The added quantities need not be temporally continuous (though continuity has its social advantages). People are attracted to the possibility of long-term suspended animation or freezing, followed by the resumption of conscious life, because they can regard it from within simply as a *continuation* of their present life. If these techniques are ever perfected, what from outside appeared as a dormant interval of three hundred years could be expe-
_____ the subject as nothing more than a sharp discontinuity
_____ acter of his experiences. I do not deny, of course, that
_____ own disadvantages. Family and friends may have died in

the meantime; the language may have changed; the comforts of social, geographical, and cultural familiarity would be lacking. Nevertheless these inconveniences would not obliterate the basic advantage of continued, though discontinuous, existence.

If we turn from what is good about life to what is bad about death, the case is completely different. Essentially, though there may be problems about their specification, what we find desirable in life are certain states, conditions, or types of activity. It is *being* alive, *doing* certain things, having certain experiences, that we consider good. But if death is an evil, it is the *loss of life*, rather than the state of being dead, or nonexistent, or unconscious, that is objectionable.[1] This asymmetry is important. If it is good to be alive, that advantage can be attributed to a person at each point of his life. It is a good of which Bach had more than Schubert, simply because he lived longer. Death, however, is not an evil of which Shakespeare has so far received a larger portion than Proust. If death is a disadvantage, it is not easy to say when a man suffers it.

There are two other indications that we do not object to death merely because it involves long periods of nonexistence. First, as has been mentioned, most of us would not regard the *temporary* suspension of life, even for substantial intervals, as in itself a misfortune. If it ever happens that people can be frozen without reduction of the conscious lifespan, it will be inappropriate to pity those who are temporarily out of circulation. Second, none of us existed before we were born (or conceived), but few regard that as a misfortune. I shall have more to say about this later.

The point that death is not regarded as an unfortunate *state* enables us to refute a curious but very common suggestion about the origin of the fear of death. It is often said that those who object to death have made the mistake of trying to imagine what it is like to *be* dead. It is alleged that the failure to realize that this task is logically impossible (for the banal reason that there is nothing to imagine) leads to the conviction that death is a mysterious and therefore terrifying prospective *state*. But this diagnosis is evidently false, for it is just as impossible to imagine being totally unconscious as to imagine being dead (though it is easy enough to imagine oneself, from the outside, in either of those conditions). Yet people who are averse to death are not usually averse to unconsciousness (so long as it does not entail a substantial cut in the total duration of waking life).

If we are to make sense of the view that to die is bad, it must be on the ground that life is a good and death is the correspondir deprivation or loss, bad not because of any positive features but because of the desirability of what it removes. We must now turn to the serious difficulties which this hypothesis raises, difficulties about loss and privation in general, and about death in particular.

Essentially, there are three types of problem. First, doubt may be raised whether *anything* can be bad for a man without being positively unpleasant to him: specifically, it may be doubted that there are any evils which consist merely in the deprivation or absence of possible goods, and which do not depend on someone's *minding* that deprivation. Second, there are special difficulties, in the case of death, about how the supposed misfortune is to be assigned to a subject at all. There is doubt both as to *who* its subject is, and as to *when* he undergoes it. So long as a person exists, he has not yet died, and once he has died, he no longer exists; so there seems to be no time when death, if it is a misfortune, can be ascribed to its unfortunate subject. The third type of difficulty concerns the asymmetry, mentioned above, between our attitudes to posthumous and prenatal nonexistence. How can the former be bad if the latter is not?

It should be recognized that if these are valid objections to counting death as an evil, they will apply to many other supposed evils as well. The first type of objection is expressed in general form by the common remark that what you don't know can't hurt you. It means that even if a man is betrayed by his friends, ridiculed behind his back, and despised by people who treat him politely to his face, none of it can be counted as a misfortune for him so long as he does not suffer as a result. It means that a man is not injured if his wishes are ignored by the executor of his will, or if, after his death, the belief becomes current that all the literary works on which his fame rests were really written by his brother, who died in Mexico at the age of 28. It seems to me worth asking what assumptions about good and evil lead to these drastic restrictions.

All the questions have something to do with time. There certainly are goods and evils of a simple kind (including some pleasures and pains) which a person possesses at a given time simply in virtue of his condition at that time. But this is not true of all the things we regard as good or bad for a man. Often we need to know his history to tell whether something is a misfortune or not; this applies to ills like deterioration, deprivation, and damage. Sometimes his experiential ____ely unimportant—as in the case of a man who wastes his ____ heerful pursuit of a method of communicating with as- ____ nts. Someone who holds that all goods and evils must be temporally assignable states of the person may of course try to bring difficult cases into line by pointing to the pleasure or pain that more complicated goods and evils cause. Loss, betrayal, deception, and ridicule are on this view bad because people suffer when they learn of them. But it should be asked how our ideas of human value would have to be constituted to accommodate these cases directly instead. One advantage of such an account might be that it would enable us to explain *why* the discovery of these misfortunes causes suffering—in a way that makes it reasonable. For the natural view is that the discovery of betrayal makes us unhappy because it is bad to be betrayed— not that betrayal is bad because its discovery makes us unhappy.

It therefore seems to me worth exploring the position that most good and ill fortune has as its subject a person identified by his history and his possibilities, rather than merely by his categorical state of the moment—and that while this subject can be exactly located in a sequence of places and times, the same is not necessarily true of the goods and ills that befall him.[2]

These ideas can be illustrated by an example of deprivation whose severity approaches that of death. Suppose an intelligent person receives a brain injury that reduces him to the mental condition of a contented infant, and that such desires as remain to him can be satisfied by a custodian, so that he is free from care. Such a development would be widely regarded as a severe misfortune, not only for his friends and relations, or for society, but also, and primarily, for the person himself. This does not mean that a contented infant is unfortunate. The intelligent adult who has been *reduced* to this condition is the subject of the misfortune. He is the one we pity, though of course he does not mind his condition—there is some doubt, in fact, whether he can be said to exist any longer.

The view that such a man has suffered a misfortune is open to the same objections which have been raised in regard to death. He does not mind his condition. It is in fact the same condition he was in at the age of three months, except that he is bigger. If we did not pity him then, why pity him now; in any case, who is there to pity? The intelligent adult has disappeared, and for a creature like the one before us, happiness consists in a full stomach and a dry diaper.

If these objections are invalid, it must be because they rest on a mistaken assumption about the temporal relation between the subject of a misfortune and the circumstances which constitute it. If, instead of concentrating exclusively on the oversized baby before us, we consider the person he was, and the person he *could* be now, then h reduction to this state and the cancellation of his natural adult development constitute a perfectly intelligible catastrophe.

This case should convince us that it is arbitrary to restrict the goods and evils that can befall a man to nonrelational properties ascribable to him at particular times. As it stands, that restriction excludes not only such cases of gross degeneration, but also a good deal of what is important about success and failure, and other features of a life that have the character of processes. I believe we can go further, however. There are goods and evils which are irreducibly relational; they are features of the relations between a person, with spatial and temporal boundaries of the usual sort, and circumstances which may not coincide with him either in space or in time. A man's life includes much that does not take place within the boundaries of his body and his mind, and what happens to him can include much that does not take place within the boundaries of his life. These boundaries are commonly crossed by the misfortunes of being deceived, or despised, or betrayed. (If this is correct, there is a simple account of what is wrong with breaking a deathbed promise. It is an injury to the dead man. For certain purposes it is possible to regard time as just another type of distance.) The case of mental degeneration shows us an evil that depends on a contrast between the reality and the possible alternatives. A man is the subject of good and evil as much because he has hopes which may or may not be fulfilled, or possibilities which may or may not be realized, as because of his capacity to suffer and enjoy. If death is an evil, it must be accounted for in these terms, and the impossibility of locating it within life should not trouble us.

When a man dies we are left with his corpse, and while a corpse can suffer the kind of mishap that may occur to an article of furniture, it is not a suitable object for pity. The man, however, is. He has lost his life, and if he had not died, he would have continued to live it, and to possess whatever good there is in living. If we apply to death the account suggested for the case of dementia, we shall say that although the spatial and temporal locations of the individual who suffered the loss are clear enough, the misfortune itself cannot be so easily located. One must be content just to state that his life is over and there will never be any more of it. That *fact*, rather than his past or present condition, constitutes his misfortune, if it is one. Nevertheless, if it is a loss, someone must suffer it, and *he* must have existed, and had a specific spatial and temporal location even if the loss itself the fact that Beethoven had no children may have been a cause of regret to him, or a sad thing for the world, but it cannot be described as a misfortune for the children that he never had. All of us, I believe, are fortunate to have been born. But unless good and ill can be assigned to an embryo, or even to an unconnected pair of gametes, it cannot be said that not to be born is a misfortune. (That is a factor to be considered in deciding whether abortion and contraception are akin to murder.)

This approach also provides a solution to the problem of temporal asymmetry, pointed out by Lucretius. He observed that no one finds it disturbing to contemplate the eternity preceding his own birth, and he took this to show that it must be irrational to fear death, since death is simply the mirror image of the prior abyss. That is not true, however, and the difference between the two explains why it is reasonable to regard them differently. It is true that both the time before a man's birth and the time after his death are times when he does not exist. But the time after his death is time of which his death deprives him. It is time in which, had he not died then, he would be alive. Therefore any death entails the loss of *some* life that its victim would have led had he not died at that or any earlier point. We know perfectly well what it would be for him to have had it instead of losing it, and there is no difficulty in identifying the loser.

But we cannot say that the time prior to a man's birth is time in which he would have lived had he been born not then but earlier. For aside from the brief margin permitted by premature labor, he *could* not have been born earlier: anyone born substantially earlier than he was would have been someone else. Therefore the time prior to his birth is not time in which his subsequent birth prevents him from living. His birth, when it occurs, does not entail the loss to him of any life whatever.

The direction of time is crucial in assigning possibilities to people or other individuals. Distinct possible lives of a single person can diverge from a common beginning, but they cannot converge to a common conclusion from diverse beginnings. (The latter would represent not a set of different possible lives of one individual, but a set of distinct possible individuals, whose lives have identical conclusions.) Given an identifiable individual, countless possibilities for his continued existence are imaginable, and we can clearly conceive of what it would be for him to go on existing indefinitely. However inevitable it is that this will not come about, its possibility is still that of the continuation of a good for him, if life is the good we take it to be.[3]

We are left, therefore, with the question whether the nonrealization of this possibility is in every case a misfortune, or whether it depends on what can naturally be hoped for. This seems to me the most serious difficulty with the view that death is always an evil. Even if we can dispose of the objections against admitting misfortune that is not experienced, or cannot be assigned to a definite time in the person's life, we still have to set some limits on *how* possible a possibility must be for its nonrealization to be a misfortune (or good fortune, should the possibility be a bad one). The death of Keats at 24 is generally regarded as tragic; that of Tolstoy at 82 is not. Although they will both be dead for ever, Keats' death deprived him of many years of life which were allowed to Tolstoy; so in a clear sense Keats' loss was greater (though not in the sense standardly employed in mathematical comparison between infinite quantities). However, this does not prove that Tolstoy's loss was insignificant. Perhaps we record an objection only to evils which are gratuitously added to the inevitable; the fact that it is worse to die at 24 than at 82 does not imply that it is not a terrible thing to die at 82, or even at 806. The question is whether we can regard as a misfortune any limitation, like mortality, that is normal to the species. Blindness or near-blindness is not a misfortune for a mole, nor would it be for a man if that were the natural condition of the human race.

The trouble is that life familiarizes us with the goods of which death deprives us. We are already able to appreciate them, as a mole is not able to appreciate vision. If we put aside doubts about their status as goods and grant that their quantity is in part a function of their duration, the question remains whether death, no matter when it occurs, can be said to deprive its victim of what is in the relevant sense a possible continuation of life.

The situation is an ambiguous one. Observed from without, human beings obviously have a natural lifespan and cannot live much longer than a hundred years. A man's sense of his own experience, on the other hand, does not embody this idea of a natural limit. His existence defines for him an essentially open-ended possible future, containing the usual mixture of goods and evils that he has found so tolerable in the past. Having been gratuitously introduced to the world by a collection of natural, historical, and social accidents, he finds himself the subject of a *life*, with an indeterminate and not essentially limited future. Viewed in this way, death, no matter how inevitable, is an abrupt cancellation of indefinitely extensive possible goods. Normality seems to have nothing to do with it, for the fact that we will all inevitably die in a few score years cannot by itself imply that it would not be good to live longer. Suppose that we were all inevitably going to die in *agony*—physical agony lasting six months. Would inevitability make *that* prospect any less unpleasant? And why should it be different for a deprivation? If the normal lifespan were a thousand years, death at 80 would be a tragedy. As things are, it may just be a more widespread tragedy. If there is no limit to the amount of life that it would be good to have, then it may be that a bad end is in store for us all.

Notes

1. It is sometimes suggested that what we really mind is the process of *dying*. But I should not really object to dying if it were not followed by death.
2. It is certainly not true in general of the things that can be said of him. For example, Abraham Lincoln was taller than Louis XIV. But when?
3. I confess to being troubled by the above argument, on the ground that it is too sophisticated to explain the simple difference between our attitudes to prenatal and posthumous nonexistence. For this reason I suspect that something essential is omitted from the account of the badness of death by an analysis which treats it as a deprivation of possibilities. My suspicion is supported by the following suggestion of Robert Nozick. We could imagine discovering that people developed from individual spores that had existed indefinitely far in advance of their birth. In this fantasy, birth never occurs naturally more than a hundred years before the permanent end of the spore's existence. But then we discover a way to trigger the premature hatching of these spores, and people are born who have thousands of years of active life before them. Given such a situation, it would be possible to imagine *oneself* having come into existence thousands of years previously. If we put aside the question whether this would really be the same person, even given the identity of the spore, then the consequence appears to be that a person's birth at a given time *could* deprive him of many earlier years of possible life. Now while it would be cause for regret that one had been deprived of all those possible years of life by being born too late, the feeling would differ from that which many people have about death. I conclude that something about the future *prospect* of permanent nothingness is not captured by the analysis in terms of denied possibilities. If so, then Lucretius' argument still awaits an answer. . . .

Study Questions

1. If death is not an evil for a person who dies, does it follow that death is not an evil for anyone?
2. Do you agree with Nagel that a man who devotes himself to cheerful pursuit of a method of communicating with asparagus plants has wasted his life?
3. Do you agree with Nagel that all of us are fortunate to have been born?
4. If we accept without regret not having lived in the past before we were born, should we also accept without regret not living in the future after we die?

CHAPTER 46

The Badness of Death

Shelly Kagan

Shelly Kagan is Professor of Philosophy at Yale University. He considers the puzzle, discussed in the previous section by Thomas Nagel, that was originally posed by the Roman thinker Lucretius (c. 94–c. 55 B.C.E.). He asked why we should be concerned about not being alive after the time of our death, although we are unconcerned about not being alive before the time of our birth.

Let me turn to . . . a puzzle that we get from Lucretius, a Roman philosopher.[1] Lucretius was one of those who thought it a mistake to claim that death could be bad for us. He thinks we are confused when we find the prospect of our death upsetting. He recognizes, of course, that most of us *are* upset at the fact that we're going to die. We think death is bad for us. Why? In my own case, of course, it's because after my death I won't exist. . . . [A]fter my death it will be true that if only I were still alive, I could be enjoying the good things in life.

Fair enough, says Lucretius, but wait a minute. The time after I die isn't the *only* period during which I won't exist. It's not the only period in which it is true that if only I were alive, I could be enjoying the good things in life. There's *another* period of nonexistence: the period before my birth. To be sure, there will be an infinite period after my death in which I won't exist—and realizing that fills me with dismay. But be that all as it may, there was of course also an infinite period *before* I came into existence. Well, says Lucretius, if nonexistence is so bad—and by the deprivation account it seems that we want to say that it is—shouldn't I be upset at the fact that there was also this eternity of nonexistence before I was born?

From Shelly Kagan, *Death*. Yale University Press, 2012. Reprinted by permission of the publisher.

But, Lucretius suggests, that's silly, right? Nobody is upset about the fact that there was an eternity of nonexistence *before* they were born. In which case, he concludes, it doesn't make any sense to be upset about the eternity of nonexistence *after* you die.

Lucretius doesn't offer this as a puzzle. Rather, he offers it as an argument that we should not be concerned about the fact that we're going to die. Unsurprisingly, however, most philosophers aren't willing to go with Lucretius all the way to this conclusion. They insist, instead, that there must be something wrong with this argument someplace. The challenge is to figure out just where the mistake is.

What are the options here? One possibility, of course, is to simply agree with Lucretius. There is nothing bad about the eternity of nonexistence before I was born. So, similarly, there is nothing bad about the eternity of non-existence after I die. Despite what most of us think, death is not bad for me. That's certainly one possibility—completely agreeing with Lucretius.

A second possibility is to partly agree with Lucretius. Perhaps we really do need to treat these two eternities of nonexistence on a par; but instead of saying with Lucretius that there was nothing bad about the eternity of nonexistence before birth and so nothing bad about the eternity of nonexistence after death, maybe we should say, instead, that just as there is something bad about the eternity of nonexistence after we die, so too there must be something bad about the eternity of nonexistence before we were born! Maybe we should just stick with the deprivation account and not lose faith in it. The deprivation account tells us that it's bad for us that there's this period after we die, because if only we weren't dead then, we would still be able to enjoy the good things in life. So maybe we should say, similarly, that it *is* bad for us that there's this period before we come into existence. After all, if only we had existed then, we would have been able to enjoy the good things in life. So maybe Lucretius was right when he tells us that we have to treat both periods the same, but for all that he could be wrong in concluding that neither period is bad. Maybe we should think *both* periods are bad. That's a possibility, too.

What other possibilities are there? We might say that although Lucretius is right when he points out that there are two periods of nonexistence, not just one, nonetheless there is a justification for treating them differently. Perhaps there is an important difference between the two periods, a kind of asymmetry that explains why we should care about the one but not the other.

Most philosophers want to take this last way out. They say that there's something that explains why it makes sense, why it's reasonable, to care about the eternity of nonexistence after my death in a way that I don't care about the eternity of nonexistence before my birth. But then the puzzle, of course, is to point to a difference that would *justify* that kind of asymmetrical treatment of the two periods. It's easy to *say* that it's reasonable to treat the two periods differently; the philosophical challenge is to point to something that explains or justifies that asymmetrical treatment.

One very common response is to say something like this. Consider the period after my death. I'm no longer alive. I have *lost* my life. In contrast, during the period before my birth, although I'm not alive, I have not *lost* my life. I have never yet been alive. And, of course, you can't lose something you've never yet had. So what's worse about the period after death is the fact that death involves *loss*, whereas prenatal nonexistence does *not* involve loss. And so (the argument goes), we can see why it's reasonable to care more about the period after death than the period before birth. The one involves loss, while the other does not.

This is, as I say, a very common response. But I am inclined to think that it can't be an adequate answer. It is true, of course, that the period after death involves loss while the period before birth does not. The very definition of "loss," after all, requires that in order to have lost something, it must be true that you don't have something that at an earlier time you did have. Given this definition, it follows trivially that the period after death involves loss, while the period before birth does not. After all, as we just observed, during the period before birth, although I do not *have* life, it is also true that I haven't had life previously. So I haven't *lost* anything.

Of course, there's another thing that's true about this prenatal period, to wit, I don't have life and I'm *going* to get it. So I don't yet have something that's going to come in the future. That's not true about the postlife period. After death I've *lost* life. But it's not true of this postdeath period that I don't have life and I'm going to get it in the future. So this period after death isn't quite like the period before birth: in the period after death, I am not in the state of not yet having something that I am going to get. That's an interesting difference.

As it happens, we don't have a name for this other kind of state—where you don't yet have something that you will get later. It is similar to loss, in one way, but it's not quite like loss. Let's call it "schmoss." When I have *lost* something, then, I don't have it, but I did have it earlier. And when I have *schmost* something, I don't have it yet, but I will get it later.

So here's the deal. During the period after death, there's a loss of life, but no schmoss of life. And during the period before birth, there's no loss of life, but there is a schmoss of life. And now, as philosophers, we need to ask: why do we care more about *loss* of life than *schmoss* of life? What is it about the fact that we don't have something that we used to have, that makes this worse than not having something that we're going to have?

It's easy to overlook the symmetry here, because we've got this nice word "loss," and we don't have the word "schmoss." But that's not really explaining anything, it's just pointing to the thing that needs explaining. Why do we care more about not having what once upon a time we did, than about not having what once upon a time we will? That's really quite puzzling.

Various proposals have been made to explain this difference in attitude toward the two periods of nonexistence. One of them comes from Thomas Nagel, a contemporary philosopher.[2] Nagel starts by pointing out how easy it is to imagine the possibility of living longer. Suppose I die at the age of eighty. Perhaps I will get hit by a car. Imagine, though, that if I didn't die then, I would have continued living until I was ninety or even one hundred. That certainly seems possible, even if in fact I am going to die at eighty. The fact that I am going to die at eighty is a *contingent* fact about me. It is not a necessary fact about me that I die at eighty. So it is an easy enough matter to imagine my living longer, by having my death come later. That's why it makes sense to get upset at the fact of my death coming when it does: I could have lived longer, by having death come later.

In contrast, Nagel notes, if I am going to be upset about my nonexistence before my birth, we have to imagine my being born earlier. We have to imagine my living longer by having my birth come sooner. Is this possible? I was born in 1954. Can I be upset about the fact that I was born in 1954 instead of, say, 1944?

Nagel thinks, however, that I shouldn't be upset about the fact that I wasn't born in 1944, because in fact it isn't *possible* for me to have an earlier birth. The date of my *death* is a contingent fact about me. But the date of my *birth* is not a contingent fact about me. Well, that's not quite right. We could change the time of birth slightly, perhaps by having me delivered prematurely, or through Caesarean section, or what have you. Strictly speaking, of course, the crucial moment is the moment at which I come into *existence*. Let's suppose that this is the time when the egg and the sperm join. Nagel's thought is that this is not a contingent moment in my life story. That's an *essential* moment in my life story.

How could that be? Can't we easily imagine my parents having had sex ten years earlier? Sure we can. But remember, if they had had sex ten years earlier, it would have been a different egg and a different sperm coming together, so it wouldn't be *me*. It would be some sibling of mine that, as it happens, never got born. Obviously, there could have been some sibling of mine that came into existence in 1944, but *I* couldn't have come into existence in 1944. The person we are imagining with the earlier birth date wouldn't be *me*. What this means, Nagel suggests, is that although we can *say* the words "if only I had been born earlier," this isn't really pointing to a genuine metaphysical possibility. So there is no point in being upset at the nonexistence before you started to exist, because you couldn't have had a longer life by coming into existence earlier. (In contrast, as we have seen, you could have a longer life by going out of existence later.)

I must say, that's a pretty intriguing suggestion. But I think it can't be quite right. Or rather, it cannot be the complete story about how to answer Lucretius's puzzle. For in some cases, I think, we *can* easily imagine the possibility of having come into existence earlier. Suppose we've got a fertility clinic that has some sperm on hold and has some eggs on hold. Perhaps they keep them there frozen until they're ready to use them. And they thaw a pair out in, say, 2025. They fertilize the egg and eventually the person is born. That person, it seems to me, can correctly say that he could have come into existence earlier. He could look back and say that if only they had put the relevant sperm and egg together ten years earlier, he would have come into existence ten years earlier. It wouldn't be a sibling; it would have been *him*. After all, it would have been the very same sperm and the very same egg, resulting in the very same person. So if only they had combined the sperm and egg ten years earlier, he would have been born ten years earlier.

If that's right—and it does seem to me to be right—then Nagel is wrong in saying it's not possible to imagine being born earlier. In at least some cases it is. Yet, if we imagine somebody like this, somebody who's an offspring of this kind of fertility clinic, and we ask, "Would they be upset that they weren't born earlier?" it still seems as though most people would say, "No, of course not." So Nagel's solution to our puzzle doesn't seem to me to be an adequate one.

Here's another possible answer. This one comes from Fred Feldman, another contemporary philosopher.[3] If I say, "if only I would die later," what am I imagining? Suppose I will get hit by a car in 2034, when I am eighty. We can certainly imagine what would happen if I *didn't* get killed at that point. What do we imagine? Something like this, I suppose: instead of my living a "mere" eighty years, we imagine that I would live to be eighty-five or ninety, or more. We imagine a longer life. When we imagine my dying later, we imagine my having a longer life.

But what do I imagine when I say, "if only I had been born *earlier*"? According to Feldman, you don't actually imagine a longer life, you just *shift* the entire life and start it earlier. After all, suppose I ask you to imagine being born in 1800 instead of the year you were actually born. Nobody thinks, "Why, if I had been born in 1800, I'd still be alive. I would be more than two hundred years old!" Rather, you think, "If I had been born in 1800 I would have died in 1860, or 1870, or some such."

When we imagine being born earlier, we don't imagine a longer life, just an *earlier* life. And of course there is nothing about having a life that takes place earlier that makes it particularly better, [according to the deprivation account]. So there is no point in bemoaning the fact that you weren't born earlier. But in contrast, when we imagine dying later, it's not as though we shift the life *forward*. We don't imagine being *born* later, keeping the life the same length. No, we imagine a *longer* life. And so, Feldman says, it's no wonder that you care about nonexistence after death in a way that you don't care about nonexistence before birth. When you imagine death coming later, you imagine a longer life, with more of the goods of life. But when you imagine birth coming earlier, you don't imagine more goods in your life, you just imagine them taking place at a different time.

That too is an interesting suggestion, and I imagine it is probably part of a complete answer to Lucretius. But I don't think it can be the complete story. Because we can in fact imagine cases where the person reasonably thinks that if only she had been born earlier she *would* have had a longer life.

Let's suppose that next week astronomers discover the horrible fact that there's an asteroid that's about to land on the Earth and wipe out all life. Suppose that it is going to crash into the Earth on January 1st of next year. Now imagine someone who is currently only thirty years old. It seems to me to be perfectly reasonable for such a person to think to herself that she has only had thirty years of life, and if only she had been born ten years earlier, she would have had forty years before she died, instead of thirty; if she had been born twenty years earlier, she would have had fifty years, instead of thirty. That all seems perfectly intelligible. So it does seem as though, if we work at it, we can think of cases where an earlier birth does result in a longer life and not merely a shifted life. In cases like this, it seems, we can imagine making life longer in the "pre-birth" direction rather than in the "postdeath" direction.

What does that show us? I am not sure. When I think about the asteroid example, I find myself thinking that maybe symmetry is the right way to go here after all. Maybe in a case like this, the relevant bit of prenatal nonexistence *is* just as bad as a corresponding bit of post-mortem nonexistence. Maybe Feldman is right when he says that normally, when thinking about an earlier birth, we just shift the life, instead of lengthening it. But for all that, if we are careful to describe a case where an earlier birth would truly mean a longer life for me, maybe it really is bad that I didn't get started sooner. (Feldman would probably agree.)

Here's one more answer to Lucretius that's been proposed. This is by yet another contemporary philosopher, Derek Parfit.[4] Recall the fact that even though nonexistence before birth doesn't involve loss, it does involve schmoss. So it would be helpful if we had an explanation of why loss is worse than schmoss. Why should we care more about the former than the latter? Parfit's idea, in effect, is that this is not an arbitrary preference on our part. Rather, it's part of a quite general pattern we have of caring about the future in a way that we don't care about the past. This is a very deep fact about human caring. We are oriented toward the future and concerned about what will happen in it, in a way that we're not oriented toward and concerned about what happened in the past.

Parfit's got a very nice example to bring the point home. He asks you to imagine that you've got some medical condition that will kill you unless you have an operation. So you're going to have the operation. Unfortunately, in order to perform the operation, they can't have you anesthetized. You have to be awake, perhaps in order to tell the surgeon, "Yes, that's where it hurts." You've got to be awake during the operation, and it's a *very* painful operation. Furthermore, we can't give you painkiller, because then you won't be able to tell the surgeon where it hurts. In short, you need to be awake while you are, in effect, being tortured. Of course, it's still worth it, because this will cure your condition, and you can go on to have a nice long life. But during the operation itself, it is going to hurt like hell.

Since we can't give you painkillers and we can't put you out, all we can do is this: after the operation is over, we'll give you this very powerful medication, which will induce a very localized form of amnesia, destroying your very recent memories. You won't remember anything about the operation itself. And in particular, then, you won't ever have to revisit horrible memories of having been tortured. Any such memory will be completely destroyed. Indeed, *all* memories from the preceding twenty-four hours will be completely wiped out. In sum, you are going to have a horrendously painful operation, and you are going to be awake during it. But after the operation you will be given medication that will make you completely forget the pain of the operation, indeed forget everything about the entire day.

So you're in the hospital and you wake up and you ask yourself, "Have I had the operation yet or not?" And of course, you don't know. You certainly don't remember having had it. But that doesn't tell you anything. On the one hand, if you haven't had it yet, it is no wonder you have no memories of having had it. But on the other hand, even if you *have* had the operation, you would have been given the medication afterwards, so would have no memories of it now. So you ask the nurse, "Have I had the operation yet or not?" She answers, "I don't know. We have several patients like you on the floor today, some of whom have already had the procedure, and some of whom are scheduled to have it later today. I don't remember which group you are in. Let me go look at your file. I'll come back in a moment and I'll tell you." So she wanders off. She's going to come back in a minute or two. And as you are waiting for her to come back, you ask yourself, what do you want the answer to be? Do you care which group you're in? Do you prefer to be someone who has *already* had the operation? Someone who *hasn't* had it yet? Or are you indifferent?

Now, if you're like Parfit, and for that matter like me, then you're going to say that *of course* you care. I certainly want it to be the case that I have *already* had the operation. I don't want to be someone who hasn't had the operation yet.

We might ask, how can that make any sense? You are going to have the operation sooner or later. At some point in your life history, that operation is going to have occurred. And so there's going to be the same amount of pain and torture at some point in your life, regardless of whether you're one of the people that had it yesterday or one of the people that are going to have it later today. But for all that, says Parfit, the fact of the matter is perfectly plain: we *do* care. We want the pain to be in the past. We don't want the pain to be in the future. We care more about what's happening in the future than about what's happened in the past.

That being the case, however, it is no surprise that we care about our nonexistence in the future in a way that we don't care about our nonexistence in the past. So perhaps that is the answer that we should give to Lucretius: the future matters in a way that the past does not.

That too is an intriguing suggestion. And it may well provide us with a convincing explanation of our asymmetrical attitudes. But we might still wonder whether it gives us any kind of *justification* for them. The fact that we've got this deep-seated asymmetrical attitude toward time doesn't in any way, as far as I can see, yet tell us whether or not that's a *justified* attitude. Maybe evolution built us to care about the future in a way that we don't care about the past, and this expresses itself in all sorts of places, including Parfit's hospital case and our attitude toward loss versus schmoss, and so forth and so on. But the fact that we've got this attitude doesn't yet show that it's a *rational* attitude.

How could we show that it's a rational attitude? Perhaps we would have to start doing some heavy-duty metaphysics (if what we have been doing so far isn't yet heavy-duty enough). Maybe we need to talk about the metaphysical difference between the past and the future. Intuitively, after all, the past is fixed, while the future is open, and time seems to have a direction, from past to future. Maybe somehow we could bring all these things in and explain why our attitude toward time is a reasonable one. I'm not going to go there. All I want to say is, it's not altogether obvious what the best answer to Lucretius's puzzle is. . . .

But for all that, it seems to me that . . . what's bad about death is that when you're dead, you're not experiencing the good things in life. Death is bad for you precisely because you don't have what life would bring you if only you hadn't died.

Notes

1. Lucretius, *On the Nature of Things*.
2. Thomas Nagel, "Death," in *Mortal Questions* (Cambridge, 1979).
3. Fred Feldman, *Confrontations with the Reaper* (Oxford, 1992), pp. 154–156.
4. This example comes from Derek Parfit, *Reasons and Persons* (Oxford, 1984), pp. 165–166. I should note, however, that Parfit isn't here explicitly discussing Lucretius. I am simply applying some of his ideas to that puzzle. (Parfit's own discussion of the puzzle can be found in *Reasons and Persons*, pp. 174–177.)

Study Questions

1. Are you concerned about not being alive before the time of your birth?
2. Do you agree with Lucretius that we should be unconcerned about not being alive after the time of our death?
3. How do you assess Nagel's reply to Lucretius?
4. How do you assess Feldman's reply to Lucretius?

K. The Meaning of Life

CHAPTER 47

The Meaning of Life

Richard Taylor

What is the essence of a good life, one in which you live well and find
meaning? An answer is proposed by Richard Taylor (1919–2003), who
was Professor of Philosophy at the University of Rochester. He discusses
the case of Sisyphus who, according to Greek myth, was condemned for
his misdeeds to the eternal task of rolling a huge stone to the top of a
hill, only each time to have it roll down to the bottom again. Is the activity of Sisyphus meaningless? Taylor concludes that the answer depends
on whether Sisyphus has a desire to roll stones up hills. If he does, then
he has found meaning in his life. In short, if your activities match your
wishes, then your life is successful.

The question whether life has any meaning is difficult to interpret,
and the more you concentrate your critical faculty on it the more it
seems to elude you, or to evaporate as any intelligible question. You
want to turn it aside, as a source of embarrassment, as something
that, if it cannot be abolished, should at least be decently covered.
And yet I think any reflective person recognizes that the question it
raises is important, and that it ought to have a significant answer.

If the idea of meaningfulness is difficult to grasp in this context,
so that we are unsure what sort of thing would amount to answering
the question, the idea of meaninglessness is perhaps less so. If, then,
we can bring before our minds a clear image of meaningless existence, then perhaps we can take a step toward coping with our original question by seeing to what extent our lives, as we actually find
them, resemble that image, and draw such lessons as we are able to
from the comparison.

Meaningless Existence

A perfect image of meaninglessness, of the kind we are seeking, is found in the ancient myth of Sisyphus. Sisyphus, it will be remembered, betrayed divine secrets to mortals, and for this he was condemned by the gods to roll a stone to the top of a hill, the stone then immediately to roll back down, again to be pushed to the top by Sisyphus, to roll down once more, and so on again and again, *forever*. Now in this we have the picture of meaningless, pointless toil, of a meaningless existence that is absolutely *never* redeemed. It is not even redeemed by a death that, if it were to accomplish nothing more, would at least bring this idiotic cycle to a close. If we were invited to imagine Sisyphus struggling for a while and accomplishing nothing, perhaps eventually falling from exhaustion, so that we might suppose him then eventually turning to something having some sort of promise, then the meaninglessness of that chapter of his life would not be so stark. It would be a dark and dreadful dream, from which he eventually awakens to sunlight and reality. But he does not awaken, for there is nothing for him to awaken to. His repetitive toil is his life and reality, and it goes on forever, and it is without any meaning whatever. Nothing ever comes of what he is doing, except simply, more of the same. Not by one step, nor by a thousand, nor by ten thousand does he even expiate by the smallest token the sin against the gods that led him into this fate. Nothing comes of it, nothing at all.

This ancient myth has always enchanted people, for countless meanings can be read into it. Some of the ancients apparently thought it symbolized the perpetual rising and setting of the sun, and others the repetitious crashing of the waves upon the shore. Probably the commonest interpretation is that it symbolizes our eternal struggle and unquenchable spirit, our determination always to try once more in the face of overwhelming discouragement. This interpretation is further supported by that version of the myth according to which Sisyphus was commanded to roll the stone *over* the hill, so that it would finally roll down the other side, but was never quite able to make it.

I am not concerned with rendering or defending any interpretation of this myth, however. I have cited it only for the one element it does unmistakably contain, namely, that of a repetitious, cyclic activity that never comes to anything. We could contrive other images of this that would serve just as well, and no myth-makers are needed to supply the materials of it. Thus, we can imagine two persons transporting a stone—or even a precious gem, it does not matter—back and forth, relay style. One carries it to a near or distant point where it is received by the other; it is returned to its starting point, there to be recovered by the first, and the process is repeated over and over. Except in this relay nothing counts as winning, and nothing brings the contest to any close; each step only leads to a repetition of itself. Or we can imagine two groups of prisoners, one of them engaged in digging a prodigious hole in the ground that is no sooner finished than it is filled in again by the other group, the latter then digging a new hole that is at once filled in by the first group, and so on and on endlessly.

Now what stands out in all such pictures as oppressive and dejecting is not that the beings who enact these roles suffer any torture or pain, for it need not be assumed that they do. Nor is it that their labors are great, for they are no greater than the labors commonly undertaken by most people most of the time. According to the original myth, the stone is so large that Sisyphus never quite gets it to the top and must groan under every step, so that his enormous labor is all for nought. But this is not what appalls. It is not that his great struggle comes to nothing, but that his existence itself is without meaning. Even if we suppose, for example, that the stone is but a pebble that can be carried effortlessly, or that the holes dug by the prisoners are but small ones, not the slightest meaning is introduced into their lives. The stone that Sisyphus moves to the top of the hill, whether we think of it as large or small, still rolls back every time, and the process is repeated forever. Nothing comes of it, and the work is simply pointless. That is the element of the myth that I wish to capture.

Again, it is not the fact that the labors of Sisyphus continue forever that deprives them of meaning. It is, rather, the implication of this: that they come to nothing. The image would not be changed by our supposing him to push a different stone up every time, each to roll down again. But if we supposed that these stones, instead of rolling back to their places as if they had never been moved, were assembled at the top of the hill and there incorporated, say, in a beautiful and enduring temple, then the aspect of meaninglessness would disappear. His labors would then have a point, something would come of them all, and although one could perhaps still say it was not worth it, one could not say that the life of Sisyphus was devoid of meaning altogether. Meaningfulness would at least have made an appearance, and we could see what it was.

That point will need remembering. But in the meantime, let us note another way in which the image of meaninglessness can be altered by making only a very slight change. Let us suppose that the gods, while condemning Sisyphus to the fate just described, at the same time, as an afterthought, waxed perversely merciful by implanting in him a strange and irrational impulse; namely, a compulsive impulse to roll stones. We may if we like, to make this more graphic, suppose they accomplish this by implanting in him some substance that has this effect on his character and drives. I call this perverse, because from our point of view there is clearly no reason why anyone should have a persistent and insatiable desire to do something so pointless as that. Nevertheless, suppose that is Sisyphus' condition. He has but one obsession, which is to roll stones, and it is an obsession that is only for the moment appeased by his rolling them—he no sooner gets a stone rolled to the top of the hill than he is restless to roll up another.

Now it can be seen why this little afterthought of the gods, which I called perverse, was also in fact merciful. For they have by this device managed to give Sisyphus precisely what he wants—by making him want precisely what they inflict on him. However it may appear to us, Sisyphus' fate now does not appear to him as a condemnation, but the very reverse. His one desire in life is to roll stones, and he is absolutely guaranteed its endless fulfillment. Where otherwise he might profoundly have wished surcease, and even welcomed the quiet of death to release him from endless boredom and meaninglessness, his life is now filled with mission and meaning, and he seems to himself to have been given an entry to heaven. Nor need he even fear death, for the gods have promised him an endless opportunity to indulge his single purpose, without concern or frustration. He will be able to roll stones *forever*.

What we need to mark most carefully at this point is that the picture with which we began has not really been changed in the least by adding this supposition. Exactly the same things happen as before. The only change is in Sisyphus' view of them. The picture before was the image of meaningless activity and existence. It was created precisely to be an image of that. It has not lost that meaninglessness, it has now gained not the least shred of meaningfulness. The stones still roll back as before, each phase of Sisyphus' life still exactly resembles all the others, the task is never completed, nothing comes of it, no temple ever begins to rise, and all this cycle of the same pointless thing over and over goes on forever in this picture as in the other. The *only* thing that has happened is this: Sisyphus has been reconciled to it, and indeed more, he has been led to embrace it. Not, however, by reason or persuasion, but by nothing more rational than the potency of a new substance in his veins.

The Meaninglessness of Life

I believe the foregoing provides a fairly clear content to the idea of
meaninglessness and, through it, some hint of what meaningfulness,
in this sense might be. Meaninglessness is essentially endless point-
lessness, and meaningfulness is therefore the opposite. Activity, and
even long, drawn out and repetitive activity, has a meaning if it has
some significant culmination, some more or less lasting end that can
be considered to have been the direction and purpose of the activity.
But the descriptions so far also provide something else; namely, the
suggestion of how an existence that is objectively meaningless, in
this sense, can nevertheless acquire a meaning for him whose existence it is.

Now let us ask: Which of these pictures does life in fact resemble?
And let us not begin with our own lives, for here both our prejudices
and wishes are great, but with the life in general that we share with
the rest of creation. We shall find, I think, that it all has a certain pattern, and that this pattern is by now easily recognized.

We can begin anywhere, only saving human existence for our last
consideration. We can, for example, begin with any animal. It does
not matter where we begin, because the result is going to be exactly
the same.

Thus, for example, there are caves in New Zealand, deep and dark,
whose floors are quiet pools and whose walls and ceilings are covered
with soft light. As you gaze in wonder in the stillness of these caves it
seems that the Creator has reproduced there in microcosm the heav-
ens themselves, until you scarcely remember the enclosing presence
of the walls. As you look more closely, however, the scene is explained.
Each dot of light identifies an ugly worm, whose luminous tail is
meant to attract insects from the surrounding darkness. As from
time to time one of these insects draws near it becomes entangled in
a sticky thread lowered by the worm, and is eaten. This goes on month
after month, the blind worm lying there in the barren stillness waiting to entrap an occasional bit of nourishment that will only sustain
it to another bit of nourishment until. . . . Until what? What great
thing awaits all this long and repetitious effort and makes it worthwhile? Really nothing. The larva just transforms itself finally to a tiny
winged adult that lacks even mouth parts to feed and lives only a day
or two. These adults, as soon as they have mated and laid eggs, are
themselves caught in the threads and are devoured by the cannibalis-
tic worms, often without having ventured into the day, the only point

to their existence having now been fulfilled. This has been going on for millions of years, and to no end other than that the same meaningless cycle may continue for another millions of years.

All living things present essentially the same spectacle. The larva of a certain cicada burrows in the darkness of the earth for seventeen years, through season after season, to emerge finally into the daylight for a brief flight, lay its eggs, and die—this all to repeat itself during the next seventeen years, and so on to eternity. We have already noted, in another connection, the struggles of fish, made only that others may do the same after them and that this cycle, having no other point than itself, may never cease. Some birds span an entire side of the globe each year and then return, only to insure that others may follow the same incredibly long path again and again. One is led to wonder what the point of it all is, with what great triumph this ceaseless effort, repeating itself through millions of years, might finally culminate, and why it should go on and on for so long, accomplishing nothing, getting nowhere. But then you realize that there is no point to it at all, that it really culminates in nothing, that each of these cycles, so filled with toil, is to be followed only by more of the same. The point of any living thing's life is, evidently, nothing but life itself.

This life of the world thus presents itself to our eyes as a vast machine, feeding on itself, running on and on forever to nothing. And we are part of that life. To be sure, we are not just the same, but the differences are not so great as we like to think; many are merely invented, and none really cancels the kind of meaninglessness that we found in Sisyphus and that we find all around, wherever anything lives. We are conscious of our activity. Our goals, whether in any significant sense we choose them or not, are things of which we are at least partly aware and can therefore in some sense appraise. More significantly, perhaps, we have a history, as other animals do not, such that each generation does not precisely resemble all those before. Still, if we can in imagination disengage our wills from our lives and disregard the deep interest we all have in our own existence, we shall find that they do not so little resemble the existence of Sisyphus. We toil after goals, most of them—indeed every single one of them—of transitory significance and, having gained one of them, we immediately set forth for the next, as if that one had never been, with this next one being essentially more of the same. Look at a busy street any day, and observe the throng going hither and thither. To what? Some office or shop, where the same things will be done today as were done yesterday, and are done now so they may be repeated tomorrow. And if we think that, unlike Sisyphus, these labors do have a point, that they culminate in something lasting and, independently of our own deep interests in them, very worthwhile, then we simply have not considered the thing closely enough. Most such effort is directed only to the establishment and perpetuation of home and family; that is, to the begetting of others who will follow in our steps to do more of the same. Everyone's life thus resembles one of Sisyphus's climbs to the summit of his hill, and each day of it one of his steps; the difference is that whereas Sisyphus himself returns to push the stone up again, we leave this to our children. We at one point imagined that the labors of Sisyphus finally culminated in the creation of a temple, but for this to make any difference it had to be a temple that would at least endure, adding beauty to the world for the remainder of time. Our achievements, even though they are often beautiful, are mostly bubbles; and those that do last, like the sand-swept pyramids, soon become mere curiosities while around them the rest of human-kind continues its perpetual toting of rocks, only to see them roll down. Nations are built upon the bones of their founders and pioneers, but only to decay and crumble before long, their rubble then becoming the foundation for others directed to exactly the same fate. The picture of Sisyphus is the picture of existence of the individual man, great or unknown, of nations, of the human race, and of the very life of the world.

On a country road one sometimes comes upon the ruined hulks of a house and once extensive buildings, all in collapse and spread over with weeds. A curious eye can in imagination reconstruct from what is left a once warm and thriving life, filled with purpose. There was the hearth, where a family once talked, sang, and made plans; there were the rooms, where people loved, and babes were born to a rejoicing mother; there are the musty remains of a sofa, infested with bugs, once bought at a dear price to enhance an ever-growing comfort, beauty, and warmth. Every small piece of junk fills the mind with what once, not long ago, was utterly real, with children's voices, plans made, and enterprises embarked upon. That is how these stones of Sisyphus were rolled up, and that is how they became incorporated into a beautiful temple, and that temple is what now lies before you. Meanwhile other buildings, institutions, nations, and civilizations spring up all around, only to share the same fate before long. And if the question "What for?" is now asked, the answer is clear: so that just this may go on forever.

The two pictures—of Sisyphus and of our own lives, if we look at them from a distance—are in outline the same and convey to the mind the same image. It is not surprising, then, that we invent ways of denying it, our religions proclaiming a heaven that does not crumble, their hymnals and prayer books declaring a significance to life of which our eyes provide no hint whatever.[1] Even our philosophies portray some permanent and lasting good at which all may aim, from the changeless forms invented by Plato to the beatific vision of St. Thomas and the ideals of permanence contrived by the moderns. When these fail to convince, then earthly ideals such as universal justice and brotherhood are conjured up to take their places and give meaning to our seemingly endless pilgrimage, some final state that will be ushered in when the last obstacle is removed and the last stone pushed to the hilltop. No one believes, of course, that any such state will be final, or even wants it to be in case it means that human existence would then cease to be a struggle; but in the meantime such ideas serve a very real need.

The Meaning of Life

We noted that Sisyphus' existence would have meaning if there were some point to his labors, if his efforts ever culminated in something that was not just an occasion for fresh labors of the same kind. But that is precisely the meaning it lacks. And human existence resembles his in that respect. We do achieve things—we scale our towers and raise our stones to the hilltops—but every such accomplishment fades, providing only an occasion for renewed labors of the same kind.

But here we need to note something else that has been mentioned, but its significance not explored, and that is the state of mind and feeling with which such labors are undertaken. We noted that if Sisyphus had a keen and unappeasable desire to be doing just what he found himself doing, then, although his life would in no way be changed, it would nevertheless have a meaning for him. It would be an irrational one, no doubt, because the desire itself would be only the product of the substance in his veins, and not any that reason could discover, but a meaning nevertheless.

And would it not, in fact, be a meaning incomparably better than the other? For let us examine again the first kind of meaning it could have. Let us suppose that, without having any interest in rolling stones, as such, and finding this, in fact, a galling toil, Sisyphus did nevertheless have a deep interest in raising a temple, one that would be beautiful and lasting. And let us suppose he succeeded in this, that after ages of dreadful toil, all directed at this final result, he did at last complete his temple, such that now he could say his work was done, and he could rest and forever enjoy the result. Now what? What picture now presents itself to our minds? It is precisely the picture of infinite boredom! Of Sisyphus doing nothing ever again, but contemplating what he has already wrought and can no longer add anything to, and contemplating it for an eternity! Now in this picture we have a meaning for Sisyphus' existence, a point for his prodigious labor, because we have put it there; yet, at the same time, that which is really worthwhile seems to have slipped away entirely. Where before we were presented with the nightmare of eternal and pointless activity, we are now confronted with the hell of its eternal absence.

Our second picture, then, wherein we imagined Sisyphus to have had inflicted on him the irrational desire to be doing just what he found himself doing, should not have been dismissed so abruptly. The meaning that picture lacked was no meaning that he or anyone could crave, and the strange meaning it had was perhaps just what we were seeking.

At this point, then, we can reintroduce what has been until now, it is hoped, resolutely pushed aside in an effort to view our lives and human existence with objectivity; namely, our own wills, our deep interest in what we find ourselves doing. If we do this we find that our lives do indeed still resemble that of Sisyphus, but that the meaningfulness they thus lack is precisely the meaningfulness of infinite boredom. At the same time, the strange meaningfulness they possess is that of the inner compulsion to be doing just what we were put here to do, and to go on doing it forever. This is the nearest we may hope to get to heaven, but the redeeming side of that fact is that we do thereby avoid a genuine hell.

If the builders of a great and flourishing ancient civilization could somehow return now to see archaeologists unearthing the trivial remnants of what they had once accomplished with such effort—see the fragments of pots and vases, a few broken statues, and such tokens of another age and greatness—they could indeed ask themselves what the point of it all was, if this is all it finally came to. Yet, it did not seem so to them then, for it was just the building, and not what was finally built, that gave their life meaning. Similarly, if the builders of the ruined home and farm that I described a short while ago could be brought back to see what is left, they would have the same feelings.

What we construct in our imaginations as we look over these decayed and rusting pieces would reconstruct itself in their very memories, and certainly with unspeakable sadness. The piece of a sled at our feet would revive in them a warm Christmas. And what rich memories would there be in the broken crib? And the weed-covered remains of a fence would reproduce the scene of a great herd of livestock, so laboriously built up over so many years. What was it all worth, if this is the final result? Yet, again, it did not seem so to them through those many years of struggle and toil, and they did not imagine they were building a Gibraltar. The things to which they bent their backs day after day, realizing one by one their ephemeral plans, were precisely the things in which their wills were deeply involved, precisely the things in which their interests lay, and there was no need then to ask questions. There is no more need of them now—the day was sufficient to itself, and so was the life.

This is surely the way to look at all of life—at one's own life, and each day and moment it contains; of the life of a nation; of the species; of the life of the world; and of every thing that breathes. Even the glow worms I described, whose cycles of existence over the millions of years seem so pointless when looked at by us, will seem entirely different to us if we can somehow try to view their existence from within. Their endless activity, which gets nowhere, is just what it is their will to pursue. This is its whole justification and meaning. Nor would it be any salvation to the birds who span the globe every year, back and forth, to have a home made for them in a cage with plenty of food and protection, so that they would not have to migrate anymore. It would be their condemnation, for it is the doing that counts for them, and not what they hope to win by it. Flying these prodigious distances, never ending, is what it is in their veins to do, exactly as it was in Sisyphus's veins to roll stones, without end, after the gods had waxed merciful and implanted this in him.

You no sooner drew your first breath than you responded to the will that was in you to live. You no more ask whether it will be worthwhile, or whether anything of significance will come of it, than the worms and the birds. The point of living is simply to be living, in the manner that it is your nature to be living. You go through life building your castles, each of these beginning to fade into time as the next is begun; yet it would be no salvation to rest from all this. It would be a condemnation, and one that would in no way be redeemed were you able to gaze upon the things you have done, even if these were beautiful and absolutely permanent, as they never are.

What counts is that you should be able to begin a new task, a new castle, a new bubble. It counts only because it is there to be done and you have the will to do it. The same will be the life of your children, and of theirs; and if the philosopher is apt to see in this a pattern similar to the unending cycles of the existence of Sisyphus, and to despair, then it is indeed because the meaning and point he is seeking is not there—but mercifully so. The meaning of life is from within us, it is not bestowed from without, and it far exceeds in both its beauty and permanence any heaven of which men have ever dreamed or yearned for.

Note

1. A popular Christian hymn, sung often at funerals and typical of many hymns, expresses this thought:

    Swift to its close ebbs out life's little day;
    Earth's joys grow dim, its glories pass away:
    Change and decay in all around I see:
    O thou who changest not, abide with me.

Study Questions

1. Can a life be enjoyed yet meaningless?
2. Can a life be immoral yet meaningful?
3. If you find meaning in a task, can you be mistaken?
4. Would Taylor agree with Thomas Nagel's claim in a previous article that a man who devotes himself to cheerful pursuit of a method of communicating with asparagus plants has wasted his life?

CHAPTER 48

Meaning in Life
Susan Wolf

Susan Wolf is Professor of Philosophy at the University of North
Carolina at Chapel Hill. She defends the view that the only meaningful
life is one in which a person actively engages in projects of worth. Thus,
unlike Taylor, Wolf would not find meaning in the life of Sisyphus, even
if his fondest desire was to roll stones up hills.

A meaningful life is, first of all, one that has within it the basis for an
affirmative answer to the needs or longings that are characteristically described as needs for meaning. I have in mind, for example,
the sort of questions people ask on their deathbeds, or simply in con-
templation of their eventual deaths, about whether their lives have
been (or are) worth living, whether they have had any point, and the
sort of questions one asks when considering suicide and wondering
whether one has any reason to go on. These questions are familiar
from Russian novels and existentialist philosophy, if not from personal experience. Though they arise most poignantly in times of
crisis and intense emotion, they also have their place in moments of
calm reflection, when considering important life choices. Moreover,
paradigms of what are taken to be meaningful and meaningless lives
in our culture are readily available. Lives of great moral or intellectual accomplishment—Gandhi, Mother Teresa, Albert Einstein—
come to mind as unquestionably meaningful lives (if any are); lives
of waste and isolation—Thoreau's "lives of quiet desperation," typically anonymous to the rest of us, and the mythical figure of
Sisyphus—represent meaninglessness.

From "Happiness and Meaning: Two Aspects of the Good Life," *Social Philosophy & Policy*,
Vol. 24, 1997. Reprinted with the permission of Cambridge University Press.

To what general characteristics of meaningfulness do these images lead us and how do they provide an answer to the longings mentioned above? Roughly, I would say that meaningful lives are lives of active engagement in projects of worth. Of course, a good deal needs to be said in elaboration of this statement. Let me begin by discussing the two key phrases, "active engagement" and "projects of worth."

A person is actively engaged by something if she is gripped, excited, involved by it. Most obviously, we are actively engaged by the things and people about which and whom we are passionate. Opposites of active engagement are boredom and alienation. To be actively engaged in something is not always pleasant in the ordinary sense of the word. Activities in which people are actively engaged frequently involve stress, danger, exertion, or sorrow (consider, for example: writing a book, climbing a mountain, training for a marathon, caring for an ailing friend). However, there is something good about the feeling of engagement: one feels (typically without thinking about it) especially alive.

That a meaningful life must involve "projects of worth" will, I expect, be more controversial, for the phrase hints of a commitment to some sort of objective value. This is not accidental, for I believe that the idea of meaningfulness, and the concern that our lives possess it, are conceptually linked to such a commitment.[1] Indeed, it is this linkage that I want to defend, for I have neither a philosophical theory of what objective value is nor a substantive theory about what has this sort of value. What is clear to me is that there can be no sense to the idea of meaningfulness without a distinction between more and less worthwhile ways to spend one's time, where the test of worth is at least partly independent of a subject's ungrounded preferences or enjoyment.

Consider first the longings or concerns about meaning that people have, their wondering whether their lives are meaningful, their vows to add more meaning to their lives. The sense of these concerns and resolves cannot fully be captured by an account in which what one does with one's life doesn't matter, as long as one enjoys or prefers it. Sometimes people have concerns about meaning despite their knowledge that their lives to date have been satisfying. Indeed, their enjoyment and "active engagement" with activities and values they now see as shallow seems only to heighten the sense of meaninglessness that comes to afflict them. Their sense that their lives so far have been meaningless cannot be a sense that their activities have not been chosen or fun. When they look for sources of meaning or ways to add meaning to their lives, they are searching for projects whose justifications lie elsewhere.

Second, we need an explanation for why certain sorts of activities and involvements come to mind as contributors to meaningfulness while others seem intuitively inappropriate. Think about what gives meaning to your own life and the lives of your friends and acquaintances. Among the things that tend to come up on such lists, I have already mentioned moral and intellectual accomplishments and the ongoing activities that lead to them. Relationships with friends and relatives are perhaps even more important for most of us. Aesthetic enterprises (both creative and appreciative), the cultivation of personal virtues, and religious practices frequently loom large. By contrast, it would be odd, if not bizarre, to think of crossword puzzles, sitcoms, or the kind of computer games to which I am fighting off addiction as providing meaning in our lives, though there is no question that they afford a sort of satisfaction and that they are the objects of choice. Some things, such as chocolate and aerobics class, I choose even at considerable cost to myself (it is irrelevant that these particular choices may be related); so I must find them worthwhile in a sense. But they are not the sorts of things that make life worth living.[2]

"Active engagement in projects of worth," I suggest, answers to the needs an account of meaningfulness in life must meet. If a person is or has been thus actively engaged, then she does have an answer to the question of whether her life is or has been worthwhile, whether it has or has had a point. When someone looks for ways to add meaning to her life, she is looking (though perhaps not under this description) for worthwhile projects about which she can get enthused. The account also explains why some activities and projects but not others come to mind as contributors to meaning in life. Some projects, or at any rate, particular acts, are worthwhile but too boring or mechanical to be sources of meaning. People do not get meaning from recycling or from writing checks to Oxfam and the ACLU. Other acts and activities, though highly pleasurable and deeply involving, like riding a roller coaster or meeting a movie star, do not seem to have the right kind of value to contribute to meaning.

Bernard Williams once distinguished categorical desires from the rest. Categorical desires give us reasons for living—they are not premised on the assumption that we will live. The sorts of things that give meaning to life tend to be objects of categorical desire. We desire them, at least so I would suggest, because we think them worthwhile.

They are not worthwhile simply because we desire them or simply because they make our lives more pleasant.

Roughly, then, according to my proposal, a meaningful life must satisfy two criteria, suitably linked. First, there must be active engagement, and second, it must be engagement in (or with) projects of worth. A life is meaningless if it lacks active engagement with anything. A person who is bored or alienated from most of what she spends her life doing is one whose life can be said to lack meaning. Note that she may in fact be performing functions of worth. A housewife and mother, a doctor, or a busdriver may be competently doing a socially valuable job, but because she is not engaged by her work (or, as we are assuming, by anything else in her life), she has no categorical desires that give her a reason to live. At the same time, someone who is actively engaged may also live a meaningless life, if the objects of her involvement are utterly worthless. It is difficult to come up with examples of such lives that will be uncontroversial without being bizarre. But both bizarre and controversial examples have their place. In the bizarre category, we might consider pathological cases: someone whose sole passion in life is collecting rubber bands, or memorizing the dictionary, or making handwritten copies of *War and Peace*. Controversial cases will include the corporate lawyer who sacrifices her private life and health for success along the professional ladder, the devotee of a religious cult, or—an example offered by Wiggins[3]— the pig farmer who buys more land to grow more corn to feed more pigs to buy more land to grow more corn to feed more pigs.

We may summarize my proposal in terms of a slogan: "Meaning arises when subjective attraction meets objective attractiveness." The idea is that in a world in which some things are more worthwhile than others, meaning arises when a subject discovers or develops an affinity for one or typically several of the more worthwhile things and has and makes use of the opportunity to engage with it or them in a positive way.

Notes

1. This point is made by David Wiggins in his brilliant but difficult essay "Truth, Invention, and the Meaning of Life," *Proceedings of the British Academy*, vol. 62 (1976).

2. Woody Allen appears to have a different view. His list of the things that make life worth living at the end of *Manhattan* includes, for example "the crabs at Sam Woo's," which would seem to be on the level of chocolates. On the other hand, the crabs' appearance on the list may be taken

to show that he regards the dish as an accomplishment meriting aesthetic appreciation, where such appreciation is a worthy activity in itself; in this respect, the crabs might be akin to other items on his list such as the second movement of the *Jupiter Symphony*, Louis Armstrong's recording of "Potatohead Blues," and "those apples and pears of Cézanne." Strictly speaking, the appreciation of great chocolate might also qualify as such an activity.

3. See Wiggins, "Truth, Invention, and the Meaning of Life," p. 342.

Study Questions

1. Based on the examples she provides, what does Wolf mean by "a project of worth"?
2. How would Wolf decide whether some activity was a project of worth?
3. In your view, are the lives of a college professor, a professional golfer, a janitor, and a hobo equally meaningful?
4. Would studying certain subjects add more meaning to life than studying other subjects?

CHAPTER 49

Meaningful Lives

Christine Vitrano

Christine Vitrano is Associate Professor of Philosophy at Brooklyn College of The City University of New York. She considers the views of a meaningful life offered by both Richard Taylor and Susan Wolf but finds neither convincing. Vitrano argues that Taylor's view is defective in not requiring that a meaningful life display any concern for the welfare of others, whereas Wolf's view depends on an unexplained notion of a project of worth. Vitrano herself proposes that a meaningful life is one in which a person acts morally while achieving satisfaction, whether doing so by engaging in scholarship, athletics, business, gardening, or rolling stones up hills.

Richard Taylor and Susan Wolf offer contrasting visions of a meaningful life. I find each account partially persuasive, but neither by itself entirely satisfactory.

For Wolf, a meaningful life is one in which you are actively engaged in projects of worth. To be engaged is to be "gripped, excited, involved." If you find your life dreary, then it is not meaningful.

Enjoying activities, however, does not by itself render them meaningful; they also need to be worthwhile. As she says, "When someone looks for ways to add meaning to her life, she is looking . . . for worthwhile projects about which she can get enthused" and "whose justifications lie elsewhere," specifically in "objective value."

According to Wolf, worthwhile activities include "[r]elationships with friends and relatives . . . [a]esthetic enterprises (both creative and appreciative), the cultivation of personal virtues, and religious practices." Specific examples include "writing a book, climbing a mountain, training for a marathon." Among the activities the lack such worth are solving crossword puzzles, watching sitcoms, playing computer games, and eating chocolate, as well as "collecting rubber bands, or memorizing the dictionary, or making handwritten copies of *War and Peace*." Controversial cases are the paths of the "corporate lawyer who sacrifices her private life and health for success along the professional ladder, the devotee of a religious cult, or . . . the pig farmer who buys more land to grow more corn to feed more pigs, to buy more land to grow more corn to feed more pigs."

An obvious problem with Wolf's position is that by her own admission she has "neither a philosophical theory of what objective value is nor a substantive theory about what has that sort of value." She relies on supposedly shared intuitions regarding the worth of various activities, but to assume such agreement is unjustified. Some people appreciate an activity Wolf disparages, yet dismiss one she values highly. For example, spending thousands of hours training for a marathon strikes many as wearisome; they may be far more engaged by computer games. On the other hand, grappling with a *New York Times* Sunday Magazine crossword puzzle is a popular intellectual challenge, holding far more appeal for most than reading an article on meta-ethics, a subject Wolf finds fascinating.

She might respond to these observations by claiming that the problem with crossword puzzles lies not in their essential unimportance but in their use as mere pastimes. In other words, even those who enjoy solving them don't take them seriously.

This reply, however, only deepens Wolf's difficulty, because the same activity could be judged as meaningful or meaningless depending on why a person engages in it. Consider, for instance, a physicist who does scientific research because of the enjoyment it brings but is devoted to chess problems for their intellectual challenge. For that scholar, pursuing physics would be meaningless, but composing and solving chess problems would be meaningful—hardly the conclusion Wolf is seeking.

Furthermore, suppose that in order to distract myself from the monotony of caring for my two children, I read an article on metaphysics. Why should the motive affect the worthiness of the activity?

Because Wolf's position is weakened by her commitment to an objective value that she cannot explain, we might drop that aspect of her position and accept Richard Taylor's view that a meaningful life is one that affords you long-term satisfaction, regardless of the activities you choose. Thus the life of Sisyphus would be meaningful if Sisyphus relished rolling stones up hills.

Yet even if a person's life is enjoyable, if it is morally unworthy, displaying no concern for the welfare of others, then such a life does not deserve to be judged positively by anyone with moral compunctions.

I would suggest, however, that by combining insights from Taylor and Wolf, we can understand the nature of a meaningful life. It is one in which an individual acts morally while achieving happiness.

To be happy is to be satisfied with one's life, content with one's lot, not suffering excessively from anxiety, alienation, frustration, disappointment, or depression. Satisfied people may face problems but view their lives overall more positively than negatively.

The crucial point is that how satisfaction may be achieved differs from person to person. One individual may be satisfied only by earning ten million dollars. Another may be satisfied by going each day with friends to a favorite club to swim, eat lunch, and play cards. Another may be satisfied by acting in community theatre productions. Their paths to contentment are different, yet their degree of satisfaction may be the same.

Some may be poor, yet satisfied. Others may be alone, yet satisfied. Still others may find satisfaction regardless of the depth of their learning or self-knowledge and irrespective of whatever illness or disability they may face. In any case, the judgment of satisfaction is the individual's, not anyone else's.

Does satisfaction depend on achieving one's goals? Not necessarily. You may achieve your aims only to find that doing so does not provide the satisfaction for which you had hoped. For example, you might eagerly seek and gain admission to a prestigious college only to find that its rural location, which seemed an advantage when you applied, turns out to be a disadvantage when you develop interests better pursued in an urban environment.

Furthermore, some people don't have specific goals. They can happily live here or there, engage in a variety of hobbies, or even pursue various careers. They find delight in spontaneity. Perhaps that approach doesn't appeal to you, but so what? If it works for others, why not let them have their enjoyment without derogating it?

How do you achieve satisfaction, considering that it has eluded so many? The key lies within yourself, because you cannot control the events outside you. If your satisfaction depends on whether others praise you, then they control how satisfied you will be with your life. If you wish to avoid being subject to the power of others, then you have to free yourself from dependence on their judgments.

Some, such as Philippa Foot, warn against a life spent in "childish pursuits."[1] But which pursuits are childish? How about collecting dolls, telling jokes, planting vegetables, selling cookies, running races, recounting adventures, or singing songs? While children engage in all these activities, so do adults, who may thereby find satisfaction in their lives. Assuming they meet their moral obligations, why disparage them or their interests?

An obituary provides information about an individual's life, detailing accomplishments. What we don't learn therein, however, is whether that individual found satisfaction. If so, and assuming the person displayed due respect for others, then that person's life was meaningful.[2]

Notes

1. Philippa Foot, *Natural Goodness* (Oxford: Clarendon Press, 2001), p. 86.
2. This theory is developed at length in Steven M. Cahn and Christine Vitrano, *Happiness and Goodness: Philosophical Reflections on Living Well* (New York: Columbia University Press, 2015).

Study Questions

1. What is Vitrano's objection to Wolf's account of a meaningful life?
2. What is Vitrano's objection to Taylor's account of a meaningful life?
3. Do you believe that some activities are more conducive to a meaningful life than others?
4. Can a person who is without friends and without any appreciation for beauty nevertheless live a meaningful life?

L. Conclusion

CHAPTER 50

The Trolley Problem

Judith Jarvis Thomson

A philosophical puzzle offers a hypothetical situation in which the available alternatives are problematic, leading to a conceptual challenge. One such perplexity in the moral realm that has attracted much attention from contemporary ethical theorists is known as "the trolley problem." Here it is explained by Judith Jarvis Thomson, whose work we read previously.

Some years ago Philippa Foot drew attention to an extraordinarily interesting problem.[1] Suppose you are the driver of a trolley. The trolley rounds a bend, and there come into view ahead five track workmen, who have been repairing the track. The track goes through a bit of a valley at that point, and the sides are steep, so you must stop the trolley if you are to avoid running the five men down. You step on the brakes, but alas they don't work. Now you suddenly see a spur of track leading off to the right. You can turn the trolley onto it, and thus save the five men on the straight track ahead. Unfortunately Mrs. Foot has arranged that there is one track workman on that spur of track. He can no more get off the track in time than the five can, so you will kill him if you turn the trolley onto him. Is it morally permissible for you to turn the trolley?

Everybody to whom I have put this hypothetical case says, Yes, it is. Some people say something stronger than that it is morally *permissible* for you to turn the trolley: They say that morally speaking, you must turn it—that morality requires you to do so. Others do not agree that morality requires you to turn the trolley, and even feel a certain

From *The Yale Law Journal*, 94 (1985) by permission of *The Yale Law Journal* and William S. Hein Company.

discomfort at the idea of turning it. But everybody says that it is true, at a minimum, that you *may* turn it—that it would not be morally wrong for you to do so.

Now consider a second hypothetical case. This time you are to imagine yourself to be a surgeon, a truly great surgeon. Among other things you do, you transplant organs, and you are such a great surgeon that the organs you transplant always take. At the moment you have five patients who need organs. Two need one lung each, two need a kidney each, and the fifth needs a heart. If they do not get those organs today, they will all die; if you find organs for them today, you can transplant the organs and they will all live. But where to find the lungs, the kidneys, and the heart? The time is almost up when a report is brought to you that a young man who has just come into your clinic for his yearly check-up has exactly the right blood-type, and is in excellent health. Lo, you have a possible donor. All you need do is cut him up and distribute *his* parts among the five who need them. You ask, but he says, "Sorry. I deeply sympathize, but no." Would it be morally permissible for you to operate anyway? Everybody to whom I have put this second hypothetical case says, No, it would not be morally permissible for you to proceed.

Here then is Mrs. Foot's problem: *Why* is it that the trolley driver may turn his trolley, though the surgeon may not remove the young man's lungs, kidneys, and heart? In both cases, one will die if the agent acts, but five will live who would otherwise die—a net saving of four lives. What difference in the other facts of these cases explains the moral difference between them? . . .

Consider a case—which I shall call *Fat Man*—in which you are standing on a footbridge over the trolley track. You can see a trolley hurtling down the track, out of control. You turn around to see where the trolley is headed, and there are five workmen on the track where it exits from under the footbridge. What to do? Being an expert on trolleys, you know of one certain way to stop an out-of-control trolley: Drop a really heavy weight in its path. But where to find one? It just so happens that standing next to you on the footbridge is a fat man, a really fat man. He is leaning over the railing, watching the trolley; all you have to do is to give him a little shove, and over the railing he will go, onto the track in the path of the trolley. Would it be permissible for you to do this? Everybody to whom I have put this case says it would not be. But why?

Note

1. See Philippa Foot, "The Problem of Abortion and the Doctrine of the Double Effect," in *Virtues and Vices, and Other Essays in Moral Philosophy* (Berkeley and Los Angeles: University of California Press, 1978), p. 19.

Study Questions

1. Can you imagine another hypothetical case akin to that of the trolley?
2. In what crucial ways, if any, does the case Thomson calls "Fat Man" differ from the original trolley case?
3. Do you believe that turning the trolley is morally permissible?
4. Do you believe that not turning the trolley is morally permissible?

CHAPTER 51

Turning the Trolley

Judith Jarvis Thomson

More than two decades after publishing a lengthy discussion of the trolley problem from which the previous selection was excerpted, Judith Jarvis Thomson returned to the issue. Influenced by the work of a doctoral student, she offers a surprising solution that casts doubt on a widely accepted assumption critical to the case.

I

In an article provoked by Foot's, I suggested that we should take our eyes off the driver; we should eliminate him. (Make him have dropped dead of a heart attack.) Then let us imagine the situation to be as in the case I will call Bystander's Two Options. A bystander happens to be standing by the track, next to a switch that can be used to turn the tram off the straight track, on which five men are working, onto a spur of track to the right on which only one man is working. The bystander therefore has only two options:

> Bystander's Two Options: he can
> (i) do nothing, letting five die, or
> (ii) throw the switch to the right, killing one.

Most people say that he may choose option (ii). . . .

II

A few years ago, an MIT graduate student, Alexander Friedman, devoted a chapter of his thesis to a discussion of the most interesting

From Judith Jarvis Thomson, "Turning the Trolley," *Philosophy & Public Affairs* 36 (2008). Reprinted by permission of John Wiley & Sons. The principles are renumbered.

solutions to the trolley problem on offer in the literature.[1] He did a very good job: he showed clearly that none of them worked. What was especially interesting, though, was what he concluded. He said: the reason why no adequate solution has been found is that something went wrong at the outset. He said: it just isn't true that the bystander may choose option (ii) in Bystander's Two Options. . . .

Friedman therefore said that we should see the (so-called) trolley problem "for what it really is—a very intriguing, provocative, and eye-opening non-problem."

Well, there's an unsettling idea! But if you mull over Friedman's unsettling idea for a while, then perhaps it can come to seem worth taking very seriously. So let us mull over it.

III

Here is a case that I will call Bystander's Three Options. The switch available to this bystander can be thrown in two ways. If he throws it to the right, then the trolley will turn onto the spur of track to the right, thereby killing one workman. If he throws it to the left, then the trolley will turn onto the spur of track to the left. The bystander himself stands on that left-hand spur of track, and will himself be killed if the trolley turns onto it. Or, of course, he can do nothing, letting five workmen die. In sum,

> Bystander's Three Options: he can
> (i) do nothing, letting five die, or
> (ii) throw the switch to the right, killing one, or
> (iii) throw the switch to the left, killing himself.

What is your reaction to the bystander's having the following thought? "Hmm. I want to save those five workmen. I can do that by choosing option (iii), that is by throwing the switch to the left, saving the five but killing myself. I'd prefer not dying today, however, even for the sake of saving five. So I'll choose option (ii), saving the five but killing the one on the right-hand track instead."

I hope you will agree that choosing (ii) would be unacceptable on the bystander's part. If he *can* throw the switch to the left and turn the trolley onto himself, how dare he throw the switch to the right and turn the trolley onto the one workman? The bystander doesn't feel like dying today, even for the sake of saving five, but we can assume, and so let us assume, that the one workman also doesn't feel like dying today, even if the bystander would thereby save five.

Let us get a little clearer about why this bystander must not choose option (ii). He wants to save the five on the straight track ahead. That would be good for them, and his saving them would be a good deed on his part. But his doing that good deed would have a cost: his life or the life of the one workman on the right-hand track. What the bystander does if he turns the trolley onto the one workman is to make the one workman pay the cost of his good deed because he doesn't feel like paying it himself.

Compare the following possibility. I am asked for a donation to Oxfam. I want to send them some money. I am able to send money of my own, but I don't feel like it. So I steal some from someone else and send *that* money to Oxfam. That is pretty bad. But if the bystander proceeds to turn the trolley onto the one on the right-hand track in Bystander's Three Options, then what he does is markedly worse, because the cost in Bystander's Three Options isn't money, it is life.

In sum, if A wants to do a certain good deed, and can pay what doing it would cost, then—other things being equal—A may do that good deed only if A pays the cost himself. In particular, here is a . . . *ceteris paribus* [other things being equal] principle:

> *First Principle:* A must not kill B to save five if he can instead kill himself to save the five.

So the bystander in Bystander's Three Options must not kill the one workman on the right-hand track in furtherance of his good deed of saving the five since he can instead save the five by killing himself. Thus he must not choose option (ii).

On the other hand, morality doesn't require him to choose option (iii). If A wants to do a certain good deed, and discovers that the only permissible means he has of doing the good deed is killing himself, then he may refrain from doing the good deed. In particular, here is a second *ceteris paribus* principle:

> *Second Principle:* A may let five die if the only permissible means he has of saving them is killing himself.

So the bystander in Bystander's Three Options may choose option (i).

Let us now return to Bystander's Two Options. We may imagine that the bystander in this case can see the trolley headed for the five workmen, and wants to save them. He thinks: "Does this switch allow for me to choose option (iii), in which I turn the trolley onto myself? If it does, then I must not choose option (ii), in which I turn the trolley onto the one workman on the right-hand track, for as the *First*

Principle says, I must prefer killing myself to killing him. But I don't want to kill myself, and if truth be told, I wouldn't if I could. So if the switch does allow for me to choose option (iii), then I have to forgo my good deed of saving the five: I have to choose option (i)—thus I have to let the five die. As, of course, the *Second Principle* says I may."

As you can imagine, he therefore examines the switch *very* carefully. Lo, he discovers that the switch doesn't allow him to choose option (iii). "What luck," he thinks, "I can't turn the trolley onto myself. So it's perfectly all right for me to choose option (ii)!" His thought is that since he can't himself pay the cost of his good deed, it is perfectly all right for him to make the workman on the right-hand track pay it—despite the fact that he wouldn't himself pay it if he could.

I put it to you that that thought won't do. Since he wouldn't himself pay the cost of his good deed if he could pay it, there is no way in which he can decently regard himself as entitled to make someone else pay it.

Of how many of us is it true that if we could permissibly save five only by killing ourselves, then we would? Doing so would be altruism, for as the *Second Principle* says, nobody is required to do so, and doing so would therefore be altruism; moreover, doing so would be doing something for others at a major cost to oneself, and doing so would therefore be major altruism. Very few of us would. Then very few of us could decently regard ourselves as entitled to choose option (ii) if we were in the bystander's situation in Bystander's Two Options.

Note

1. A. W. Friedman. *Minimizing Harm: Three Problems in Moral Theory.* Unpublished doctoral dissertation, Department of Linguistics and Philosophy, Massachusetts Institute of Technology (2002).

Study Questions

1. Is your judgment affected by which role in the story you imagine yourself playing?
2. Would your judgment be different if turning the trolley saved the lives of many more people?
3. Do you agree that you should not make someone else pay a cost if in the same circumstances you yourself would not be willing to pay it?
4. If you could save thousands of lives by sacrificing your own, would you have a moral obligation to do so?

CHAPTER 52

Moral Saints

Susan Wolf

We have reached our last reading, and here Susan Wolf, whose work we read previously, challenges the view that the best life is that of the moral saint, a person whose every action is as good as possible. She argues that such an individual would necessarily sacrifice other ideals, such as academic, artistic, or athletic excellence, whose pursuits are incompatible with maximum devotion to morality. She concludes that our values should not be understood as a hierarchy with morality at the top.

I don't know whether there are any moral saints. But if there are, I am glad that neither I nor those about whom I care most are among them. By *moral saint* I mean a person whose every action is as morally good as possible, a person, that is, who is as morally worthy as can be. Though I shall in a moment acknowledge the variety of types of person that might be thought to satisfy this description, it seems to me that none of these types serve as unequivocally compelling personal ideals. In other words, I believe that moral perfection, in the sense of moral saintliness, does not constitute a model of personal well-being toward which it would be particularly rational or good or desirable for a human being to strive.

Outside the context of moral discussion, this will strike many as an obvious point. But, within that context, the point, if it be granted, will be granted with some discomfort. For within that context it is generally assumed that one ought to be as morally good as possible and that what limits there are to morality's hold on us are set by features of human nature of which we ought not to be proud. If, as

From Susan Wolf, "Moral Saints," in *The Journal of Philosophy*, Vol. 79. Copyright © 1982. Reprinted by permission of the author and *The Journal of Philosophy*.

I believe, the ideals that are derivable from common sense and philosophically popular moral theories do not support these assumptions, then something has to change. Either we must change our moral theories in ways that will make them yield more palatable ideals, or, as I shall argue, we must change our conception of what is involved in affirming a moral theory. . . .

Consider first what, pretheoretically, would count for us—contemporary members of Western culture—as a moral saint. A necessary condition of moral sainthood would be that one's life be dominated by a commitment to improving the welfare of others of society as a whole. As to what role this commitment must play in the individual's motivational system, two contrasting accounts suggest themselves to me which might equally be thought to qualify a person for moral sainthood.

First, a moral saint might be someone whose concern for others plays the role that is played in most of our lives by more selfish, or at any rate, less morally worthy concerns. For the moral saint, the promotion of the welfare of others might play the role that is played for most of us by the enjoyment of material comforts, the opportunity to engage in the intellectual and physical activities of our choice, and the love, respect, and companionship of people whom we love, respect, and enjoy. The happiness of the moral saint, then, would truly lie in the happiness of others, and so he would devote himself to others gladly, and with a whole and open heart.

On the other hand, a moral saint might be someone for whom the basic ingredients of happiness are not unlike those of most of the rest of us. What makes him a moral saint is rather that he pays little or no attention to his own happiness in light of the overriding importance he gives to the wider concerns of morality. In other words, this person sacrifices his own interests to the interests of others, and feels the sacrifice as such.

Roughly, these two models may be distinguished according to whether one thinks of the moral saint as being a saint out of love or one thinks of the moral saint as being a saint out of duty (or some other intellectual appreciation and recognition of moral principles). We may refer to the first model as the model of the Loving Saint: to the second, as the model of the Rational Saint.

The two models differ considerably with respect to the qualities of the motives of the individuals who conform to them. But this difference would have limited effect on the saints' respective public personalities. The shared content of what these individuals are motivated to be—namely, as morally good as possible—would play the dominant role in the determination of their characters. Of course, just as a variety of large-scale projects, from tending the sick to political campaigning, may be equally and maximally morally worthy, so a variety of characters are compatible with the ideal of moral sainthood. One moral saint may be more or less jovial, more or less garrulous, more or less athletic than another. But, above all, a moral saint must have and cultivate those qualities which are apt to allow him to treat others as justly and kindly as possible. He will have the standard moral virtues to a nonstandard degree. He will be patient, considerate, even-tempered, hospitable, charitable in thought as well as in deed. He will be very reluctant to make negative judgments of other people. He will be careful not to favor some people over others on the basis of properties they could not help but have.

Perhaps what I have already said is enough to make some people begin to regard the absence of moral saints in their lives as a blessing. For there comes a point in the listing of virtues that a moral saint is likely to have where one might naturally begin to wonder whether the moral saint isn't, after all, too good—if not too good for his own good, at least too good for his own well-being. For the moral virtues, given that they are, by hypothesis, all present in the same individual, and to an extreme degree, are apt to crowd out the nonmoral virtues, as well as many of the interests and personal characteristics that we generally think contribute to a healthy, well-rounded, richly developed character.

In other words, if the moral saint is devoting all his time to feeding the hungry or healing the sick or raising money for Oxfam, then necessarily he is not reading Victorian novels, playing the oboe, or improving his backhand. Although no one of the interests or tastes in the category containing these latter activities could be claimed to be a necessary element in a life well lived, a life in which *none* of these possible aspects of character are developed may seem to be a life strangely barren.

The reasons why a moral saint cannot, in general, encourage the discovery and development of significant nonmoral interests and skills are not logical but practical reasons. There are, in addition, a class of nonmoral characteristics that a moral saint cannot encourage in himself for reasons that are not just practical. There is a more substantial tension between having any of these qualities unashamedly and being a moral saint. These qualities might be described as going against the moral grain. For example, a cynical or sarcastic wit, or a sense of humor that appreciates this kind of wit in others, requires that one take an attitude of resignation and pessimism toward the flaws and vices to be found in the world. A moral saint, on the other hand, has reason to take an attitude in opposition to this—he should try to look for the best in people, give them the benefit of the doubt as long as possible, try to improve regrettable situations as long as there is any hope of success. This suggests that, although a moral saint might well enjoy a good episode of *Father Knows Best*, he may not in good conscience be able to laugh at a Marx Brothers movie or enjoy a play by George Bernard Shaw.

An interest in something like gourmet cooking will be, for different reasons, difficult for a moral saint to rest easy with. For it seems to me that no plausible argument can justify the use of human resources involved in production a *paté de canard en crois* against possible alternative beneficent ends to which these resources might be put. If there is a justification for the institution of haute cuisine, it is one which rests on the decision *not* to justify every activity against morally beneficial alternatives, and this is a decision a moral saint will never make. Presumably, an interest in high fashion or interior design will fare much the same, as will, very possibly, a cultivation of the finer arts as well.

A moral saint will have to be very, very nice. It is important that he not be offensive. The worry is that, as a result, he will have to be dull-witted or humorless or bland. . . .

One might suspect that the essence of the problem is simply that there is a limit to how much of *any* single value, or any single type of value, we can stand. Our objection then would not be specific to a life in which one's dominant concern is morality, but would apply to any life that can be so completely characterized by an extraordinarily dominant concern. The objection in that case would reduce to the recognition that such a life is incompatible with well-roundedness. If that were the objection, one could fairly reply that well-roundedness is no more supreme a virtue than the totality of moral virtues embodied by the ideal it is being used to criticize. But I think this misidentifies the objection. For the way in which a concern for morality may dominate a life, or, more to the point, the way in which it may dominate an ideal of life, is not easily imagined by analogy to the dominance an aspiration to become an Olympic swimmer or a concert pianist might have.

A person who is passionately committed to one of these latter concerns might decide that her attachment to it is strong enough to be worth the sacrifice of her ability to maintain and pursue a significant portion of what else life might offer which a proper devotion to her dominant passion would require. But a desire to be as morally good as possible is not likely to take the form of one desire among others which, because of its peculiar psychological strength, requires one to forego the pursuit of other weaker and separately less demanding desires. Rather, the desire to be as morally good as possible is apt to have the character not just of a stronger but of a higher desire, which does not merely successfully compete with one's other desires but which rather subsumes or demeans them. The sacrifice of other interests for the interest in morality then, will have the character, not of a choice, but of an imperative.

Moreover, there is something odd about the idea of morality itself, or moral goodness, serving as the object of a dominant passion in the way that a more concrete and specific vision of a goal (even a concrete *moral* goal) might be imagined to serve. Morality itself does not seem to be a suitable object of passion. Thus, when one reflects, for example, on the Loving Saint easily and gladly giving up his fishing trip or his stereo or his hot fudge sundae at the drop of the moral hat, one is apt to wonder not at how much he loves morality, but at how little he loves these other things. One thinks that, if he can give these up so easily, he does not know what it is to truly love them. There seems, in other words, to be a kind of joy which the Loving Saint, either by nature or by practice, is incapable of experiencing. The Rational Saint, on the other hand, might retain strong nonmoral and concrete desires—he simply denies himself the opportunity to act on them. But this is no less troubling. The Loving Saint one might suspect of missing a piece of perceptual machinery, of being blind to some of what the world has to offer. The Rational Saint, who sees it but foregoes it, one suspects of having a different problem—a pathological fear of damnation, perhaps, or an extreme form of self-hatred that interferes with his ability to enjoy the enjoyable in life.

In other words, the ideal of a life of moral sainthood disturbs not simply because it is an ideal of a life in which morality unduly dominates. The normal person's direct and specific desires for objects, activities, and events that conflict with the attainment of moral perfection are not simply sacrificed but removed, suppressed, or subsumed. The way in which morality, unlike other possible goals, is apt to dominate is particularly disturbing, for it seems to require either the lack or the denial of the existence of an identifiable, personal self.

This distinctively troubling feature is not, I think, absolutely unique to the ideal of the moral saint, as I have been using that phrase. It is shared by the conception of the pure aesthete, by a certain kind of religious ideal, and, somewhat paradoxically, by the model of the thorough-going, self-conscious egoist. It is not a coincidence that the ways of comprehending the world of which these ideals are the extreme embodiments are sometimes described as "moralities" themselves. At any rate, they compete with what we ordinarily mean by "morality." Nor is it a coincidence that these ideals are naturally described as fanatical. But it is easy to see that these other types of perfection cannot serve as satisfactory personal ideals: for the realization of these ideals would be straightforwardly immoral. It may come as a surprise to some that there may in addition be such a thing as a *moral* fanatic.

Some will object that I am being unfair to "commonsense morality"—that it does not really require a moral saint to be either a disgusting goody-goody or an obsessive ascetic. Admittedly, there is no logical inconsistency between having any of the personal characteristics I have mentioned and being a moral saint. It is not morally wrong to notice the faults and shortcomings of others or to recognize and appreciate nonmoral talents and skills. Nor is it immoral to be an avid Celtics fan or to have a passion for caviar or to be an excellent cellist. With enough imagination, we can always contrive a suitable history and set of circumstances that will embrace such characteristics in one or another specific fictional story of a perfect moral saint.

If one turned onto the path of moral sainthood relatively late in life, one may have already developed interests that can be turned to moral purposes. It may be that a good golf game is just what is needed to secure that big donation to Oxfam. Perhaps the cultivation of one's exceptional artistic talent will turn out to be the way one can make one's greatest contribution to society. Furthermore, one might stumble upon joys and skills in the very service of morality. If, because the children are short a ninth player for the team, one's generous offer to serve reveals a natural fielding arm or if one's part in the campaign against nuclear power requires accepting a lobbyist's invitation to lunch at Le Lion d'Or, there is no moral gain in denying the satisfaction one gets from these activities. The moral saint, then, may, by happy accident, find himself with nonmoral virtues on which he can capitalize morally or which make psychological demands to which he has no choice but to attend. The point is that, for a moral saint, the existence of these interests and skills can be given at best the status of happy accidents—they cannot be encouraged for their own sakes as distinct, independent aspects of the realization of human good.

It must be remembered that from the fact that there is a tension between having any of these qualities and being a moral saint it does not follow that having any of these qualities is immoral. For it is not part of commonsense morality that one ought to be a moral saint. Still, if someone just happened to want to be a moral saint, he or she would not have or encourage these qualities, and on the basis of our commonsense values, this counts as a reason *not* to want to be a moral saint.

One might still wonder what kind of reason this is, and what kind of conclusion this properly allows us to draw. For the fact that the models of moral saints are unattractive does not necessarily mean that they are unsuitable ideals. Perhaps they are unattractive because they make us feel uncomfortable—they highlight our own weaknesses, vices, and flaws. If so, the fault lies not in the characters of the saints, but in those of our unsaintly selves.

To be sure, some of the reasons behind the disaffection we feel for the model of moral sainthood have to do with a reluctance to criticize ourselves and a reluctance to commit ourselves to trying to give up activities and interests that we heartily enjoy. These considerations might provide an *excuse* for the fact that we are not moral saints, but they do not provide a basis for criticizing sainthood as a possible ideal. Since these considerations rely on an appeal to the egoistic, hedonistic side of our natures, to use them as a basis for criticizing the ideal of the moral saint would be at best to beg the question and at worst to glorify features of ourselves that ought to be condemned.

The fact that the moral saint would be without qualities which we have and which, indeed, we like to have, does not in itself provide reason to condemn the ideal of the moral saint. The fact that some of these qualities are good qualities, however, and that they are qualities we *ought* to like, does provide reason to discourage this ideal and to offer other ideals in its place. In other words, some of the qualities the moral saint necessarily lacks are virtues, albeit nonmoral virtues, in the unsaintly characters who have them. The feats of Groucho Marx, Reggie Jackson, and the head chef at Lutèce are impressive accomplishments that it is not only permissible but positively appropriate to recognize as such. In general, the admiration of and striving toward achieving any of a great variety of forms of personal excellence are character traits it is valuable and desirable for people to have. In advocating the development of these varieties of excellence, we advocate nonmoral reasons for acting, and in thinking that it is good for a person to strive for an ideal that gives a substantial role to the interests and values that correspond to these virtues, we implicitly acknowledge the goodness of ideals incompatible with that of the moral saint. Finally, if we think that it is *as* good, or even better for a person to strive for one of these ideals than it is for him or her to strive for and realize the ideal of the moral saint, we express a conviction that it is good not to be a moral saint. . . .

In pointing out the regrettable features and the necessary absence of some desirable features in a moral saint, I have not meant to condemn the moral saint or the person who aspires to become one. Rather, I have meant to insist that the ideal of moral sainthood should not be held as a standard against which any other ideal must be judged or justified, and that the posture we take in response to the recognition that our lives are not as morally good as they might be need not be defensive. It is misleading to insist that one is *permitted* to live a life in which the goals, relationships, activities, and interests that one pursues are not maximally morally good. For our lives are not so comprehensively subject to the requirement that we apply for permission, and our nonmoral reasons for the goals we set ourselves are not excuses, but may rather be positive, good reasons which do not exist *despite* any reasons that might threaten to outweigh them. In other words, a person may be *perfectly wonderful* without being *perfectly moral.* . . .

The role morality plays in the development of our characters and the shape of our practical deliberations need be neither that of a universal medium into which all other values must be translated nor that of an ever-present filter through which all other values must pass. This is not to say that moral value should not be an important, even the most important, kind of value we attend to in evaluating and improving ourselves and our world. It is to say that our values cannot be fully comprehended on the model of a hierarchical system with morality at the top.

Study Questions

1. How does Wolf distinguish "the Loving Saint" and "the Rational Saint"?
2. Does the desire to be as morally good as possible conflict with the desire to be an outstanding scholar, musician, or athlete?
3. Would you admire a moral saint?
4. Would you want to be a moral saint?

Glossary

This collection of key terms with their meanings is drawn from *Exploring Moral Problems: An Introductory Anthology*, edited by Steven M. Cahn and Andrew Forcehimes, published in 2018 by Oxford University Press.

***A posteriori* proposition**   A proposition whose truth-value can be known only through experience. For example, "Some swans are black" is true *a posteriori*, because we need to examine the swans in the natural world to discover if some of them are black.

***A priori* proposition**   A proposition whose truth-value can be known independently of experience. For example, "triangles have three sides" is true *a priori*, because we do not need to examine any triangles in the natural world to discover that they have three sides.

Absolutism   The view that certain types of acts are impermissible no matter the consequences.

Act-consequentialism   The view that you are required to perform an action if and only if (and because) of the acts now available to you, this act will uniquely bring about the most good.

Active euthanasia   Directed action taken by a physician, at the request of a terminally ill patient or the immediate family, to kill the patient.

Argument   A series of statements, one of which (the conclusion) is claimed to be supported by the others (the premises).

Autonomy   Having control over one's life. For Kant, autonomy is a property of the will—namely, to be a law unto oneself.

Average utilitarianism   The view that, for all persons, each person is permitted to do (of the available actions) only what will bring about the maximum average utility— in other words, the total utility divided by the number of persons.

Beneficence   The act of benefiting of others. (Or, conceived of as a character trait, the disposition to do so).

Consequentialist theory   A theory that treats the status of an act to be fully determined by the goodness of outcomes the act would bring about.

Consistency   A set of claims is consistent if it is logically possible for all of the claims in the set to be true at the same time.

Constitutive value   Something's having value by being a part of a larger valuable whole—for example, a piece of glass in a beautiful mosaic.

Cultural relativism   The view that you are required to perform an action if and only if (and because) your performance of the act is called for by the norms of your culture.

Decisive (or conclusive) reasons   Reasons to act in a certain way that outweigh any other reason (or combination of reasons) not to act in this way.

Deontic verdict   A claim about the normative status of an action—for example, impermissible, permissible, required, optional, supererogatory.

Deterrence   The use of praise, blame, punishment, or reward to increase the likelihood that one will refrain from performing a certain act.

Dignity   Having moral standing that makes one the appropriate object of respect.

Distributive justice   The fair allocation of benefits and burdens among the members of a society.

Divine command theory   The view that you are required to perform an action if and only if (and because) your performance of such acts is commanded by God.

Ecosystem   The collection and interaction of living organisms and their environment.

Egalitarianism   The view that justice requires equality, or perhaps the elimination of inequality.

Extrinsic value   Something's having value because of the value some other intrinsically valuable thing bestows on it—for example, a family heirloom.

Fetus   The unborn offspring of a mammal (usually taken to be in the later stages of development).

Good will   A will that is able to reliably identify and carry out its duty for the sake of the duty.

Hedonism   The view that your well-being consists exclusively in facts about pleasure and pain.

If and only if   A sentence that states both a necessary and sufficient condition—a biconditional. The "if" captures the sufficient condition. The "only if" captures the necessary condition.

Instrumental value   Something's having value because of what it brings about via its consequences—for example, money.

Intrinsic value   Something's having value in and of itself, or for its own sake—for example, pleasure.

Liberalism   A view in political philosophy that takes individuals as primary, emphasizing their freedom and equality.

Maxim   A subjective principle of action that consists of the actor's intention and reason for so intending.

Moral worth   The praiseworthy feature of an action associated with the motive that led the agent to perform the action. For Kant, an action has moral worth if and only if it is a dutiful action done from the motive of duty.

Necessary condition   A condition p is a *necessary condition* for some q when the falsity of p guarantees the falsity of q. That is, q cannot be true unless p is true. For example, one is a mother only if one is female. That is, being female is a necessary condition for being a mother.

Negative duties   A requirement to refrain from performing certain kinds of acts—for example, killing the innocent.

Normative (as opposed to descriptive) claims   A claim that tells us what should, ought, or must be the case. By contrast, a descriptive claim tells us what is, was, or will be the case.

Normative reason   A consideration that counts in favor of, or justifies, acting in certain ways.

Objective claim   A claim that depends on how things are, independent of the speaker's psychology.

Objective list theory   The view that your well-being consists in having your life contain certain objective goods and lack certain objective bads. To the extent that (and because) your life contains these goods, you are benefited. To the extent that (and because) your life contains these bads, you are harmed.

Obligatory   An action is obligatory if and only if it is an action that is required.

Optimific   An action is optimific if and only if (of the actions available) it is the action that makes things go best—in other words, no other action would produce a better outcome.

Optional   An action is optional if and only if it is permissible to perform or not perform the action.

Passive euthanasia   The withholding of treatment at the request of a terminally ill patient (or the immediate family) in order that the patient might be allowed to die.

Permissible   An action is permissible if and only if it is an action that is not impermissible.

Pornography   The depiction of sexually explicit material whose main purpose is the sexual arousal of the consumer. More controversially, the depiction and endorsement of degrading and abusive sexual behavior whose main purpose is the sexual arousal of the consumer.

Positive duties   A requirement to perform certain kinds of acts—for example, helping those in need.

Predicate   A term that tells us something about the subject of the sentence. For example, in the sentence "The cat is fat," the portion "is fat" is the predicate. The predicate here tells us that the subject (the cat) possesses a certain attribute (fatness). But predicates can also be used to tell us that there is a certain relation between two things. For instance, in the sentence "The cat is north of New York City," the portion "is north of " is the predicate.

Pro tanto reason   A consideration that counts in favor of acting in a certain way, but may not do so decisively.

Psychological egoism   The view that people are motivated exclusively by the promotion of their own well-being.

Racism   Believing or acting on the view that certain racial groups are inherently inferior to others.

Reason   A consideration that counts in favor of, or justifies, acting in certain ways.

Required   An action is required if and only if there is decisive (or conclusive) reason to perform the action. That is, an action is required if and only it is the only permissible action available.

Rights   Broadly, for S to have a right is for S to have a claim to be treated in a certain way. Narrowly, for S to have a right is for S to have a claim that corresponds to someone else's having a positive or negative duty to treat S in a certain way. Rights attached to a negative duty are called *negative rights*—e.g., freedom of speech. Rights attached to a positive duty are called *positive rights*—e.g., the right to be loved.

Rights infringement   An action that breaches someone's rights but, given the circumstances, this breach is justified.

Rights violation   An action that breaches someone's rights and, given the circumstances, this breach is unjustified.

Rule-consequentialism   The view that, for all persons, each person is required to conform to the rules whose general internalization will (of the available sets of rules) bring about the most good.

Self-evident claims   A claim whose truth one is justified in believing simply by virtue of adequately understanding it.

Sexism   Believing or acting on the view certain members of one sex (usually female) are inherently inferior to another.

Singer's *key claim*   You are obligated to prevent something bad from happening if you can do so without thereby sacrificing anything of comparable moral importance.

Soundness   A valid argument that has true premises.

Speciesism   A term to designate systematic discrimination based on species membership, analogous to racism or sexism.

Sufficient condition   A condition p is a *sufficient condition* for q when the truth of p guarantees q. That is, p's being true is enough for q's being true.

For example, if one is a mother, then one is female. Being a mother is a sufficient condition for being female.

Supererogatory   An action is supererogatory if and only if it is an action that is good but not required—in other words, an action that goes beyond the call of duty.

Synthetic propositions   A proposition that is not analytic. For example, "all creatures with hearts have kidneys" is true because of the way the world is, not because the predicate concept is contained within the subject concept.

Universal egoism   The view that you are required to perform an action if and only if (and because), of the acts now available to you, this act will uniquely bring about the most good-for-you. That is, you ought to perform the action whose outcome is uniquely best-for-you.

Universalizability   The requirement that deontic verdicts must apply to all persons in relevantly similar circumstances.

Utilitarianism   The view that you are required to perform an action if and only if (and because) of the acts now available to you, this act will uniquely bring about the greatest sum-total of well-being. That is, you ought to perform the action whose outcome maximizes total well-being.

Validity   The form of an argument is such that if all of the premises are true, then its conclusion must be true.

Vices   Bad dispositions, or defects of character. Lead to negative assessments of attributive goodness.

Virtue ethics   The view that you are required to perform an action if and only if (and because) this action is what a fully virtuous person (acting in character) would do in the circumstances. That is, you ought to do whatever the completely virtuous agent would characteristically do.

Virtues   Good dispositions, or excellences of character. Lead to positive assessments of attributive goodness.

Index